Encyclopaedia of modern architecture

Edited by   Wolfgang Pehnt

Contributors   Kyösti Alander, Helsinki
Reyner Banham, London
Maurice Besset, Paris
Peter Blake, New York
Max Cetto, Mexico City
G. F. Chadwick, Hale Barns, Cheshire
Alexandre Cirici-Pellicer, Barcelona
Robert L. Delevoy, Brussels
Tobias Faber, Copenhagen
Giuseppe Giordanino, Turin
Vittorio Gregotti, Novara
Henry-Russell Hitchcock, Northampton, Mass.
Hubert Hoffmann, Graz
John M. Jacobus Jr., Berkeley, Calif.
Jürgen Joedicke, Stuttgart
William H. Jordy, Providence, R.I.
Shinji Koike, Tokio
Björn Linn, Bromma
Harold Meek, Belfast
Henrique E. Mindlin, Rio de Janeiro
Leonardo Mosso, Turin
Herbert Ohl, Ulm
Margit Staber, Zurich
Klaus-Jakob Thiele, Berlin
Mark Hartland Thomas, Sittingbourne, Kent
Giuseppe Varaldo, Turin
Giulia Veronesi, Milan
J. J. Vriend, Amsterdam
Arnold Whittick, Crawley, Sussex
Gian Pio Zuccotti, Turin

Encyclopaedia
of modern
architecture

General editor: Gerd Hatje

446 illustrations

Thames and Hudson London

Translations from the German
by Irene and Harold Meek
from the French, Spanish and Italian
by Harold Meek
from the Danish by G. D. Liversage
from the Dutch by E. van Daalen

Asterisks preceding names in the text indicate that separate entries devoted to them appear elsewhere in the book.

Originally published as
Knaurs lexikon der modernen architektur
© Droemersche Verlagsanstalt Th. Knaur Nachf.
Munich and Zurich 1963
This edition © Thames and Hudson London 1963
Printed by Jarrold and Sons Limited, Norwich

Joseph Paxton. Crystal Palace. London, 1851

Introduction

In the year 1850, Prince Albert delivered a remarkable speech at a banquet for the chief magistrates of the City of London. His Royal Highness attempted to secure the support of the representatives of this thriving metropolis for his pet scheme for a Great International Exhibition; and the plan he unfolded testified to no mean optimism: 'Nobody who has paid any attention to the peculiar features of our present era will doubt for a moment that we are living at a period of most wonderful transition, which tends rapidly to accomplish that great end, to which indeed, all history points—the realization of the unity of mankind. . . .' Distances between continents were vanishing, scholarship and knowledge were becoming common property, and the products of all nations were available to the citizens to choose from. Gratitude to the Almighty would overwhelm the viewer of this vast exhibition, concluded the Prince.

As amazing as the exhibition itself, the first ever of such proportions, was the building in which it was housed: Joseph *Paxton's Crystal Palace. This huge building, erected in the breathtakingly short period of nine months, seized on the imagination of its contemporaries as did few structures of the 19th century before the Eiffel Tower. The delicate filigree of the metalwork, filled in by glass panes, the immensity of the boundless interior, and

the transparency and weightlessness of the walls seemed to the public of the day to herald the arrival of a new style—unless, like Ruskin, they were of the opinion that the Crystal Palace was a greenhouse like others, only larger. Glass and iron were the building materials which made a new aesthetic conception of architecture possible. It was not these materials that were new. The tradition of iron construction went back to the 18th century and had already produced some excellent schemes in the first half of the century. After all, the prize-winning competition design for the Crystal Palace by Hector Horeau, which was not actually used, also envisaged a light iron structure. But the conquest of this vast space by a seemingly insubstantial and unreal tracery of walls and the apparent merging of interior and exterior were new. Contemporary prints prefer to show an interior partly suffused by sunlight and yet shaded in turn by clouds, a hazy light that seems to abolish the limitations of space. New, too, was the impression of a labyrinth without narrowness and weight, similar to the three-dimensional openwork effect of the Eiffel Tower's steel frame three decades later.

The Crystal Palace was no bolt from the blue. As early as 1832, the French social reformer and sectarian Barthélemy Prosper Enfantin unfolded the vision of a new architecture which assigns a principal rôle

Thomas Telford. Design for a bridge over the Thames. London, 1801

to iron, compares parts of the structure with the molecular composition of the body, and speaks of the 'open form' of such an architecture of the future. The 'metallurgical architecture' demanded by an only recently rediscovered architectural theorist, William Vose Pickett, in a book published in 1845 seems to have anticipated modern architecture with its framed and suspended structures and its *brise-soleil*. Paxton's Crystal Palace was not such an unqualified

William Le Baron Jenney. Home Insurance Building. Chicago, 1883–5

success because it surprised and amazed its generation but because it had fulfilled their secret hopes and ambitions.

Architectural historians have investigated the 19th century for its pioneer works such as the Crystal Palace, and have long seen in these undoubtedly bold achievements the first steps towards modern architecture. They have pointed to early examples of bridge-building, cast- and wrought-iron vaulting and suspension and girder type bridges, which were already achieving astonishing spans in England and North America. In high structures there were buildings that combined load-bearing masonry and iron frames. The aesthetic charm that emanates from such factory and warehouse buildings with their heavy, solid outer walls and light, internal columns of iron may not have been obvious to contemporaries, but buildings to which the public had access such as Henri *Labrouste's Sainte-Geneviève Library in Paris (1843–50) already display it. American firms were experimenting with façades made up of prefabricated cast-iron units as early as the middle of the century, and these permitted extensive penetration of the outer walls too.

But materials alone do not create a new style. A new style is born only when an individual genius such as Paxton or Eiffel or an ambitious group such as the architects of the so-called *Chicago School after 1880, adopt the new building materials. *Burnham, *Root and *Sullivan arrived at their imposing, clear and withal lively designs for multi-storey buildings, not, in the first place, thanks to the new system of framed structures, but mainly due to their notions of style derived from the great *Richardson. William Le Baron *Jenney did not know himself that he had created the first steel-frame structure with his Home Insurance Building (1883–5)—that was only discovered when it was later pulled down; and one of the main examples of this school, the Monadnock Building (1889–91) is structurally a traditional solid masonry building. The Chicago School was a special case; it did not found a tradition. Until the advent of the department stores around 1900, the new steel structures were hardly noticeable in the townscape; the façades of the city stations only rarely betrayed the bold lines of the halls hidden beyond the entrance lobbies. Reinforced concrete structures became aesthetically attractive only in the new century, although the effective patents were taken out in the sixties of the 19th century. Despite the Crystal Palace, despite the Machinery Hall and the Eiffel Tower of the World Exhibition of 1889, the type of architecture in which the taste of the age was expressed did not make use of the new opportunities. The Paris Opera by Charles Garnier (1861–74) was more a symptom of its times than the elliptical exhibition galleries (1867) of Frédéric Le Play.

If Prince Albert in his speech before the city fathers praised the availability of all the world's merchandise, his generation exercised this sovereignty with regard to history. The 19th century was the century of stylistic imitations. The boundless availability of forms, which history had taken several thousand years to develop, was at the ready disposal of this well-informed century. The reversion to a distant past had in the first instance a concrete significance. The memory of Greek forms was a memory of classicism, Greek intellect, simplicity, nobility and greatness. Behind the protagonists of the Gothic Revival, too, there were ideas other than simply the reawakening of dead history, for most European countries connected reminiscences of their first national glory with the Gothic epoch. Disregarding the fact that English and German Gothic were unthinkable without Saint-Denis and Chartres, neo-Gothic buildings like the Houses of Parliament in London (1840–65) and the reconstructed Cologne Cathedral became memorials to a national consciousness which had grown stronger during the romantic age. Karl Friedrich von *Schinkel's design for a Prussian national

Ferdinand Dutert and Contamin. Machinery Hall at the International Exhibition. Paris, 1889 cathedral, of course, is in the most romantic fairy-tale Gothic.

Such arguments did not apply to the attempts to revive the other styles. The town became a populated museum, a permanent exhibition. The great architects of the century already built in heterogeneous styles. John *Nash was not only responsible for magnificent Ionic columns but also for the bizarre effects of the Brighton Pavilion (1815–23) with its oriental trappings.

John Nash. Brighton Pavilion, 1815–23

John Nash and James Thomson. Cumberland Terrace, Regents Park. London, 1826–7

Schinkel supplied Gothic and Renaissance schemes to choose from for his Werdersche Church in Berlin (built from 1825 to 1831). Eventually not only were alternative proposals such as these possible, but even the combination of different styles in the same building. Friedrich Schmidt, architect of the Vienna Town Hall (started 1872) declared in reply to the question whether the building was conceived more in the Gothic or the Renaissance vein: 'It is the accomplishment of an artist who has absorbed the architecture of past centuries.' The 'cold synthesis', in which the elements do not merge but remain separate and recognizable with their different origins, became the ideal. It was typical of the arrogance of the age to force successive periods to exist side by side.

The 19th century not only had styles, it had a style—*its* style. Development may appear to have resolved itself into an endless reprise of architectural fashions, but in reality this carnival of imitation followed consistent rules. The 18th century bequeathed its successors an architecture that loved large stereometric buildings, used decoration with restraint and tried to preserve continuity of surfaces. The classical motifs of column, entablature and arch were set off by plain wall surfaces or confronted by them. The pillars on John *Soane's Bank of England (1803) look like cut-out vertical wall panels. On twin-tower façades of churches (The Ludwigskirche in Munich by Friedrich von Gärtner, 1829–40; Saint-Vincent-de-Paul, Paris, 1824–44, by Lepère and Hittorff) the individual towers remain tied in by surface continuity and only appear as separate parts of the building in the upper storeys.

The historic styles employed by architects at this time were interpreted in this sense. Klenze and his contemporaries at Munich at the time of Ludwig I built Renaissance palaces in the new Ludwigsviertel part of the town, but they took as their model the Early Florentine Renaissance, not the Roman High Renaissance with its strongly accentuated wall relief. And Gothic examples fascinated them not primarily by their spatial interpenetration. A late building by Schinkel, the neo-Gothic castle of Kamenz in Silesia (1838–65) still shows an unsurpassed refinement in its treatment of wall surfaces. The unpierced walls make up a sculptural whole—the purer and more severe in style the earlier the masters are of this romantic classicism. It was not without reason that the twenties and early thirties of this century, with their inclination to stereometric form, discovered an affinity with Ledoux, Boullée, Durand, Sobre, Lequeu, Soane, Gilly, Weinbrenner, Haller von Hallerstein and partly even with Schinkel! It is significant that a book by Emil Kaufmann which came out in 1933 was called *From Ledoux to Le Corbusier*.

As the century progressed, so did the tendency to carve up surfaces. Architecture became picturesque. Clearly defined massing gave way to something that looked as if it had been nibbled at from outside, and plebeian wealth replaced noble poverty. Details that were formerly precise and clearly legible became clumsy, complicated and restless, and could only be understood as part of the whole building—and sometimes not even then. Picturesque arrangements took over from the—still valid—symmetrical plan. A large structure was now subdivided into so many main and subsidiary parts that the orderly effect of symmetry, especially as seen from a narrow street, was considerably weakened. What applies to the exterior also applies to the inside. Niches and bays hived off the drawing-rooms to conform with late-bourgeois notions of comfort and ease. If multiplicity of forms was a tacit demand, then the mixture of heterogeneous forms was its consequence. At the beginning of the 19th century architects selected their models from the stylistic conceptions of their time. In the second half of the century anything goes: distinguished antique, heavy Romanesque, riven Gothic, opulent Renaissance and, finally, Baroque, whose hour struck only when the plastic treatment and spatial exploitation of the walls had sufficiently progressed.

In the field of town planning 19th-century architecture failed almost completely. The romantic classicism prevalent around 1800 already had a tendency to break down the walls of the 'place' and isolate buildings that were of any significance in the design of the town. Open space was no longer

Friedrich Gilly. Theatre. Berlin, 1800. Project

Gottfried Semper. Opera House. Dresden, 1837–41

Charles Garnier. Opera House. Paris, 1861–74

considered as a positive shape, a spatial concept, which created its own limits as it were, in the way the Baroque squares had done so admirably. Open space was now an element pressing in from an undefined distance, which was framed by architectural shapes, but was not moulded by them.

The transition to such town planning layouts was an early development. Already the Place de la Concorde in Paris (since 1753) is no longer formed by its peripheral buildings, by its architectural frame, but is open in several directions. A generously proportioned plan like that by Ludwig Förster for the Vienna Ringstrasse (1857–8)—the highest level of spatial luxury that town planning afforded itself in this economical century—strings together a series of open spaces and groups of buildings. The open spaces are arranged axially about each part of the polygonal *Ring*-Strasse, but are not in any relationship to each other,

nor do they set each other off. Undefined open space surrounds the prominent buildings, which are grouped as though at an exhibition. This scheme, dismantled ramparts done up as boulevards with prestige buildings strung out alongside, was a customary town-planning recipe of the 19th century and in line with the contemporary need for display. More rigorous measures, such as the breaches driven by Baron Haussmann at the time of Napoleon III through the chaos that was Paris, are among the few effective solutions. These sanitary measures, however, did not develop any new conception of town life, and behind the new façades everything remained the same. The outer peripheries of the towns were completely left to look after themselves and spread along the traffic arteries.

The rapid growth of cities was the worst problem. In 1860, the USA had nine

Ludwig Förster. Project for the Ringstrasse. Vienna, 1857–8

cities with more than 100,000 inhabitants; by 1910 there were fifty. London increased its size eightfold within a hundred and fifty years, Mannheim and Düsseldorf went up by more than fourfold in forty years, while Chicago doubled its size in a single decade from 1880 to 1890. Building regulations were restricted to a minimum. The Berlin by-laws allowed any height of building in streets over fifty feet wide and permitted back yards seventeen feet square! The old town centres had to assume the civic functions of vastly increased living conglomerations. The attention of architects was focused on the monumental buildings; for the decorative treatment of apartment house façades there existed pattern books. Structural engineers were kept fully occupied with the enormous task of maintaining the services for this mammoth organization. When the buildings they erected needed an architect's touch, details familiar from other types of edifice were employed to meet the new requirements as far as was practical. But for factories, abattoirs, power stations, market halls, and water towers the academies had no models.

The reaction to these circumstances, which was especially marked in England in the *Arts and Crafts movement, was as heroic as it was helpless. Especially as the understandable discontent with the industrial age often went together with an antagonism towards machinery and thus seemed to rule out in advance any hopes of far-reaching efficiency. The diagnosis was correct, the cure imperfect. The furniture, furnishing materials and wallpapers made by William *Morris in his workshops with the help of his Pre-Raphaelite friends were new and original creations which contrasted favourably with the stylistic imitations of the eclectics. But the era of the machine could only be successfully combated by the use of machinery—not without it. The distrust of the division of labour and the manufacturing methods of industry survived until late in the present century; it echoes still in the slogan of the early *Bauhaus days: 'Architects, sculptors, painters, we must all return to handicraft!'

A great change in attitude to the machine had by no means yet occurred around 1900 when enthusiasm for 'the beauty in the tremendous force of its vast but calm outlines' and 'the clean, smooth, polish of the machine' inspired progressive spirits.

Charles Annesley Voysey. Perrycroft House. Colwall, 1893

Obrist and van de *Velde praised the 'wonderful fitness for purpose' of ocean liners, locomotives, and aeroplanes, and yet Obrist's embroideries and van de Velde's silver service were not intended for mass production by machinery but required the tools of a craftsman. *Le Corbusier, for example, talked of *prefabrication early on in his career, but when he called the house 'a machine for living in' he was not only thinking of the smooth functioning of these buildings but of the formal properties of the machine as well. What fascinated him in the motor-car to such an extent that he called his projects after motor-car marques, and what he tried to achieve in his houses, was not least the 'simple shell, which creates space for manifold organs'. The smooth and perfect shapes, the dynamic appearance and the sound of speed appealed to his aesthetic senses, which carefully selected the objects of his admiration. A typewriter or a sewing-machine with their visually complex mechanisms had to wait for the Surrealists before they were aesthetically acceptable. And it was but one step further from aesthetic appraisal to the recognition that the new and rational methods of construction, already long employed by structural engineers, were eminently compatible with 'great' architecture, the architecture of architects.

This step was not yet taken by the *Art Nouveau. But at least it combined the various tendencies towards a new architecture within a consistent style. Scant justice is done to the era between 1880 and 1910 when it is merely looked on as a transitional period to modern art and architecture, for within it lay the presuppositions of the

Joseph Olbrich. Ernst-Ludwig-Haus. Darmstadt, 1901

20th century. The awareness of what the functions of a house should be that characterized the pioneers of the Arts and Crafts movement, led to the epoch-making houses of *Voysey and *Mackintosh; parallel development in North America was due to the work of the young Frank Lloyd *Wright and a number of Californian architects. The elegant surface treatment which the anonymous London town house had preserved since the beginning of the 19th century entered into a fascinating combination with the idiosyncratic sense of proportion of the nineties (Ashbee, Godwin, *Shaw, Voysey). The cubic building fantasies of the time of Soane and the architects of the French Revolution were echoed in the Late Art Nouveau period, by Viennese practitioners in particular. Iron and glass, which structural engineers had boldly introduced into their designs time and again in the course of the century, were made to serve the new style's need for ornamental expression, and employed to perform tricks of decoration (*Horta, *Guimard).

But above all Art Nouveau starting from

Frank Lloyd Wright. Martin House. Buffalo, N.Y., 1904

Page 13. Antoni Gaudí. Casa Milà. Barcelona, 1905–10

Jacobus Johannes Pieter Oud. Workers' housing.
Hook of Holland, 1924

Michael de Klerk. De Dageraad housing estate.
Amsterdam, 1920–2

mere surface decoration advanced to a fully
three-dimensional expression of architecture which formed a direct link with
*Expressionism. The transition from Art
Nouveau to Expressionism is everywhere
fluid. Expression was aimed at by both
movements, even if Expressionism hardly
took over the flowing contours and the
ostensibly soft masses of Art Nouveau,
with its manifold reminiscences of and
associations with the organic world of
nature. But the darkly menacing cubic
forms of Mackintosh's Glasgow School of
Art (1893–1909), the unadorned blocks of

Adolf *Loos, betraying so much of Art
Nouveau proportions, Rudolf Steiner's
Goetheanum at Dornach near Basle
(1925–8) or the phantasmagoria of Antoni
*Gaudí's late work can be interpreted both
as products of Art Nouveau and as manifestations of Expressionism.
It is much more difficult to find connections
between Expressionism and the style of the
twenties, although they were close and
manifold. Only in the *Netherlands was
the situation sharpened by controversy as
the School of *Amsterdam opposed the
Rotterdam Group. *Wendingen on the
one side, De *Stijl on the other; picturesque individual homes here and rows of
whitewashed disciplined houses there; pic-
turesque-plastic thinking as against fascination with objective form; this was the
sharply defined antithesis despite a common derivation from the forerunner of
modern Dutch architecture, Hendrik
Petrus *Berlage, and despite the great impact made by Frank Lloyd *Wright on both
Wendingen and De Stijl.
But in Central Europe, the fronts overlapped, just as did Art Nouveau and Expressionism. Nearly every great architect of
the twenties went through an Expressionist
phase. Peter Behrens's Turbine Factory in
Berlin (1908–9), which is looked on as the
manifesto of functional architecture, has
massive corner piers, a huge cornice formed
by the side windows canting inwards, and
a heavy roof, features dictated by an urge
for Expressionism—not by structural necessity. The glazed façades of the factories
by Walter *Gropius have exerted a
revolutionary effect. They did not preclude
the fact that the model factory at the
Cologne Werkbund Exhibition of 1914 was
built on a strictly axial plan and confronts

Adolf Loos. Small house. 1923. Model

the viewer with a heavy Egyptian-type façade, properties that seem to be out of keeping with the modernity of the staircase towers. Bruno *Taut's pavilions at various exhibitions set out to demonstrate not so much the practicality as the poetic magic of the new building materials, steel and glass. The first *Bauhaus Manifesto is decorated with a woodcut by Lyonel Feininger, which idealizes the Gothic cathedral and expresses the affinity of the Bauhaus idea with the thinking of medieval building craftsmen—Expressionism of the purest water. In the years immediately after the First World War, when commissions were hard to come by, visionary drawings were made by numerous architects who later played a part in the Berlin association Der *Ring, and these, together with those of *Sant'Elia are among the most beautiful architectural esquisses of our time. *Mies van der Rohe's glass-house projects with their poetic quality are a part of this trend no less than the avowed expressiveness of *Poelzig's space caverns and *Mendelsohn's architectural sculpture.

A new development in the twenties, which affected Expressionism as well, is the involvement of time in the experience of a

Lyonel Feininger. Woodcut from the first Bauhaus manifesto. 1919

Walter Gropius and Adolf Meyer. Model factory at the Werkbund Exhibition. Cologne, 1914

work of architecture. Three-dimensional shapes, whether sculpture or architecture, are only revealed in all their aspects when the viewer moves around them, i.e. after the passage of a certain time. But the plastic buildings of Expressionism were uniformly constructed; Gaudí's Casa Milà does not reveal new vistas from whatever side it is looked at. An outstanding building of the twenties, on the other hand, such as the Bauhaus at Dessau (1925) or Le Corbusier's project for the League of Nations (1927), is only fully appreciated if the observer constantly changes his viewing position. The intersections of different parts of the building, the ever-changing perspectives, the constant variations in visual scale, and the alternation from high to low, large to small, nearness to distance, horizontal to vertical have been carefully worked out in the design. As the eye can only make what is meant to be a three-dimensional

Le Corbusier. League of Nations Palace. Geneva, 1927. Project

composition into a flat picture from a fixed viewpoint, the original aesthetic intent of the building can only be fulfilled by a person in motion. 'It is essential to walk round a building in order to grasp its shape and the function of its parts' writes Gropius in relation to the Bauhaus scheme.

From this a new vocabulary of shapes emerged: in particular the dissolution of the mass into slender members of changing dimensions; asymmetry of plan; locating individual wings at angles apart; and the creation of vistas by means of ground floor columns or space-spanning bridges. No part of the building demands prior attention, so special features and wall reliefs are dispensed with. The eye travels over white, smooth walls and is led on by horizontal strips of window, rows of columns or wall openings. Baroque architecture also 'led the eye', but by means of intersecting streets which revealed a building at right angles or diagonally; oval or circular open spaces, parterres or fountains were obstacles on the prescribed route. The architecture of the twenties knows no such routes. The spectator goes his own way, and the building is meant to be seen from any angle.

Already the 'Città Nuova' by the Italian Sant'Elia had included movement as part of its architectural and urbanistic conception, in conformity with the Futurist delight in the dynamics of modern city traffic. But Sant' Elia was not so much concerned with the movement of the spectator and not at all with the free rhythm and calmness of tempo which are the prerequisites of such building schemes of the twenties as the Bauhaus or the Weissenhof housing estate at Stuttgart. Sant'Elia was concerned with the movement of the object, not of the beholder: the rushing

traffic on several levels, arriving and departing trains, escalators and elevators, motor cars, and aeroplanes landing and taking off. Sant'Elia, and not Le Corbusier, first wrote of the modern house that was to resemble a gigantic machine. Sant' Elia's architectural shapes are compact and monumental, as though rooted in the ground; they are often symmetrical, and can be grasped from one viewpoint.

Many practitioners of modern architecture were only concerned with the new aesthetic inasfar as it served a new social attitude. 'We know no problems of form, only problems of building', Mies van der Rohe said in 1923. There have probably seldom been times in which architects were less aware of an aesthetic ideal. The aims of the spatial organization of a house were correct exploitation of the site, appropriate orientation, sound insulation, short, time-saving circulation for the housewife, and clear distinctions between individual zones of function. The preoccupation with these basic problems of human habitation was accompanied by growing scientific precision, and by no means only in Europe but in South America, for example, too.

The key word of this era is a concept whose history reaches back into the 19th century but which ultimately lies behind every type of architecture in some form or other: *Functionalism. The relationship of building to function has been the subject of many interpretations, in the light of the purpose for which the building is to be used, its materials, structure and environment. The opinion has often been voiced that the expression of function is beautiful in itself. As Bruno Taut said in 1929: 'Serviceability becomes the actual content of aesthetics.' The second assumption, which remained unspoken at the time, was that the factors determining functional architecture are themselves unchangeable and are not for their part postulated by any one style. Philip *Johnson recounted to students at Harvard University the re-action of visitors to his Barcelona chairs, designed by Mies van der Rohe: 'When people come who like them, they exclaim "What wonderful chairs!" Which they really are. And when they sit down, they remark ". . . and how comfortable!" But if someone comes who dislikes chairs made from strips of curved steel, he will gener-ally say: "How uncomfortable!"'

In the twenties we find numerous examples of people thinking their chairs comfortable because they liked their design. Architec-ture was then expressing functions founded on aesthetic ideals. Thus extensive use of glass walls met the demand for well-lit living and working areas and for close con-tact between interior and exterior, but the practice was unwisely introduced before the problem of protection from the sun had been solved. Sun louvres only appeared again during the thirties in the wake of new aesthetic ideas for enlivening façades three-dimensionally.

The twenties were a great Utopian period. The new architecture had to be quite dif-ferent from the historical styles of the past. Divorced from art-historical development, this architecture was meant to be timeless and valid in the encounter between purpose and material. That is why the functional argument carried such weight. It seemed to guarantee that architecture was now orientated towards viewpoints that were constant and lay within the nature of man or the characteristics of materials. 'The objectivization of personal and national features is clearly recognizable in modern architecture' (Gropius, 1924). An inter-national agreement seemed possible. For the attribute 'international' also appears among the designations which the period conferred upon itself. Gropius called his 'picture book of modern architecture' in 1924 Internationale Architektur, and the tag *International Style, coined in a publi-cation of the year 1932 by Hitchcock and Johnson, took its place beside Rationalism or Neue Sachlichkeit. Regional variations of this general canon were permissible, but only as voices that were part of a polyphonic harmony. Team-work like the Weissenhof

housing estate of the *Deutscher Werk-bund, to which sixteen architects from different countries contributed, the found-ing of the architectural organization *CIAM and the work submitted in the large international competitions of the twenties, forcefully demonstrated the new spirit of unity, even if the judges themselves still awarded the prizes to reactionaries.

It was not only Central Europe—the *Netherlands, *Germany and *Switzerland —that was in the throes of the new move-ment. When Gropius compiled the first Bauhaus book in 1924, the Internationale Architektur, more than half of the eighty-five examples of the new style were designs or models only. But in the course of one decade, the International Style established itself. In *Italy, the young *gruppo 7 was formed. In *France an avant-garde emer-ged whose clients were generally private patrons. In *Finland there were promising beginnings. *Sweden's eminent architect Erik Gunnar *Asplund wheeled round and openly joined the new movement with the Stockholm Exhibition of 1930. Modern architecture emerged in Hungary, Poland and above all in Czechoslovakia.

But already the two enormous reservoirs of power were considered to be the United States and the Soviet Union. The *United States had silos and factories whose sober pathos delighted Gropius, Le Corbusier and Mendelsohn. Even though architects such as *Schindler or *Neutra only con-cerned themselves with private building, the victory of the new idea was only a question of time in this land of phenomenal activity. Russia made such remarkable contributions as *Constructivism. With his 'Suprematist architektona' Malevich created abstract compositions in which the interplay and spatial relationship between rectangular shapes is explored; the Bau-haus published his work in the Bauhaus Books series which as a rule were reserved for their own products.

The ideas of the Russian architects at this time were informed by a technological mystique. Structure is exposed. El *Lis-sitzky projected multi-storey buildings as 'Cloud Props'; in a scheme for the Lenin Institute, Moscow, in 1927, J. J. Leonidov designed a glass sphere suspended by steel ropes to house an auditorium for 4,000 people. Even the less ambitious designs for offices and industrial plants show a graphic

Chemical works. Detail. Moscow, before 1929.
Project

Palace of the Soviets in Moscow (1931) on the other, stemmed from similar considerations! America and Russia were the lands of promise for modern architecture.

But this ideal of international unity was impossible without some simplifications. Already two of the greatest exponents did not fit into the picture which the new movement had of itself. Frank Lloyd Wright, who had been of great influence since the turn of the century, possessed too much poetry, pathos and stubbornness to allow his work to be derived from 'utilitarian elements'. *Oud, the Dutch protagonist of the new architecture, called Wright one of the greatest architects of his time. But he also gave a warning that the 'lyric enchantment that sounded from the pipes of this architectural pied piper was at the same time damaging the purity of tone' of the new architecture. How little inspiration Wright's work derived from the strict and disciplined architecture of that period is borne out by the fact that there is a temporary falling off in his industry in the twenties. Le Corbusier, too, aroused some misgivings, although his individual forms (the features on his villa

Alvar Aalto. Sanatorium. Paimio, 1929–33

brilliance and precision which betray a fascination for all that is technical. The defeat of the huge but badly equipped Russian army in the First World War had relentlessly revealed the need for technology: now technology was looked on as the means of salvation that would safeguard the future of the new order. Erich Mendelsohn, who knew the architecture of the USSR and the USA at first hand, saw the problem as a need to create a synthesis of America's 'rational intelligence' and Russia's 'vehement feeling', and he thought such a task was capable of achievement. Perhaps the attraction which big competitions had for the world's greatest architects, like the one for the Chicago Tribune Skyscraper (1922) on the one hand and those for the Kharkov Theatre (1930) and the roofs) at this time could not yet be understood as anticipations of his later sculptural play with forms. Bruno Taut wrote that it was Le Corbusier's greatest weakness that 'he was an abstract painter as well and that he mixed up architectural problems with those of painting', and Mendelsohn reproached him with lack of economy in his Weissenhof flats.

To the extent that the architecture of smooth white surfaces, rectangles, clearly articulated groupings, lightness and transparency, encountered new and hitherto unexplored fields, it changed. Alvar *Aalto's early buildings indicate already how design determined by function leads to a new style image, as soon as stylistic attitude is freer and gesture more liberal. For example, Le Corbusier's design for the League of Nations Building at Geneva (1927) envisaged a curved ceiling above the auditorium descending in great waves, clearly breaking back from each other, to the speaker's desk. The lecture hall in Aalto's library at Viipuri (1927–35) also has a ceiling suspended from the structural roof for the same acoustic reasons, but it is now developed in a freely undulating flow, sometimes rising, sometimes flat, a shape that only a few years earlier would not have been acceptable in the citadels of the International Style.

Aalto's architecture with its organic materials, its adaptation to the surrounding countryside and its avoidance of all dogma is the most conspicuous example of this change, because it is the work of a great architect. The new relationship to nature, as shown by his buildings, is not confined to him. The architects of the twenties had a preference for unadorned precise technological shapes. Their buildings, too, showed a fruitful relationship to exterior space and to nature; the opening up of the wall, the way a building's parts reach out to the open air and the invasion of the living areas by nature (Le Corbusier's buildings on *pilotis*, and his roof gardens!) all bear witness to it. But this relationship was one of contrasts. Here stood the man-made structure with its taut, clean lines and pure homogeneous surfaces, while there lay luxuriant untamed nature. As Oud put it in 1921: 'Instead of the natural charm of uncultivated material, the broken effect of glass, intricately textured surfaces, clouded colours, fused enamels and the weathering of walls

Le Corbusier. Villa Savoye. Poissy, 1927–31

we now have the attraction of cultivated material, clear glass, shining curved surfaces, the sparkling and brilliance of colour and the glitter of steel.' After 1930 and again after 1950 'natural charm' began to break through again.

Frank Lloyd Wright. Offices for S. C. Johnson and Son. Racine, Wis., 1936–9

A. Aubert, J. C. Dondel, M. Dastugue, P. Viard.
Museum of Modern Art. Paris, 1937

A new appreciation of the lively rather than
the stylized surface, as expressed by Aalto's
choice of building materials, gained ground
in many places. In southern countries the
necessity for protection from sun and glare
provides a functional reason for this. Le
Corbusier put honeycombed screens on the
elevations in his designs for multi-storey
blocks. In *Denmark, the new University
at Aarhus founded in 1932 affords an
example of the effects that can be achieved

Frank Lloyd Wright. Kalita Humphreys Theater.
Dallas, Texas, 1960

by the use of bricks without any detriment
to the modernity of its idiom. Lively surface textures are featured at *Gardella's
elegant clinic at Alessandria (1936–8) and
at the entrance to the Finsbury Health
Centre, London (1938). The aptitude of
Brazilian architects in the field of plastic
and free-form inventions first revealed
itself before a great public at the New York
World's Fair of 1939 in the pavilion by
*Costa and *Niemeyer. Modern architec-
ture was no longer essentially confined to
a small area in Central Europe but made
its appearance now all along the periphery
of its former centre.

The geographic decentralization coincided
with a stylistic one. Architecture in the
thirties is more divided, perhaps richer in
possibilities, but also less grandiose than
in the preceding period. The stylistic
formula of the twenties would no longer
wear. Frank Lloyd Wright's individual
type of art, which had derived little benefit
from a climate of spiritual sobriety and
ascetic poetry, now flourished, but concerned itself with the large-scale disposition
of masses and with less detailed ornament.
The other great architects of the older
generation did not build much, mainly for
reasons beyond their creative powers. Le
Corbusier received only a few commissions,
as measured against the wealth of his ideas.
Gropius, forced into exile after 1933, had
to adapt himself twice to new surroundings,
once in England and once in America.
Finally, Mies van der Rohe did not succeed
in building a single large project between
his Tugendhat House at Brno in 1930 and
the Illinois Institute in Chicago, started in
1940!

Just as in the 19th century, the architecture
of the engineers was separate from that of
the architects. *Shell constructions, which
have played an important part since the
end of the Second World War, were mainly
used for industrial schemes, and not as yet
for public buildings except by *Torroja.
*Nervi's large-span steel or reinforced con-
crete halls were at first only used as aircraft hangars; his world-wide reputation
was only established after the war.

Periods of modern architecture when the
contemporary style's powers of expansion
flag for a while, are usually characterized
by an emergence of classicism. Classicism
is the temptation of the century. Architects
of all generations gave in to it: Peter Beh-

rens as well as Walter Gropius, and both with buildings of national prestige to their credit, the German Embassy in St Petersburg (1911–12) and the United States Embassy in Athens (1961). Fascists everywhere under the sun encouraged this more or less secret leaning, and made classicism the official style of architecture. The accessories of the style such as columns, pillars, pilasters, cornices, and flights of steps were raised to an imperial pseudo-grandeur and, in their violation of human scale, personified the inhuman power that raised these buildings. Fascist, National Socialist, and Soviet types of government architectures were presented at the Paris International Exhibition of 1937; their declamatory gesticulations laid bare the ideology behind the style. Even nations that had no need of such hollow forms of self-assertion succumbed to the attractive force of neoclassicism. The buildings which were put up in Paris at the same time on the opposite bank of the Seine, the Musée d'Art Moderne and the Palais Chaillot, were close behind the concrete pamphlets of the dictatorships for dreary amplitude.

Classicism was not only a temptation but also a legitimate possibility. Nobody will deny the respect due to Asplund's Stockholm Crematorium (1935–40) which the quiet dignity of this building deserves. The Lincoln Memorial in Washington (1914–22) and the National Gallery of Art there (1937) are honest examples which are all the more justified as the first public buildings of the newly created country were in this style at the very beginning of the North American tradition in building. Classicism in America meant memories of independence and the wars of liberation. Apart from the imitation of column and pillar, gable and abacus, latent classicism is evident in more than one important modern building (*neoclassicism). Mies van der Rohe has built in an unmistakable idiom, free of all imitation, after his early villas with their reminiscences of Schinkel. But the way he places steel sections in front of a wall in order to reveal the play of forces in the framework hidden in the wall, recalls the symbolism of forces expressed by the individual parts of a building in classical architecture. In the designs for the layout of the Illinois Institute of Technology in Chicago, which preceded the final scheme of 1940, there is an axial

arrangement of the architecture—and hence also of the people it serves—which corresponds to the clear orientation and axial stress of classical architecture. The Seagram Building in New York (1958) has remained the most clearly defined expression of this style so far. Related tendencies, albeit less strongly marked, are to be found in the decorative variants of current North American architecture.

What is modern architecture? Is it architecture based on the latest possibilities of building technique, from the earliest cast-iron structures to prestressed reinforced concrete? Architecture that aims at realizing a new style of living, perhaps in the manner of CIAM's ideals? Architecture which believes in a new spatial conception, the open plan that links indoors and outdoors and combines both in a single continuum? Or is modern architecture a provisional expression that will pass away by itself, because only after a period of time can clear and precise notions of style develop?

The situation became clear four or five years after the end of the Second World War. Around 1950, Olympus was unanimous and the gods distributed their gifts. Walter Gropius had trained himself a team of young American architects. Mies van der Rohe's ideal of the clear and crystalline

Ludwig Mies van der Rohe. Alumni Memorial Hall, Illinois Institute of Technology. Chicago, 1945–6. Detail cube was accepted by the great American architectural firms and eventually by post-war European architects also. An unpleasant episode, that of the erection of the United Nations Building in New York (1950–1), indicates how effortlessly the conceptions of the great authorities—in this case Le Corbusier's—could be carried out, even if association with the great masters of modern architecture was uncomfortable, as association with genius has always been. International Style, Functionalism, Rationalism or whatever they were called, were of equal importance in 1950. This kind of architecture, however, was no longer as dogmatic as it had been in the twenties, and regional and personal variations were admitted in considerably greater measure. Surfaces were more lively and textured and natural materials held their ground against the smooth white planes of the twenties—tendencies that continued from the thirties into the fifties. Colour began to assume a greater importance; but after all Le Corbusier and

Bruno Taut had already pleaded for colour in building in the twenties.

In all, there was a mandatory stock of forms in 1950, which could be summarized, as they had been twenty-five years before, under headings such as transparency, visual lightness, and apparent weightlessness. Only a few years after the middle of the century the scene changed. There are times that favour the formation of traditions and those that react with neurotic vehemence to its every onset. Wright, Gropius, Mies van der Rohe, Le Corbusier: at what time did a new generation have the opportunity to build alongside their own forebears and to debate with their living exemplars? Frank Lloyd Wright, however much he had acted as a motive force at decisive moments, was no teacher in the sense of being a schoolmaster; his protean individualism did not lend itself to ready transference. Le Corbusier, in his Unité d'Habitation at Marseilles (under construction in 1950), created the type of the slab-shaped high apartment block, with

Ludwig Mies van der Rohe. Chemotechnics and Metallurgy Building, Illinois Institute of Technology. Chicago, 1946

Edward Durell Stone. Gallery of Modern Art.
New York, c. 1957. Model

and Merrill, which has an exceptional feeling for the trends of the time, completed Lever House, the model prototype of the multi-storey office block in which the load-bearing frame remains concealed and a fully glazed outer skin forms a *curtain wall. With its precise rectilinear shape in the thoroughgoing Miesian tradition, and free of all decoration, this building proved the starting point of a new tendency in architectural decoration. Verticals and horizontals are equally distributed in the treatment of the glass façade; the surfaces which envelop Lever House are completely devoid of directionality. The division by storeys is shown up clearly and the structural frame is discernible through the transparent panes. More recent buildings play decorative tricks with the curtain walling. The walls, which are not load-bearing, consist of pressed aluminium panels, handicraft-type metal grilles, or prefabricated concrete or plastic units which are assembled in monumental patterns. In

Skidmore, Owings and Merrill. Lever House.
New York, 1952

internal service passages and two-storey flats; a building that had, or could have had, the force of a model. But since Ronchamp (1950–4) at the latest, his architecture has assumed an individual look, even to the untrained eye, that is unrepeatable. Gropius seems to have become a victim of his own pedagogic virtue in giving his pupils and collaborators a clear field for their own development; the University at Bagdad (under construction), which he designed with his *TAC team, is not likely to become such an important example as the Dessau Bauhaus (1926) and the Harvard Graduate Center at Cambridge, Mass. (1949–50) had been.

The most spectacular is the decline of van der Rohe's pupils. Mies himself has probably built more since 1950 than during the first four decades of his creative life. Each year, these apparently simple structures spring up, standing or reclining boxes of sublime proportions and finely modelled profile. But his former disciples have long since renounced his ideal of ascetic nobility. In 1952 the large firm of Skidmore, Owings

Vittoriano Viganò. Istituto Marchiandi. Milan, 1957

the American Pavilion at the Brussels International Exhibition by Edward D. *Stone (1958) this divagation received the accolade of official prestige.

The excessively smooth form of this boneless type of decorative architecture is confronted by the rugged forms of a number of others, mainly the work of Italian architects. This faction, to which the architecture of *Japan and the later Le Corbusier also belongs, has declared its opposition to the jewel-like wall mem-

Eero Saarinen. TWA Airport Terminal Building. Idlewild, New York, 1962. Model

branes of the Americans. The wall becomes heavy and solid even where it is not load-bearing. Building materials are preferred with rough, granular, and contrasty textures such as brick and exposed concrete with the shuttering marks showing up as coarsely as possible. The predilection for weighty loads is carried to such extremes that the Torre Velasca in Milan (1957) has been provided with a huge crown-like top. Acute or obtuse angles reign supreme, with a tendency to hard, dissonant articulation of the individual parts of a building. The visual scale is constantly jumping and small units are abruptly confronted with large ones. Detail, like overall form, is block-shaped and heavy in appearance. The cultivated elegance of the decorator-architects is faced with brutal Expression, while the hedonists confront men wrestling with problems.

In all this antagonism between the two camps, a form of unity subsists in more than just the affront towards the classical concept of balance between load and support found in the creations of a Mies van der Rohe. Both parties exist in a deeply thought-out relationship to the history of architecture. Even the classic phase of modern architecture, the twenties, was not divorced from history, however much its protest against the style-imitations of the 19th century would have us believe it. Gropius sold Napoleon's table linen which his family had owned, in order to acquire building land for the Bauhaus in Weimar: an act which has its symbolic overtones. At least the twenties did not sell history completely for the sake of the present. Then, too, there was a historic revival but it was, so to say, ahistoric: it preferred those periods of time that had an anonymous character: the classical temples of Greece, which Le Corbusier had learnt to admire on his travels, the grain silos of the 19th century in North America, the farmhouse.

In the architecture of 1960, on the other hand, the past is admitted in almost every shape. In Italy, silhouettes appear that recall the baptistries of Parma and Cremona, and office blocks which recall medieval fortress towers. The Americans build semicircular structures amid gardens which invite comparison with the English 18th-century 'crescents', and there is constant borrowing from various exotic styles, mainly the Islamic ones but also from late

BBPR. Torre Velasca. Milan, 1957

Gothic. *Yamasaki attempted to combine 'the typical English character of the Palace of Westminster with the elegant lightness of the Doge's Palace' in his design for the American Embassy in London. His project was completely in accord with the ideas behind the huge building programme of the United States. A decade earlier, a country that erected prestige buildings abroad would have wanted these to reflect its own way of living and building. As a matter of fact, the American consulates in post-war Germany were images of what had just manifested itself in the Lever Building, New York, as the most recent tendency in United States architecture. The new buildings of the US State Department, over fifty diplomatic missions, reflect on the contrary the environment in which they are erected; a case of applied diplomacy. The competition for the Embassy in London explicitly demanded 'an architectural style which creates an atmosphere of good will by its intelligent appreciation and consideration of the site and by its adaptation of the architecture to its surroundings'.

The relationship of modern architecture to itself is already being reflected on—a situation that is alien to the historic styles. High and Late Renaissance knew no reversions to Early Renaissance; but modern architecture reminds itself with verbal quotations of Art Nouveau ('neo-Liberty'), De Stijl ('neo-neoplasticism') or the functionalism of the twenties, an

Minoru Yamasaki. McGregor Memorial Community Conference Center. Detroit, Mich., 1959 important phase of its own evolution. A new eclecticism is in the air.

The tendency to a literary programme is hence boundless. It stretches from an expression of certain psychological states to pure symbolism of form. Paul *Rudolph, one of the most talented of the younger American architects, demands that architects should concern themselves 'with considerations of vision, symbolism, and content'. Yamasaki advocated a 'friendly, more gentle kind of building', and attacks 'muscular boasting' in architecture; Edward D. Stone talks of a 'need for richness, exuberance and pure unadulterated freshness'. A picturesque character has been more and more demanded for buildings in recent years. The famous south-east

Carlos Raúl Villanueva. Building for the Faculty of Architecture and Town Planning, University City, Caracas, 1957

corner of Le Corbusier's Ronchamp Chapel (1950–4) suggests the bold curve of a ship's bow by legitimate means, i.e. through the expressiveness of its abstract shape. Eero *Saarinen's Idlewild Airport Terminal Building (1962) must have been inspired by the thought of a bird in flight. But it is pushing architecture too far if it has to express freedom of speech (*Stubbins's Congress Hall, Berlin, 1957) or if the pools on the model of a Capitol for the fiftieth State of the USA are meant to represent the sea surrounding the Hawaiian Islands.

It is the eternal privilege of contemporaries to think of their own times as being particularly complex and involved. Hence modern architecture, too, is a mass of contradictions. A revaluation of the historic styles has led to a plurality of expression that would have been unthinkable even as recently as 1950. Countries that were on the periphery of architectural development before, now offer individual and unmistakable solutions of their own—South America, Japan. The great architects have lost much of their power to serve as models. Art form seems to triumph over residential form, and architecture as formal expression over architecture as social design. At the same time the problem of the modern city is becoming ever more pressing, while the demand for prefabrication and the industrialization of building is undeniable.

Architectural critics from all over the world have their say in this book. They would probably not agree on all points as regards matter, method and even basic conceptions if they came together round a table. But they would be unanimous in their belief that the forms and problems of contemporary architecture must be debated passionately. It is right to take an interest in the history of modern architecture. not only because modern architecture has arrived at a stage in its development where architects themselves have again become interested in history, but above all because modern times have lasted long enough to provide the answers to many questions.

WOLFGANG PEHNT

Page 27. Le Corbusier. Notre-Dame du Haut, South-east Angle. Ronchamp, 1950–4

Aalto, Hugo Henrik Alvar, b. Kuortane, Finland, 1898. Aalto studied under Sigurd Frosterus at Helsinki Polytechnic, where he graduated in architecture in 1921. In the years immediately following he travelled in Scandinavia and Central Europe, worked for a short time in the planning office of the 1923 Gothenburg Fair, and made his official début with the Tampere Industrial Exhibition of 1922, though his first work was really the remodelling of his mother's house, the Mammula of Alajärvi, carried out when he was still a student. He opened his first office in Jyväskylä, and in 1925 married Aino Marsio, who until her death in 1949 was his principal collaborator, especially in the work connected with the organization and production of Artek timber furniture, first designed in 1928 for Paimio Sanatorium.

In Jyväskylä Aalto erected a number of 'pre-functionalist' buildings including the Trade Union Theatre (1923–5). He moved to Turku in 1927, and collaborated with Erik *Bryggman in 1929 on the Jubilee Exhibition organized to celebrate the seventh centenary of the city. This exhibition displayed an exemplary feeling of coherence, and considerable originality as a graphic structure. It also marks an important stage in the history of Finnish architecture, for with it both Aalto and Bryggman reached the culmination of their development towards *Functionalism, abandoning the decorative elements of their former classic style to produce the first expression of modern architecture in Scandinavia.

The works which Alvar Aalto carried out over these years already reveal the fully developed character of his art, which may be set beside that of the greatest artists, because it succeeds both in being of its time and, simultaneously, timeless. They include the Library at Viipuri (1927–35), newspaper offices for the Turun Sanomat (1929–30), and Paimio Sanatorium (1929–33). This first 'white' period continued right up to the Second World War, and is

Alvar Aalto. Municipal Library. Viipuri, 1927–35

Alvar Aalto. Cellulose factory. Sunila, 1936–9

Alvar Aalto. Town Hall. Säynätsalo, 1950–2

Page 29. Alvar Aalto. Church. Vuoksenniska, near Imatra, 1956–8

Alvar Aalto. Church. Vuoksenniska, near Imatra, 1956–8

rich in projects such as those at Paimio and Viipuri, which will always be considered among the classics of modern architecture: the architect's own house at Riihitie 10, Helsinki (1935–6), a delightful and little-known masterpiece; the Finnish Pavilions at the International Exhibitions in Paris (1937) and New York (1939); the terraced house of Kauttua and the Villa Mairea (1938–9); and a number of industrial buildings such as the cellulose factory at Toppila (1930–1), and the huge industrial

Alvar Aalto. Maison Carré. Bazoches, 1956–8

and residential Sunila complex (1936–9, completed 1951–4).

After the intermission of the war years, Alvar Aalto applied himself to rebuilding his native land. In 1944–5 he drew up a master-plan for the development of Rovaniemi, the capital of Finnish Lapland, in conjunction with Y. Lindegren, B. Saarnio, M. Tavio, and K. Simberg. The works built or projected in the first ten years after the war may be ascribed to what we shall call the artist's middle or mature period. It may also be referred to as his 'red' or 'Cézanne' period, from the intense hues of the bricks he employed and his manner of handling volumes, but above all from the way that light is broken into facets in the manner of Cézanne; or his 'Italian' period, from the affectionate memories that are embodied of the severe Tuscan contours of towers and strongholds, and from the way he contrives internal courtyards, often raised at a higher level, where the explicit feeling of authority is tempered to a human scale. The work which embodies and concludes the structural and spatial experiments of this period, while constituting its highest and most perfect expression, is the Town Hall at Säynätsalo (1950–2). Mention should also be made of the imposing campus of Jyväskylä Teachers' Training College (1952–7), and the Funeral Chapel for Malmi, near Helsinki, a fine design that has remained unbuilt.

It was at this time that Alvar Aalto's intense work on civic schemes began, which are altering the face of Helsinki. His buildings of the fifties, such as the Rautatalo office block, 1952–4, one of his greatest projects; the Engineers' Institute, 1952; the National Pensions Institution, 1952–6; and the Cultural Centre, 1955–8, are of an intermediate stage between his 'red' and second 'white' periods, which may be literally referred to as 'bronze'. Aalto's command of plastic design had become enriched to an extraordinary degree, backed as it was by thirty years of building experience. The butterfly roof of Säynätsalo Town Hall and the great hull of the Stadium at Otaniemi may serve as symbols of this supreme mastery of technology and three-dimensional design in the handling of wood: Finland's most typical and traditional, if modest, building material. The following schemes date from the same years: the design for Seinajoki Episcopalian

Church (1952), completed in 1958 as part of a more extensive town-planning layout currently in course of realization; the Enso-Gutzeit paper mill at Summa (1953); the cemetery and chapels for Kongens Lyngby, near Copenhagen, in collaboration with Jean-Jacques Baruel (not built); the design for Vienna Municipal Hall (1953, not built); the Oulu Theatre project (1955); Otaniemi Polytechnic (1955, under construction); the development plan for Imatra (1947–53) and the regional plan for Lapland (1950–7).

Meanwhile, Aalto's second 'white' period begins in 1953, with the country house he built himself, of a somewhat experimental character, on the island of Muuratsalo. In 1955 came his masterly studio, completely in white, where Aalto's habitual attention to the psychological effects of colour reaches its ultimate stage in surroundings with no colour at all, intended to be conducive to work and quiet meditation. His eight-storey block of flats for the Berlin Interbau dates from 1955–7; then came the project for the Municipal Centre at Gothenburg (1956), the Church at Vuoksenniska near Imatra, and the Maison Carré, in the neighbourhood of Paris (both between 1956 and 1958). The latter work was carried out in collaboration with Elissa Makkinheimo, whom Aalto married in 1952. The almost 'Mycenaean' articulation of spaces gives the interiors of these buildings less volumetric definition, as grouping becomes ever more complex. Space is no longer simply fluid in the way it was at Viipuri, but grows, and, as it were, breathes in every direction around man. This treatment characterizes Aalto's most recent works, in course of construction or projected: the museums for Aalborg (Denmark) and Bagdad; Kiruna Town Hall; the Volkswagen Cultural Centre at Wolfsburg, and the tower house at Bremen. All these schemes were drawn up in 1958, and the last two are under construction. Later works include the Enso-Gutzeit office block at Helsinki (1959–62), the Opera House at Essen, and the Cultural Centre in Helsinki. Numerous other schemes are at the planning stage.

No other architecture of the present day exerts quite the same fascination as Alvar Aalto's: rich in allegory, unforeseeable, at once mystical and sensual, rationalist and anti-rationalist. As an outstanding prac-

Alvar Aalto. Cultural Centre. Helsinki, 1955–8

titioner of *organic architecture, he is aristocratically remote from all the mannerisms that have appeared due to a misunderstanding of this term. In the present state of architecture, where the need to provide accommodation for ever-increasing masses of people has led, and too often still leads to a frightful deterioration in the human and psychological qualities of housing and urban environments, to say nothing of the aesthetic considerations involved, the work of this poet amongst architects, so rich in affectionate attention to all human needs, expressed and latent, recognized or forgotten, is a source of comfort and hope. With the current spread of 'new' materials, whether used with greater commercial brashness or more barbarous insipidity it is difficult to say, Aalto's lamps and chairs, and the materials he employs, speak to us with an ancient wisdom whose very memory we seem to have lost. His work is a protest against everything stupid, unnatural and impoverished that goes under the name of 'modern', against fashionable clichés and trick photography. It is the contradictory and coherent work of a genius who does not adapt himself to the conventions of today or yesterday, because he is one of the men of our time who understands with the greatest clarity what the word tradition really means, and how, having grasped its spirit perfectly, one becomes part of it: without nostalgia, or complexes, though with all the respect due to it: in fine, a free man.

Bibliography: Alvar Aalto, 'Zwischen Humanismus und Materialismus', in *Der Bau*, No. 7/8, Vienna 1955; reprinted in *Baukunst und Werkform*, Volume IX, No. 6, Darmstadt 1956; Alvar Aalto, 'Problemi di architettura', in *Quaderni* ACJ, Turin 1956; Alvar Aalto, RIBA Annual Discourse, London in *RIBA Journal*, May 1957; Ed. and Cl. Neuenschwander, *Alvar Aalto and Finnish Architecture*, London 1954; Pier Carlo Santini and Göran Schildt, 'Alvar Aalto from Sunila to Imatra: Ideas, Projects and Buildings' in *Zodiac 3*, Milan 1958; Frederick Gutheim, *Alvar Aalto*, New York 1960; Göran Schildt and Leonardo Mosso, *Alvar Aalto*, Jyväskylä 1962.
                                LEONARDO MOSSO

Aberdeen, David du Rieu, b. 1913. Studied at Bartlett School of Architecture, London University; later lecturer at the Atelier of Advanced Design there (1947–53). Won the open competition for the TUC Memorial Building, London (1953–56). Housing at Basildon, Harlow and N. Southgate (London), the latter featuring a thirteen-storey point block. Redevelopment of Paddington Hospital; commercial buildings; aircraft hangars.

Abramovitz, Max, b. Chicago 1908. Studied at the University of Illinois and at Columbia University. In partnership with Wallace K. *Harrison.

Adler, Dankmar, b. near Weimar, Saxony 1844, d. Chicago 1900. Central Music Hall in Chicago (1879). In 1879 Louis *Sullivan joined Adler's firm and became a partner two years later. Their collaboration, in which Sullivan was responsible for the formal design of projects, lasted till 1895.

Albini, Franco, b. Robbiate, Como 1905. Graduated 1929 at Milan, where he now lives. His first essays in architecture were made during the thirties, in connection with the Milan Triennali and Trade Fairs. The fine pavilion for the Istituto Nazionale delle Assicurazioni dates from 1935. It was the first of his designs to be built, and already unmistakable. Having come to maturity of outlook and architectural practice during the years when Persico and Pagano were conducting their polemics in the pages of *Casabella* on behalf of a rationalist architecture in the European manner, and against the current of the *Novecento Italiano*, Albini has kept faith with those distant premisses to a greater degree than perhaps any other of his companions. This will be readily perceived if his entire work is analysed; in this way it would be seen how he likes thinking of architecture in essentially rational terms, to which he restricts the emotions of fantasy. Of course, there is more to it than that: there is his consciousness of profound underlying reasons, social and historic order and architectural rationalism.

For many years Albini's fantasy played on the contrast between his lively, spatial intuitions (as expressed by his frequent clever use of transparent, i.e. luminous, diaphragms, and reticulated panels, i.e. openwork panels which let the light flow in) and the clear orthogonal geometry of his structures. The contrast was finally resolved by identifying the formal element in the structure itself and from then onwards Albini's style has been more strongly expressed. This is exemplified in the field of architecture from his first villa in Milan, 1938, and his workers' flats there, 1936–8, to the Palazzo INA at Parma, 1951, the new municipal offices at Genoa, 1959 and on through to the large department store La Rinascente in Rome, 1961, his most recent and most discussed work. In the field of town planning, it may be traced from his first studies and projects, produced in conjunction with Pagano, Camus and Palanti before the war, down to the development plan for Reggio Emilia (1947–8, in collaboration); in industrial design: from the metal chair, in whose design he collaborated for the 1936 Triennale, to the circular armchair, designed in collaboration with Franca Helg for the Triennale of 1960; in the fitting out of shops, houses and museums: from the Museo di Palazzo Bianco at Genoa in 1951, a high-water mark in international museology, to the Museo del Tesoro di San Lorenzo at Genoa, 1954–6, which is one of the most intense and interesting works of recent Italian architecture, starting from its plan, laid out with a pure organic geometry, like that of a crystal.

Albini, who has attained world stature as a museum architect, has been entrusted with the project for the great new museums of Egyptian art at Cairo, currently under construction. He was a member of the executive committee of the 1951 Triennale; has lectured for some years at the Venice Istituto Universitario di Architettura; and was awarded the Olivetti national prize for architecture in 1957.

Bibliography: Giuseppe Samonà, 'Franco Albini e la cultura architettonica in Italia', in *Zodiac 3*, Milan 1958; G. C. Argan, *Franco Albini*, Milan 1962. See also: *Architectural Review*, March 1957 and December 1960.
                                    GIULIA VERONESI

Almqvist, Osvald, b. Trankil near Karlstad 1884, d. Stockholm 1950. Studied at Stockholm Technical College. The 'first Swedish functionalist'. He founded a School of Architecture in 1910, together with *Asplund, Bergsten, *Lewerentz, and other young architects, which lasted only a short time but contributed to a clarification of the situation in Sweden. Housing, power stations.

Amsterdam, School of. Group of architects that started from the break with *Berlage and provided a parallel movement in the twenties and thirties of this century to contemporary German *Expressionism. Their mouthpiece was the journal *Wendingen*. The plastically conceived shapes of their brick buildings were in sharp contrast to the buildings of De *Stijl. Most eminent exponents were Kramer, van der Mey, and Michael de *Klerk.

Antonelli, Alessandro, b. Ghemme, Novara 1798, d. Turin 1888. Professor at the Accademia di Belle Arti at Turin. He built the multi-shell cupolas of St Gaudenzio at Novara (1841–81) and of the Mole Antonelliana at Turin (1863–88), bold feats of engineering, which relied in the main on Classic Revival forms of decoration.

Franco Albini. Museo di Palazzo Bianco. Genoa, 1951

Franco Albini. La Rinascente department store. Rome, 1958–61. Model (first version)

Architects' Co-Partnership. Practice originally founded by C. K. Capon, P. L. Cocke, M. H. Cooke-Yarborough, L. M. de Syllas, J. M. Grice and M. A. R. Powers. Their rubber factory at Brynmawr, South Wales (1949) with its repetition of simple but powerful shapes gave the first indication of the feeling for sculptural effect which characterizes the firm's style. This has been displayed since in a series of educational buildings, including schools in London, Warwickshire, Hertfordshire and Dorsetshire, and university premises at Leicester, Carmarthen and Cambridge. Their hall of residence for undergraduates at St John's College, Oxford has an ingenious plan comprising a series of related hexagons, whose cellular character provides an interesting silhouette in sympathy with the existing medieval building.

HAROLD MEEK

Aronco, Raimondo d', b. Gemona, Udine 1857, d. Naples 1932. Graduate of Venice Academy. Together with *Basile and *Sommaruga he was the most important exponent of *Art Nouveau in Italy. D'Aronco designed the main building of the Turin Industrial Exhibition (1902), a bizarre mixture of the most varying influences including the Viennese. Worked in Turkey. Later, like *Horta and partly also *Behrens, he turned to designing in the Classic Revival style.

Art Nouveau. Extensive romantic, individualist and anti-historical movement which affected the whole of Europe between 1890 and 1910. It was known in England at the time as the 'modern style'; in Belgium as the *coup de fouet* (whiplash) or *paling* (eel) style (from the flexible line introduced by *Horta), or the *style des Vingt* (in view of the important part played by a group of this name led by Octave Maus); in Germany it was called the *Jugendstil*, from the Munich periodical *Jugend*; in France the *style nouille* (noodle style) or *style Guimard* (after the architect Henri *Guimard, who designed the decorative entrances to the Paris Métro in 1899). The Austrians named it the *Sezessionsstil* (after the Viennese *Sezession* group, led from 1897 on by the painter Klimt and the architects *Hoffmann and *Olbrich); in Italy it was the *stile Liberty* or *stile floreale*, and in Spain *modernismo*.

Known more generally as the *style 1900*, Art Nouveau expresses an essentially decorative trend that aims to highlight the ornamental value of the curved line, which may be floral in origin (Belgium, France) or geometric (Scotland, Austria). This line gives rise to two-dimensional, slender, sinuous, undulating and invariably asymmetrical forms. The applied arts were the first to be affected (textiles by William Morris, 1880; wood-engraved title page to *Wren's City Churches* by Arthur H. Mackmurdo, 1883; vases by Émile Gallé, 1884; ornamental lettering by Fernand Khnopff and Georges Lemmen, 1890–1; mural tapestry *The Angels' Vigil* by Henry van de Velde, 1891; furniture by Gustave Serrurier-Bovy, 1891; title page for *Dominical* by van de Velde, 1892).

Next came architecture, represented by the house which the architect Victor *Horta built at Brussels in 1892 for the engineer Tassel, a key-work of the new style, which was to find a dazzling counterpart a few years later in the Elvira studio at Munich by August *Endell (1897–8, destroyed). Among the most characteristic architectural products of Art Nouveau, albeit widely differing in purpose and plastic expression, may be counted the houses built by Paul *Hankar in Brussels (1893–1900); the works of Willem Kromhout (1864–1940), Th. Sluyterman (1863–1931) and L. A. H. Wolf in the Netherlands; Guimard's Castel Béranger (1897–8), Métro stations and the auditorium of the Humbert de Romans building (1902, destroyed) at Paris; Horta's Maison du Peuple (1896–99) and the former Hôtel Solvay (1895–1900) in Brussels; the overhead Stadtbahn station at the Karlsplatz, Vienna (1897) by Otto *Wagner; and the Folkwang Museum laid out by van de Velde at Hagen (1900–2). All these works are the result of a deliberate attempt to put an end to imitations of past styles; in its place is offered a florid type of architecture which exploits craft skills, using coloured materials (faience cabochons, stoneware, terracotta panels, stained glass), exotic veneers, moulded stonework, grilles, balconies, and tapered brackets in wrought-iron; and burgeoning with asymmetrical door- and window-frames, bow and horse-shoe windows, etc. We are in the presence of a type of architecture which is seeking a relationship between surface and ornament, rather than a spatial expression of plan. An exception to this may be found in buildings designed in the tradition of the English country house (*Voysey, *Mackintosh), with their principle of building from inside to out; and the Continental examples based on them (Olbrich's houses on the Mathildenhöhe at Darmstadt). In the later phases of Art Nouveau, façade decoration was accompanied by a powerful plastic treatment of the whole building, either by the dramatic accentuation of individual parts of the structure (Glasgow Art School, 1898–1909, by Mackintosh) or by the sculptural modelling of the whole building mass (Werkbundtheater, Cologne, 1914 by van de Velde; Casa Milà, Barcelona, 1905–10, by *Gaudí).

Art Nouveau was first and foremost an aesthetic undertaking, based on social theories and inspired by aesthetes such as Ruskin, Morris and Oscar Wilde. It was born from a panic fear of the rise of industrialism, and from a determination to create a new style, in view of the 19th century's stylistic bankruptcy, which would affect the design of objects of everyday use and leave its mark ultimately on the décor and surroundings of daily life.

In theory, from the ethical and political point of view, it appears as an attempt to integrate art with social life; in practice, and from the cultural point of view, it assumes the manner of a reactionary bourgeois movement. Art Nouveau tried, in effect, to relieve man from the pressures of a technological milieu. Faced with the machine, which it regarded as the work of the devil, it aimed at renewing contact with nature and rehabilitating the tool in its rôle of the 'lengthener of the hand': by the same token, it obliged the artist to express himself in the margin of the living forces of technology. On the other hand, it claimed to be able to fashion a three-dimensional universe, independent of the fundamental support of the true creators of the epoch (Cézanne, Gauguin, Van Gogh, Munch) or rather, only borrowing the most external trappings of their inspiration. The point may thus be seen at which Art Nouveau (in the midst of its romantic, sentimental and social outbursts) posed in contradictory terms the problem of the social relations of art. It may also be seen how it brought about, in all fields, a real severance between life and thought, and partially destroyed the 'relation between plant and soil'.

August Endell. Elvira photographic studio. Munich, 1897–8

Art Nouveau may thus be compared to a short circuit; by confounding style and surface ornament, and by basing all its efforts on theories of decoration, it appeared as a parenthesis in the organic development of history. At a time of the most prodigious industrial development, which saw the works of *Eiffel, Contamin and Dutert, and the early *Gropius, Art Nouveau kept painters, sculptors and architects at a respectful distance from the complex of technology, and inveigled them into a concern for virtuous craftsmanship rather than for machines and machine

Hector Guimard. Entrance to a Métro station. Paris, 1900

Victor Horta. Hôtel Tassel. Brussels, 1892–3

Antoni Gaudí. Casa Batlló. Barcelona, 1905–7

products. Hence, despite the ever-increasing tempo of human life, Art Nouveau wished to protect the quiet little world dreamt of by Ruskin, Morris, Tolstoy, Dickens, Renan, Zola and many others. Distinguished architects of the Art Nouveau style, such as Mackintosh, *Behrens and the Viennese masters became pioneers of modern architecture, it is true, but with their forward-looking buildings they overstepped the frontiers which the style had imposed upon its adherents.

Bibliography: Fritz Schmalenbach, *Jugendstil. Ein Beitrag zu Theorie und Geschichte der Flächenkunst*, Würzburg 1934; Stephan Tschudi Madsen, *Sources of Art Nouveau*, New York 1956; Helmut Seling (editor), *Jugendstil. Der Weg ins 20. Jahrhundert*, Heidelberg 1959; Peter Selz and Mildred Constantine (editors) *Art Nouveau. Art and Design at the Turn of the Century*, New York 1959; Louis Gans, *Nieuwe Kunst. De Nederlandse Bijtrage tot de 'Art Nouveau'*, Utrecht 1960; Jean Cassou, Emil Langui, Nikolaus Pevsner, *Durchbruch zum 20. Jahrhundert, Kunst und Kultur der Jahrhundertwende*, Munich 1962; Robert Schmutzler, *Jugendstil-Art Nouveau*, Stuttgart 1962.

ROBERT L. DELEVOY

Arts and Crafts. In 1861 William *Morris, together with a group of Pre-Raphaelite painters and architects in London, founded the firm of Morris, Marshall and Faulkner, Fine Art Workmen in Painting, Carving, Furniture and the Metals. He thus took the first step in a movement that was to lead over the next thirty years to an ultimate crystallization in C. R. Ashbee's Arts and Crafts Exhibition Society of 1888. The route was marked by a series of experiments, researches and battles, including the foundation of various other associations for the purpose of reviving craft production and fighting the encroachments of machinery on life. In its progress, the movement was to exercise a profound influence on the development of new ideas, tastes and methods of work over the whole of Europe. Inspired by the example of medieval craftsmen, Morris conducted a passionate campaign throughout these years to restore a genuine feeling of creativity to the decorative arts (i.e. those pertaining to domestic interiors), and indirectly to architecture as well. He fought against the

Charles Robert Ashbee. House in Cheyne Walk. London, 1904

Its influence is clear, too, especially on van de Velde's work in this sphere, and in the developments which gave rise to the *Deutscher Werkbund. An important rôle in this respect was played by the German architect Hermann *Muthesius, who spread the knowledge of modern English domestic architecture throughout Germany in the early years of this century with his numerous well-documented books on the English house and the exhibitions he organized abroad of English furniture and decorative schemes.

With the question of taste, however, things were more complex and difficult, not least because Walter Crane, the first president of the Arts and Crafts Society was still personally bound up with the old Pre-Raphaelite aesthetic, and sometimes opposed a greater 'opening-up' of the movement, although some of the most advanced architects of the day were to be found amongst the first members and exhibitors, men such as C. F. A. *Voysey, C. R. Ashbee, W. R. Lethaby, George Walton and E. L. Lutyens. Crane, in fact, always categorically excluded from the Society's exhibitions the works of the young C. R. *Mackintosh, and the whole Glasgow School, which was to exert such an influence on the Continent, particularly in Vienna.

It may nevertheless be affirmed that the Arts and Crafts movement made a lasting impression in both the aesthetic and technical spheres. Its abandonment of the

lowering of standards that had been brought about when the market was flooded with cheap mass-produced goods which brought not truth and beauty, but falsehood and ugliness into everyday life. Behind this attitude lay the moralizing aesthetics of John Ruskin.

But in the years that had passed since Morris & Co. was founded, the rise of industrial mass-production methods and the abhorred machine were facts that could no longer be suppressed or ignored. Ashbee, indeed, took account of them, and accepted, at least in theory, the need for collaboration with industry. In this may be seen the beginnings of industrial design, which ever since the time of the Crystal Palace had been a desideratum of the machine age.

The social, or even Socialist, presuppositions of this process are clear: to raise to the dignity of art the cheap, widely distributed, mass-produced standard product.

Philip Webb. Red House. Bexley Heath, Kent, 1859

stylistic imitations of the 19th century, its disavowal of illusionistic patterns and its preference for continuous forms laid the basis for the creative fantasies of *Art Nouveau and Jugendstil, and for the break with the aesthetic outlook of the 19th century, which the art of the present century was to consummate.

Bibliography: Nikolaus Pevsner, *An Enquiry into Industrial Art in England*, New York 1937; Nikolaus Pevsner, *Pioneers of Modern Design from William Morris to Walter Gropius*, New York 1949; Jean Cassou, Emil Langui, and Nikolaus Pevsner, *Durchbruch zum 20. Jahrhundert, Kunst und Kultur der Jahrhundertwende*, Munich 1962.

GIULIA VERONESI

Aslin, Charles Herbert, b. Sheffield 1893, d. 1959. Studied at Sheffield University Department of Architecture. After a career in various local authority offices Aslin became County Architect for Hertfordshire in 1945, where he stayed till his retirement in 1958.

At the end of the Second World War, acute shortage of school places in Hertfordshire, together with lack of manpower and craftsmen in the building trade moved Aslin to tackle the problem as a quasi-military 'planned operation'. Taking advantage of the production potential of light industry, built up during the war, he organized a system of school *prefabrication from factory-made parts, of sufficient flexibility to allow each school to be treated individually.

Erik Gunnar Asplund. Law Courts Extension. Gothenburg, 1934–7

The prototype was Cheshunt Primary School, built in 1946 on an 8 foot 3 inch grid. In 1947, eleven schools were projected on a serial production basis, with flat roofs, solid floors, and standardized stanchions and beam connections; in 1948–49, development proceeded on twenty-one primary schools, while the 1947 schools were being completed. Development on these lines has continued ever since, with the 8 foot 3 inch grid successfully applied to multi-storey buildings, though a later development has led to the introduction of a 2 foot 8 inch planning module. The hundredth school of this type was opened in 1955.

Aslin also pioneered the use of bold clear colours in schools. He was President of the RIBA in 1954–6.

Bibliography: C. H. Aslin, 'Specialized developments in school construction' in *Journal of the RIBA*, November 1950; K. C. Twist, J. T. Redpath and K. C. Evans, 'Hertfordshire Schools Development' in *Architects' Journal* (London), 12 and 26.5.1955, 11.8.1955, 19.4.1956 and 2.8.1956.

HAROLD MEEK

Asplund, Erik Gunnar, b. Stockholm 1885, d. Stockholm 1940. The architecture of Erik Gunnar Asplund, one of the most prominent of Swedish architects of the first half of the twentieth century, is of historical significance because it shows the transition from traditional to modern architecture. Asplund received his architectural training at the Technical High School and the Academy of Art, Stockholm. He completed his training and began practice in 1909. His early work consisted mainly of houses. In 1913–14 he went to Italy and Greece to study the architecture of these countries; the visit made a profound impression on him and the influence of classical architecture can be discerned in almost all his work.

Among the buildings for which he was responsible on his return, from about 1914 to 1928 which represents his early period, were the layout of the Stockholm South Cemetery in collaboration with Sigurd Lewerentz, the Woodland Chapel in the same cemetery (1918–20), the Snellman villa, Djursholm (1917), the Skandia Cinema (1922–3) and the Stockholm City Library (1924–7). The last two mentioned are among Asplund's most important works, and they are both strongly classical in design. The Skandia Cinema, which was much admired at the time it was built, is rectangular in shape with side balconies and a design that depends for its aesthetic effect on a balance of verticals and horizontals, with a restrained use of classical decoration. The City Library is symmetrical in plan with a large cylindrical lending hall enclosed on three sides by rectangular blocks containing reading and study rooms and offices. The central part was originally designed to be surmounted by a dome, but this was abandoned for a flat roof over the cylinder. The whole work is a classical conception with an accent on simplicity and severity which was a trend of the time. If Asplund had continued designing in the style of the Skandia Cinema and the Stockholm City Library, he would have been regarded as another competent traditional architect, but with the buildings of the Stockholm Exhibition of 1930, for which he was responsible, he showed himself a modern architect expressively handling glass and steel with the lightness of effect that these materials create. This is seen especially in the Paradise Restaurant with its slender supports, its glass walls, its circular glass tower, and large coloured sun blinds, the very epitomization of the new architecture in Europe.

After this exhibition Asplund designed the Bredenberg store in Stockholm (1933–5), which has something of the lightness of the exhibition buildings; the State Bacteriological Laboratory, Stockholm (1933–7); the Gothenburg Law Courts Extension (1934–7), the design of which is modern in spirit yet harmonizes in scale with the original building in the classical style; and lastly the Forest Crematorium, Stockholm South Cemetery, begun in 1935 and completed in 1940. This building is generally regarded as his masterpiece. The work involved the remoulding of the site: the transformation of a gravel pit to a wind-swept hill on the summit of which the crematorium was built. Near it is a large pool, to reflect the sky, and a large marble cross. The group of buildings consists of three chapels, the crematorium and the columbarium; at the main entrance is a large portico with numerous plain shafts. Simple, dramatic and original as is the

Erik Gunnar Asplund. Stockholm Exhibition, 1930

Erik Gunnar Asplund. Forest Crematorium. Stockholm, 1935–40

design for a purpose of this kind it is essentially Greek in conception, the feeling of repose that it creates depending on the relation of verticals and horizontals; it demonstrates how Greek architectural feeling can live in architecture that seems to be imbued with the modern spirit.

Bibliography: Bruno Zevi, *E. Gunnar Asplund*, Milan 1948; Holmdahl and Odeen (eds), *Gunnar Asplund, Architect*, Stockholm 1950; Eric de Maré, *Gunnar Asplund —A great modern architect*, London 1955.

ARNOLD WHITTICK

Athens Charter. A manifesto published by the international architectural organization *CIAM in 1933, setting out data and requirements connected with the problem of the modern city under five main headings (Dwellings, Recreation, Work, Transportation, Historic Buildings).

Austria. The wealth and power of the old monarchy on the Danube found its chief expression in the concentration of culture at Vienna, which reached a climax around 1900 in *Art Nouveau. The extensive diffusion of Austrian architecture, arts and crafts to other countries has never been achieved again. *Wagner, *Hoffmann, *Olbrich and *Loos triumphed over senseless eclecticism and produced outstanding examples of new conceptions of space. It is characteristic of the Vienna School that it never quite cut itself loose from tradition, whether it condemned

Otto Wagner. Station building for the Vienna Stadtbahn. Vienna, 1896–7

ornament radically like Loos, or sought to give it a new purpose like Hoffmann. It always adhered to the native tradition, especially to Kornhäusel.

Decimated Austria was hit harder by the consequences of the First World War than any other country. The new style in building, that second great attempt to do away with the influences of the past, had only met with a weak response in Austria. Furthermore, the puritanical and ascetic features of the movement, of the kind the Bauhaus embodies for example, are properties that are alien to the Austrian mentality. That is why significant Austrian architects became successful only when they went abroad: *Schindler, *Neutra, Bieber, Brenner, Schuster, Gottwald, Steinbüschel, *Seidler and Petschnigg.

Others transformed the influences entering from the north and west to achieve a charming compromise, as did Lichtblau and Haertl, or Strnad, who started off with classical shapes and modified them subjectively. Frank produced typical examples with a clear directness and cultivated the Viennese arts and crafts in new shapes.

Adolf Loos. Steiner House. Vienna, 1910

Roland Rainer. Municipal Hall. Vienna, 1954–8

Schuster revived the Biedermeier tradition. *Holzmeister, too, starting off in the traditional idiom, developed strong and capricious forms (churches and Salzburg Festival Theatre).

After the Second World War, economic stagnation was even more paralysing than between the wars. It is largely due to the vitality of Roland *Rainer and his school that this lethargy has been overcome.

Karl Schwanzer. Austrian Pavilion at the International Exhibition. Brussels, 1958

Arbeitsgruppe 4. Parish Church. Salzburg-Parsch, 1955–6

Rainer combines strict economy and rationality with a sure feeling for the expression of any building function. His Vienna Municipal Hall (1954–8) for 16,000 people, a steel structure with aluminium cladding, is of a new type for this class of building; one which he has employed again for halls at Bremen and Ludwigsburg. In conscious contrast to the fortress-like blocks of flats built in Vienna during the twenties, Rainer, in conjunction with Auböck, put up an experimental estate of detached prefabricated houses adjoining the old Vienna Werkbund estate. These examples, like others inspired by him in housing estates by younger architects (Windbrechtinger/Ketterer, Sekler, Freyler), propagate his theories on low buildings in cities. Only after a hard struggle has Rainer been able to carry into effect his general plan for rebuilding in Vienna.

A characteristic combination of the principles of modern architecture with the traditions of the Vienna School of 1900 has been achieved by architects such as Lorenz, who combines restraint in outer shape with a three-dimensional feeling for space, or Gottwald, a typical engineer-architect who

has built some remarkable schools and industrial buildings in Germany. His four-storey block of flats in the Hansa district of Berlin is an interesting solution of the problem of flexibility in the provision of dwelling space. A lucid demonstration of Austrian architecture is afforded by the exhibition pavilion at Brussels (1958) by Schwanzer which was re-erected in Vienna for the Museum of the Twentieth Century. Strict logicality in the manner of Loos is perpetuated in the work of Arbeitsgruppe 4 (Holzbauer, Kurrent, Spalt): church near Salzburg, shops. There are also manifestations of individuality in sports buildings such as the Gänshäufel Baths, Vienna, by Fellerer and Wörle, and in the simple and clear shapes of the airport buildings at Schwechat by the architects Klaudy, Pfeffer, Hoch and Schimka.

HUBERT HOFFMANN

Bakema, Jacob B., b. Groningen 1914. Studied architecture and hydraulic engineering in his home town, graduated at evening classes in advanced architecture in Amsterdam (HBO), and attended lectures part-time at the Delft Technical College. After that he worked for a few years under

J. H. van den Broek and Jacob B. Bakema. Lijnbaan pedestrian precinct. Rotterdam, 1953

Professor Cor van *Eesteren, in the town-planning department of the City Architect's office in Amsterdam, and in the office of Van Tijen and Maaskant. Went into partnership with J. H. van den *Broek in 1948. Solely responsible for the art centre 't Venster in Rotterdam (1947) and the Civic Centre Plan for St Louis, Missouri (1955).

J. J. VRIEND

Baldessari, Luciano, b. Rovereto near Trento 1896. Graduated Milan 1922. Architect, painter, stage designer. Exhibition architecture, including the free forms of the Breda Pavilion, Milan (1951).

Bartning, Otto, b. Karlsruhe 1883, d. Darmstadt 1959. Studied at the Technical Colleges of Berlin and Karlsruhe. Industrial, administrative, domestic and hospital buildings and, in particular, Protestant churches. Steel church on the Pressa, Cologne (1928); Church of the Resurrection, Essen, on a circular plan (1930); emergency churches of prefabricated timber construction for the German Evangelical Relief Organization (designed 1946).

Basile, Ernesto, b. Palermo 1857, d. Palermo 1932. Built shortly after the turn of the century in the Italian *Art Nouveau style (Casa Basile, 1904; Casa Frassini, 1906, both at Palermo). Later changed over to a Classic Revival style and opposed the *Functionalist architecture of the twenties.

Baudot, Anatole de, b. Saarburg 1834, d. Paris 1915. Pupil of *Labrouste and *Viollet-le-Duc. De Baudot, 'Romantic of Reinforced Concrete', introduced the new building material to ecclesiastical architecture (St Jean-de-Montmartre, Paris, 1894–7). Besides designing buildings he carried out restorations and worked as an architectural writer.

Bauhaus. The Bauhaus was a school of design, building, and craftsmanship founded by Walter *Gropius in Weimar in 1919. It was transferred to Dessau in 1925, where it continued until 1928, and then transferred to Berlin, ultimately closing in 1933. The ideas and teaching of the Bauhaus have exercised a profound influence throughout the world.

Oskar Schlemmer. Bauhaus symbol, 1922

Before the First World War the Belgian architect Henry van de *Velde had been director of the Grossherzogliche Sächsische Kunstgewerbeschule and the Grossherzogliche Sächsische Hochschule für Bildende Kunst at Weimar, and he had recommended to the Grand Duke of Saxe-Weimar that Walter Gropius should be his successor. The Grand Duke summoned Gropius for an interview in 1915, and Gropius asked for and was given full powers to reorganize the schools; when he took up his appointment in 1919 he united the two schools under the name of Das Staatliche Bauhaus Weimar. This was of profound significance because it made clear at the outset that one of the main purposes of the new school was to unite art and craft which had for too long been divorced from each other. Gropius contended that the artist or architect should also be a craftsman, that he should have experience of working in various materials so that he knew their qualities and that he should at the same time study theories of form and design. The traditional distinction between artist and craftsman should, Gropius thought, be eliminated. He also believed that a building should be the result of collective effort, and that each artist-craftsman should contribute his part with a full awareness of its purpose in relation to the whole building. Gropius was therefore an advocate of team-work in the creation of a building and in the production of furniture,

Georg Muche. Bauhaus experimental house. Weimar, 1923. Elevation and plan

pottery, and all the various architectural arts.

The teaching thus comprehended industrial production. Gropius was not opposed, as was William *Morris, to the increasing use of machinery in the production of well-designed objects, but he believed that the machine should be made absolutely subservient to the will of the creative designer. This part of Gropius's teaching has perhaps been most difficult for many people to understand. Many critics have asked why it is necessary for students to master a craft in a material and yet acquiesce in industrial production. But Gropius regarded machinery merely as an elaboration of the hand tool of the craftsman, and thought it was necessary to know the nature of the material and all its potentialities before the tool or machine could be used to the best advantage.

There is obviously a correlation of team-work in building and the necessary division of labour in industrial production, but the best results are likely to be obtained in both if members of the team not only master their own particular part but grasp its relation to the complete building or indus-

trial product. By thus using the machine to the best advantage the training at the Bauhaus was directed not to works of hand craftsmanship but to the creation of type-forms which could serve as models for mass production. And in the creation of this type-form the artist himself produces the prototype, that is if it is a teapot he makes this in the clay with his own hands as the model for mass production; he is no longer merely the drawing-board designer, but the designer-craftsman.

The curriculum of training consisted of two parallel courses of instruction, one devoted to the study of materials and craft (Werklehre) and the other to the theories of form and design (Formlehre). In the early years of the school it was necessary for the student to be taught by two masters, one in each section, an artist and a craftsman, because of the difficulty at that time of finding teachers who were sufficiently masters of both. These two teachers worked in close collaboration. Instruction at the school began with a preliminary course of six months, during which period the student worked with various materials—stone, wood, metal, clay, glass, pigments, and textiles—while he received elementary instruction in the theory of form. The purpose of working and experimenting with materials was to discover with which particular material the student had naturally the most creative aptitude, for it was an essential purpose to bring out the latent creative faculties of the individual. It might be that one student had a strong feeling for wood, another for the harder materials, stone and metal, another for textiles, another for pigments and colour. He was instructed in the use of tools and later in the use of machines that in industry have supplanted these tools. In the school devoted to form and design, instruction was given in the study and representation of natural form, in geometry and principles of building construction, in composition and the theories of volume, colour, and design.

Gropius was fortunate in gathering together some very able teachers, many of whom afterwards became famous in their various spheres. Among the first was Johannes Itten, who joined the school in 1919 and whom Gropius had first met a year earlier teaching in a private school in Vienna. Gropius was impressed with Itten's methods of education and invited him to the Bauhaus to direct the preliminary course. Itten's teaching included the study of the physical character of natural materials by representation and experiment, for it was contended that representing a material intelligently was one way of appreciating its structure. And in working in a particular material the student must not only develop a feeling for it in all its aspects, but he must appreciate its relation to other materials so as to be aware of its qualities by comparison and contrast. Other teachers at the Bauhaus at Weimar were Lyonel Feininger, printer and graphic artist, and Gerhard Marcks, sculptor and potter, both of whom joined in 1919; Georg Muche, painter and writer, who joined in 1920; Paul Klee, painter, graphic artist, and writer; and Oskar Schlemmer, painter and stage designer, who joined in 1921; Wassily Kandinsky, painter and graphic artist, who joined in 1922; and László Moholy-Nagy, painter, theatrical designer, photographer, and typographer, who joined in 1923.

In 1923, at the request of the Thuringian Legislative Assembly, the Bauhaus held an exhibition of its work which was to serve as a report on the four years of the life of the Bauhaus. Gropius felt that this was a bit premature; he would have preferred to wait until more mature results could be presented. The theme of the exhibition was 'Art and Technics, a New Unity', and included in the exhibition were designs in various materials, various products of the different workshops, examples of theoretical studies, and a one-family house called 'Am Horn' which was built and furnished by the Bauhaus workshops. This house was planned as a large square with several small rooms arranged round a central larger one; it was enthusiastically acclaimed by many critics, among them Dr E. Redslob, the National Art Director of Germany, who praised its organic unity.

In spite of the progress and success of the Bauhaus it met with much local opposition from the more conservative members of the community, while the whole enterprise was associated with Socialism in the minds of many because it happened to be established at a time when there was a Socialist régime. It also met with considerable hostility from the Thuringian Government, which more or less forced Gropius to a decision at the end of 1924 to close the

Walter Gropius. Bauhaus. Dessau, 1925–6

school. Both teachers and students wholeheartedly supported Gropius; the Director and masters notified the Government of Thuringia on 26 December of their decision to close the institution, created by them, on the expiration of their contracts on 1 April 1925.

Various cities discussed the possibility of transplanting the Bauhaus, among them Frankfurt, Hagen, Mannheim, Darmstadt and Dessau. The Mayor of Dessau succeeded in securing the transfer of the Bauhaus to his town. He appropriated seven houses for the use of the school while a new building was being erected. This building, designed by Gropius in response to the request of the City Council, was begun in the autumn of 1925 and completed in December 1926. It consisted of three principal wings, a school of design occupying one, workshops another, and a students' hostel a third. The first two were linked by a bridge over a roadway, and in

Walter Gropius. Bauhaus. Dessau, 1925-6

this bridge were administrative rooms, club rooms, and a private atelier for Professor Gropius. The students' hostel was a six-storey building consisting of twenty-eight studio-dormitory rooms. The building was constructed partly of *reinforced concrete. In the workshops' wing reinforced concrete floor slabs and supporting mushroom posts were employed with the supports set well back to allow a large uninterrupted *glass screen on the façade extending for three storeys. This was probably the first time so ambitious a use of glass screen was employed in an industrial building, and it helped to lead the way to similar constructions throughout Europe and America.

With the re-establishment of the Bauhaus at Dessau, the opportunity was taken to revise the curriculum. The earlier method of joint instruction by two masters, an artist and a craftsman, was abandoned and was supplanted by that of one master who was trained as both. This was becoming increasingly possible because several former Bauhaus students were now appointed masters: Josef Albers, Herbert Bayer, Marcel *Breuer, Hinnerk Scheper, and Joost Schmidt. Seven of the masters who had been with the Bauhaus at Weimar continued at Dessau. Gerhard Marcks left because there were not sufficient funds to install his pottery workshop at Dessau. Johannes Itten had left in the spring of 1923 owing to differences of opinion on

the conduct of the preliminary course, and his work was continued by Moholy-Nagy and Josef Albers, who jointly broadened its scope. In revising the course at Dessau the opportunity was also taken to reaffirm the principles which guided the Bauhaus system of education: these could be summarized as training in design, technics, and craftsmanship for all kinds of creative work, especially building; the execution of experimental work, especially building and interior decoration; the development of models or type-forms for industrial production and the sale of such models to industry. As a general doctrine the Bauhaus sought to establish the common citizenship of all forms of creative work and their interdependence on each other.

The Bauhaus continued at Dessau under the direction of Walter Gropius until early in 1928, when he resigned because he wished to devote himself more freely to his creative work without being restricted by official duties; on his recommendation Hannes *Meyer, the Swiss architect, who had been head of the department of architecture, became director. Meyer resigned in June 1930 as the result of differences with the municipal authority, who then tried to persuade Gropius to take over again. Instead, Gropius recommended the appointment of Ludwig *Mies van der Rohe, who accepted the position. In October 1932, after the National Socialist party had taken over the Government of

Anhalt, the Bauhaus moved to Berlin; in April 1933 it was closed by the National Socialists. From April 1933 the building at Dessau was used for the training of political leaders.

Although the school was closed, its teaching and methods were by no means dead, and they continued to exercise a wide influence throughout the world. Indeed, it may be said that its influence has been strongest since it ceased to exist, probably because it takes time for such ideas to spread. Many art schools in Europe and America have adopted in part its methods of teaching, especially as many of its masters and students have taken positions in art schools and institutes throughout Europe and America. For example, Moholy-Nagy became director of the New Bauhaus—now the Institute of Design—at Chicago, where Bauhaus methods were employed. They have also been introduced partially at the school of architecture at Harvard University, the Laboratory School of Industrial Design in New York, and in the School of Design in southern California. It would be a mistake to think that the ideas that prompted Bauhaus training are universally accepted, but it is doubtful whether any method of art teaching of the century has had quite the same impact.

Bibliography: Walter Gropius, *Idee und Aufbau des Staatlichen Bauhauses*, Weimar 1923; *Neue Arbeiten der Bauhauswerkstatten*, 1925 (English translation, *The New Architecture and the Bauhaus*, London 1935, reprinted 1955); Herbert Bayer, Walter Gropius, and Ise Gropius, *Bauhaus 1919–1928* (London 1939, Boston 1952); Hans Maria Wingler, *Das Bauhaus*, *Weimar*, *Dessau, Berlin*, Cologne 1962.

ARNOLD WHITTICK

BBPR. Partnership of architects Lodovico Barbiano di Belgioioso, Enrico Peressutti, Ernesto N. *Rogers, and (until his death in 1945) Gian Luigi Banfi. The team achieved international fame with its Sanatorium at Legnano (1937–8); more recent buildings such as the Torre Velasca, Milan (1957), endeavour to establish a poetic style by reference to tradition and local atmosphere. Housing and industrial buildings; exhibition architecture (children's maze at the Milan Triennale 1954); restoration work; interior decoration (Museum at the Castello Sforzesco, Milan, 1952–6).

Beaudouin, Eugène, b. Paris 1898. Student at the French Academy in Rome. In collaboration with Marcel *Lods he designed, in 1933, the Cité de la Muette at Drancy, near Paris, a mixed development estate where prefabricated reinforced concrete units were used; the Pavilion School at Suresnes (1932–5); and the Maison du Peuple at Clichy (1939). Cité Rotterdam suburb at Strasbourg (1951–3). Town and regional planning.

Beaux-Arts. *École des Beaux-Arts.

Behrens, Peter, b. Hamburg 1868, d. Berlin 1940. In a society torn between archaic mental attitudes and a blind faith in the lightning progress of technology, Behrens was one of the first architects of the 20th century to develop a form of architectural thought that would answer to the demands of an industrialized civilization. At a period when the moral and social demands put forward by the Expressionist painters of Dresden (*Die Brücke*) were leading to new directions in the graphic arts, he was in at the birth of modern architecture in Germany, where he exerted a leading influence between 1900 and 1914. Furthermore, the sidelines derived from architecture in which he engaged inaugurated (1907) a form of specialization that has become widely known in our times under the name of Industrial Design. Here, too, he deeply influenced the development of technology and style at a time when the propagation of craft-derived forms by the exponents of *Art Nouveau was threatening to undermine any attempts to formulate design principles in conformity with new ways of living.

Behrens did not discover his true vocation from the first. Like *van de Velde and *Le Corbusier, he was a painter at first, and came to architecture via the so-called applied arts. From 1886 to 1889 he attended painting classes at the art schools of Karlsruhe and Düsseldorf. In 1890 he was impressed by the work of the *luministes* (Israels) in Holland, and the work of painters such as Leibl in Munich; he was a founder-member of the Münchner Sezession in 1893. Already interested in the graphic arts, his early compositions (coloured woodcuts, frontispieces for books, etc.) are still permeated by the decorative influence of Art Nouveau.

Peter Behrens. Behrens House. Darmstadt, 1901

After travelling in Italy (1896), Behrens turned in 1898 to problems of industrial production and designed a number of prototype flasks for mass production by a large glass works; these are already notable for their plain, straightforward shapes. In 1899 the Grand Duke Ernst Ludwig invited him to stay at Darmstadt and join a group of young artists (the architects J. M. *Olbrich and P. Huber, the painters and interior decorators H. Christiansen and P. Bürck, and the sculptors L. Habich and R. Bosselt) who under the name of *Die Sieben* (The Seven) had as their aim the establishment of effective relationships between all the plastic arts. It was then that

Peter Behrens. AEG Turbine Factory. Berlin, 1908–9

Behrens took up architecture and, as van de Velde had done at Uccle five years before, he built his own house and fitted it out completely in a unitary style that betrayed the influence of both van de Velde and *Mackintosh. At the instance of *Muthesius, he was appointed head of the Düsseldorf School of Art in 1903, a post he held until 1907. From this period onwards his classical temperament led him to design sober, powerful and massive works, of mathematical severity and uncompromisingly functionalist in style. The houses he built for Obenauer (Saarbrücken, 1905–06), Cuno and Schroeder (Eppenhausen near Hagen, 1908–10) express this rationalistic tendency, that was ultimately to distinguish the work of Behrens from the plastic dynamism and lyricism of *Poelzig and *Mendelsohn.

In 1907, the year the Deutscher Werkbund was founded, Behrens was summoned to Berlin by the AEG (the German General Electrical Company). His duties comprised the design not only of pieces of electrical equipment (cookers, radiators, ventilators, lamps, etc.) but also of the firm's packaging, catalogues, leaflets, posters, letterheads, showrooms, shops, and, to boot, factories and workshops. The circumstance is of much importance: it marks the emergence, in the midst of industry, of a desire to humanize technology. By employing an architect to ensure a good visual appearance for their products, the AEG was bringing objects into daily life that were not only functionally efficient, but were harmoniously and sensitively designed as well, permeated as they were by an authentically creative style which, in the last analysis, projected the brand image of an industrial power. At the same time, and under the same auspices, Behrens introduced a new expression of monumentality to European architecture with his turbine factory for the AEG (Berlin, 1908–9)—the first German building in glass and steel—the high tension plant (1910) and the factory for small motors (1910–11), etc. Behrens also built a complete district of flats for AEG workers at Henningsdorf, near Berlin (1910–11). Apart from numerous factories which he erected throughout his career, mention should be made of certain other

Page 49. Peter Behrens. Entrance hall of the Hoechst Dyeworks offices. 1920–5

Peter Behrens. Offices of the Hoechst Dyeworks, 1920–5

major works of his, designed in a neo-classic style that expressed their owners' need for prestige. These include the Mannesmann offices at Düsseldorf (1913–23), those for the Continental Rubber Company at Hanover (1911–12), and the German Embassy in St Petersburg (1911–12).
In 1922 Behrens was appointed director of the School of Architecture at the Vienna Academy; some of the buildings he designed in the following years may be considered as examples of German *Expressionism (Hoechst Dyeworks, 1920–5). In 1936 he became head of the department of architecture at the Prussian Academy of Arts, Berlin. His most outstanding pupils are: Le Corbusier, who worked in his Berlin office from 1910 to 1911; Gropius, from 1907 to 1910; and Mies van der Rohe, from 1908 to 1911.
Bibliography: Peter Behrens, Feste des Lebens und der Kunst, Jena 1900; Fritz Hoeber, Peter Behrens, Munich 1913; Paul Joseph Cremers, Peter Behrens, Sein Werk von 1909 bis zur Gegenwart, Essen 1928; K. M. Grimme, Peter Behrens und seine Wiener akademische Meisterschule, Vienna 1930

ROBERT L. DELEVOY

Belluschi, Pietro, b. Ancona 1899. From 1927 chief designer in an architect's office at Portland, Oregon; since 1943 has intermittently run an office of his own. Now mainly a consultant and designer in collaboration with other architects. Residential and office buildings, shopping centres, ecclesiastical buildings. Equitable Savings Building at Portland, Oregon (1948), in which all façade units together with the aluminium-clad stanchions are arranged flush with the wall plane.

Berg, Max, b. Stettin 1870. Studied at Technical College, Berlin-Charlottenburg. City Architect, Breslau (1912–13). His Centenary Hall at Breslau, a huge cupola with exposed ribs, was one of the boldest reinforced concrete structures of its time. Exhibition Hall Messehof (1925) and hydro-electric station at Breslau.

Berlage, Hendrik Petrus, b. Amsterdam 1856, d. The Hague 1934. Berlage studied at Zurich, and had his own practice in Amsterdam from 1889 onwards; he is regarded as one of the great innovators of architecture around the year 1900. Reacting against 19th-century eclecticism, he aimed at an 'honest awareness of the problems of architecture' and a craftsmanlike approach to materials and construction. Berlage revealed once more to his contemporaries the meaning and magic of brickwork. Plastering a wall was tantamount to falsification in his eyes, and he eschewed its use even in the rooms of private houses. Berlage's 'moral' outlook was in harmony with the social climate of the times, which since c. 1895 was strongly influenced by the rising labour movement.
Despite his rejection of all historic styles, Berlage felt attracted by the massive gravity of the Romanesque, which is reflected in his semicircular arches and his large unbroken wall surfaces. These features also recall the work of the American architect H. H. *Richardson, who probably influenced him during his trip to America. Characteristic works of his include the Diamond-workers' House, Amsterdam (1899–1900), Holland House, London (1914), and above all Amsterdam Stock Exchange, completed in 1903. The Stock Exchange was the outcome of a competition held in 1897, which Berlage

won with a design he subsequently altered in many details. In this monumental work, Berlage used a light-coloured stone for special features, in addition to brick. The steel roof structure over the main hall is left exposed. There is a certain aridity of conception here which cannot be overlooked; it appears also in Berlage's earliest designs for furniture.

As an architectural writer, Berlage exerted great influence through his numerous publications and lectures. Many buildings, especially in the *Netherlands, are based on Berlage's work, even though they differ formally from it. He himself, in

Bill, Max, b. Winterthur 1908. Painter, sculptor, exhibition designer, architect. Studied at Zurich Art School and (1927–9) at the *Bauhaus. From 1951 to 1956 rector of the Hochschule für Gestaltung at Ulm and head of the departments of architecture and industrial design. Private houses, offices. The buildings of the Ulm Hochschule (1953–5) embody a complex scheme in an open, easily graspable layout, which harmonizes well with its setting.

Bibliography: Tomás Maldonado, *Max Bill*, Stuttgart 1956; Margit Staber, 'Max Bill und die Umweltgestaltung', in *Zodiac* 9, Milan 1962.

Hendrik Petrus Berlage. Stock Exchange. Amsterdam, 1897–1903

Hendrik Petrus Berlage. Stock Exchange. Amsterdam, 1897–1903

his later years came under the influence of the young *Expressionist architects. In 1928 he attended the first congress of *CIAM at La Sarraz, but felt himself too committed to a more traditional conception of architecture to be able to join the CIAM.

Bibliography: Hendrik Petrus Berlage, *Gedanken über den Stil in der Baukunst,* Leipzig 1905; Hendrik Petrus Berlage, *Grundlagen und Entwicklung der Architektur,* Berlin 1908; Hendrik Petrus Berlage, *Studies over Bouwkunst, Stijl en Samenleving,* Rotterdam 1910; Jan Gratama, *Dr. H. P. Berlage Bouwmeester,* Rotterdam 1925.

J. J. VRIEND

Bogardus, James, b. Catskill, New York 1800, d. New York 1874. Manufacturer and inventor, who built multi-storeyed factory buildings in the mid-19th century, where the outer walls were assembled from cast-iron units (his own factory in New York, 1848–9; Harper and Brothers Building, New York, 1854). The publicity Bogardus gave his buildings resulted in the widespread adoption of cast-iron façades, which paved the way for steel-frame structures (*Steel).

Böhm, Dominikus, b. Jettingen, Bavaria 1880, d. Cologne 1955. Studied at Stuttgart Technical College under Theodor *Fischer. Catholic ecclesiastical buildings

Rino Levi. Art Palacio Cinema. São Paulo, 1936

(e.g. Church at Mainz-Bischoffsheim, 1926;
St Engelbert at Cologne-Riehl, 1930; St
Maria Königin at Cologne-Marienburg,
1954).
Bibliography: August Hoff and H. Muck,
Böhm, Leben und Werk, Munich and
Zurich 1962.

Bonatz, Paul, b. Solgne, Lorraine 1877,
d. Berlin 1951. Pupil and successor of
Theodor *Fischer at Stuttgart Technical
College. Main station at Stuttgart (1913–27,
together with F. E. Scholer). Cultural,
commercial, and industrial buildings.

Bourgeois, Victor, b. Charleroi 1897, d.
Brussels 1962; 1914–19 student at the
Académie Royale des Beaux-Arts, Brussels.
His conception of architecture as the
mirror of society led him early in his career
to the problem of municipal housing. The

Attilio Correia Lima. Santos Dumont de Hidros
Airport. Rio de Janeiro, 1938

Cité Moderne at Berchem-Ste-Agathe near
Brussels (1922–5) seeks to relieve the
monotonous character of the estate by
varying the articulation of terraced housing
and by the use of open squares and courtyards and lively façade elements. Social
buildings, schools, estates, town planning.
Professor at the École Nationale Supérieure d'Architecture.
Bibliography: Georges Linze, *Victor Bourgeois*, Brussels 1961.

Brazil. When in 1943 the Museum of
Modern Art of New York presented its
exhibition on old and new architecture in
Brazil, the world was suddenly made aware
that in a faraway country the International
Architecture of the 1920s had blossomed
into a tropical version. Characterized by its
daring formal expression, its lyrical content, and its regional connotations, it also
had strong spiritual links with the colonial
past of the country. As a matter of fact, it
had sprung up in the wake of two rebel
movements, the Modern Art Week in São
Paulo, 1922, and the Regionalist movement in Recife, 1926, led by Gilberto
Freyre, which aimed at giving new shape
to Brazilian intellectual and artistic life,
not only by bringing it up to a truly contemporary outlook, rooted in the most
genuine sources of Brazilian life, but also
by attempting to destroy the alien influences which had dominated the country
since the arrival in 1806 of the King of
Portugal, D. João VI, when he fled the
Napoleonic invasion and transferred his
court to Rio de Janeiro. In 1816 D. João VI
invited a French mission of painters,
sculptors, and architects to 'civilize' the
country, with the result that the organic
development of a local architecture,
brought about throughout the colonial
period by an ecological assimilation of the
Portuguese Baroque style, was disrupted,
and all kinds of foreign pseudo-styles were
introduced, turning the 19th century into
an uncharacteristic interval, chiefly taken
up by copies of whatever might be done
abroad—not only in architecture but in all
the arts.

Page 53. Lúcio Costa, Oscar Niemeyer, Jorge
Machado Moreira, Affonso Eduardo Reidy,
Ernani Vasconcellos and Carlos Leão;
consultant architect, Le Corbusier. Ministry of
Education. Rio de Janeiro, 1937–43

Jorge Machado Moreira. House for Antonio
Ceppa. Rio de Janeiro, 1958

A few years before these two movements,
scientific studies of the effect of sunlight
on buildings had been started by Alexandre
Albuquerque, who in 1916 succeeded in
incorporating into the Building Code of
the city of São Paulo precise requirements
as to the minimum provision of sunlight in
a new building. There existed thus in the
1920s not only an intellectual atmosphere
receptive to the new ideas in architecture
but also a sound regional approach to the
basic problem of the exposure of buildings,
both in order to assure a minimum of sunlight and also to control its excess. In 1927
in São Paulo, G. *Warchavchik, a new-
comer from Russia, presented his first
cube-like houses to the public, and was
later joined in partnership by Lúcio *Costa.
When the Revolution of 1930, led by
Getulio Vargas, upset all the conventional
political and cultural values of the country
and launched a programme of important
new public works, the younger architects
were in a way prepared for the decisive, if
paradoxical, episode of the new building
for the Ministry of Education and Health.
A competition was held for the design of
this building, and all the modern projects

were disqualified by a conservative jury.
But the Minister of Education, Gustavo
Capenema, who was surrounded by a
group of far-seeing collaborators, had the
daring, after paying the prizes awarded by
the jury, to invite Lúcio Costa, one of the
disqualified competitors, to design the final
project. Lúcio Costa insisted on a team of
all the other rejected candidates being
formed, and this was done. Lúcio Costa,
Oscar *Niemeyer, Jorge Machado Moreira,
Affonso Eduardo *Reidy, Ernani Vasconcellos, and Carlos Leão were thus responsible for the development of the final design.
In 1936, *Le Corbusier was invited as a
consultant on this project, as well as on one
for the new University City. He stayed in
Brazil only three weeks, working with the
group and giving a few public lectures, but
during this short stay the turning-point
was reached and modern architecture was
irrevocably established. Le Corbusier's
main ideas fell on fertile ground. The
concept of *pilotis* was especially good for
the Brazilian climate, the *brise-soleil* were
in many cases an absolute necessity, and
his basically lyrical formal approach was
thoroughly suited to the Brazilian spirit.
A local version of International Architecture thus emerged. Prior to this, Warchavchik's houses, from 1928 on, and Rino
Levi's outstandingly direct Art Palacio
Cinema in São Paulo (1936) must of course
be mentioned.
In the years that followed, i.e. from 1937
to 1943, an impressive number of distin-
guished jobs show how quickly maturity
was achieved. They include: Oscar Nie-
meyer's Day Nursery in Rio (1937), his
Ouro Preto Hotel (1940), his Casino, Yacht
Club and Dance Hall (1943), and the São
Francisco Chapel (1944) at Pampúlha; Luiz
Nunes's (with Fernando Saturnio de Brito)
Water Tower at Olinda (1937); Attilio
Correia Lima's Santos Dumont de Hidros
Airport in Rio (1938), with Jorge Ferreira,
Thomaz Estrella, Renato Mesquita dos
Santos and Renato Soeiro; Lúcio Costa's
and Oscar Niemeyer's (with Paul Lester
Wiener) Brazilian Pavilion at the New York
World's Fair (1939); Marcelo and Milton
Roberto's ABI—the Brazilian Press Asso-
ciation Building (1938), the Instituto de
Resseguros Building (1942), and the Santos
Dumont Airport Building (1944), all in
Rio; Alvaro Vital Brasil's Edificio Esther
apartment building (with Adhemar Marin-

Henrique E. Mindlin. Avenida Central Building.
Rio de Janeiro, 1961

ho) in São Paulo (1938) and his Vital
Brasil Institute, in Niteroi (1941); Olavo
Redig de Campos's Social Centre in Rio
(1942); Firmino Saldanha's Mississippi
(1938) and Mossoró (1940) apartment
buildings in Rio, not to mention the
Ministry of Education and Health itself,
started in 1937 and finished in 1943. All
these are landmarks which have already
endured the test of time.

After the war years the country entered
into a phase of fast industrialization which
helped to raise the level of construction,
also of tremendous real estate speculation,
which of course resulted in a number of
second-rate jobs. However, the initial impulse persisted and today a large number
of good buildings may be credited to the
movement. To the architects whose work
has become better known abroad belong
Paulo Antunes Ribeiro, João Vilanova Artigas, Sergio Bernardes, Francisco Bolonha,
Oswaldo Bratke, Icaro Castro Mello, Ary

Affonso Eduardo Reidy. Museum of Modern Art.
Rio de Janeiro, commenced 1954

Garcia Roza, Henrique E. Mindlin, and
Giancarlo Palanti. The most important
events in the history of Brazilian architec-
ture since 1950 are Oscar Niemeyer's
Ibirapuéra Exhibition Pavilions in São
Paulo (1953); in Rio, Lúcio Costa's Parque
Guinle apartment buildings (1948–50–54);
Affonso Eduardo Reidy's Pedregulho
Housing Estate and his Museum of
Modern Art in Rio de Janeiro (1954 –);
Jorge Machado Moreira's University City
(1953–), as well as, of course, Niemeyer's
superb buildings in Brasilia.

In spite of obvious individual differences,
there is in most Brazilian work a deliberate
formal research, an attempt at lightness
and airiness and, in many cases, a trans-
literation into contemporary terms of old
elements from the colonial past (such as
open ceramic tile work, various forms of
'jalousies', or the renewed use of ceramic
murals in tiles, i.e. *azulejos*, or in mosaic)
which give it a common character. There
is in general, however, much less use of
colour in the exterior than might be
expected by the foreign visitor. It is

Oscar Niemeyer, Zenon Lotufo, Helio Uchôa
and Eduardo Kneese de Mello. Palace of
Industry, Ibirapuéra Park. São Paulo, 1951–4

Oscar Niemeyer. President's Palace. Brasilia, completed 1959

probably felt that the brilliance of the sky and of the sunlight, as well as the gorgeous landscape, need no further reinforcement. A great deal of the colour which serves to emphasize the best architectural jobs is due to the surrounding gardens, in connection with which the immense contribution of Roberto Burle Marx must be stressed. The rôle played by Brazilian painters, starting with Candido Portinari's murals and *azulejo* designs for the Ministry of Education must also be noted.

Modern architecture in Brazil has had a paradoxical development, leading it to the summits of creative achievement almost from the start, a result perhaps of the fact that it was handed down and imposed from above by an intellectual *élite* under exceptionally fortunate circumstances. Monumental buildings were put up before any real attempt had been made at solving the urgent problems of providing schools or hospitals or low-cost housing. Until recent times city planning and interior decoration were neglected in favour of more spectacular undertakings. Architects were satisfied with traditional Brazilian furniture or the best that could be brought from Europe, contemporary if possible.

The most striking example of this peculiar development is the dramatic creation by President Juscelino Kubitschek of Brasilia, the new capital for the country, about 1,000 kilometres from the Atlantic coast, in a hitherto virgin territory. Located on gently sloping highlands, half surrounded by a huge artificial lake, this new city, planned for 600,000 inhabitants, was formally inaugurated as the new seat of the Federal Government on 21 April 1960, only three years, one month, and five days after an international jury had selected Lúcio Costa's deceptively simple plan in an open competition among Brazilian architects. In a general outline reminiscent of an aeroplane, the wings are devoted to the super blocks of apartment dwellings; the main axis, along what would correspond to the body of the plane, to the monumental distribution of the Ministries and the Plaza of the Three Powers (Presidential Palace, Supreme Court, and Congress), with the business and entertainment districts round the intersection, which is emphasized by the bus depot, arranged on several levels. Thoroughly planned with deep human concern, yet deliberately aiming at a clear symbolic expression of the city's unique function, Brasilia has carried to the man-in-the-street the concept of planning to an unsurpassed degree, especially through the total elimination of traffic intersections, one of the aspects of planning most easily grasped by the general public.

The unity and integrated character of Brasilia derive not only from Costa's lucid plan but also from Oscar Niemeyer's striking design for most of the buildings carried out to date. There can be no question that the building of Brasilia, in very difficult economic and financial circumstances and involving considerable

sacrifices for the country as a whole, con-
stitutes a magnificently constructive state-
ment of the collective will of the people.
Bibliography: Philip L. Goodwin, *Brazil
Builds*, Museum of Modern Art, New
York 1943; Henry-Russell Hitchcock,
Latin American Architecture since 1945,
New York 1955; Henrique E. Mindlin,
Modern Architecture in Brazil, Colibris,
Amsterdam 1956.

HENRIQUE E. MINDLIN

Breuer, Marcel, b. Pecs, Hungary 1902.
In 1920 Breuer moved to Vienna, intending to become a painter and sculptor. After
a brief attendance at the Art Academy he
became disillusioned with its 'tired eclecticism' and looked around for a practical
apprenticeship in one of the crafts, which
would bring him into direct contact with
tools and materials. Before long, he heard
of Walter *Gropius's *Bauhaus, then
located in Weimar; and, late in 1920, he
left Vienna for Weimar and became one of
the youngest members of the first generation of Bauhaus students. Under the
influence of Breuer and others then at the
Bauhaus, the emphasis of the school began
to shift from 'arts and crafts' to 'art and
technology'—or from romanticism and
impressionism to rationalism and objectivity in design. Breuer's principal interest,
from the start, was in the area of furniture
design, and by 1924, at the age of twenty-
two, he took over the direction of the
Bauhaus's furniture department. Before
long his preoccupation with standardized,
modular unit furniture led him to interior
design and standardized, modular unit
housing—and, thus, to architecture.
Breuer's most notable contribution to contemporary design in the 1920s was in the
field of furniture, for he had invented, as
early as 1925, a series of systems that
employed continuously bent steel tubes
(painted or chromium-plated) to form the
structural frames of stools, chairs, and
tables. Indeed, between 1925 and 1928
Breuer literally designed almost every
single piece of modern, tubular steel furniture in use today all over the world. Among
his finest designs was the S-shaped cantilever chair of 1928, which remains the most
commonly used modern commercial chair
in the world today. Much of this important
experimental work in furniture design was
made possible by the move, in 1925, of the

Marcel Breuer. Elberfeld Hospital, 1928. Project

Marcel Breuer, Alfred and Emil Roth. Doldertal
apartments. Zurich, 1935–6

Marcel Breuer. Breuer House. New Canaan,
Conn., 1947

Marcel Breuer. Gymnasium, Litchfield High School. Litchfield, Conn., 1954–6

Bauhaus to Dessau, and the construction of the new Bauhaus by Gropius. Breuer was commissioned to design all the furniture needed in the new buildings, and this commission provided an important stimulus to his work in this field. In later years —especially in Switzerland and in England —Breuer again advanced the art of furniture design by developing some of the first bent and moulded plywood chairs ever manufactured in quantity, as well as some of the first chairs using aluminium as a structural supporting frame.

Meanwhile his interest in architecture had grown, and he left the Bauhaus in 1928 to practise as an architect and interior designer in Berlin. During the next half-dozen years Breuer built several houses and apartments easily as radical as—and often more practical than—the contemporary work of the time by *Le Corbusier and others. Moreover, he entered a number of competitions and otherwise prepared theoretical projects for cities, theatres, factories, etc., that greatly influenced his contemporaries. With the advent of Hitler in 1933, Breuer made preparations to leave Germany and soon entered into partnership with F. R. S. *Yorke in London. The partnership lasted until 1937, when Walter Gropius, who had been appointed Chairman of the Department of Architecture at Harvard, asked Breuer to join him on that faculty. At the same time, Gropius and Breuer formed an architectural partnership in Cambridge, Massachusetts. This partnership lasted until 1941.

While it is difficult, if not impossible, to separate the individual contributions of Gropius and Breuer both to the teaching at Harvard and to the houses designed in their office, it is fair to say that Breuer's contact with individual Harvard students was especially close (he was closer to them in age, and he tended to be extremely practical in his approaches to design problems); and it is fair, also, to say that much of Breuer's attention to detail is evident in the work completed by the Gropius and Breuer partnership. In any event, both Breuer's teaching and Breuer's completed buildings left a profound impression on a new generation of American architects. Among his students, for example, were such men as Philip *Johnson, Paul *Rudolph, John *Johansen, Edward L. Barnes, Landis Gores, and Willo von Moltke—all of them prominent in American architecture and planning today.

In 1946 Breuer moved to New York City, and he has practised there ever since. For the first few years of that practice, Breuer's work was limited largely to houses and smaller, institutional buildings; but in 1952 he was selected to be one of the three architects for the new Headquarters for UNESCO, in Paris. (The other two were the Italian Pier Luigi *Nervi, and the Frenchman Bernard H. *Zehrfuss.) From that moment on, Breuer's work became increasingly important internationally, and larger in scale: his UNESCO Headquarters were completed in 1958; a monastery in Minnesota was under construction at the same time; college buildings all over the

Page 59. Marcel Breuer. St John's Abbey Church. Collegeville, Minnesota, 1953–61

US, large urban projects in South America and in Asia, factories and office buildings in Europe and the US all came his way. At long last he had arrived.

In a sense, Breuer is the last of the true functionalists. In the early 1920s he was greatly influenced by the spirit of the *Constructivist movement, both in Russia and in Western Europe. All his designs were highly articulated: a Breuer chair would express every element separately, both in form and in material; a Breuer house would express different areas of activity in different and separate forms (his H-plans for houses, which separate the day-time areas from the night-time areas, are especially well known); in his construction details, every element of the structure was always clearly defined and separately articulated; and even in his large buildings, such as the UNESCO Headquarters, there was always a clear distinction and separation of functionally different elements—whether different kinds of buildings or different parts of the same building. The resulting clarity in his work has done much to keep modern architecture from becoming eclectic and formalistic. Although some of Breuer's separately articulated elements tended to be poetic rather than purely practical, they always did describe, very literally, what was happening in plan, structure, or building equipment. Still, this clarity of organization has certain drawbacks, for it is often difficult to create a coherent architectural grouping if each part of the group is given separate and equal importance. For this reason, some of the larger projects Breuer undertook in the years after 1952 have consisted of buildings which were individually impressive but failed to add up to truly significant architectural groupings. The UNESCO Headquarters, for example, consists of several separate structures, each of which is highly successful in itself; but as a group these separate structures do not, at present, form a successful architectural unity.

It is too early to evaluate Breuer's work in its entirety, but it is possible to evaluate his influence upon his contemporaries and upon younger generations of architects. Because of the great clarity of his structures and the great clarity of organization of his plans, he has become an enormously successful teacher, for in his work all the fundamentals of modern architecture are clearly distinguishable and presented with imagination and with art.

Bibliography: Peter Blake, Marcel Breuer, Architect and Designer, New York 1949; Marcel Breuer, Sun and Shadow, the Philosophy of an Architect, New York 1956; Marcel Breuer, 1921–1962, Stuttgart 1962; Marcel Breuer: 1921–1961, Buildings and Projects, ed. Cranston Jones, London 1962.
                                                          PETER BLAKE

Brinkman, Johannes Andreas, b. Rotterdam 1902, d. 1949. From 1925 in partnership with L. C. van der *Vlugt. The Van Nelle tobacco factory in Rotterdam (1928–30), to whose design Mart Stam also contributed, is, with its transparent structure, one of the most important industrial buildings of the twenties. The slab-shaped Bergpolder point block in Rotterdam was built in 1933–4 (Brinkman, van der Vlugt and W. van Tijen), an early prototype of buildings on stilts. Partnership with J. H. van den *Broek (1937).

Broek, J. H. van den, b. Rotterdam 1898. The names of J. H. van den Broek and Jacob B. *Bakema are inseparably connected with post-war building in the Netherlands, and the reconstruction of Rotterdam in particular. Van den Broek is a professor at Delft Technical College, where he himself graduated in 1924. He started his own practice in 1927 at Rotterdam, entering into partnership with J. A. *Brinkman in 1937 and J. B. Bakema in 1948.

Architecture and social outlook are closely linked in the work of van den Broek and Bakema. The Lijnbaan shopping centre in Rotterdam (1953), a systematically laid-out pedestrian street with low-built shops, was a distinctive contribution to current town-planning practice. The civic centre at Marl (under construction) gives a modern interpretation to the old idea of a citadel, while providing a comprehensive centre for a rising industrial town. A considerable proportion of the two architects' practice is taken up with housing and schools (school buildings at Brielle, 1948–57; Montessori Lyceum, Rotterdam, 1958). Van den Broek and Bakema have carried out other projects also, in which Bakema's description of architecture as the three-

dimensional expression of human activity
has been realized. These include exhibition buildings (Dutch pavilions at the
International Expositions at Paris, 1937,
and Brussels, 1958), offices (Van Om-
meren, Antwerp, 1939; N. B. ten Cate,
Almelo, 1954), department stores (Wassen
van Vorst, 1951; Galeries Modernes,
1956, both in Rotterdam), and industrial
layouts, laboratories, and research buildings for the Technical High School at
Delft. The two churches at Schiedam
(1957) and Nagele, in the Nordostpolder
(1959) are severely rectilinear buildings
which achieve their effects through the
interplay of large glazed areas and plane
surfaces.

Bibliography: J. H. van den Broek,
*Creative krachten in de architectonische
conceptie,* Delft 1948; Jürgen Joedicke,
*Architektur und Städtebau, Das Werk der
Architekten van den Broek und Bakema,*
Stuttgart, in preparation.

J. J. VRIEND

J. H. van den Broek and Jacob B. Bakema. Town
Hall Complex. Marl, under construction. Model

Brutalism. Brutalism gave conscious form
to a mood that was widespread among
younger architects in the 1950s, but in
spite of the fact that it expressed a sentiment that was felt in most parts of the
Westernized world its origins can be pin-
pointed in space and time with some
precision. Although Giedion is wrong in
his etymology ('Brute + Alison') he is right
in identifying the Smithson family as the
source of the word—either Alison *Smithson or the Smithson's family friend Guy
Oddie (who used to call Peter Smithson
'Brutus') was the first person to utter the
phrase *The New Brutalism,* some time in
the early summer of 1954.

This much being established, what was the
intended content of the phrase? The basis
was a mood of frustration brought on
partly by the difficulties of building in
Britain after the Second World War, and
partly by disgust at the smugness of the
compromising elders who were still able to
build because they were well placed with
the 'Establishment'. The stylistic preferences of these elders were known as 'The
New Humanism' by the political Left, 'The
New Empiricism' by the political Right.
'The New Brutalism' as a phrase was
intended as a mockery of both, but it also
drew attention to certain real qualities in
the architecture that was being admired or

designed by the Smithsons and their
generation.

They set as their standard the uncompromising ruthlessness of *Mies van der Rohe
and *Le Corbusier, their intellectual
clarity, their honest presentation of structure and materials. At the same time, they
sensed in the work of these masters a
continuing tradition, an architecture that
lay above and beyond styles and fashions
—among the work of the past they admired the clarity and formality of Palladio,
the heroic scale of the Anglo-Baroque
architects Vanbrugh and Hawksmoor, and
the clear-cut and massive forms of early
19th-century engineering structures.

J. H. van den Broek and Jacob B. Bakema.
Church of the Resurrection. Schiedam, 1957

But the architecture that emerged from these admirations was, in the beginning, purely Miesian. No doubt a streak of English puritanism accounts for this initial selection of a simple, elegant structural system, for it was allied to an absolute horror of any pretence or concealment; not only were structure and materials honestly expressed, but services as well. In the school at Hunstanton, England, the first true Brutalist building, not only are steel and brick expressed with an honesty that goes even beyond the acceptable subterfuges of Mies, but pipe runs, electrical conduits, and other services are exposed to view. The austerity of this design was so remarkable that it attracted world-wide attention, and international comparisons were sought. Of these, Louis *Kahn's Art Centre at Yale University was in some ways more convincing than Mies's own work, because Kahn seemed equally preoccupied with the raw nature of the materials and concerned with the expression of the services.

By the time that this was happening, however, the original puritanical extremism of

Jack Lynn and Ivor Smith. Park Hill Housing Estate. Sheffield, 1955–61

Le Corbusier. Unité d'Habitation. Marseilles, 1947–52. Detail of piers at ground floor level

the English Brutalists was beginning to merge with an international movement of different origins and only remotely comparable aims. This movement could be characterized by developments as diverse as the a-formal painting of Jackson Pollock and the a-formal planning of the Chapel at Ronchamp, the *art brut* of Dubuffet and the *béton brut* of the *Unité* at Marseilles. The Brutalism of the uncompromising exhibition of materials became allied to a Brutalism of form; the expressed symmetry of the Hunstanton School and the concealed symmetry of the Yale Art Centre were abandoned in favour of a ruthless honesty in expressing the functional spaces and their inter-relationships. Even that adaptable rectangular geometry, derived from abstract painting, that the older functionalists had been able to accept, was now cast aside, in favour of modes of composition based on the topography of the site and the topology of internal circulation—as may be seen very clearly in the siting and planning of Park Hill, Sheffield, designed in the city architect's office by the newly graduated Jack Lynn and Ivor Smith.

Once the Brutalism of a building such as
Park Hill is understood it becomes clear
that the application of the term to such
fashionably sentimental architecture as
that of Leonardo Ricci is improper, as is
any attempt to make 'Brutalists' out of—
say—Juan *O'Gorman or Paolo *Soleri.
Brutalism implies some sort of attempt to
make manifest the moral imperatives that
were built into the tradition of modern
architecture by the pioneers of the 19th
century, and the use of shutter-patterned
concrete or exposed steel-work is only a
symptom of this intention—as Peter Smithson has said, 'We also admire the nature of
gold paint, where it is necessary.' The
fundamental aim of Brutalism at all times
has been to find a structural, spatial,
organizational and material concept that is
'necessary' in this metaphysical sense to
some particular building, and then express
it with complete honesty in a form that
will be a unique and memorable image. In
the creation of this definitive image the
other plastic arts provide, not an aesthetic,
but an exemplar of method or a standard
of comparison—thus, the admirations of
the Brutalists have covered subjects as
diverse as US car-styling and the Ise
shrines in Japan. Neither have had any
visible influence on Brutalist architecture,
but both are examples of images created
out of the kind of necessary conditions the
Brutalists believe to be fundamental, also,
to the conception of buildings today. It is
this insistence on the primacy of the given
and necessary factors in the conception
of a building that has caused Sir John
Summerson to compare the beliefs of the
Brutalists to the Rigorism of Lodoli and
other radical theorists of late 18th-century
Italian Illuminism.

On this ground, the only Brutalist building
in Italy is the Istituto Marchiondi by
Vittoriano Viganò, even though at first
sight its departures from the common
practices of the modern movement appear
less extreme than those of the neo-Liber-
tarian sentimentalists. Stylistically, the

Alison and Peter Smithson. Hunstanton School.
Norfolk, 1954

Alison and Peter Smithson. Economist Building.
London, under construction. Model

Vittoriano Viganò. Istituto Marchiondi. Milan,
1957

Istituto Marchiondi consciously echoes the ideas, if not the work, of Giuseppe *Terragni and the period of *l'architettura razionalista*, which provide an image that is entirely expressive of the stern, reformative necessities that underlie the conception of this building.

Nevertheless the Istituto Marchiondi draws attention to the relationship of Brutalism to the traditions of architecture. For all its aggressive tone and uncompromising attitudes, Brutalism does not represent a radical departure from the traditional conception of architecture—it is in no way comparable to the technological extremism of Buckminster *Fuller, nor even to the methods of radical functional analysis developed in England by the Nuffield Trust. The most instructive comparisons to be made on this subject are with action-painting and *musique-concrète*. Action-painting abandoned the last vestiges of formal composition but still accepted such 'outworn' traditions as paint, canvas, and a rectangular format for the picture, all of which had been previously rejected at various times by modern painters; *musique-concrète* abandoned the polite fictions of the sounds made by artificial musical instruments in favour of recordings of 'real noises', but it abandoned very little else of what had been left of the traditions of music by earlier modernist composers. Similarly the Brutalists, while abandoning fictitious surface for the 'reality' of steel and concrete and the concept of formal composition as necessary to the art of architecture, have still practised and theorized within the basic traditions of architecture.

To make another comparison between the Brutalists and one of the architects whom they admire, without now imitating his forms: the Smithsons's project for the Economist Building in London has the three component buildings informally grouped around an irregular piazza, whereas the Seagram Building in New York is a single classicist slab, axially sited behind a formal forecourt. The irregular Economist piazza gives a truer image of the organizational and topological necessities of that particular functional programme than an imitation of the Seagram composition would have done, and yet this project accepts the siting of the main built volumes on a pedestrian platform from which

vehicles are banished, as does the Seagram, rather than providing some radical solution of the relationship between building, pedestrians and wheeled traffic.

Brutalism, then, is a tough-minded reforming movement within the framework of modern architectural thought, not a revolutionary attempt to overthrow it. On the other hand, the implicit intention of the Brutalists to return to fundamental functionalist principles in order to make them fulfil their apparent promise may involve the refusal of so many marginal compromises that an effective revolution may unintentionally result.

                                        REYNER BANHAM

Bryggman, Erik William, b. Turku 1891, d. Turku 1955. Bryggman studied at the Design School of the Turku Art Society from 1906 to 1909, and later at Helsinki Polytechnic, where he graduated in architecture in 1916. Directly afterwards he began his professional career with a series of important works in collaboration: the Helsinki War Memorial, with the sculptor Ilkka; the Monument to Liberty at Oulu, with the sculptor Sakselin; and the restoration of the medieval Cathedral at Turku, carried out from 1921 to 1923. In the same year Bryggman opened his own office in the old capital, where he always lived, and where he was joined a few years later by Aino and Alvar *Aalto. The Aaltos's propinquity and collaboration with Bryggman did not last long, however, as the former afterwards moved on to Helsinki, but it came during the most critical period in the development of their architectural thought and resulted in a unique work of collaboration, of great importance in the history of Finnish architecture: the Seven Hundredth Anniversary Exhibition of the City of Turku, which took place in 1929 and is considered to be the first example of modern architecture in Scandinavia.

Bryggman, who was seven years older than Aalto, had carried out a good many works before the Turku Exhibition; they mark the most important stages in that process leading to *Functionalism which was silently developing in the architecture of the young nation. Amongst them may be noted a block of flats for employees of the Finnish Sugar Company at Turku (1923–4), some houses in Turku and elsewhere, and two hotels in Turku: the Seurahuone, with very sophisticated décor (1928), and the Hospitz Hotel (1927–9). His finest work was carried out, however, between 1930 and 1940, starting with Parainen Cemetery Chapel, the Kinopalatsi Cinema at Turku, and the Finnish Pavilion at the Antwerp International Exhibition, all dating from 1930. Next came a series of delightful white country houses, set like crystals amid the virgin nature of the islands in the archipelago: those at Ruissalo and Hirvenssalo (1933); the Villa Kaino at Kaskerta (1935); the Villa Jaatinen (1939); and Vierumäki Sports Club, another work in a purely rationalist style (1930–6). Finally, in this period, we may mention the Library of Turku Academy (1935), and the cemetery chapel in the same city, built between 1938 and 1941. The book tower of the Academy rises in a district of the old city, over which the dark mass of the Cathedral looms in the distance. It is remarkable for the balance of its voids in the large white walls, and for the perfect way it fits in with its surroundings, via a subtle handling of proportions and a complete understanding of the *genius loci*. Turku Cemetery Chapel is Bryggman's best known work, and it is undoubtedly a very fine one, especially in the magical lightness of its internal space, but taken as a whole it is certainly less great, already revealing in certain points the germ of that progressive decline that ultimately affected his performance. The chapel was built to replace one originally erected in 1877 to the designs of F. A. Sjöstrom. Construction commenced in 1938, and was finished with much labour in 1941, despite the war and the great difficulties of supply. In this project more than any other of Bryggman's designs, one feels that the architect has reached deeply into himself and brought to the surface all his most intimate and painful sensibility, but that in doing so he has passed the inexorable limit beyond which it becomes a weakness not to control one's own powers of suggestion. Nevertheless, Turku Chapel is the work in which the architect's personality is expressed most fully, through the medium of a serene rationalism, rarefied and infused by the subtle *frisson* of a pervading romanticism, in a placid and almost still atmosphere, where the dominating whiteness finds its essential complement in the light, which, as it varies, alters the

Erik Bryggman. Cemetery Chapel. Turku, 1938–41

weight and the consistency of the architectural elements.

Bryggman's post-war works, in the decade from 1945 to 1955, the year of his untimely death, confirm that Turku Chapel marked the end of his rationalist period in the thirties, just as the 1929 Exhibition proved the turning point between his previous classicism and the functionalism which followed. The buildings of this final period, which we may call one of romantic decline, are numerous, and often very good: they include an estate of timber houses at Pansio, near Turku (1946), the Students' Union and the chemistry laboratory of Turku Academy (1948–50), the Villa Nuuttila on the island of Kuusisto, finely tailored to the site (1947–51) and Riihimäki Water Tower (1951–2).
The last designs which bear Bryggman's

name are probably, in part at least, the work of his office, over which the architect, by now a sick man, gradually lost control. They show a decline towards more complex forms, at times tending to *organic practice, with the careful siting of buildings in the landscape, at others showing a more strictly 'national' inspiration in the handling of volumes, materials and colours, as in his last cemetery chapels. Then his life drew to a premature close, leaving us as a consolation for his loss those authentic works of art, reflecting in their essential forms of line and volume the clear simplicity of his own life and spirit, which have made Turku, already famous for its ancient architectural traditions, Erik Bryggman's city.

Bibliography: Leonardo Mosso, 'L'opera di Erik Bryggman nella storia dell' architetture finlandese', in *Atti SJA*, Turin December 1958.

LEONARDO MOSSO

Bunshaft, Gordon, b. Buffalo, New York 1909. Studied at the Massachusetts Institute of Technology, Cambridge, Mass. In 1937 he joined the architectural firm

Félix Candela. Church of the Miraculous Virgin. Mexico, 1954

of *Skidmore, Owings and Merrill; since 1946 partner. Bunshaft was responsible for the design, among others, of the Lever Building (New York, 1952), one of the most influential buildings of the last two decades, and the Connecticut General Life Insurance Building (Bloomfield, Conn., 1957).

Burnham, Daniel Hudson, b. Henderson, New York 1846, d. Heidelberg 1912; 1873–91 in partnership with John W. *Root. Burnham and Root designed the Reliance Building at Chicago (1890–4), a classical example of early American steelframe construction, and the Monadnock Building (1889–91), a skyscraper with load-bearing outer walls of gently modulated profile. After Root's death in 1891, the firm, which had been entrusted with the preparation of the World's Columbian Exposition at Chicago in 1893, veered towards an academic eclecticism. Planning of city centres with axial layouts (Washington, Cleveland, San Francisco, Chicago).

Candela, Félix, b. Madrid 1910. Studied at the Escuela Superior de Arquitectura, Madrid. Towards the end of his studies, Candela had the opportunity of watching one of the best known structures by *Torroja, the Frontón Recoletos, being built. This double barrel-vault spanning 197 feet by 118 feet, or other works by Torroja, probably awakened Candela's interest in *shell vaulting. At all events, he was determined to visit the German shell vaulting specialists Dischinger and Finsterwalder, when the outbreak of the Spanish Civil War in July 1936 prevented his trip. It is anybody's guess if Candela and the exponents of the highly developed German methods of calculation would have seen eye to eye. After Candela had fought in the Civil War on the Republican side, he came to *Mexico in the summer of 1939 via the refugee camps at Perpignan. After twelve years in his adopted country, during which time he, and later his brother Antonio, picked up a living as architects and builders, he began advocating the use of shell vaulting, at first in articles and lectures. The building of the University City gave him an opportunity to construct the first hyperbolic paraboloids, which enabled him to reduce the roof of the Cosmic Ray Building to a thickness of $\frac{5}{8}$ inch. A special advantage of this shape as compared with the sphere or other types of vault, is that the shuttering for hyperbolic paraboloids can be made from straight boards. Due to the relative simplicity of this process, and the great saving in material, Candela's constructions are more economical than other rigid roofs, and this fact alone won his firm numerous industrial commissions. Candela increased his spans with every project and became increasingly bolder in the exploitation of shell vaulting. When he maintains that he is guided less by exact calculation than by an intuitive feeling 'in the manner of the old master builders of cathedrals' we must recall that his intuition has a very firm foundation in his knowledge of materials and stresses, which grows with each new building. As an architect and designer, Candela has distinguished himself with his Church of the Miraculous Virgin in Mexico City (1954) which shows the unmistakable influence of *Gaudí, even though Candela departs widely from the building methods of the lonely Catalan. Later buildings of a non-industrial nature such as the Stock Exchange, several churches and pavilions in Mexico and Cuernavaca and a restaurant in Xochimilco were executed in collaboration with different architects, who were glad to avail themselves of the free outlines of his structures in their search for organic or baroque shapes.

Candela is not lacking in official recognition these days. In 1961 he was awarded the gold medal of the Institute of Structural Engineers in London and almost simultaneously the Auguste Perret Prize of the Union Internationale des Architectes. Shortly afterwards, Harvard appointed him Norton Professor of Poetry.

Bibliography: Max Cetto, *Modern Architecture in Mexico*, Stuttgart and New York 1960; Colin Faber, *Candela, the architect of shell construction*, New York and Munich, in preparation.

MAX CETTO

Candilis, Georges, b. Baku, Russia 1913. Studied in Greece where he met *Le Corbusier in 1933 at the *CIAM Congress in Athens. A scholarship made a stay in Paris possible (1945), and after that (until 1950) he worked for Le Corbusier. Residential buildings in Morocco (with Dony, Josic, and Woods). Planning for Le Mirail near Toulouse. The new town of Bagnols-

Félix Candela and Enrique de la Mora. Chapel of the Missionaries of the Holy Ghost. Coyoacán, 1956

sur-Cèze in the Rhône valley (started in 1956, with Bodiansky, Woods and Piot), adjoining an old urban centre with which it shares a cultural and sports precinct.

Casson, Sir Hugh Maxwell, b. Southampton 1913. Studied at Cambridge; Craven Scholar, British School at Athens. In private practice from 1937 with the late C. Nicholson; resumed 1946, after war service, latterly with Neville Conder. Professor of Interior Design, Royal College of Art, since 1953. His directorship of architecture at the *Festival of Britain, 1948–51, ensured its remarkable triumph as a piece of organized *townscape; the same powers of urbanistic control are evident in his schemes for Cambridge University (with N. Conder). His Youth Hostel at Holland Park, London, blends sympathetically with the remains of Holland House (17th century), while making no concessions to historicism.

HAROLD MEEK

Castiglioni, Enrico, b. Busto Arsizio near Milan 1914. Designs for complex sculpturally modelled shell constructions, which vault wide areas and mould spaces with the help of light. (Project for the main station in Naples, 1954; for the pilgrimage Church of the Madonna delle Lacrime at Syracuse, 1957.)

Chamberlin, Powell and Bon: Peter
Chamberlin, Geoffrey Powell, and Christof
Bon. First attracted attention in 1952 in
their prize-winning scheme for high-
density housing at Golden Lane, London
(1953–7), a controversial layout with
interesting treatment of multiple ground
levels, a preoccupation later (1957) developed in their plan for the Barbican district of
London, with separate routes for traffic and
pedestrians. Their Bousfield Primary
School with its *Miesian exteriors, was
awarded the London Bronze Medal for
Architecture in 1956; Newington Secondary School, also in London, features a
complex folded roof over the assembly hall.
Among their other schemes mention may
be made of the Sports Centre for Birmingham University, with sculpturesque
buildings atop a large podium, and the
development plan for Leeds University,
which closely integrates the academic layout
with the city centre.
Bibliography: 'Detailed Proposals for the
Barbican Redevelopment', in *Architects'
Journal* (London), 4.6.1959. HAROLD MEEK

Chiattone, Mario, b. Lugano 1891.
Studied architecture and painting at the
Brera, Milan. Became a member of the
*Futurist movement and together with his
fellow-student *Sant'Elia exhibited a col-
lection of drawings at Milan in 1914 under
the heading 'Structures for a modern
Metropolis'.

Daniel Hudson Burnham and John Wellborn
Root. Monadnock Building. Chicago, 1889–91

Chicago School. This is a term conventionally applied to the characteristic commercial architecture of the American
mid-west, especially Chicago, in the last
quarter of the 19th century. It has also
occasionally been used, but inappro-
priately, to cover the domestic Prairie style
of 1900 that was evolved by Frank Lloyd
*Wright and his followers in the same
region. The Chicago style of commercial
architecture is dominated by two features:
the metal frame, as the basic structural
system, together with its clear expression

Henry Hobson Richardson. Marshall Field
Warehouse. Chicago, 1885–7

on the building's exterior in a simple, often non-historical vocabulary. The Chicago fire of 1871 demonstrated the importance of fire-proof construction and the inability of exposed cast-iron structures to withstand the heat, but the definitive solution to this problem, the protective combination of a metal frame sheathed by brick or masonry, was not arrived at until the construction of the Home Insurance Building, 1883–5, by William Le Baron *Jenney, a ten-storey structure which was subsequently extended. However, this building's structural system was only tentatively expressed in the somewhat conventional detailing and awkward articulation of the exterior, which has none of the suavity of subsequent skyscrapers of the 1890s by *Adler and *Sullivan, *Burnham and *Root, or *Holabird and *Roche. Indeed, the outward appearance of Jenney's pioneer structure does not break with the eclectic Victorian and Second Empire vernacular modes that had been employed previously in Chicago by H. H. *Richardson in the American Express Building, 1872, and by Dankmar Adler in the Central Music Hall, 1879, both typical examples of Chicago architecture before the advent of the skyscraper. Furthermore, a significant stylistic predecessor (though not a specific inspiration) for the Home Insurance Building is the ten-storey mansarded Tribune Tower, New York, 1872–5, by Richard Morris Hunt (1827–95). While this earlier instance of eastern commercial architecture did not employ the metal frame, its pronounced vertical conception certainly is as deserving of the label 'skyscraper' as are the later, more structurally sophisticated towers in Chicago.

If Jenney's structure helped to provide the freedom from height restrictions that were imposed by load-bearing masonry construction, the 'style' of the Chicago School was reoriented by the simple monumentality of Richardson's rusticated, roundarched, but only nominally revivalistic Marshall Field Warehouse, 1885–7, a building which depended for its effect upon an epic expression of its surface material. At first its forms were imitated, as in Adler and Sullivan's Auditorium Building, 1886–9, or in Burnham and Root's Rookery, 1885–7. These derivative structures were rather more elaborate and historically detailed versions of the Richardsonian paradigm, and the external walls of both were of conventional masonry construction. Subsequently the letter of Richardson's style was dropped, but his direct, expressive compositional principle was transformed into a mode fit for the metal frame and the large glazed openings which now became possible. Jenney's second Leiter Building (now Sears, Roebuck & Co.), 1889–90, is a bold, regular eight-storey volume in which the lines of the structure and the regular window rhythms dominate the almost invisible touches of classicizing detail. Similar qualities are to be observed in the pronounced verticality of the Reliance Building, 1890–4, by Daniel H. Burnham and

Daniel Hudson Burnham and John Wellborn Root. Reliance Building. Chicago, 1890–4

John W. Root, one of the most startling anticipations of the metal and glass style of the mid-20th century. The lower floors of the Reliance Building were built at the same time as Burnham and Root were completing the last masonry skyscraper, the sixteen-storey Monadnock Building, 1889–91, whose simple, rugged elevation contrasts with its light if somewhat inelegant contemporary. Two of Sullivan's finest Chicago School metal-frame skyscrapers of this period were built in St Louis (Wainwright Building, 1890–1) and Buffalo (Guarantee Building, 1894–5), but his most characteristic efforts of the late 1890s are in Chicago: the Carson, Pirie and Scott Store, 1899, and his portion of the façade of the tripartite Gage Building, 1898–9. The Gage Building was the work of William Holabird and Martin Roche (who had made a skeleton framed addition to Burnham and Root's massive Monadnock Building in 1893), and Sullivan was employed to design the façade of the larger right third of the building, accommodating himself to the established structural grid. A comparison of the differing parts of this façade points up the multiple virtues of the Chicago School: the directness and simplicity of the Holabird and Roche portions is in contrast to the more refined, complicated, yet beautifully integrated Sullivan design.

The expressive originality of the Chicago School did not outlast the beginning of the 20th century. The admiration for the academic modes of design, popularized by the Columbian Exposition of 1893 (originally projected in a romantic, almost Richardsonian mode by Root in 1891, but finally executed in a frigid *beaux-arts* manner), did not take hold immediately, but by 1900 the great period of Chicago commercial architecture was over. It did, however, produce a notable, if somewhat isolated, aftermath in such works as Richard E. Schmidt's (b. 1865) Nepeenauk Building, 1901–2, and Montgomery Ward Warehouse (actually by the firm Schmidt, Garden and Martin), 1906–8, in Dwight Perkins's Carl Schurz High School, 1910, and, most provocatively, in Frank Lloyd Wright's Larkin Building, Buffalo, 1904.

Bibliography: Early Modern Architecture: Chicago 1870–1910, New York 1940; Thomas S. Tallmadge, *Architecture in Old Chicago*, Chicago 1941; F. Randall, *History of the Development of Building Construction in Chicago*, Urbana, Illinois 1949; G. Condit, *The Rise of the Skyscraper*, Chicago 1952.

JOHN M. JACOBUS, JR

CIAM (Congrès Internationaux d'Architecture Moderne). The foundation of CIAM in 1928 has been called the beginning of the 'academic' phase of modern architecture: the time certainly appeared propitious for the introduction of some kind of international order into the scattered and independent essays towards a new architecture whose international unity of intention and style had been demonstrated at the Weissenhof exhibition of the previous year.

The effective impetus towards the foundation of CIAM came from Hélène de Mandrot, a sincere and intelligent woman who had aspirations towards being a patroness of the arts. She proposed in the first place a reunion of creative spirits at her château at La Sarraz, Switzerland, but this romantic project was turned to something more purposeful after consultation with Sigfried Giedion and *Le Corbusier. The preparatory document, issued to intending delegates, stated: 'This first congress is convened with the aim of establishing a programme of action to drag architecture from the academic impasse' (it was, in fact, to drag it into another) 'and to place it in its proper social and economic milieu. This congress should ... determine the limits of the studies and discussions shortly to be undertaken by further congresses.' Although a distinction was thus made between the preparatory congress and later meetings, the date of 26, 27, and 28 June 1928 at La Sarraz is remembered and recorded as CIAM I, in spite of the fact that the properly constituted series of *Congrès Internationaux d'Architecture Moderne* did not begin until after the declaration of 28 June. The contents of the declaration embodied most of the best aspirations as well as the most fashionable fetishes of the architecture of the time. Sample statements read: 'It is only from the present that our architectural work should be derived', and 'The intention that brings us together is that of attaining a harmony of existing elements—a harmony indispensable to the present—BY PUTTING ARCHITECTURE BACK ON ITS REAL PLANE, THE

ECONOMIC AND SOCIAL PLANE; therefore architecture should be freed of the sterile influence of the Academies and of anti-quated formulas', and again, 'The most efficacious production is derived from rationalization and standardization.'

The historical irony of these repeated invectives against the Academies is under-lined by the dry, formalistic statement of aims that appears as the preamble to the statutes drawn up at Frankfurt-am-Main in 1929 (CIAM II). The aims are given as: (a) to state the contemporary architectural problem; (b) to restate the idea of modern architecture; (c) to disseminate this idea throughout the technical, economic and social strata of contemporary life; (d) to remain alert to the problems of architec-ture.

The Frankfurt Statutes also gave CIAM three operative organs: (1) the Congrès or general assembly of the members; (2) CIRPAC (Comité Internationale pour la Résolution des Problèmes de l'Architecture Contemporaine) to be elected by the Congrès; and (3) working groups, to apply themselves to specific subjects in collabora-tion with non-architectural specialists. At the same time the hierarchy of membership was stabilized in the form of national member-groups, to which individuals belonged.

It must be stated that this academic flavour (doubtless given by the 'clerics' such as Giedion, rather than the practising archi-tects) was in no way representative of the work actually being undertaken in these years. The Frankfurt Congress had been called under the auspices of Ernst *May, the city architect and Europe's greatest expert on low-cost housing, and its out-come was a serious report, Die Wohnung für das Existenzminimum. CIAM III was held in Brussels in 1930, through the good offices of Victor *Bourgeois, and applied itself to basic problems of land-organiza-tion for housing, publishing an equally important report, Rationelle Bebauungs-weisen. Both reports were at once dogmatic and realistic, somewhat in the manner of the town-planning studies being pursued at the Bauhaus under Hannes *Meyer, and these documents close the 1920s with the last genuine group-efforts of the architects who had met together to build Weissenhof. The next three years were to see funda-mental changes.

Already in 1930 it was becoming apparent that CIAM was neither intellectually nor organizationally prepared for the problem to which the logic of its discussions had driven it—town planning. In order to deal with this situation CIAM set to work to standardize the graphic techniques, scales, and methods of presentation used by its members (an enterprise that was not really completed until the adoption of the Grille-CIAM after 1949). The Dutch national group, under Cor van *Eesteren, became the working group entrusted with the evolution of an effective symbol language for town planning. These labours, con-ducted against a background of growing political tensions and disintegrating inter-national relations, proved to be protracted, and CIRPAC met three times (Berlin, 1931, Barcelona, 1932, and Paris, 1933) before it was felt that work was sufficiently advanced for another plenary Congrès to be called. This delay of almost three years proved crucial to the whole future of the move-ment; CIAM underwent a subtle and irrevocable change and took on the character which it was to preserve until its collapse more than twenty years later.

CIAM IV—theme 'The Functional City' —took place in July and August 1933 aboard the S.S. Patris, in Athens, and in Marseilles at the end of the voyage. It was the first of the 'romantic' congresses, set against a background of scenic splendour, not the reality of industrial Europe, and it was the first Congrès to be dominated by Le Corbusier and the French, rather than the tough German realists. The Mediter-ranean cruise was clearly a welcome relief from the worsening situation of Europe, and in this brief respite from reality the delegates produced the most Olympian, rhetorical, and ultimately destructive docu-ment to come out of CIAM: the *Athens Charter. The hundred and eleven propo-sitions that comprise the Charter consist in part of statements about the conditions of towns, and in part of proposals for the rectification of those conditions, grouped under five main headings: Dwellings, Recreation, Work, Transportation, and Historic Buildings.

The tone remains dogmatic, but is also generalized and less specifically related to immediate practical problems than were the Frankfurt and Brussels reports. The generalization had its virtues, where it brought with it a greater breadth of vision and insisted that cities could be considered only in relation to their surrounding regions, but this persuasive generality which gives the Athens Charter its air of universal applicability conceals a very narrow conception of both architecture and town planning and committed CIAM unequivocally to: (*a*) rigid functional zoning of city plans, with green belts between the areas reserved to the different functions, and (*b*) a single type of urban housing, expressed in the words of the Charter as 'high, widely-spaced apartment blocks wherever the necessity of housing high densities of population exists'. At a distance of thirty years we recognize this as merely the expression of an aesthetic preference, but at the time it had the power of a Mosaic commandment and effectively paralysed research into other forms of housing. The Paris *Congrès* of 1937 (CIAM V) which was to be the last before the war, did little more than make marginal annotations to the Charter.

By the time the war was over, twelve years had passed since the Charter was drawn up, and its proposals had become the established dogma of progressive town planning. In the first years of peace there could be seen attempts to apply the Charter as a universal blueprint all over the world. But even while the *Système-CIAM* was being enforced in the schools and in planning offices its fatal weakness had been recognized, as is made clear by the insertion of a section in *Can Our Cities Survive?* that had no warrant in the Charter: the Civic Centre. At first this appears to be little more than a place where the citizen can go to escape from the Cartesian prison of Dwelling / Work / Recreation / Transportation, but as the study of centres proceeded it became apparent that CIAM's Functional City had been conceived in ignorance of the city's specific functions. Thus the Charter defines Dwelling as the first urban function; but it is also the first rural function; Work and Transportation are functions even of the nomadic life of the desert; Recreation is not specific to cities. The attempt to isolate the specifically urban functions of the city was to be the prime task of CIAM after the war, and since it led to the overthrow of the categories and categorical imperatives of the Athens Charter it was to lead to the

destruction of CIAM, to which the Charter had become more central than either the preparatory document of 1928 or the Statutes of 1929. At first there was no sign of trouble. CIAM VI met in 1947 at Bridgwater, England, a joyous reunion of the heroes of Weissenhof and the followers they had collected in the 1930s; its outcome, a review of buildings erected since CIAM V by the members, edited by Giedion and published under the title of *A Decade of New Architecture*. But at CIAM VII, held at Bergamo in 1949, a new pattern was beginning to emerge, with the growing importance of the Italian delegation and the gathering of numbers of war-toughened students on the fringes of the *Congrès* in order to sit at the feet of the men who were, to them, legendary figures, the makers of modern architecture.

At CIAM VIII, held at Hoddesdon in England, in honour of the Festival of Britain, 1951, the new pattern of CIAM was becoming plain—increasing numbers of students, and official recognition of the inadequacy of the Charter, since the theme was 'The Urban Core'. For this theme the delegates were as unprepared intellectually as they had been for town planning in 1930, and the Congress report, edited by Jacqueline Tyrwhitt, José Luis *Sert, and Ernesto *Rogers, is little more than a compendium of fashionable clichés, such as the need to integrate painting and sculpture into architecture, while at the heart of these so-called studies appears an intellectual and urbanistic vacuum: the centre of the city is considered simply as yet another functionally designated area, an open space, to which the citizens were to be attracted by some mysterious quality of 'spontaneity'.

It was not long before the failure of CIAM VIII was recognized, but in the meantime CIAM IX at Aix-en-Provence had taken place; its theme was officially 'Habitat', but the *Congrès* will be chiefly remembered as a mass rally of Le Corbusier's student fan-club and the proceedings, culminating in an impromptu striptease performance on the roof of the Unité at Marseilles, were marked by adolescent *bonhomie* rather than mature cerebration. Yet it was to be the young who undertook to deliver CIAM from the new 'academic impasse' into which it had lapsed. The group who were entrusted with the preparation of CIAM X (who were therefore known as Team-X) took up a position that, though it drew to some extent on the programme documents for CIAM IX, nevertheless represented a clean break with both the mood and the content of the Athens Charter. Against the large-scale diagrammatic generalizations of the Athenian tradition, Team-X set up the personal, the particular, and the precise: 'Each architect is asked to appear with his project under his arm, ready to commit himself. Today we recognize the existence of a new spirit. It is manifest in our revolt from mechanical concepts of order . . . CIAM X must make it clear that we, as architects, accept the responsibility for the creation of order through form . . . the responsibility for each act of creation, however small.' Though the theme of CIAM X was still nominally 'Habitat', the real business of the *Congrès*, which took place in Dubrovnik in 1956, was the direct challenge presented to the established members by the young radicals of Team-X, *Bakema, *Candilis, Gutmann, the *Smithsons, Howell, van *Eijck, and Voelcker. By the end of the congress, CIAM was in ruins and Team-X stood upon the wreckage of something that they had joined with enthusiasm, and— with equal enthusiasm—destroyed. The sense of the end of an epoch was so strong that the *Congrès* accepted the fact of death with comparative calm; the national groups were instructed to wind up their affairs, and the project of a memorial volume covering twenty-five years of work was seriously discussed. But there were national groups, notably the Italian, who felt that CIAM could still be of service. In addition, Team-X were not averse to international meetings as such, and the combination of these two parties produced, in 1959, a further congress in Otterlo, Holland. In content this was to be similar to what Team-X had intended for CIAM X, and particular projects were indeed discussed, individual responsibility was accepted, and the results, edited by Oscar Newman, were published as *CIAM 59 in Otterlo*. These published documents reveal that close discussion of the particular could often be as trivial as broad discussion of generalities, while the title of the report conceals a bitter dispute among the delegates who, in fact, voted to dissociate their activities from the word 'CIAM'. But the vote was disputed by some of the delegates who left before the final meeting, and as a result accusations of bad faith were launched against Team-X by founder-members Giedion, Sert, *Gropius, and Le Corbusier (none of whom had been in any way involved with the congress).

This was neither a productive nor a dignified outcome to thirty years of international activity, and the blame for the final collapse of CIAM must be laid chiefly on the inability of the founder-members to resist the temptation to *faire école*. They failed to guard against the academic tendencies in their midst, and became the victims of what Cor van Eesteren termed 'a too formal structure' to which work-programmes had to be subordinated. Nevertheless, in two vital periods—1930–4 and 1950–5—CIAM was the major instrument through which the ideas of modern architecture and town planning were made known to the world, while it performed an equally vital function during the war years in maintaining the nucleus of an international network of communications between progressive-minded architects. It is quite possible that these achievements may ultimately prove to be of greater historical importance than any of the documents that CIAM produced, even the Athens Charter. *Bibliography: Die Wohnung für das Existenzminimum*, Stuttgart 1930; *Rationelle Bebauungsweisen*, Stuttgart 1931; *Logis et loisirs*, Paris 1938; (Le Corbusier) *La Charte d'Athènes*, Paris 1941; J. L. Sert and CIAM, *Can Our Cities Survive?*, Cambridge, Massachnsetts 1942; S. Giedion, *A Decade of New Architecture*, Zurich 1951; Oscar Newman (ed.), *CIAM 59 in Otterlo*, Stuttgart 1961.

REYNER BANHAM

CLASP. Acronym for Consortium of Local Authorities Special Programme. In 1957, a group of local education authorities in England banded together to exploit a system of *prefabricating schools, originally devised in Nottingham under Donald *Gibson to counteract subsidence in mining areas and later extended, as in C. H. *Aslin's Hertfordshire schools, to allow buildings to be erected rapidly from mass-produced prefabricated units at low cost and with a small labour force. Consortium components amount to about half the cost of CLASP schools; £7 million worth of

CLASP school. West Bridgford, Nottinghamshire, 1962

work was built in 1961–2, and a second Consortium has been formed of other authorities (SCOLA).

A 3 foot 4 inch planning grid is used, with external walls that can change direction at 6 foot 8 inch and 10 foot intervals. An organic grouping of elements with carefully controlled relationships between the spaces creates a deceptive, though usually successful feeling of informality. The same informality, however, when evoked in the choice of external cladding components often appears arbitrary and visually confused, lessening the effect of the carefully related spaces.

A CLASP school was exhibited at the 1960 Milan Triennale, where it aroused great interest.

Bibliography: Ministry of Education (Building Bulletin No. 19): *The Story of CLASP*, London 1960; 'CLASP in Italy', in *Architectural Review*, May 1963.

HAROLD MEEK

Concrete. *Reinforced concrete.

Constructivism. The movement known as Constructivism originated in Moscow just after the First World War in the work and theories of the two sculptor brothers Naum Gabo and Antoine Pevsner, who issued a Realistic Manifesto in 1920 which indicated the aims of the movement. Other Russian artists associated with the move-

ment in those early years were Vladimir *Tatlin, painter, sculptor, and architect; Kasimir *Malevich, painter and sculptor and founder of the Suprematist movement; and El *Lissitzky, painter and architect. The purpose of the group has perhaps been most succinctly indicated by Naum Gabo, writing in *Abstraction-Création* in 1932, when he said that constructivists no longer paint pictures or carve sculptures but make constructions in space. The distinction between painting and sculpture is thus eliminated and both enter the domain of architecture. Thus Constructivism is a movement that affects all the visual arts, but it emanates in the first place from sculpture. This sculpture being constructions of various elements is essentially the same aesthetically as the constructions in architecture.

Constructivist sculpture consists of constructions in various materials—metals, glass, plastic, and nylon—and one work may be composed of many materials. It was the purpose in making such sculpture to express in symbolic forms the conceptions of life and the universe prompted by modern science. Materials provided by modern industry were logically the most appropriate for this purpose, and thus the constructions of Gabo and Pevsner are expressions mainly in abstract or associative forms that stem from modern science. Constructivism has, by some, been closely associated with Cubism. It was regarded as exhibiting the simple relations of geometric forms to which all natural forms can be reduced according to the dictum of Cézanne that 'Everything in Nature is shaped according to the sphere, cone, and cylinder.' Geometric forms were thus, to some Constructivists, the essential structural forms and Cubist painting was, therefore, either symbolical of Constructivism or actual Constructivist painting. In architecture Constructivism can be regarded as part of the broader movement of *Functionalism, with an accent on constructional expression. Construction in all its aspects was emphasized to the full and in that emphasis all the traditional accessories of a building, such as ornament and style, were discarded so that the aesthetic effect depended on the formal relations of mass and space emanating from the most efficient construction. Any object that was efficiently made for its purpose was regarded as a model to follow; thus the most modern methods of construction, involving the use of new materials made available by industry, whereby structural efficiency could be secured superior to traditional methods, were encouraged, while the efficient machine was cited as a standard of excellence. In this theory there was a good deal of kinship with the early theories of *Le Corbusier, who in his book *Vers une Architecture* cited modern machines, such as the motor-car and aeroplane, as examples of efficient constructions, involving the logical relations of parts to the whole.

In 1921 El Lissitzky, one of the Russian members of the Constructivist movement, came to Berlin and in the following year a Constructivist International was founded with which, in addition to El Lissitzky, the well-known Dutch artist and architect, Theo van *Doesburg, was associated. The manifesto accompanying the foundation, published in *De *Stijl*, affirms the importance of the machine in modern life, and declares that, being designed strictly for its purpose without irrelevancies, it should form a model for building. The principle of Elementarism is also introduced, a kind of philosophy of the elements that form the structure of a building. The manifesto was not a very profound state-

Alexander and Vladimir Vesnin. Pravda Building. Leningrad, 1923. Project

ment of aims and hardly survives critical examination. For example, in the cult of the machine there is a suggested independence of nature and belief in a 'mechanical aesthetic'. Further thought would have made it clear that all machines originate in natural organisms and their functions, while the manifesto is in part a contradiction of the evolution of Cubism based on the principle that geometric forms are, basically, essentially natural forms.

Other members of the Dutch De Stijl group who were associated with the Constructivist movement were Cor van *Eesteren, Gerrit T. *Rietveld, Mart Stam, the painter Piet Mondrian, and the Belgian artist Georges Vantongerloo. In 1923 a further manifesto was issued under the title of *Vers une Construction Collective*, by Theo van Doesburg, Cor van Eesteren, and G. T. Rietveld. In this manifesto it is asserted that the laws of space and colour have been studied and that it was found that their variations and relationships can be resolved into a definite unity, while the

Vladimir Tatlin. Monument to the Third International in Moscow, 1920. Project.

Kasimir Malevich. Suprematist architectural model. 1920–2

El Lissitzky and Mart Stam. 'Cloud Props'. Project. 1924

result of the study of the relation of space and time is that the two through colour give a new dimension, and that means have been secured whereby the duality of the interior and exterior of a building can be eliminated. The main point here is, of course, that all the diverse elements which make a construction in the arts can be composed into a unity satisfying to the human spirit, which was repeating in different words what had been said many times before.

Works that might be cited as examples of Constructivism are many and varied. A significant early example is Vladimir Tatlin's design for a monument to the Third International made in 1920, a design of a spiral character in which the bare bones of steel construction are manifest and which could be regarded as either sculpture or architecture. Very much in the same spirit is a much later work, the immense Construction in Space completed by Naum Gabo in 1957 and placed near the Bijenkorf building in Rotterdam. Many of the most interesting Constructivist architectural works are projects, and include a design for the Leningrad *Pravda* offices by the Vesnin brothers made in 1923; a scheme by El Lissitzky and Mart Stam in 1924 for office blocks erected on huge supports bestriding a city thoroughfare, known as the 'Cloud Props' project; Marcel *Breuer's scheme for a theatre in Kharkov made in 1930; and the many industrial fantasies in Jacob Tchernykhov's *Architectural Fictions*, published in Leningrad in 1933. There is one scheme in this book (No. 74) in which buildings at various points are perched on vast cantilevered structures, suggesting construction for construction's sake.

The influence of Constructivism on modern European architecture is difficult to assess. Certain it is that there has been a marked impulse to stress constructional elements in creating architectural effects. Among these is the emphasis given to the structural supporting members of a building, often by leaving the ground floor wholly or partially open, which play a decided part in the architectural ensemble. Such designing has been chiefly associated with Le Corbusier, and it is possible he was influenced by Constructivist theories, although it is equally possible that his theories, resolved independently, gave

Marcel Breuer. Theatre at Kharkov, 1930. Project

strength to the early Constructivists. The display of structural members in a building, especially large supporting elements, is becoming a more prominent feature of much modern architecture, and formal decorative effects are increasingly dependent on the emphasis on structure. Indeed, in some designs the simulation of structure is actually introduced as a decorative motif and this may be in part due to the movement.

Perhaps the tenet of the Constructivists that has most strongly survived in architectural thought is the identity of efficient construction with beauty, which is a variant of the theory that true and economical fitness for purpose results in beauty. It is a theory held by many noted architects and engineers. For example, the Italian structural engineer, Pier Luigi *Nervi, who has been responsible for some of the most beautiful constructions in concrete, believes that the best chance of a building being beautiful is for it to be structurally right.

Bibliography: El Lissitzky, Russland, Die Rekonstruktion der Architektur in der Sowjetunion, Vienna 1930; Jacob Tchernykhov, Architectural Fictions, Leningrad 1933; Naum Gabo, The Constructive Idea in Art, London 1937; Rex Martienssen, 'Constructivism and Architecture. A new chapter in the history of formal building', South African Architectural Record, vol. 26, 1941.

ARNOLD WHITTICK

Costa, Lúcio, b. Toulon 1902. The acknowledged dean of modern architecture in *Brazil as well as its most articulate thinker, Lúcio Costa epitomizes, both in his work and in his writings, all that is more deeply typical of this movement, i.e. the continuing emotional relationship with the colonial past and the lyrical and humanistic approach to the problems of our time.

After graduating in 1924 from the Escola Nacional de Belas Artes in Rio de Janeiro, Costa entered into an early partnership with Gregori *Warchavchik, a Russian architect who had studied in Rome and settled in Brazil and who was responsible for the first modern, cube-like houses built in the country. In 1931, in the wake of the drastic changes brought about by the successful Vargas Revolution of 1930, Lúcio Costa was appointed to the directorship of the School of Fine Arts, which included the School of Architecture, and attempted a renewal of teaching methods, thus bringing to life a whole new generation of young architects oriented in a contemporary direction. Subsequently, in several projects which figure among the most significant milestones of the movement in Brazil, Lúcio Costa was able to express his discriminating good taste and his synthetic vision of the traditional past and the dynamic present of the country. The Ministry of Education and Health, (1937) for which *Le Corbusier was consulting architect and Lúcio Costa for a time the leader of the team of architects, the Brazilian Pavilion at the New York World's Fair, with Oscar *Niemeyer (1939), the Parque Guinle apartment buildings in Rio (1948–50–54), inspire young Brazilian architects to this day.

When in 1937 the DPAHN (National Historical and Artistic Patrimony Department) was formed Lúcio Costa joined it from the start and has never interrupted his devoted study of the history of Brazilian architecture or his work for the restoration and preservation of artistic monuments. Throughout his career, Lúcio Costa has always selflessly supported the work of Oscar Niemeyer, whose extraordinary talent was singled out by him in the early days when the Ministry of Education and Health was being designed, and who thus rose to his decisive role in the development of modern architecture in Brazil.

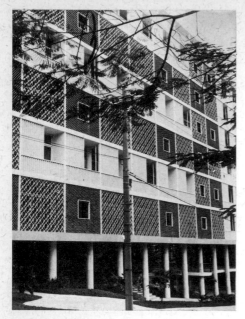

Lúcio Costa. Parque Guinle apartment buildings.
Rio de Janeiro, 1948–54

Recently Lúcio Costa has become more
and more involved in city planning. His
master-plan for Brasilia, which was selected
by an international jury in an open competition in 1956, and which provides a
superb framework for Niemeyer's monumental buildings as well as a beautiful and
rational setting for a better organized
community life in a dignified capital city,
is justly famous.
Bibliography: Except for an article on 'The
Architect and Contemporary Society' published by UNESCO, and one on 'The New
Scientific and Technological Humanism'
published by the Massachusetts Institute
of Technology, Lúcio Costa has to be read
in Portuguese, but the result will be worth
the trouble, especially in the case of the
articles 'A Necessary Documentation',
'Portuguese-Brazilian Furniture', 'Jesuitic
Architecture in Brazil', published in the
*Revista do Serviço do Patrimônio Historico
Artistico*, nos. 1, 3, 5, and of the publications of the Ministry of Education and
Culture of his 'Thoughts on Contemporary Art' and 'A great deal of Building,
a bit of Architecture, and a Miracle'.

                                HENRIQUE E. MINDLIN

Cuijpers, Petrus Josephus Hubertus, b.
Roermond 1827, d. Roermond 1921.
Studied at Antwerp Academy, follower of
*Viollet-le-Duc. Cuijpers stood at the
watershed between historicism and the
modern movement in the *Netherlands.
Numerous Catholic churches in a freely
adapted Gothic manner. Rijksmuseum
(1885) and main station at Amsterdam
(1889).

Curtain wall. In the evolution of structural
systems two basic types can be distinguished, deriving at various times from
the particular contingencies of place and
civilization: massive structures and skeleton
ones.
In buildings of the first type (Palazzo
Strozzi, Florence, 1489–1507; Notre-Dame
du Haut, Ronchamp, by *Le Corbusier,
1954) every part of the walls performs, without differentiation, the functions both of
loadbearing and of separation; in the second
type (Chartres Cathedral, 1194–1220; Promontory Apartments, Chicago, by *Mies
van der Rohe, 1949) on the other hand, a
system of high strength units, which may
be connected together in various ways,
performs the special functions of a load-
bearing framework, while the other parts
of the wall are devoted exclusively to the
tasks of closing off and separation. All non-
loadbearing walls, adopted at any time by
whatever structural tradition, could in a
certain sense be called curtain walls; in fact
they possess in some respects both the
qualities of a wall (which is immovable,
heavy, and definitive) and those of a curtain
(which is movable, light, and temporary).
In this broad sense the Gothic cathedrals
with their large windows between piers,
the frame buildings of Japan which close
off space with panels of wood and paper,
and those of Central and Northern Europe
which employ brick walls, sometimes
plastered, for partitioning, may be considered authoritative examples of curtain
wall architecture.
However, the feature called by the modern
name of curtain wall (the English term has
universal currency) signifies a particular
kind of external, non-loadbearing wall,
composed of repeating modular elements,
shop-manufactured and erected on site,
which performs all the functions (and only
these) of separation between indoors and
out, and in particular those of defence

against external agencies (atmospheric and otherwise), thermal and acoustical insulation, and regulation of view, light and air. This definition, however, is not always strictly adhered to, either because curtain walling is of recent invention, and has thus not yet been the subject of any deep critical examination, or because its typology is being constantly enriched, thanks to the continual efforts of designers and manufacturers to find better methods of production and application.

The curtain wall is the end-product of a process of development that has involved a number of interrelated considerations connected with technical progress, social and cultural factors, and the emergence of the modern style in architecture. The introduction and perfecting of new structural techniques making use of *steel at the beginning of the 19th century and *reinforced concrete in its second half, gave the impulse to a spreading use of framed structures (Chocolate factory at Noisiel-sur-Marne, by Saulnier, 1871–2; second Leiter Building, Chicago, by Le Baron *Jenney, 1889–90; house in the Rue Franklin, Paris, by *Perret, 1903). The increased employment of this type of walling showed the importance of aiming at two characteristics in particular: slenderness, to keep the maximum floor area available for use, and lightness, so that by reducing the load on the steel frame, the latter might be designed with correspondingly smaller members.

The small dimensions of the steel frames and the progress made by the glass industry permitted an increase in window sizes, a development that was also stimulated by the demand for as much natural light as possible in industrial and commercial buildings. Between 1850 and the early years of the 20th century the window gradually turned into the window wall (Chatham Dockyard Museum, 1867; Reliance Building, Chicago, by *Burnham and *Root, 1890–4; Samaritaine department store, Paris, by Jourdain, 1905), sometimes taking over the whole basic area defined by the façade (Maison du Peuple, Brussels, by *Horta, 1896–9; AEG works, Berlin, by *Behrens, 1908–9). The use of large areas of glass had meanwhile become widespread in greenhouses and winter gardens, pedestrian galleries, railway station roofs and large exhibition pavilions (Crystal Palace, London, by *Paxton, 1851; Machinery Hall, Paris, by Dutert and Contamin, 1889).

The transformation of the window into the window wall and the employment of large glazed areas drew attention to a number of problems and evoked the first solutions to them; they included such questions as that of insulation, eliminating condensation, developing the secondary glazing framework (Hallidie Building, San Francisco, by *Polk, 1918) and countering the effects of expansion by the careful design of joints and fixing systems. Large industrial buildings and tall office blocks, conceived as endless repetitions of identical cell units, led to the use of a uniform grid for the structural frames. Between the eve of the First World War and the beginning of the Second, the architects of the modern movement carried out a series of experiments, each of which may be considered as perfecting some particular aspect of curtain walling by the use of modern methods of industrial production (Fagus factory, Alfeld, 1911; model factory at the Werkbund Exhibition, Cologne, 1914; Bauhaus, Dessau, 1925–6, all by *Gropius; Bijenkorf department store, Rotterdam, by *Dudok, 1929–30; Maison Suisse, University City, Paris, 1930–2; Salvation Army Hostel, Paris, 1932; Maison Clarté, Geneva, 1932, all by Le Corbusier).

At the same time the theoretical principles of this new means of architectural

Jules Saulnier. Chocolate factory. Noisiel-sur-Marne, 1871–2

Walter Gropius. Bauhaus. Dessau, 1925–6

Gian Antonio Bernasconi, Annibale Fiocchi and
Marcello Nizzoli. Palazzo Olivetti. Milan, 1954.

expression were being formulated via educational experiments (*Bauhaus), writings (Le Corbusier) and projects (various schemes of Mies van der Rohe between 1919 and 1922; Gropius and Meyer's design for the Chicago Tribune competition, 1922). It was only after the Second World War, however, that the first experiments began in the real industrialization of the building trade on a vast scale. It was this period that saw the development and spread of the curtain wall in the United States (UN Secretariat Building, New York by *Harrison and others, 1947–50; Lake Shore Drive Apartments, Chicago, 1951 and Seagram Building, New York, 1956, by Mies van der Rohe) and Europe. Architects experimented with its application to different types of building, and discovered new possibilities of expression, with the close collaboration of manufacturers on the alert for new materials and methods.

The classification of curtain wall types is still in its early stages, though certain criteria based on technical and structural considerations seem to provide a valid instrument for critical inquiry:

1. Presence or otherwise of spatial modelling of the façade, obtained with strongly projecting or recessed units. Some types feature three-dimensional treatment: main elevation of the Palazzo Olivetti, Milan, 1954, by Bernasconi, *Fiocchi and *Nizzoli; others employ a flat or two-dimensional treatment: Phoenix-Rheinrohr Building, Düsseldorf, 1960, by Hentrich and Petschnigg.

2. Relationship to the structure's loadbearing frame. Some types do not bring out the framework at all, but cover it like a sheath: Lever House, New York, 1952 by *Skidmore, Owings and Merrill; some pick out only the verticals: Inland Steel Company Building, Chicago, 1954 by Skidmore, Owings and Merrill; or only the horizontals: headquarters of the Fédération Nationale du Bâtiment, Paris, 1950, by Gravereaux and Lopez. Yet others feature both verticals and horizontals: Equitable Savings Building, Portland, Oreg., 1948 by *Belluschi.

3. Differentiation between the wall unit and its frame. Some types are in the form of panels set in a secondary frame, which in its turn is fixed to the loadbearing structure: Crown Hall of the IIT, Chicago, 1955 by Mies van der Rohe. Others use panels of an appropriately rigid section, which is

anchored direct to the main structure: Alcoa Building, Pittsburgh, 1953 by *Harrison and *Abramovitz.

4. Structural make-up of the secondary frame, where it exists. Some types feature vertical elements, others horizontal ones, others again use a grid of both.

5. Method of assembly of individual elements. Some come in single units, others have to be put together from various parts.

6. Method of connecting adjacent units. Some types have edge sections which interlock with the next unit, others use an intermediate feature.

7. Method of packing joints. Some types have rigid joints (welded), others use non-rigid packing (mastic, plastic, etc.).

Bibliography: Curtain Walls, Milan 1956; *Construire en acier*, Zurich 1956; Ian McCallum (editor), 'Machine-Made America' in *The Architectural Review*, London, May 1957, No. 724; W. Dudley Hunt, *The Contemporary Curtain Wall*, New York 1958; R. Schaal, *Vorhangwände —Curtain Walls*, Munich 1961; R. McGrath and A. C. Frost, *Glass in Architecture and Decoration*, London 1961; *Industrial Architecture* (London) 6/1963.

GIUSEPPE GIORDANINO, GIUSEPPE VARALDO, AND GIAN PIO ZUCCOTTI

Skidmore, Owings and Merrill. Inland Steel Company Building. Chicago, Ill., 1954

Left. Pietro Belluschi. Equitable Savings Building. Portland, Oreg., 1948

Wallace K. Harrison and Max Abramovitz. Alcoa Building. Pittsburgh, 1953. Erection of a prefabricated unit

Deilmann, Harald, b. Gladbeck 1920. Studied and worked as assistant at Stuttgart Technical College. Architect of the Municipal Theatre, Münster, together with Hausen, Rave, and Ruhnau (1954–6). Nordwest-Lotto offices, Münster (1960). Hospitals, cultural buildings.

Deitrick, William H., b. Danville, Va. 1905. Together with *Nowicki and Severud architect of the arena at Raleigh, N.C. (1952–3). The roof of the arena is carried by steel ropes which are suspended from two sloping parabolic arcs.

Denmark. Danish people have always drawn inspiration from the major centres of world culture, but have shown a capacity to adapt new ideas to Danish landscape and climate, customs and building practices, adopting what is new with caution and criticism. Thus the process whereby Danish architecture acquired its own character was markedly evolutionary. Securely anchored in their own tradition of craftsmanship, the Danes developed a sense for simple order, natural proportions, and rhythm, first through half-timbered work and afterwards through the *modular brick buildings of the Empire period. Emotionalism in architecture was always distrusted and the worst excesses of eclecticism were avoided. On the other hand the genuine progressive movement was slow to make itself felt.

A functional tradition runs through Danish architecture, from the simple brick buildings of the Empire period, via Gottlieb Bindesbøll onward to neoclassicism, to Ivar Bentsen and Kay *Fisker. Bindesbøll's Medical Association houses and Oringe Hospital (built in the fifties) are simple buildings of yellow brick serving a clear functional purpose. Daniel Herholdt's work of the 1860s has a clearer sense of style, but shows the same respect for simple structures and honest materials. Herholdt was also the first to use cast-iron in a major building—Copenhagen University library (1861). The master builder of Copenhagen town hall, Martin Nyrop, carried the use of this material's special properties further, while Jensen *Klint, securely rooted in the brick-building tradition, thought he had arrived at a new and timeless architecture with Grundtvig's Church (1920–40), a gigantic paraphrase of the Danish country

Gottlieb Bindesbøll. Thorwaldsen Museum. Copenhagen, 1839–48

church. The neoclassicism of 1910–15 was eclecticism's last outburst. Its two chief works were Carl Petersen's Fåborg Museum (1912); and the Police Station (1918–22, by Hack, Kampmann and his two sons, and Åge Rafn. The chief significance of the period for the future lay in a severer artistic discipline and a sharpened sense for the qualities of craftsmanship and material.

Ivar Bentsen carried on the tradition of brick building with small unpretentious houses and good blocks of flats, and since the twenties Kay Fisker has been the leading exponent of traditionalism, playing a leading part in the effort to improve the quality of ordinary housing. The most important product of Functionalism has been Århus University (begun 1931), the first part of which was designed by Fisker in collaboration with C. F. Møller and Povl Stegmann. Its many separate buildings stand skilfully related to one another in a rolling park-like campus. The laconic and precise style of the first yellow brick buildings has been continued by C. F. Møller alone during the past twenty years, without losing the originally projected unity of design. Fisker's strong personality shows to advantage in Copenhagen's Voldparken School and the Maternity Care Building of the mid-fifties. Kåre Klint carried on his father Jensen Klint's ideas in Bethlehem Church (1937) and also became the leading figure of furniture design, with semi-traditional furniture of the highest craftsmanship. In the post-war years an agreeable personal atmosphere has been given to housing developments like Søndergårdsparken (architects P. E. Hoff and Bennet Windinge) by the location of the buildings and their relation to terrain and landscape gardening. There has been especial emphasis on school building in the past decade, with low single- and double-storeyed buildings which create admirable conditions of intimacy for the pupils. One of the finest of these is F. C. Lund and Hans Christian Hansen's Hansted School in Copenhagen.

The *Art Nouveau movement left little of note in Denmark (see, however, the work of Anton Rosen and Thomas Bindesbøll). International *Functionalism first made itself seriously felt after the Stockholm Exhibition of 1930, which was a revelation for young Danish architects. Vilhelm Lauritzen became an outstanding exponent of Functionalism, coping with contem- porary problems such as Copenhagen Airport and Broadcasting House. Mogens Lassen built the first *Le Corbusier-inspired villas and Fritz Schleget became the Danish exponent of a freedom from aesthetic preconceptions established by *Perret with his reinforced concrete work (Mariebjaerg crematorium). The young Arne *Jacobsen also belonged to the revolutionary group, with the charming

Vilhelm Lauritzen. Broadcasting House. Copenhagen, 1938–45

Povl Ernst Hoff and Bennet Windinge. Høje Søborg apartment block. Copenhagen, 1949–51

Left. Peter Vilhelm Jensen Klint. Grundtvig Church. Copenhagen, 1920–40

Kay Fisker, C. F. Møller, and Povl Stegmann. Århus University. Commenced 1931 development at Bellevue and later (in collaboration with Møller and Lassen) with the Århus and Søllerod town halls. These edifices were the climax of progressive building in the thirties, before the material shortages of the war and subsequent years brought a return to the cultivation of traditional qualities.

The post-war years have been marked especially by inspiration from the USA, first by *Wright's houses and their adaptation to the landscape, later by *Mies van der Rohe's simplicity. Again Jacobsen was the leading figure, with large administrative buildings and hotels, like Rødovre town hall (1955) and the SAS building in Copenhagen (1959). In his schools and housing Jacobsen convincingly combined foreign inspiration with Danish tradition. Among the younger generation Halldor Gunnløgsson is a fine exponent of a severe classical architecture. Drawing inspiration both from Japanese architecture and from Mies van der Rohe, he has built single houses and (in co-operation with Jørn Nielsen) Kastrup town hall. Jørn *Utzon is the vital, imaginative and original talent whose prize design for Sydney Opera House is now under construction. In Denmark he has so far only completed a number of interesting houses and housing blocks. Utzon is Denmark's most important representative of a dynamic, organic architectural sense. Vilhelm Wohlert and Jørgen Bo have created a delightful background for contemporary art in Louisiana Museum, combining sensitivity with caution towards external effects.

Otherwise it is not so much by individual achievements that Denmark has acquired a certain international recognition as by the conscientious and workmanlike character of her architecture and craftsmanship.

Bibliography: Kay Fisker and Knud Millech, *Danske Arkitekturstrømninger 1850–1950,* Copenhagen 1951; Harald Langberg, *Dansk Byggeskik,* 1955; Monies, Hjort, Røgind, *Contemporary Danish Architecture,* Copenhagen 1956; (Symposium): *The Architecture of Denmark,* London 1949; Esbjørn Hjort, *Housing in Denmark since 1930,* London 1952.

TOBIAS FABER

Deutscher Werkbund. The genesis of the Deutscher Werkbund, which was founded on 6 October 1907 by the German architect Hermann *Muthesius, can be traced back, in part, to the movement in England led by William *Morris and his associates in the middle of the 19th century to revive the standards of craftsmanship in the arts of everyday life that had obtained in the Middle Ages. This movement was associated with the moral requirement that the craftsman should find pride and joy in his labour, and it led to an antagonism to machinery and its crude productions in contemporary industrial art, although it should be emphasized that the antagonism was less to machinery itself than to its bad use by the continual stamping out of crude imitations of historical styles. It must be acknowledged, however, that Morris never really came to terms with machinery, which he felt was responsible for so many of the social and aesthetic evils of the 19th century. Yet the movement led by William Morris revived much of the excellent medieval craftsmanship, with the emphasis on quality of design, of material, and of individual skill. The movement also contributed to the revival of a high standard of domestic architecture which began with the Red House designed by William Morris's architect Philip *Webb in 1859. This was the first of a series of excellent houses designed by Webb, which together with those by C. F. A. *Voysey and Norman *Shaw showed at that time (that is, the last forty years of the century) a new spirit in domestic architecture. Instead of

Jørgen Bo and Vilhelm Wohlert. Louisiana Museum. Humlebaek near Copenhagen, 1958 formal symmetrical elevations with planning to match as in Late Renaissance buildings, houses were designed more in accordance with the best fulfilment of their purpose, with rooms in convenient relation to each other, and orientation in accordance with sunlight. This meant design more on medieval lines with often irregular plans, while it was accompanied with an expressive use of the best materials.

From 1896 to 1903 Hermann Muthesius was attached to the German Embassy in London, and during his sojourn he made a thorough study of English contemporary architecture and of industrial art. He returned to Germany with enthusiastic admiration for English domestic architecture and applied art in the Morris tradition and wrote several books on these subjects. He deplored the poor condition of industrial art in Germany, its constant repetition of dead historical styles, and as head of the Prussian Board of Trade for Schools of Arts and Crafts in 1907 he took steps to effect improvements and to infuse new life into industrial art by forming the Deutscher Werkbund. His criticisms of contemporary German art met with a good deal of opposition, both in art circles and from industrialists, but he was able to exercise some influence on the latter by emphasizing the economic aspect of good design and craftsmanship in industrial production, because without these there was a risk that Germany would lose ground in world markets. Several industrialists seemed to realize this and it is not without significance that they appointed well-known architects and designers as design consultants about the same time as the foundation of the Deutscher Werkbund, the most notable being Peter *Behrens, appointed in this capacity to the AEG.

The avowed objects of the Deutscher Werkbund were to select the best representatives of the arts and crafts, industry and trades, to make all necessary efforts to secure high quality in industrial art, and to form a centre for all who aimed at this high quality in their work. Among those who were associated with the venture in its early years, in addition to Muthesius, were Karl Schmidt, Theodor *Fischer, Richard *Riemerschmid, Hans *Poelzig, Heinrich Tessenow, Josef *Hoffmann, and Henri van de *Velde. There was a great insistence on quality of craftsmanship and

Fritz Hellmut Ehmcke. Poster for the Werkbund Exhibition. Cologne, 1914

material, and it is a question whether aesthetic aspects were sufficiently considered, but this was rectified later when the whole question of aims was considered at the Convention in 1911. The attitude of the members to the use of machinery in production was very different from that of William Morris. They not only came to terms with it, but they welcomed it as a valuable means of large-scale output of quality goods. They viewed machinery as a development of the hand tool, but, like the hand tool, something to be fully controlled and wholly subservient to the artist-craftsman. Another factor that probably influenced the acceptance of the machine by the Deutscher Werkbund was the gradual realization that many machines are beautiful things in themselves, and that such objects as the modern locomotive, motor-car, aeroplane, and modern liner can compare in beauty with the finest of modern buildings.

At the congress held in 1911 Muthesius reasserted the aims of the Deutcher Werkbund, but in addition he placed emphasis on aesthetic qualities and spiritual values which he associated with ideas of form, and he advocated turning for inspiration to that architecture of the past where the realization of form had been of the highest excellence, in the Greek temple, the Roman baths and the Gothic cathedral. This perfection of form was associated, to some extent, in the mind of Muthesius with mathematical calculation, which, together with the acceptance of machine production, led to a belief and advocacy of standardization that he expressed at the annual meeting of the Werkbund in 1914. This point of view, however, met with opposition from Henri van de Velde, a prominent member of the Werkbund, who could not reconcile standardization and the acceptance of canons with the individual creative work of artists. An artist, he contended, was always an individualist, who would never submit to rules and standards. These two lines of thought existed in the ranks of the Werkbund, as indeed they have always existed in discussions of art and architecture.

In this same year, 1914, the Deutscher Werkbund held a very important exhibition of industrial art at Cologne, which some have regarded in retrospect as the most important of the century. Several of the buildings for this exhibition were designed by pioneer modern architects, including Henri van de Velde, Walter *Gropius, Peter Behrens, Josef Hoffmann, and Bruno *Taut, and include some of the most significant early examples of modern architecture in steel, concrete and glass.

Weissenhof Housing Exhibition. Stuttgart, 1927

Van de Velde's contribution was a theatre which contained several innovations. Perhaps the most notable building of the exhibition and that which marked the greatest advance was the model factory administrative block and garage designed by Walter Gropius in collaboration with Adolf *Meyer. The contribution of Bruno Taut was a pavilion for the German glass industry which consisted of a twelve-sided glass drum with a pointed glass dome. The First World War arrested the work of the Deutscher Werkbund, but it had already exerted considerable influence throughout Europe and many institutions were formed in other countries to follow its example. An Austrian Werkbund was formed in 1910 and a Swiss in 1913. The Swedish Slöjdsforening was reorganized about the same time to conform with the Werkbund, while in England in 1915 the Design and Industries Association was established which was frankly modelled on the Deutscher Werkbund.

The next really great event in the history of the Werkbund was the exhibition of 1927 which included a housing exhibition on a hill in Weissenhof, a suburb of Stuttgart. It was superintended by Ludwig *Mies van der Rohe, then a vicepresident of the Deutscher Werkbund, who invited several European architects to submit designs. Those who accepted invitations were the German architects: Peter Behrens, Walter Gropius, Hans Poelzig, Bruno Taut, Hans *Scharoun, Adolf G. Schneck, Ludwig *Hilberseimer, R. Döcker, Adolf Rading, and Max *Taut; the Austrian architect, Josef Frank; the French architect, *Le Corbusier; and the Dutch architects, J. J. P. *Oud and Mart Stam, while Mies van der Rohe himself designed a block of flats for the scheme. He gave the architects complete freedom in their designs with the one proviso that all the houses should have flat roofs. This housing exhibition proved to be one of the most important events in domestic architecture in the period between the two wars. Its historical value is that it demonstrates, in a concentrated form, the stages reached in the evolution of house design and construction in 1927 by the most progressive architectural thought in Europe. In some of the houses a degree of standardization is employed which would make it possible to build them economically on a large scale.

For example, in the two houses designed by Walter Gropius a steel-framed construction is employed on a grid of about one metre, with asbestos cement sheets as external facing on slabs of cork with suitable internal facing, a method which lends itself not only to mass production but to dry assembly. This is also the case with the block of flats designed by Mies van der Rohe constructed of a light steel frame with standardized wall sections and windows. Similarly the house designed by Hans Poelzig consists of timber sheets fixed to a framed structure. Several of the houses are built of reinforced concrete, including those designed by Le Corbusier in which the essential structure consists of reinforced concrete and steel posts or columns placed at intervals on which the houses are suspended. Flexibility in the design and use of the houses was one of the principal motifs in the designs.

The housing exhibition of the Deutscher Werkbund at Stuttgart was in many ways an exemplification of the principles of modern building advocated by the Werkbund's founder, Muthesius, in 1911. It took place in the year of his death, and its success—for it attracted attention among architectural circles throughout the world —was a reward for his early pioneer efforts. A further triumph for the Deutscher Werkbund was its very successful participation in the Paris exhibition of 1930. The German Government entrusted the task to the Deutscher Werkbund, which appointed Walter Gropius to organize the German section. He was assisted by three of his former colleagues at the Bauhaus, L. Moholy-Nagy, Marcel *Breuer, and Herbert Bayer. The exhibition was dedicated to building and the industrial arts and had two main themes, which were a continuation of those of the Stuttgart housing exhibition: standardization in all fields of building and the mass production of well-designed housing units.

With National Socialism the Deutscher Werkbund was disbanded. It was revived after the end of the Second World War.

Bibliography: Die Form, Berlin, especially IX—1927, and VII—1932; Nikolaus Pevsner, *Pioneers of the Modern Movement*, especially chapter 1, London 1936; Reyner Banham, *Theory and Design in the First Machine Age*, 1–5, London 1960.

ARNOLD WHITTICK

Doesburg, Theo van, b. Utrecht 1883, d. Davos 1931. Van Doesburg, whose real name was Chr. E. M. Küpper, began his career as a painter; his pictures were shown for the first time at an exhibition in The Hague in 1912. In collaboration with the architects *Oud and Wils, van Doesburg endeavoured to transfer his painting of the two-dimensional into something spatial and connect it organically with architecture. In 1916 he founded the *Sphinx* group in Leiden together with Oud, but it did not last long. A year later, he joined a group of artists and architects in De *Stijl, a movement set up to achieve a 'radical renewal of art'. Van Doesburg became the spokesman of the group, whose ideology he helped to formulate.

In 1917, together with Oud, he designed the hall of the latter's house at Noordwijkerhout, near Leiden, in which he sought to reinforce and stress the architecture by means of painting. His use of primary colours, tiled flooring and geometrical leading on the windows is in line with De Stijl methods. In the years that followed, van Doesburg was invited to lecture on the movement's activities at the *Bauhaus in Dessau, and in Berlin. The Bauhaus also took over his book on the basic principles of art, originally published in Dutch (Amsterdam 1919), as the sixth publication in the Bauhaus Books series (*Grundbegriffe der bildenden Kunst*, Munich 1924).

When the Aubette, a dance hall and amusement centre in Strasbourg was reconstructed in 1926–7, van Doesburg was able to realize his ideas on space and colour on a larger scale, in collaboration with Hans Arp. Moving to Paris, he built a studio for himself at Meudon-Val-Fleury (1930–1), which soon became the focus of the Stijl movement. He worked once more in collaboration with Cor van *Eesteren, as he had done already in the early twenties, and turned his attention to applying the principles of De Stijl to town planning. Van Doesburg's death in 1931 meant the end of the Stijl group, but its concepts of space, which he helped to define, have remained a living issue to the present time.

Bibliography: Theo van Doesburg, *De Nieuwe Beweging in de Schilderkunst*, Delft 1917; Theo van Doesburg, *Drie voordrachten over de nieuwe beeldende*

Theo van Doesburg. Aubette. Strasbourg, 1926–7

Kunst, Amsterdam 1919; Theo van Doesburg, *Klassiek, barok, modern*, The Hague 1920; Theo van Doesburg, *L'Architecture vivante*, Paris 1925.

J. J. VRIEND

Drew, Jane Beverly, b. 1911. Studied at the Architectural Association School of Architecture, London. In partnership with J. T. Allison, 1934–9. Independent practice, 1939–45. In partnership with Maxwell *Fry (whom she married in 1942) since 1945. Early work in Kenya led to specialization in tropical architecture. Assistant Town Planning Adviser, West Africa, 1944–5. Schools, housing and colleges in Ghana. Joint work with Maxwell Fry on the University of Ibadan, Nigeria. Projects in Kuwait (1,000-bed hospital); India (hospitals, housing, and a large high school; senior architect at Chandigarh in collaboration with *Le Corbusier); Singapore; Ceylon; South Persia (housing, town planning, hospital extensions, cinemas); and Mauritius (hospitals and housing). Jane Drew served as Bemis Professor at the Massachusetts Institute of Technology in 1961, and has lectured widely elsewhere.

Dudok, Willem Marinus, b. Amsterdam 1884. Although deriving something from both the School of *Amsterdam and De *Stijl, Dudok evolved an independent position of his own. The contrast of solid and void areas, horizontals and verticals recalls De Stijl, but Dudok's brick buildings nearly always retain a massive weightiness. Numerous buildings at Hilversum, where Dudok became municipal architect in 1915: Vondel School (1928–9), Town Hall (1928–30). Netherlands House at the Paris Cité Universitaire (1927–8), Bijenkorf department store at Rotterdam (1929–30, now replaced by the new building designed by Marcel *Breuer).
Bibliography: W. M. Dudok, Übersicht über sein Werk, Amsterdam 1954.

Duiker, Johannes, b. The Hague 1890, d. Amsterdam 1935. Studied at Delft Technical College. Member of De *Stijl and the group connected with the journal *De 8 en Opbouw*. Zonnestraal Sanatorium at Hilversum (1928, together with B. Bijvoet); open-air school at Amsterdam (1930–2), a five-storey fully glazed structure with terraces for open-air lessons.

Eames, Charles, b. St Louis, Missouri 1907. Broke off his studies at Washington University, St Louis, after eighteen months. Architect and designer. Together with his wife Ray he undertakes almost any sort of design from toys to furniture. His own house at Santa Monica, California (1949), a steel-frame building constructed from prefabricated units, is reminiscent of an old Japanese house in its proportions and light appearance.

Ecole des Beaux-Arts. Most influential School of Art and Architecture in the 19th century. The Parisian École goes back to its foundation by Colbert in 1671. Its teaching system rests on lectures and practical work in artists' studios and architects' offices. The Grand Prix de Rome offered by the École provides several years of study at the French Academy in the Villa Medici in Rome. The institute's basic conceptions of architecture lie in the composition of well-proportioned elements in a well-proportioned whole. In practice, the École, where many eminent architects have been trained, has often opposed modern trends in architecture.

Eesteren, Cor van, b. Ablasserdam 1897. Studied at the Academy in Rotterdam, the Sorbonne, and the *École des Beaux-Arts. Belonged from 1923 to the De *Stijl movement. Collaboration with van *Doesburg, especially on housing projects in 1923. For many years President of the *CIAM. Municipal buildings (Amsterdam Plan, 1936).

Eiermann, Egon, b. Neuendorf, near Berlin 1904. Together with Hans *Scharoun, Egon Eiermann is among the most discussed architects of post-war Germany. The work of these two men denotes the span of modern German architecture. If Scharoun designs with a feeling for the possibilities of sculptural massing, Eiermann lays stress on perceptible articulation, logical expression of the structural frame and precise detailing. His buildings create an impression of extraordinary clarity and taut organization. Architecture means to him 'making order visible, from town planning to the smallest building'. Structure and function can nearly always be read off, and his industrial plants reveal the aesthetic charm of visibly displayed technical apparatus. Eiermann develops his designs from functional analysis, in the widest sense of the word, including an assessment of the cultural and geographical background. Two office blocks, built over the same period, for the Essener Colliery (1960) and the Müller Steel Works at Offenbach (1960) depend in their different conceptions on the character of their surroundings: relatively blank wall areas with smallish window openings and quiet, dark panel cladding in the Ruhr town; brightly coloured façades with shady galleries and variable protection from the sun on the Upper Rhine. The tendency towards dogmatic preference for certain shapes is less pronounced in Eiermann than in other architects who are still under the influence of *Mies van der Rohe's image of a clear-cut rectilinear architecture.

Egon Eiermann. Handkerchief Mill. Blumberg, 1951

Egon Eiermann. Neckermann Mail Order
Company Building. Frankfurt, 1958–60. Detail
of elevation

Eiermann, who studied under *Poelzig in
Berlin, wrote his thesis on a department
store, and worked at first in the architects'
office of the Karstadt multiple store company. He retained a liking for this type of

Gustave Eiffel. Truyère Bridge. Garabit, 1880–4

work even after the war (Merkur Department Store at Heilbronn, 1951). The Blumberg Handkerchief Mill (1951) represents
a culminating point in his work, with the
slender tracery of its various viewpoints.
Of Eiermann's church designs, St Matthew's at Pforzheim (1953) and the
Memorial Church in Berlin (1961) have
been built; the war damaged stump of the
latter's tower was preserved and surrounded
by the simple stereometric buildings of the
new church.
For these ecclesiastical buildings Eiermann
used pierced blocks with coloured glazing,
which the light filters through. Similar
textured wall surfaces, which have a purely
decorative purpose, occur at his two depar-
ment stores, the Horten at Heidelberg and
the Merkur at Stuttgart (1961); they are
reminiscent of Edward D. *Stone's work.
But these buildings do not stand comparison with that of the export firm of Neckermann at Frankfurt (1958–60). In contrast
to the patterned surfaces of the two department stores, the Frankfurt building is
vigorously enlivened by external galleries,
fire-escapes, and air conditioning and stair
towers. Eiermann's buildings for the German government display more delicate
outlines and elegant proportions; they include the German pavilion at the Brussels
World Fair (in collaboration with Sep Ruf,
1958) and the German Embassy in Washington, which rises in steps on a sloping
site (work still in progress).
Eiermann, who lectures at Karlsruhe
Technical College, has also made a name
for himself as an industrial designer.
                                        WOLFGANG PEHNT

Eiffel, Gustave, b. Dijon 1832, d. Paris
1923. Gustave Eiffel, a Burgundian by
birth, was intended to be a chemist and
only by chance became a structural
engineer. As consultant to several building
firms and later as an independent consulting engineer, he had the opportunity of
making himself familiar with all the problems occasioned to bridge designers by the
advance of the railways into ever more
difficult territory. He soon realized that
these problems could not be solved if the
metal used was, as hitherto, in the form of
the comparatively heavy and inelastic cast-
iron. New materials, such as rolled iron
and steel had to be used, and these were
now being commercially produced in

sufficient quantities, but new methods and shapes had also to be invented that did justice to the better static behaviour of these materials.

When Eiffel founded his own firm in 1867 he already commanded a sufficiently extensive experience. He also realized the importance of collaborating with outstanding men such as Nouguier and Koechlin, and he introduced new methods, whose precision gave his firm great advantages over his mostly foreign competitors. Soon after the end of the Franco-German war, commissions came in from all over the world (France, Switzerland, Austria, Hungary, Russia, Portugal, Peru, etc.). Thus he had ample opportunity of testing the versatility of the lattice beam he had developed and which he made the most important component of a novel structural system. Apart from numerous bridges, stations, roof projects, and other structures, nearly all of which brought technical advances, his three main designs were: the Maria Pia Bridge over the Douro near Oporto (1877–8), the Truyère Bridge near Garabit in the French Massif Central (1880–4), and the Eiffel Tower in Paris (1887–9). These three enormous structures are all closely related. All three rely throughout on the application of the principle on which the lattice beam is based, viz. the subdivision of beams into three-dimensional space frames built up from individually small members and riveted together from commercially available angle irons or flats, which afford maximum rigidity for minimum weight. The Eiffel Tower is nothing but an extension of the solution tried out at Oporto and Garabit for extremely tall bridge supports.

The Tower, in particular, marks an important stage in the development of modern architecture for the impressive proof it gives of the fecundity of the engineering approach: intuitions, substantiated by calculation, led to entirely new shapes. The Tower brought the realization of a new spatial image, made up of joints and fields of force, to which indeed only graphic artists like Robert Delaunay and Antoine Pevsner were receptive, and then hardly before 1910. Through their intermediation, and thanks to the interpretations they gave

Gustave Eiffel. Eiffel Tower. Paris, 1887–9

of this spatial image, it was beamed back to architecture. The work of *Wachsmann and Le Ricolais on space structures has aroused the interest of architects and for some years now they have been working on Eiffel's multi-centred conception of space.

Eiffel himself pursued the logical direction of his research on the greatest adversary his giant constructions had to contend with: the wind. From 1910 on, he devoted himself to aerodynamic studies, which led to the building of the first wind-tunnel to meet the needs of the aircraft industry (1911), and to the development of the first aeroplane tested in a wind-tunnel (Bréguet LE, 1918).

Bibliography: Gustave Eiffel, *Mémoire présenté à l'appui du projet définitif du Viaduc de Garabit*, Paris 1889; Gustave Eiffel, *La Tour de Trois Cents Mètres*, Paris 1900 (2 folio vols.); Gustave Eiffel, *La Résistance de l'air et l'aviation*, Paris 1913 and 1914; Jean Prévost, *Eiffel*, Paris 1929; Maurice Besset, *Gustave Eiffel*, Milan 1957, Paris 1959.

MAURICE BESSET

Eijck, Aldo van, b. Driebercen 1918. Eijck, who has shown particular interest in problems of education (children's playgrounds at Amsterdam), created 'a house like a small town' when he built the Municipal Orphanage at Amsterdam (1955). This consists of a number of square space units which make up a growing complex of buildings. Municipal work (collaboration in the Nagele Plan).

Ellwood, Craig, b. Clarendon, Texas 1921. Mainly private dwellings of unusually elegant proportions and careful detailing which are reminiscent of *Mies van der Rohe with their slender sections. Carson-Roberts Building, Los Angeles (1961).

Endell, August, b. Berlin 1871, d. Breslau 1925. Self-taught. Designer and architect in the *Art Nouveau style. His most important buildings, the Elvira Photo Studio at Munich (1897–8) and the Bunte Theatre at Berlin (1901), are both distinguished by ingenious surface decoration.

Ervi, Aarne, b. Tammela, Finland 1910. Tapiola Garden City near Helsinki was based on Ervi's 1953 plan, and he himself carried out several of the projects there. Buildings for Turku University (1956–9).

Expressionism. Expressionist architects, like Expressionist painters, had no cultural groupings, with unified programmes and activities, and most architects who came within the ambit of Expressionism did so only for a short period of their development, although this often proved to be the zenith of their artistic careers. In the work of the best of them, various influences must be recognized as existing simultaneously side by side, or at different levels; these may vary from *Art Nouveau to romantic nationalism, from Expressionist art to a kind of late-romantic surrealism, and from rationalism and a search for objectivity to a view of the creative act as an unrepeatable gesture of self- and world-knowledge.

In Germany, during the years immediately prior to 1914, the true artistic avant-garde consisted of architects who owed their allegiance to the *Jugendstil, the course of whose history overlaid that of Expressionism for upwards of ten years. If we look more closely at the anti-classical, anti-internationalist traits that characterize the German version of Art Nouveau, its considerable hang-over from the historical styles and its general tendency to picturesqueness and a taste for organic forms, not projected on to plane surfaces but conceived plastically almost from the start, we shall readily perceive the numerous connecting links with avant-garde German Expressionist movements such as the *Brücke* and the *Blauer Reiter*. In this context one thinks of the work of Eckmann, Pankok, Obrist, *Endell, Joseph Maria *Olbrich, who played a key-rôle at this period with his activities at Darmstadt, and above all of Richard *Riemerschmid with his Hellerau factory (1910) and Henry van de *Velde, for their direct influence on the architects of Expressionism.

A typical feature of the situation in Germany at the time was the way the country was divided up between different cultural centres, each with a strong individual character and relatively independent of all the others, with its own schools of architecture and the applied arts. Efforts were being made to develop a romantic-national style, as a form of escape from eclecticism, that would provide the new German nation with a suitable form of architecture. With Alfred Messel's Wertheim department store (1896) a series of attempts began at simplifying the eclectic Wilhelminian language of the times which implicated all the most distinguished architects currently practising: Theodor *Fischer who taught at Munich (Ulm Garrison Church, 1911), Ludwig Hoffmann, Paul *Bonatz (Main Railway Station, Stuttgart, 1913–27, with F. E. Scholer), and Fritz Schumacher, Professor at Dresden, and later at Hamburg, who had already before 1914 clearly worked out and established an expressive style of his own.

It was Peter *Behrens who achieved the transition to Expressionism with his buildings for the AEG in Berlin (1908–13). We are not concerned here with those elements which clearly anticipate the rationalist style. Behrens's factories are not designed with the kind of utilitarian character associated with the functional tradition, but rather as the representation of a new power, one that directly multiplies nature's goods. In his work may be seen that process of deformation of the national romantic style which is one of the fundamental sources of Expressionist architecture.

Apart from Behrens, there are only two architects before the First World War clearly distinguishable as Expressionists: Hans *Poelzig and Max *Berg. The conventional exterior of Berg's reinforced concrete Centenary Hall in Breslau (1912–13) gives no indication of the exciting three-dimensional treatment inside the enormous dome, 213 feet in diameter. It is impossible to find any reinforced concrete building before this date equally as compelling, and with as little of the schematic about it. Of these three architects, however, it is Hans Poelzig who seems to have adhered most consciously to Expressionism. His large industrial complex at Luban (1911–12) seems even more unprejudiced in design than the best works of Behrens at this period. His volumes are built up of asymmetrical blocks, whose organic unity seems to underline the peculiar individuality of the design. Three years previously, Poelzig had built a large house near Breslau, where the plastic fusion of all the elements towards a volumetric continuity recalls some of van de Velde's villas of the same epoch.

Thanks to the absence of preconceived

Hans Poelzig. Water tower. Posen, 1911

types, it was industrial architecture that offered the line of least resistance to progressive experiments at the time. This may be seen in the celebrated scheme for a water mill at Weider (1906), and above all in the great structure built by Poelzig at Posen (1911), with a water tower above and an exhibition hall below; brick is used here to clad a steel framework. The bold handling of volumes makes it one of the

Hans Poelzig. Salzburg Festival Theatre, 1920–1. Project

Mies van der Rohe. Office building, Friedrich-strasse, Berlin, 1919. Project (first version)

Fritz Höger. Chilehaus. Hamburg, 1922–3

most significant German buildings of its day—the 'total transposition of a personal idea into a work' which Kirchner demanded as the basis for art. A series of sketches dating from this period are clearly influenced in conception by certain drawings of Kokoschka, and show a desire to model a building with an aggressive immediacy that leaves no part of its surface unmarked by its author's will.

German culture in the years after the First World War became progressively more political in character. The Socialist revolution accompanied Expressionism as a form of protest for at least ten years, in an ideologically hybrid identification between cultural avant-gardism and progressive politics. Examples of this tendency may be seen in the Berlin *Arbeitsrat für Kunst* and *Novembergruppe*. The latter group, descended from pre-war anarchist papers such as *Aktion* and *Revolution*, attracted to it all the foremost representatives of German artistic life in the years 1918–20; many architects were members, including

*Gropius and *Mendelsohn. The *Novembergruppe*'s programme attributed particular importance to architecture, regarded as a direct instrument for raising social standards. The group was dissolved after the bloody suppression of the Sparticist rising, and the ensuing disillusion among the progressive spirits of the Weimar Republic contributed decisively to the emergence of *Neue Sachlichkeit*, which became the focus of much Expressionist activity.

The *Bauhaus, too, especially during its Weimar period, absorbed many features of Expressionism. The crude pragmatism; the stark expressive simplicity; a tenacious grip on reality combined with an ethical sense of human obligation; all accord well with the School's methodological programme as also with a type of design that was a frequent outcome of Expressionist theory. It is in this light that some of the works of the protagonists of rationalism built at this period may be clearly explained; works carried out in a style with close affinities to Expressionism. They include *Mies van der Rohe's design for a skyscraper (1919) and his memorial to Rosa Luxemburg and

Page 94. Hans Scharoun. Sketch. 1920

Michael de Klerk. Eigen Haard estate.
Amsterdam, 1921

Paul Bonatz. Head Office, United Steel Works.
Düsseldorf, 1922–4

Karl Liebknecht (1926), and Gropius's War Memorial at Weimar (1922) and his theatre at Jena (1923).

Numerous other buildings at this time, however, were built under the direct influence of pre-war Expressionism, thus displaying a cultural lag of about ten years. They may be roughly divided into two distinct groups: one pushing the Expressionist protest in the direction of a progressive intensification of its idiom, either in a lyric vein with Art Nouveau reminiscences, or in a desperate manner leading to the destruction of volume; the other tending towards a national-romantic style. This kind of ambiguity is typical of Expressionism, which proved a fertile source of progressive drives and rationalist activity. Emil Fahrenkamp, for example, built a series of interesting factories in 1923, but later went over to a nationalist style. Wilhelm Kreis, with his Düsseldorf skyscraper, the Wilhelm-Marx-Building (1922–4), and the interior of the planetarium in the same city, produced two works of the highest merit in a near-Expressionist idiom, but later developed a heavy simplified neoclassic manner. *Scharoun, Schneider and the *Luckhardt brothers made use of the figurative manifestations of Expressionism within the orbit of rationalist practice. Rudolf Steiner's Goetheanum at Dornach (1925–8) is linked to Expressionism by its picturesque treatment, but occupies a place apart, as it was designed in accordance with the principles of Anthroposophy.

The School of *Amsterdam, too, whose mouthpiece was the journal *Wendingen*, displayed an intensification of the national style; but the situation was somewhat different here from that in Germany, as social contrasts were less extreme. In point of fact, the largest scheme carried out by these architects was the development of low-cost housing estates in South Amsterdam. Hence the Expressionist character of the work is not a manifestation of protest; it derives from a peculiar ability to evolve an endless variety of forms, in a three-dimensional treatment that often achieves almost fairy-tale effects.

The most important Expressionist buildings erected in Germany in the first years after the war comprise: the Chilehaus (Fritz Höger), Ballinhaus (brothers Hans and Oskar Gerson) and Sprinkenhof

Rudolf Steiner. Goetheanum. Dornach, 1925–8

(Höger and the Gerson brothers), at Hamburg (1922–3), all influenced by Fritz Schumacher; the Einstein Tower by Erich Mendelsohn at Potsdam (1920); and the entrance hall of the Hoechst Dyeworks by Peter Behrens (1920–5). In Behrens's building, the wall surface features continuous punctuation by varying textures and materials, which emphasizes a feeling of unrest and instability that seems to lurk beneath the severe overall design. The brickwork is in shades which range from blue to orange and yellow, a palette which recalls the water-colours of Nolde or Kirchner. Mendelsohn, on the other hand, was influenced by the *Blauer Reiter* movement—he knew Franz Marc and Kandinsky when a student at Munich in 1911—and his Jugendstil reminiscences derive from that source. His sketches, executed between 1914 and 1920, display the same stylistic idioms, and that character of cosmic and stylistic search and lyric effusion as an act of liberation, and at the same time mystical union with the world, that is typical of the *Blauer Reiter's* spiritual posture. His use of sketches to work out his approach to a theme, without reference to structure, is typically Expressionist.

Two other architects deserve special notice: Hugo *Häring and Otto *Bartning. For Häring adherence to the Expressionist aesthetic was tantamount to a recognition of German Gothic as an anti-illuminist culture that shunned the laws of geometry and was hence organic in form (farm buildings, Garkau, 1923). For Bartning, however, architecture is growth and activity, the force of nature itself (Star church project, 1922). Poelzig's development between 1919 and 1930 is in two phases. The rebuilding of the Grosses Schauspielhaus in Berlin, the designs for the Salzburg Festival Theatre and a festival hall at Dresden carry the process of

Erich Mendelsohn. Einstein Tower. Potsdam, 1920. Project

dissolving not only the classic rules of composition but the very constituent elements of the structure itself to extraordinary lengths. A second phase witnesses the reassertion of volumetric values, with a soberer and more monumental style, as exemplified by his designs for the IG-Farben offices at Frankfurt (1928–31) and his broadcasting studios in Berlin.

Under the stress of the menacing political situation in the early thirties, the artistic forces of the time tended to crystallize into groups centring around the democratic opposition or the Nazi party. The sharpening of this crisis betokened the end of Expressionism, which by its intrinsic nature could not tolerate extreme ideological conditions, although it tended to promote and educe them. The 'white architecture of the twenties' became a symbol of the democratic opposition, while Expressionism began to acquire pan-Germanic and nationalist traits, and in its ideological uncertainty was relegated to a position of cultural insignificance.

Bibliography: Walter Müller-Wulckow, *Deutsche Baukunst der Gegenwart*, Leipzig 1929; E. M. Hajos and L. Zahn, *Berliner Architektur der Nachkriegszeit*, Berlin 1928; Vittorio Gregotti, 'L'architettura dell' espressionismo', in *Casabella Continuità*, No. 254, Milan 1961; Arnold Whittick, *European Architecture in the Twentieth Century*, Vol. 1 (up to 1924), Vol. 2 (1924–33), London 1950 and 1953.

VITTORIO GREGOTTI

Festival of Britain, South Bank Exhibition. London, 1951. Aerial view of site

Farmer and Dark. Frank Quentery Farmer, b. 1879, d. 1955 and Bernard Franklin Dark. Practice founded 1934, specializing in industrial buildings, where effects are achieved by essentially simple but carefully developed methods of planning and close attention to details; factories, mills, power stations. In 1957 a 75-inch module system was developed for one- or two-storey timber buildings (Sconce Hills School, Newark, Notts.).

Festival of Britain. A national manifestation organized throughout the United Kingdom in 1951, at the original suggestion of Sir Gerald Barry, to mark the centenary of the Great Exhibition of 1851. Its most important architectural expression was the exhibition laid out on the south bank of the Thames in London (Director of Architecture: Hugh *Casson). This was significant not only for the opportunity it afforded millions of people to see stimulating modern architecture of an almost uniformly high level of design, but because it provided an occasion for displaying the principles of *townscape which had been developing and clarifying themselves over the previous years. Eschewing the formal layouts that had been usual in earlier major exhibitions, recourse was had to a subtly planned disposition of buildings and features, an exploitation of changes of level, progressively evolving views and the dramatic long-distance backdrop of the north bank of the Thames to give an impression of exciting complexity and size that was quite extraordinary for so small a site.

Notable contributions were made by Ralph Tubbs (Dome of Discovery), Arcon (Transport), Maxwell *Fry and Jane *Drew, Edward *Mills (Administration building), R. Y. Goodden and R. D. Russell (Lion and Unicorn), H. T. Cadbury Brown (Land of Britain), Brian O'Rorke and F. H. K. Henrion (The Natural Scene and The Country), *Architects' Co-Partnership (Minerals of the Land), G. Grenfell Baines and H. J. Reifenberg (Power and Production) and Basil *Spence (Sea and Ships).

Bibliography: H. Casson, 'The 1951 Exhibition' in *Journal of the RIBA*, April 1950. See also *Architectural Review* for May 1951.

HAROLD MEEK

Misha Black, Alexander Gibson, and Design Research Unit. Regatta Restaurant. Festival of Britain, South Bank Exhibition. London, 1951

Figini, Luigi, b. Milan 1903. Graduated there 1926. Founder member of *gruppo 7*. Collaboration with Gino *Pollini. Residential buildings, factories (for Olivetti in Ivrea), exhibition architecture, and interior decoration. The Church of the Madonna dei Poveri erected on a basilica plan (Milan 1952–6) attempts to create an atmosphere of mystical faith with its exposed concrete frame, narrow light slits in the nave and its deliberate impression of a rough, unfinished state.

Finland. The counter-movement to eclecticism began to take shape in Finland in the course of the 1890s. Although preliminary development was gradual, the actual breakthrough in 1900 proved stormy. Following it, virtually no classical shapes emerged again for a long time. The victor was not *Art Nouveau in its true sense, but a Finnish version of it, the so-called National Romantic style, which was inspired by the tradition of primitive Finnish architecture. Axial symmetry was done away with and replaced by the free plan and free massing. Façade architecture gave way to layouts with separate blocks and wings. One of the essential problems of modern architecture had already been encountered: that of the continuity of space. These problems were solved in such an original way in Finland that the best examples have preserved their freshness throughout the past decades. While Art Nouveau often relied on decorative details for its artistic effect, the Finnish National Romantic style depended more on the effect of its materials as such. Timber and granite were favourite media from which strong and expressive effects were derived.

The painter Akseli Gallén-Kallela may be regarded as the spiritual father of the National Romantic movement in Finland, and his studio built in the Wildmark (1894) was the first achievement of the new style. Three architects, Gesellius, Lindgren and Eliel *Saarinen, soon took their place at its head. It was their design for the Finnish pavilion at the Paris International Exhibition of 1900 which precipitated the breakthrough, and their fortress-like loghouse building at Hvitträsk near Helsinki (1902) still makes the strongest impression on a spectator to this day. Lars Sonck, the builder of Tampere Cathedral (1902–7) is currently regarded as the most brilliant exponent of the real romantic style. By its side, International Art Nouveau also made its appearance in Finland, assuming the tasks of a rationalist school in comparison with the picturesque romantic style. Its representatives are Selim Lindqvist, Onni Tarjanne and Usko Nyström, whose aims were closer to present-day architecture than those of the romantics although they did not always measure up to them as artists.

Lars Sonck and Valter Jung. Bank. Helsinki, 1904

Sigurd Frosterus, a pupil of van de Velde's, and Gustaf Strengell were the leaders of the rationalist opposition and modern architectural ideas emerge in their writings around 1904. Even if they did not manage to defeat the romantics, the rationalists dealt them a decisive blow. The reaction was mainly due to the example set by Eliel Saarinen. He developed his own monumental style, whose fundamental idea is a vertical movement breaking through from the central feature of a horizontal mass; a subject whose pathos greatly appealed to his contemporaries. Saarinen's most important building in Finland is the main station at Helsinki (1904, built 1910–14), but it is less attractive than his general plan for the town—a fully consistent decentralization plan, conceived as early as 1918.

After the end of the First World War, it became apparent that belief in the birth of a new art and a new architecture had been vain. Classical motives, albeit freely handled, returned to architecture. Coupled with this tendency now was the influence of Swedish classicism, which prevailed among the young generation. Striving for monumentality during the classicizing intermezzo of the twenties reached its peak in J. S. Sirén's Parliament Building. For many others, such as Erik *Bryggman and Gunnar Taucher, this trend meant a process of simplification, which banished every last moulding from their smooth surfaces. The timeless, functional architecture of the Mediterranean countries was the main exemplar adduced, and in this

respect classicism too paved the way for the new architecture. Furthermore, the social thought of the twenties introduced a new element, as shown in the garden suburb of Käpylä at Helsinki (1920–5), planned by Martti Välikangas and others, which is based on old Finnish traditions as much as on the teachings of Ebenezer *Howard.

The new architecture, *Functionalism, only reached Finland in the late twenties. The exhibition at Turku, designed by Alvar *Aalto and Erik Bryggman in 1929, became the manifesto of the movement. The great Stockholm Exhibition of the following year assured the victory of Functionalism in Finland too. Compared with most other countries, the change in Finland was rapid and complete. The first new works by Bryggman, Erkki Huttunen, Yrjö Lindegren, and others showed great maturity, quite apart from Aalto's sanatorium at Paimio (1929–33) and the library at Viipuri (1927–35), which are among the classic masterpieces of modern architecture.

This 'white' Functionalism in Finland does not lack individuality despite its internationalism. A certain stress of solidity is characteristic of most of its products and gives them an expression of real monumentality, which often achieves pathos as in P. E. Blomstedt's work. Bryggman displays an outward lightness which is reminiscent of Continental rationalism but always preserves a romantic colouring.

Although the thirties were so uniform in Finnish architecture, new ideas did develop

Eliel Saarinen. Main railway station, Helsinki. Designed 1904, built 1910–14. Project

during this period, and more diverse
artistic expressions resulted. Aalto above
all, whose works from the outset attracted
attention outside Finland, demonstrated
new powers of design. His cellulose factory
at Sunila (1936–9) and the house built
along terraces at Kauttua (1938–40) are
studies in adapting architecture to landscape. Free shapes and careful use of
building materials (in particular of timber)
characterize his work from the start
(Finnish Pavilion at the New York World's
Fair, 1939).

The forties brought a reaction against the
severity of Functionalism. The Olympic
Village by Hilding Ekelund and Välikangas
(Helsinki 1940) marks the retreat of the
cube in favour of less demanding functional
shapes and the memorial chapel at Turku
cemetery (1938–41) by Bryggman appeals
to the spectator's emotions. Throughout
the war building activity was very limited
and the artistic results were modest. The
romantic reaction took refuge in eclecticist
and decorative motives, so that the fundamental character of the new architecture
seemed in some ways to be already as good
as lost.

The fifties saw a new upsurge of activity,
once more beneath the banners of rationalism and Constructivism. American influences were apparent in the work of
Aarne *Ervi and Viljo *Revell. Revell's
studio became a kind of headquarters of the
rationalist school, from which many of the
leading architects of today have emerged.
The bright and simple Kudeneule factory
at Hanko (1955) may be regarded as
Revell's most typical design. He has become widely known as the leader of the team
that won the Toronto City Hall competition.
Although the fifties were so rationalistic,
the trend that started in the thirties still
continued. The heavy, vigorous shapes of
Finnish architecture are very different from
the precise purism of the *International
Style; feeling for materials and adaptability
to natural surroundings have remained
constant. Even in such purist examples as
the chapel at Otaniemi (1957) by Kaija and
Heikki *Siren, it is for just these reasons
that a warmth has been preserved which
we generally call 'human'.

These properties are most pronounced in
Alvar Aalto's buildings. Although at first
he renounced free shapes, his designs
preserve a plastic unity despite their

Gunnar Taucher. Housing. Helsinki, 1926

Jorma Järvi. High School. Helsinki, 1955.
Assembly Hall

rectangularity (Town Hall at Säynätsalo, 1950–2; boarding school at Helsinki, 1952–6). Later he returned to free shapes and transferred them from the interiors to the way his buildings were massed (Cultural Institute at Helsinki, 1955–8; church at Vuoksenniska near Imatra, 1956–58). His palette as always is built up from natural materials and has become still richer. Apart from timber he now employs exposed brickwork, copper, ceramics and marble. Aalto has not founded a school of architects but his influence on Finnish architecture is none the less extraordinarily great, thanks to his ability to point out new directions and to serve as a criterion of architectural quality.

Lindegren (extensions to the Olympic Stadium at Helsinki, 1952; 'Snakehouse' residential district at Helsinki, 1951) and Aulis Blomstedt have also gone their own roads. The less numerous and more modest works of Blomstedt achieve their effect by their outstanding sureness of proportion to which he has devoted special research.

New trends reached Finland, too, towards the end of the fifties. The free shapes of *shell vaulting have remained more or less at the design stage, however, and this situation is not yet resolved.

Bibliography: Nils Erik Wickberg, *Byggnadskonst i Finland*, Stockholm 1959;

Alvar Aalto. Boarding School. Helsinki, 1952–6

Page 102. Yrjö Lindegren and Toivo Jäntti. Olympic Stadium. Helsinki, 1934–40 and 1952

Kaija and Heikki Siren. Chapel, Otaniemi Technical College, 1957

Viljo Revell. Kudeneule Textile Works. Hanko, 1955

Aulis Blomstedt. Extension to a Workers' Club. Helsinki, 1959

Hans J. Becker and Wolfram Schlote, *Neuer Wohnbau in Finnland*, Stuttgart 1958, Milan 1960.

KYÖSTI ÅLANDER

Fiocchi, Annibale, b. Milan 1915. Director of the architectural department of Olivetti's. Housing estates and factories in Ivrea (together with *Nizzoli, *Figini and *Pollini and Mario Oliveri), Palazzo Olivetti, Milan (with Gian Antonio Bernasconi and Nizzoli, 1954).

Fischer, Theodor, b. Schweinfurt 1862, d. Munich 1938. Collaborated with Paul Wallot on the Reichstag Building, Berlin. Taught and built in Stuttgart, Munich, and elsewhere. Evangelical Garrison Church at Ulm (1911), numerous offices, schools, museums.

Fisker, Kay, b. Copenhagen 1893. Studied at the Academy of Fine Arts, Copenhagen. The influence of international Functionalism is evident in Fisker's buildings, but he has not abandoned the tradition of Danish brick architecture. Considerable teaching activity. Architect of Århus University, together with Povl Stegmann and C. F.

Møller (work commenced 1931), school at Husum (1949–51), large housing estates.
Bibliography: Hans Erling Langkilde, *Arkitekten Kay Fisker*, Copenhagen 1960.

Floorscape. The use of patterns and textures in the ground as a design element, either contributing to overall visual appeal, suggesting lines of directivity to the pedestrian, or simply emphasizing space.
Bibliography: Elizabeth Beazley, *Design and detail of the space between buildings*, London 1960; Gordon Cullen, *Townscape*, London 1961.

France. The history of modern architecture in France is characterized by the tenacious resistance to new ideas put up by the reactionary forces and the continuance of a type of thought aiming at reform, which has been asserting itself equally stubbornly for a hundred years. From this polarity a fascinating historical picture emerges and, at the present time, a conflicting situation that can only be surveyed with difficulty. Academic resistance has centred round the Paris *École des Beaux-Arts, with practically all the means of a centralized, official apparatus at its disposal. The attitude of this court of official opinion was not only of importance to France; European and American reaction took its cue for decades from the example of the École des Beaux-Arts. Though the academicians succeeded in keeping commissions away from the younger generation and withholding from them the opportunity for experimentation, they could not prevent men in every generation who had espoused a revolutionary attitude from making their influence felt even far beyond the frontiers of their own country.
The conflict flared up when *Viollet-le-Duc, in his own feud against the Beaux-Arts, professed a doctrine relating form to material and function, which his investigations into Gothic architecture had suggested to him (*Dictionnaire de l'Architecture*, 1854 ff., *Entretiens sur l'Architecture*, 1863 –72, American translation 1875–1881). This doctrine has influenced practically all pioneers of modern architecture, from *Richardson, via *Berlage and *Horta, to *Perret, *Le Corbusier and even F. Ll. *Wright. It met with most approval from the engineers, who saw in the return of architecture to structural form an ideal

which they themselves did not dare to proclaim publicly. Their colossal structures (Douro and Garabit bridges by *Eiffel, 1877–84; Eiffel Tower and *Contamin's Machinery Hall, 1889; Arnodin's Ponts Transbordeurs at Nantes and Marseilles, 1900–5) seemed to confirm the doctrine of the essential dependence of form on function, and the new formal and spatial concepts were indeed traced back to a strict adherence to this thesis. The prestige of such works has outlasted the change of generations. No wonder then that Choisy's still influential *Histoire de l'Architecture*, which was published towards the end of that golden age of construction in 1898, tackles the history of form in a purely engineering spirit.

The iron style had just reached its Baroque phase in Art Nouveau (*Guimard's Métro station entrances, 1900, Frantz Jourdain's Samaritaine department store, 1901) when a new generation tried taking the new material of reinforced concrete as the starting point for a new style, based on the same functional principles. A clear, strictly geometrical vocabulary of form, with classical overtones in the case of Perret, takes the place of the spatially complicated iron structures. Until the First World War the architectural use of reinforced concrete was restricted to a few examples (Perret, *Garnier). But these pioneers deserve the credit for having made the new material fit for architecture, while restoring validity again to the principle of truth to structure. The conflict with official architecture now assumed a sharper character than at the time of the iron engineers whose sphere of activities only overlapped with academicism at the edges.

Only after the war did the 'new style' emerge from a combination of architectural form with the new spatial concept that had crystallized between 1907 and 1914 in the graphic arts: Cubism. Since then Le Corbusier's genius towers over the horizon of French architecture. Around him and beside him, however, though seldom quite independent of him, new paths were explored. During the twenties the interchange of ideas with other centres of the movement —Germany and Holland—was particularly active. It was promoted by such journals as *L'Esprit Nouveau* (edited by Le Corbusier and Ozenfant, 1920–6), *Les Cahiers de l'Effort Moderne* (edited by Léonce

Rosenberg, 1925–7) and the *Architecture Vivante* series (edited by Badovici and Morancé from 1923); by exhibitions such as the International Exhibition of Applied Art, Paris, 1925, the unequalled exhibition of the Deutscher Werkbund (with the *Bauhaus as a focal point) in the Salon des Artistes Décorateurs, Paris, 1930, and the participation of French architects at the Werkbund Exhibition in Stuttgart, 1927, and at the International Building Exhibition, Berlin, 1930, etc. Adolf *Loos worked in Paris from 1923 till 1928 (Maison Tzara, 1926) and exerted a deep influence

Hector Guimard. Métro entrance. Paris, 1900

Henri Labrouste. Bibliothèque Ste Geneviève. Paris, 1843–50

Le Corbusier. Salvation Army Hostel. Paris, 1931–2

on the younger architects. Le Corbusier and Jeanneret, André *Lurçat, Robert *Mallet-Stevens, Gabriel Guevrekian, Jean Badovici, Michel Roux-Spitz built houses and villas for avant-garde patrons, all typical examples of the *International Style; suffice it to mention the steel and glass house built by Pierre Chareau for Dr Dalsace, 1931.

The exponents of the new architecture, however, lacked the powerful support which their colleagues in Germany and Holland enjoyed in the form of major commissions from municipal authorities for the design of housing estates. It was only as late as 1930–5 that opportunities for other work arose on a limited scale. Thus besides a few blocks of flats (preceded twenty years earlier by those of Henri Sauvage in the Rue Vavin which had not received the attention they merited), the Hôtel Latitude 43 was built at St Tropez in 1933 by Pingusson and the school at Villejuif by Lurçat in 1931–3. The housing estates of Eugène *Beaudouin and Marcel *Lods at Drancy (the first point blocks) and Bagneux followed, with their open air school at Suresnes (1932–5) and the Maison du Peuple at Clichy (in collaboration with Jean *Prouvé). A development opened up that might have led to a kind of 'Scandinavian style' if stagnation on the property market, the hostility of the authorities and the deplorable success of the compromise-architecture at the Paris International Exhibition of 1937 had not barred the way.

The years following the Second World War created a completely new situation: a building boom, shifting the emphasis to State-backed housing schemes (annual target: 350,000 dwellings), with the problem extended to dimensions that required the creation of mixed teams of architects, engineers, and sociologists, and the emergence of town- and country-planning projects to a position of major importance. The unique opportunity of this first reconstruction period has been missed in France as thoroughly as elsewhere. Le Corbusier's advanced scheme for St Dié was not carried out; the aged Perret created a grandiose urban abstraction at Le Havre, but his pupils can breathe no life into it. Pison's research into contemporary farm buildings was not followed up. The remainder is mediocrity. It looks above all as if French architecture has succumbed to an empty inhuman geometry, from which it can at best only save itself by recourse to an inadequate, if technically brilliant, formalism in ostensibly purpose-free buildings (French Pavilion at Brussels, 1958).

Eugène Beaudouin and Marcel Lods. Cité de la Muette, Drancy near Paris, 1933

André Lurçat. School. Villejuif, 1931–3

A new generation, whose most outstanding representatives have been trained by Le Corbusier or who at least acknowledge allegiance to him has led to a marked change since about 1955. These younger men show a common tendency, which may be traced back to Le Corbusier, to consider all architectural problems in the light of a 'humanisme total', whether it is a matter of individual buildings or of town planning. In the manipulation of technical resources, apart from the influence of the masters of reinforced concrete such as *Freyssinet, André Coyne and Bernard Lafaille, the work of Jean Prouvé is exerting an increasingly more marked effect. His example makes up for the temptation offered to their followers by the monumentality of Le Corbusier's later works and the abstract transparency of Mies. Hence an original French style is beginning to establish itself, whose principal features can already be recognized in numerous buildings and projects. These include the new town of Bagnols-sur-Cèze and the planning for the Toulouse satellites at Le Mirail (*Candilis team), the blocks of flats at Croix and St Germain (Shape-Village), the Paris Museum of Folk Art (Dubuisson), the Vieille-Église housing estate at Croissy (Chemineau and Mirabaud), tall blocks of flats, shops and district heating plant at Bagneux (Gomis, Bodiansky, Gillet), residential and school buildings, the cathedral at Algiers (Herbé and Le Couteur), the Les Bureaux housing estate at Sceaux and the Museum at Le Havre (Lagneau team), the experimental plastic house by Schein and Magnant, the studio house at St Rémy, the 'Mex' type adaptable prefabricated houses and the St Antoine University Clinic by A. Wogenscky, who was the architect in charge of building the Unités d'habitation when head of Le Corbusier's office.

Men of the older generation have also contributed to this renaissance, e.g. Lods with his large housing estate, Marly (with Honegger and Beuté), André Sive with several housing schemes, Beaudouin with the Cité Rotterdam at Strasbourg and the point blocks in Berlin (Hansa district) and Pantin (with Lopez), Emile Aillaud with industrial buildings in Lorraine and the ribbon and round tower housing estates at Aubervilliers and Bobigny, Pierre *Vago with the Basilica at Lourdes (with Freyssinet), and Ecochard with town planning and large-scale buildings in North Africa and the Near East. Mention should also be made of the office buildings by Lopez and Gravereaux (Rue Lapérouse and Rue Viala in Paris, with Prouvé) and by Edouard Albert at Paris and Orly, the Technical College (INSA) at Lyons (Jacques Perrin-Fayolle with Prouvé), the Faculty of Philosophy at Poitiers (Ursault), the medical faculty at Marseilles (Egger), the training workshops of the Electricité de France near Soissons (P. and P. Sirvin), Ginsberg's residential blocks in the west of Paris, and several shopping centres and

Georges Candilis, Bodiansky, Woods and Piot. Bagnols-sur-Cèze. Commenced 1956

Eugène Beaudouin. Cité Rotterdam. Strasbourg, 1951–3

industrial and exhibition buildings. The churches form a group of their own: Rueil (Sonrel and Duthilleul), Neuilly (Coulon), Mazamet (Belmont), Baccarat (Kazis), Fontaine-lès-Grès (Marot), Pontarlier and Villejuif (Rainer Senn), the Franciscan Monastery at Orsay (Brothers Arsène-Henry) and the Dominican Monastery at Lille. The influence of the Dominican journal *Art Sacré* played a decisive rôle here.

Since 1925, Charlotte Perriand has been in the forefront of the fight for functional equipment in the home. The feud between *Formes Utiles* (André Hermant) and *Esthétique Industrielle* (Jacques Viénot) has led to the solution of many minor problems in the field of industrial design. The *Architecture Mobile* Association is carrying out basic research, the sculptor H. G. Adam encourages his pupils to co-operate with architects, and the Cercles d'Etudes Architecturales have become a forum for modern architecture and an important centre for international exchange. This revival of the spirit of experimentation on which the best French tradition has always been based can be furthered by the reform of architectural education, which was at last taken in hand in 1962 and which should lead to the suppression of the *de facto* monopoly of the Beaux-Arts.

Bibliography: S. Giedion, *Bauen in Frankreich, Eisen und Eisenbeton*, Leipzig 1929; Marie Dormoy, *L'Architecture Française*, Paris 1938; *25 Années UAM* (*Union des Artistes Modernes*), Paris 1956; J. Schein, *Paris construit*, Paris 1961.

MAURICE BESSET

Guillaume Gillet. Notre Dame de Royan, 1954–9

Camelot, De Mailly and Zehrfuss. Centre Nationale des Industries et Techniques. Paris, 1958

Freyssinet, Eugène, b. Objat, France 1879, d. 1962. Freyssinet was a pupil of the reinforced concrete pioneer Charles Rabut. In 1907, when just twenty-eight years old and employed as an engineer by a road-works authority in Central France, he built the bridges of Boutiron and Le Veurdre (destroyed 1940–4), which together with the contemporary early works of the Swiss *Maillart are considered among the boldest and most elegant creations of the early days of *reinforced concrete bridge building. A design for an arched bridge with a span of 607 feet (1913) was not executed due to the outbreak of war, but served as a basis for a number of later bridges by Freyssinet, right up to the Traneberg Bridge in Stockholm (1932, 597 foot span) and the bridges on the Caracas-to-La Guaira motorway (1950–5, average spans 476 feet). The St Pierre-du-Vauvray Bridge was built in 1922, its thin deck slab borne by a daring twin-arch 433 feet in span (destroyed 1940–44). Apart from the road and railway bridge over the Elorn estuary in Brittany, with three piers (1926–9, span 3 by 564 feet, partly destroyed 1944), Freyssinet's most popular works were the two airship hangars at Orly (1916–24, each 984 foot long and 205 foot high, destroyed 1944). These giant structures are important in the history of architecture not just because of their tremendous size and their technical innovations, but perhaps even more because of the matter-of-factness with which harmony of forms results from the choice of rational, albeit unusual, structural solutions despite unfamiliar dimensions. St Pierre-du-Vauvray and Orly are examples of pure functional beauty raised to the highest pitch of drama. Exceptionally bold intuitions of form were realized in them without their effect being weakened by any later 'cosmetic' alterations.

Eugène Freyssinet. Elorn Estuary Bridge. 1926–9

Apart from bridges, Freyssinet designed mainly industrial buildings, warehouses, etc., in his 'industrial period' (he was technical director of the Entreprises Limousin from 1913 to 1928). During this time he produced a series of now famous examples in the field of *shell and vaulted structures. Due to the difficulty of shuttering, the execution of curved shapes in reinforced concrete is troublesome and expensive. Freyssinet therefore attempted, on the one

Eugène Freyssinet. Airship hangar. Orly, 1916–24

hand, to achieve extensive standardization of these shapes, and on the other hand to improve the static behaviour of reinforced concrete by means other than stiffening deformations. He had the idea of subjecting the reinforcement to tensile stresses. These tensile stresses were intended to compensate for the compressive stresses which are engendered in the finished building by the self-weight of the concrete and the additional live loads. This led to the invention of pre-stressing, as it is now called, in experiments which go back to 1926 (his 'scientific period'). Freyssinet used it from 1933 onwards for the most varying tasks in multi-storey and underground structures (dam building in North Africa and harbour construction at Brest, 1937–9, and in particular Le Havre, 1946–52, runways at Orly, 1946–7, bridges and water tanks of up to 9,000 cubic yards capacity).

The shapes resulting from pre-stressed concrete are considerably flatter, slenderer and more highly stressed than those of normal reinforced concrete. The Marne bridges Freyssinet rebuilt with an average span of 230 feet thus have a stress ratio of 1:45. The strength of the units, which are prefabricated on the bank and assembled like steel beams, depends on the centre-piece of the bridge which is 2 feet thick. This type of construction, which was tried out on bridges, could be taken over for the underground Basilica of Pius X at Lourdes, where a maximum clear width had to be achieved for a minimum overall height. Here, as at Orly, repetition of a single technical shape worked out to the last detail, resulted in a monumental effect of

a truly architectural nature. As in certain designs by Pier Luigi *Nervi, pure structure becomes most impressive architecture.
Bibliography: Maurice Besset, *Eugène Freyssinet*, in *Les Architectes Célèbres*, Vol 2, Paris 1959.

MAURICE BESSET

Fry, Edwin Maxwell, b. 1899. Studied at Liverpool School of Architecture. Partnership with Walter *Gropius, 1934–6; with Jane *Drew, 1945–50. From 1951 to 1958 practised as Fry, Drew, Drake and Lasdun; since 1958, Fry, Drew and Partners. A pioneer of modern architecture in *Great Britain; his Kensal House housing scheme at Ladbroke Grove, London (1936, in collaboration) was the nearest British pre-war approach to a continental *Siedlung*. Schools, hospitals, housing, offices; educational buildings in West Africa, where he worked as a town planner from 1943 to 1945. Senior Architect at Chandigarh, 1951–4, in collaboration with *Le Corbusier.

Fuller, Richard Buckminster, b. Milton, Massachusetts 1895. Not an architect in the usual sense of the word, but instead a unique reflection of those 20th-century concepts related to the machine aesthetic, Fuller has received recognition from the architectural profession for his unique gifts only in the last few years. His formal education was sketchy and did not progress much beyond two years at Harvard, 1913–15. After service as a naval officer during the First World War and after occupying a number of positions in business and industry, he perfected a kind of machine for living in which he called the 'Dymaxion (dynamic plus maximum efficiency) House' in 1927. In contrast to the poetic expressions of the machine age which were so frequently manifested in the buildings of the 1920s in Europe, and especially in Le *Corbusier's lyrical Villa Savoye, 1929, Fuller's product was a machine for living in in a literal rather than in a metaphorical sense. Unlike the contemporary masterpieces of European Purism and related movements, Fuller's Dymaxion House was not in any consequential way an object for aesthetic contemplation, but is more correctly viewed as an assemblage of mechanical services in conjunction with living areas. In 1932–5 Fuller developed a motorized version of this idea in his 'Dymaxion Three Wheeled Auto'. Since then Fuller has devoted much time and effort to the art of structures, and these studies have led to the perfection of his Geodesic Domes, structures of metal, plastic, or even of cardboard based upon octahedrons or tetrahedrons. He came to use the domical shape not for a traditional, architectural reason—not, for instance, because it was an 'ideal' form—but because of its natural efficiency in providing the greatest space enclosed in relation to the surface area of the enclosing form. In their use of standardized parts, these Geodesic Domes are, in a sense, the most recent descendants of the assembly techniques that were first employed by Sir Joseph *Paxton in the Crystal Palace, London, 1851. The largest of these domes that has been erected was the repair shop for the Union Tank Car Co., Baton Rouge, La., 1958, with a diameter of 384 feet, a span that exceeds those of the mammoth 19th-century exhibition halls, such as the Machinery Hall at the World Exhibition, Paris, 1889 (362 feet). More recently Fuller has produced a new system known as

Richard Buckminster Fuller. Dymaxion House, 1927. Model

Richard Buckminster Fuller. Ford Motor
Company. Dearborn, Mich., 1953. Dome

Tenegrity Structures (a contraction of
Tensional Integrity), examples of which
were exhibited at the Museum of Modern
Art, New York, in 1960.
Understandably more popular with students
than with the established elements in the
architectural profession, Fuller has enjoyed
notable success as a visiting lecturer in
various architectural schools in the USA,
among them being Cornell, Massachusetts
Institute of Technology, University of
California, University of Pennsylvania,
Princeton University, University of Michigan and Yale University. In 1952 Fuller
received the Award of Merit of the New
York Chapter of the AIA, and in 1959 the
national organization of the same body
recognized his work with the award of an
honorary membership.
Bibliography: Robert W. Marks, *The
Dymaxion World of Buckminster Fuller*,
New York 1960.

JOHN M. JACOBUS, JR

Functionalism. 'Form follows function'
is the catchphrase that spells modern
architecture to most laymen. In the 1920s
it seemed like a strange idea, cold and
forbidding; today, although widely accepted
(and even more widely misunderstood),
'form follows function' continues to evoke
the image of modern as opposed to traditional architecture more readily than any
other slogan. Yet there is no architectural
principle that can claim a more ancient and
distinguished tradition. Form has followed
function from the paleolithic cave-dwellers
to the neolithic lake-dwellers; it followed
function in Roman forts and aqueducts, in
medieval castles and the Great Wall of
China, in 18th-century English warehouses, and in 20th-century Manhattan
office piles. Functionalism, in short, is as
old as building itself.
Critics of functionalism sometimes sug-
gest that functionalism stops where architecture begins. This is unfair both to
functionalism and to architecture. The
functionalist period in the development of
a new architecture is much like the formative childhood period in the life of a man.
As he matures, he may reject many of the
fads and prejudices of his teen-age; none
the less, the basis of his personality was
laid during those earlier years.
The personality of modern architecture
had its genesis in the 1850s, the formative
years of present-day Functionalism. Both
the followers of *Le Corbusier and of
Frank Lloyd *Wright—now apparently
poles apart—derived much of their early
inspiration from the 19th-century doc-
trines of Eugène *Viollet-le-Duc, the
French architect and theoretician, who is
best known for his restorations of medieval
castles. Less well known, but more important, are his attempts to rationalize (or
'functionalize') the art of architecture into
a logical system with simple rules. Le
Corbusier's writings of the early twenties
—for example, his *Vers une architecture*—
read like Viollet-le-Duc brought up to date;
and Wright told his architect-son to read
Viollet-le-Duc, because his writings would
give him all the basic education he needed.
The first rule of Functionalism grew
directly out of the credo that form must
reflect function—or 'express' function, as
architects like to say. This was paraphrased
to mean that all the different elements in a
building should be separately 'expressed':
for example, the structural columns and
beams should be made clearly visible,
inside and out, and separated from non-
structural wall panels and partitions, so
that the structural frame would clearly
'express' its function of holding up the
floors and the roof.

The second rule of Functionalism came about in a more roundabout way. Because the early Functionalists got much of their inspiration from the machine itself, machine forms became greatly admired. The fact that such forms did not always make much sense in buildings did not matter; after all, Louis *Sullivan used plant forms for terracotta ornament because natural organisms were something that *he* admired—so why should not machine forms like cylinders, cones, cubes, and other geometric shapes be used by the admirers of machine organisms? None of this need have come as a surprise. As early as 1920, Le Corbusier had written jubilantly: 'Thus we have the American grain elevators and factories . . . the American engineers overwhelm with their calculations our expiring architecture.' However, Le Corbusier was not quite so overwhelmed as he may have seemed. For while he was praising functional buildings put up by practical men, he also announced, in the same breath, that 'architecture is the masterly, correct, and magnificent play of masses brought together in light . . . cubes, cones, spheres, cylinders, or pyramids are the great primary forms which light reveals to advantage . . . these are *beautiful forms, the most beautiful forms* [his italics]'. In other words: Functionalism is wonderful—as long as it produces beautiful forms.

But while these sophisticated Functionalists were busy in the 1920s and 1930s developing a style out of the raw material of engineering, there grew up, on the sidelines, another kind of functionalist. He was the builder, the businessman, the engineer, who really believed all that he had read in the papers about cheaper, more practical, more form-fitting architecture. If 'form follows function', he argued, does not efficient function automatically produce beautiful form? Well, it seemed to—in some instances at least: How about aeroplanes? How about some bridges, ships, tools, factories, dams? And if you can produce beauty by some kind of automatic function-computer, why bother with all the talk about art? The output of these literal functionalists is all around us today, for everyone to see. Every big American city is studded with office and apartment buildings designed—if that is the word—by some sort of automatic 'functional' process: the exterior shape is determined

by zoning laws; the exterior surface is papered with *curtain wall patterns picked out of a manufacturer's catalogue; the interior layout is determined by rental experts, the core by the stop-watches of elevator specialists; the roof is designed by the cooling tower fabricators; and the lobby by the newspaper distributors. Result: chaos—in the name of 'functionalism'.

Unfortunately, the 'sophisticated Functionalists' have only themselves to blame. They laid the trap when they began to apologize for the new style by claiming it was less expensive to build and less expensive to maintain. Few, if any, ever came out and said publicly that Functionalism was a coherent system of organization, a completely integrated method of putting a building together, and that it should be judged entirely on its own merits.

The present confusion over Functionalism has not been caused entirely by the innocent or the opportunistic. Functionalism needs to re-examine its own premises to see how many of them still make sense. Is it really justifiable to adhere so rigidly to a machine aesthetic? Does it really make sense to articulate and to express all things —to separate a building's elements only to have to link them together again afterwards? 'Expressing structure' is fine in many kinds of buildings; in many others, however, expressing the structure may turn out to be a big headache. And when you come to expressing mechanical equipment—elevators, or cooling towers—then the question arises, why not express the plumbing, the wiring, and the heating, too? Moreover, as the need increases for flexible space uses (in schools, offices, factories, almost any type of building), the urge to articulate each plan element must be suppressed; for, after all, the plan requirements may change overnight.

Functionalism, however, though in transition, is far from dead. It remains a rigorous and demanding discipline, an excellent textbook for young architects, a fine standard by which to judge many a building put up today.

Bibliography: E. R. de Zurko, *Origins of Functionalist Theory*, New York 1957.

PETER BLAKE

Furness, Frank, b. Philadelphia 1839, d. 1912. In buildings such as the Provident Life and Trust Bank (Philadelphia 1872)

Furness employed neo-Gothic features to create an architecture of powerful gravity and impressively integrated massing. His decoration is entirely original and employs free geometric or organic shapes derived from nature. Louis *Sullivan worked in his office for a time.

Futurism. The Futurist movement, which began in 1909, ignored architecture until 1914. In that year two young architects, Antonio *Sant'Elia and Mario *Chiattone, presented a revolutionary picture in Milan of the *Città Nuova*, the city of the future, in a series of designs and projects. In the catalogue of the exhibition a powerful harangue by Sant'Elia was published, which pleads the historical and human necessity for a radical renewal of Italian architecture, that had fallen into an academic eclecticism lacking any vital spark. The author was clearly familiar with the writings of Boccioni and Marinetti, although he had not joined the Futurist movement himself, and his proposals to 'harmonize the environment with man', in the light of the extraordinary and decisive developments of science and technology, frequently chime in with the views expressed in Futurist manifestoes on the other arts.

Marinetti, discovering the Futurist elements in Sant'Elia's thought, determined to integrate the movement's programme

Mario Chiattone. Block of flats. 1914. Project

with this fascinating and open-minded piece of writing on architecture. He persuaded Sant'Elia to join the group, introduced some modifications to his text (which made no mention of Futurism in the original version) and published it again in July of the same year, 1914, under the title of *Manifesto dell'Architettura Futurista*. The manifesto proclaimed that 'everything must be revolutionized. Architecture is breaking loose from tradition. It is forcibly starting from scratch again', and a 'preference for what is light, practical, ephemeral and swift' was praised as being Futurist, in accordance with Boccioni's aesthetic theories on 'plastic dynamism'.

This manifesto was the most important objective that Futurism achieved in the field of architecture. It has become famous and has acquired great historical value because in its way it helped to bring *Italy into the mainstream of modern developments in European architecture. In actual fact, it was only a matter of words: no important Futurist work was ever built in Italy. The finest thing that has come down to us from this period of lively controversy is simply the series of splendid drawings by Sant'Elia himself, which portray, in part at least, the architecture of Futurism. To these may be added the designs of Chiattone, most of them unpublished until 1962, and based furthermore on a static system that foreshadows the aesthetics of the *Novecento Italiano*, far removed from the 'plastic dynamism' that is at the basis of Futurism.

Fourteen years had to pass before Futurist architecture was thought of again. In 1928 one of the keenest and most convinced supporters of the idea of Futurism in architecture, the painter and journalist Fillía, organized the 'First Exhibition of Futurist Architecture' (it was also to be the only one) 'under the high patronage of His Excellency Mussolini'. The artists who took part were of various origins and tendencies: Antonio Sant'Elia, Mario Chiattone, Alberto Sartoris and Virgilio Marchi (architecture); Ivo Pannaggi, Giacomo Balla and Fillía (interior decoration); Enrico Prampolini, Fillía and Nicola Diulgheroff (stage designs); Fortunato Depero, Diulgheroff and Prampolini (exhibition architecture); and various other artists with posters and objects of daily use. Most of the schemes illustrated were only

Antonio Sant'Elia. Città Nuova. 1914. Project

projects. The sole works of architecture, apart from exhibition designs, built up to then (by Sartoris) were tied in with the European rationalist movements and ignored 'plastic dynamism'. But Fillía continued to believe in the possibility of Futurist architecture developing as Fascist architecture, and to promote and spread this idea he founded and edited a number of journals (*La città futurista, La città nuova*) and wrote articles and books (*Arte Fascista*, 1928; *La nuova architettura*, 1931).

Of works that were actually built a few 'Futurist villas' may be mentioned (at Turin and Albisola), and some exhibition

pavilions (by Depero at Monza, 1924; by Fillía at Turin and Florence, 1928). Stage designs were carried out by Enrico Prampolini, Virgilio Marchi and Anton Giulio Bragaglia, amongst others, for the Teatro degli Indipendenti in Rome, which was run by Bragaglia.

The work in which Futurism, with all its poetry, culminated was the 'Exhibition of the Fascist Revolution' held in Rome in 1932. Organized by architects, painters and designers who were mostly drawn from the ranks of Futurism, it was the only manifestation of Fascist art that achieved any historic *rapport* with the rest of Europe, by displaying a kind of *Constructivism

which could be compared with that of
Russia. While the Futurist requirements
of plastic dynamism, simultaneity and
speed ('empty words in architecture'
Mario Chiattone wrote) were being met by
stage design techniques at the Exhibition,
the principles of the *Novecento Italiano*
were winning acceptance in architecture:
'plastic values' taken from national tradition, and accepted by Fascism as those
truly expressive of the times. Sant'Elia had
died twenty years before, shortly after
*Gropius's Fagus factory was built. Now
Marinetti, the leader of Futurism, was
appointed by Mussolini to the Accademia
d'Italia.

Bibliography: Virgilio Marchi, *Architettura
futurista*, Foligno 1924; F. T. Marinetti,
Enrico Prampolini and Escodame, *Sant'
Elia e l'architettura futurista mondiale*,
Milan 1931; Alberto Sartoris, *Sant'Elia e
l'architettura futurista*, Rome 1944; Fillía,
La Nuova Architettura, Turin 1931; Reyner
Banham, 'Futurism and Modern Architec-
ture' in *RIBA Journal*, February 1957;
Rafael Benet, *Futurismo y Dada*, Barcelona
1949; Drudi Gambillo and Teresa Fiori,
Archivi del Futurismo, Rome 1958; Reyner
Banham, *Theory and Design in the First
Machine Age*, London 1959.

GIULIA VERONESI

Ignazio Gardella. Block of flats for employees.
Alessandria, 1952

Gardella, Ignazio, b. Milan 1905, first
winner of the Olivetti National Prize for
architecture, is a lecturer at the University
Institute of Architecture, Venice. In the
current architectural scene in Italy, Gardella is a figure of particular importance.
In contrast to the other architects of his
generation, he has not had recourse to any
social or aesthetic ideologies for the
genuine rationalism he has displayed from
his first works. This attitude, nevertheless,

Ignazio Gardella. Mensa Olivetti. Ivrea, 1959

has permitted him to work quite naturally by the side of the most committed of his colleagues. He has collaborated with them fruitfully at the various Triennali, in architectural and town planning competitions and in projects of all kinds. His work is characterized by its elegance and purity of composition, in a lyric vein which he has used to provide magisterially free and simple solutions to the most complex problems.

He began his career with interior decoration and rebuilding schemes. The most noteworthy among the latter are: the renovation of the theatre at Busto Arsizio in 1934, and an extension of the Villa Borletti in Milan (1935), which first brought him to notice. In the following year came his finest work to that date, and one that remains 'an outstanding example of Italian rationalism' (Mazzariol): the Anti-tuberculosis Dispensary at Alessandria (1936–8), in which the most interesting lines of Gardella's architecture are defined: clarity in the handling of plane surfaces and a judicious use of materials as essential instruments of expression. In this connection, the extensive employment of brick to face a reinforced concrete building shows Gardella's tendency to respect local traditions, at least as far as the use of colour goes.

The splendid Dispensary (soon to become dilapidated through neglect on the part of the city authorities) was the first and most significant of Gardella's architectural activities in Alessandria, where he has left a distinctive imprint, building the major part of his own most important works there: the Provincial Laboratory for Hygiene and Prophylaxis (1937–9); a block of flats for employees (1952), in which he tried, by an interesting play of movement on the elevation and the use of deeply projecting eaves, to go beyond a purely 'rationalist' scheme; a building for the Borletti works, in 1951; the Children's Hospital, in 1955; and finally, a Vocational School, currently under construction. During the same period Gardella was building elsewhere too. In 1946, in a block of flats he designed at Castana, particular emphasis was laid on an attempt to reinterpret regional and traditional elements in a modern key. This characteristic has led Gardella little by little a long way from his initial standpoint; his architecture, diverging as it does some-

Tony Garnier. Residential district. Cité Industrielle. 1901–4. Project

times from strict rationalism has sparked off a good deal of controversy, though no one disputes his taste or technical skill.

He has built blocks of flats and villas, and a group of terraced houses (1952) in the new suburb of Cesate Milanese, where he also plans to erect a brick-built church with historic overtones and a layout of subtle geometric invention in the contemporary spirit. He returns again to the poetic 'rationalist' manner, albeit exceptionally, with the white annexe he designed for the Museum of Modern Art in Milan (1953). Thereafter he often subordinates the free workings of his own imagination to the promptings of the environment in his schemes, which include a house on the Grand Canal in Venice, and a villa on the Riviera. His most significant design currently under construction, apart from the Vocational School at Alessandria, is the Olivetti Studies Centre at Ivrea.

Gardella was a member of the executive committee of the 1959 Milan Triennale.
Bibliography: G. C. Argan, *Gardella*, Milan 1959; Giuseppe Mazzariol, 'Umanesimo di Gardella' in *Zodiac 2*, Milan 1957.

GIULIA VERONESI

Garnier, Tony, b. Lyons 1869, d. La Bédoule 1948. Tony Garnier is a unique case. His first job, the project for an industrial town designed in 1901–4, when he was a Rome Scholar of barely thirty, contains not only a wealth of fertile, revolutionary ideas but so many concrete suggestions as well for the most diverse architectural

Tony Garnier. Railway station. Cité Industrielle. 1901–4. Project

problems of the modern town that as a mature master later on he had only to dip into it to cope with his manifold commissions: in particular the 'Grands Travaux de la Ville de Lyon', the abattoir of La Mouche (1909–13), the Olympic Stadium (1913–16), the Grange Blanche Hospital (1915–30), the War Memorial (1924), the telephone exchange (1927) and the residential district known as 'Les États Unis' (1928–35). Even the still much-copied town hall of Boulogne-Billancourt (1931–4, in collaboration with Debat-Ponsan) can be traced back to the 'Cité Industrielle'. But this does not mean that the untiring, ever-searching Garnier even considered resting on his early-won laurels.

Even the idea that lies at the basis of Garnier's 'Cité Industrielle' is revolutionary in its novelty. The town planning of his time had not progressed beyond Camillo Sitte's *Stadtbaukunst* (1889) and the English garden city, both of which only cope with certain aspects of the problem. Thanks to his Socialist leanings, Garnier conceived a town organism which—without churches and barracks!—fully serves the human needs of an industrial age. His

choice of material which determines the shape of the individual buildings is no less bold; only a few experimental buildings were erected in reinforced concrete in 1901. In addition, Garnier invented the shapes best suited to reinforced concrete, which have become standard features in modern architecture: continuous strips of glazing, glass walls, *pilotis*, and flat roofs. The 'free plan' derives from his cantilevered structures, which (with the exception of *Perret, 1903) he was the first in Europe to achieve. In addition, there are surprising technical innovations such as electric heating, thermostats, service cores, and a novel system of ducting worked out to the last detail. The shapes are of a baffling modernity. Their ascetic geometry recalls the harmonious cuboid houses of Adolf *Loos (e.g. Garnier's own house at St Rambert, 1911). No less advanced are the designs of the buildings and the general disposition of the town: a residential district without enclosed courtyards but featuring continuous green areas and traffic-free pedestrian precincts; single-storey schools in open layouts; hospitals planned in separate blocks; numerous sports stadia;

a community centre that anticipates contemporary social centres; separation of vehicular and pedestrian traffic; clear distinction between the different functions of a town (living, work, leisure, education, traffic), in a way that has only been theoretically planned by *CIAM since 1928. All the fundamental ideas of modern architecture and town planning have not just been hinted at in Garnier's project but are carefully thought out in detail. Only the outbreak of the First World War prevented their actual realization at Lyons from 1915 to 1920.

Garnier's name was little known outside Lyons up to the time of his death. His influence, however, extended far beyond the circle of faithful pupils who had gathered round him. Long before the publication of *Une Cité Industrielle* and its later shortened version, Garnier's ideas were known in progressive architectural circles; they played a considerable part in *Le Corbusier's ideas on town planning. Only after his death was Garnier's importance fully recognized as one of the key figures of the start of the century.

Bibliography: Tony Garnier, *Une Cité Industrielle*, Paris 1917; Tony Garnier, *Les Grands Travaux de la Ville de Lyon*, Paris 1919; Jean Badovici and Albert Morancé, *L'œuvre de Tony Garnier*, Paris 1938; Giulia Veronesi, *Tony Garnier*, Milan 1948.

MAURICE BESSET

Gaudí, Antoni, b. Reus, Catalonia 1852, d. Barcelona 1926. Gaudí, who came from a family of coppersmiths, began his architectural studies in Barcelona at the age of seventeen and graduated in 1878. At school his radical nonconformity often earned him bad marks in his examinations. He felt little attraction for the official courses, whereas, during his years as a student, he was an assiduous frequenter of the philosophy classes of Llorens y Barba and the lectures on aesthetics by Pau Milà y Fontanals. In his youth Milà y Fontanals had lived in Rome during its romantic period, where he had moved in the circle of the Nazarenes, Overbeck and his fraternity. As a consequence he had developed in a direction parallel to the English Pre-Raphaelites, with a passionate attachment to the Middle Ages, symbols, mystery and a certain esotericism. In Catalonia this kind of mentality had been brought about by the nationalist movement, some seeing in a return to the Middle Ages a return to Catalonia's Golden Age, others displaying a primitivist reaction which sought the fount of life in the realm of folk-lore and in communion with the nature of one's native land.

Gaudí's ideas were decisively influenced by this school of thought, which led him to a veneration for craftwork and the honesty of medieval art; to a mechanistic logic inspired by *Viollet-le Duc's conception of medieval architecture; and to nature as a source of inspiration, not only for decorative details but for structures as well. While he was a student, he worked as an assistant to Villar and Fontseré on the

Antoni Gaudí. Palau Güell. Barcelona, 1885–9

church at Montserrat and on the waterfall in the Ciutadella Park in Barcelona. His contribution consisted of decorative details derived from a stylization of themes from nature in the Japanese manner and from the use of ironwork features with strongly accentuated joints. His workshop experience marked him off from those architects who were merely academic draughtsmen and helped him to grasp three-dimensionally the way things are made, with tangible material.

In 1878, shortly after graduating, he designed the Casa Vicens, in the Carrer de les Carolines at Barcelona, a building suggestive of Islamic prototypes with its stepped prismatic blocks, its alternations of stone and brick, and its brilliant decoration in polychrome tiles. Constructed as it was at a period when revivalism was in full flood, it had the merit of belonging to no known style. This recourse to Islamic details was one of the levers Gaudí used, in conjunction with neomedievalism, to throw off the weight of academic prejudices and try to arrive at his own means of expression, which was characterized by a feeling for the modulation of indirect light in interiors, and something that was to be as much part and parcel of his architecture as it was to be opposed to the colourless art of the academics: his polychrome use of ceramics, mosaics, glazing and painting. Although naturalism was limited at the Casa Vicens to palm leaves featured in the wrought-iron work and the decorative ceramics which displayed ivy and raspberry tendrils, Gaudí took a step further with the street lamps he designed for the Plaça Reial in Barcelona, where he imitated forms derived from the growth of plants. The same period marks the beginning of his interest in structural problems, with the parabolic arches he employed in warehouses built for the Mataró Workers' Cooperative (1878–82), and in social questions with his schemes for workers' housing drawn up for the same co-operative.

In 1883, Gaudí was commissioned to continue the work on the Church of the Sagrada Familia, a building of great size that was progressively to monopolize his activities. A neo-Gothic design by Villar was already in existence, which Gaudí

Antoni Gaudí. Church of the Sagrada Familia. Barcelona, 1883–1926

Antoni Gaudí. Casa Milà. Barcelona, 1905–10

abandoned, but the lines of the apse, the first part he built, still contain many Gothic reminiscences, although the mouldings and decorative details are drawn much more closely from nature. It is to this period that the Palau Güell belongs in the Carrer Nou de la Rambla, Barcelona, now the calle Conde del Asalto (1885–9), where Gaudí's structural experiments—the use of parabolic arches is the most evident one —create a personal style, adapted to the exclusive use of stone, timber and wrought-iron. This palace, and his designs for a large building for Catholic missions in Tangiers, with towers that recall the parabolic cupolas of villages in the Chad, formed the basis of his complete liberation from the historic styles, and his approach to a 'biological' style.

Work on the Sagrada Familia continued with the Nativity façade of the east transept. This consists of three open portals between four interpenetrating square-based towers, set diagonally, which rise to a height of 351 feet and terminate in thin, curved, circular features crowned by a piece of capricious play with intersecting surfaces, covered in mosaic. A complex and lively world, modelled for the most part by Gaudí himself and comprising an immense variety of plants and animals, throngs the great concavities below the gables, which are covered in imitation snow carved out of stone and carry a series of sculptures depicting the childhood of Christ. While in his previous works naturalism was used purely decoratively, in this instance the sculptures of living forms, connected up by a series of continuous curved surfaces, make up a form of cladding that covers the structure completely and models it independently.

Henceforth, as in the Casa Batlló in the Paseo de Gracia, Barcelona (1905–7), natural and organic forms no longer simply comprise a kind of ornament superimposed on the building but go on to constitute essential structural elements, as in the case of the bone-shaped columns, the undulating façade covered with polychrome mosaics like a sheet of sea-water set on end, and the imbricated roof like an armadillo's back. This type of effect is a transitional one between the sculptural plasticity of Gaudí's earlier years (1878–91), and the structural plasticity of his later period.

This structural plasticity has as one of its chief features the system of design Gaudí used for the Colonia Güell Church (1898–1914), which was planned by means of a string model representing the structural ribs of the building, from which were hung weights proportional to the loads which each member would have to carry. The polygons formed by these strings gave the inverted shape of the building's columns. It permitted a type of vaulted structure without buttresses of any kind, since all thrusts are taken up by suitably inclined pillars. This method was later used in designing the naves of the Sagrada Familia.

In the Güell Park (1900–14) Gaudí made systematic use of inclined supports of unwrought stone for retaining walls and bridges, where he raised great masses of stone on flimsy columns in a tense desire to flaunt gravity. An important feature in this park is the abundant employment of ceramic and glass mosaic, which presents an extraordinary ensemble of powerfully expressive abstract compositions, in which Gaudí makes frequent use of broken plates, china dolls, bottles, etc., in a fabulous fantasia, like the elements of a collage.

The Casa Milà (1905–10), called *la Pedrera* (the quarry) is perhaps Gaudí's most original work. An interesting structural feature is the way the entire weight is carried between the external elevations and the columns which surround the patios. The handling of the internal space is also noteworthy, with its numerous acute and obtuse angles and undulating walls. Plastically speaking it constitutes a great stone sculpture of organic shape, with a rhythm of undulating horizontal edges, comparable to eyebrows or lips, pierced by windows, which preserve the expression of human eyes or mouths, somewhat in the manner of sculptures by Henry Moore or Barbara Hepworth. Gaudí's structural masterpiece was reached in 1909 with his Sagrada Familia schools, walled and roofed by undulating membranes of thin brick.

Towards the end of his career, Gaudí asserted that the straight line belonged to men, the curved one to God. Shortly before his death he invented a system of well-nigh universal application, based on hyperboloids and paraboloids, though his designs were never purely geometrical. They always preserved a close tie with familiar living shapes: bones, muscles, wings and petals, and at other times with caves and even stars and clouds.

Terrifying and idyllic features may be encountered side by side in Gaudí's work, in a way that closely recalls Surrealism. This impression is accentuated by the fortuitous objects in his collages, and gives Gaudí's architecture, despite his profoundly rational approach to structure, a character that is impassioned, savage and poetical to the point of frenzy.

Bibliography: Alexandre Cirici-Pellicer, *El arte modernista catalán*, Barcelona 1951; J. F. Ràfols, *Gaudi 1852–1926*, 3rd edition, Barcelona 1952; Joan Bergós, *Antoni Gaudí, L'home i l'obra*, Barcelona 1954; George R. Collins, *Antonio Gaudí*, New York 1960; James Johnson Sweeney and Joseph Lluis Sert, *Antoni Gaudí*, London 1960.

ALEXANDRE CIRICI-PELLICER

Germany. In 1828 the architect Heinrich Hübsch published a brochure with the title *In which style should we build*? In it he put forward the thesis that it was impossible to create new and beautiful forms in architecture. But the combination of these forms, and the 'arrangement of the parts . . . could reveal much that was individual'. These words sum up the malaise of the 19th century. The romantic period in German architecture after Friedrich Gilly had omitted to develop an exclusive manner in which the whole was subjected to a common rule like its parts. In practice, of course, the combination of adopted antique or Gothic features led to a new kind of style. The German romantic period was already familiar with unlimited repetitions of particular forms, the renunciation of dominating axes, flowing plan forms and the alternating interpenetration of space and buildings, and it already took account of the optical displacements and intersections that ensue when the spectator moves about. It is not by chance that the early *Mies van der Rohe was influenced by the country house projects of *Schinkel.

In the face of the tasks confronting the 19th-century architect this anticipation of the principles of modern architecture seems to lack binding force or significance. Infinite space was one thing, back yards in the Ackerstrasse, Berlin, another. Industrial expansion and increasing population created an inescapable situation in the second half of the 19th century. There were no models for factories, commercial buildings or above all for apartment blocks on a large scale; there was a reluctance at first to accept these tasks as worthy of architecture. The readiness for technical experimentation which led to revolutionary solutions in building with iron and *steel in *Great Britain, *France and the *United States, was less pronounced in Germany. Internationally important innovations in building technique only appeared in the 20th century with the glass architecture of the years around 1910, Max *Berg's reinforced concrete dome (Centenary Hall, Breslau 1912–13), the *shell structures of the twenties and the scientific study of building as developed by the *Bauhaus. *Art Nouveau, which marked the beginning of extensive reform movements, began with private houses. *Muthesius studied English country house styles while serving as an attaché at the German Embassy in London, *Riemerschmid and *Behrens started their architectural careers by building their own houses. This limitation was not meant as a renunciation, for the new style was not going to be determined by popular taste but, as Henry van de *Velde expressed it, by the 'ethos of the most intimate of man's possessions', the ethos of his own home. The Darmstadt Exhibition on the Mathildenhöhe (1901) which mainly featured such individual homes was thus not a private but a public event of considerable significance.

German Jugendstil had a higher moral content than Art Nouveau in France or Belgium. Appreciation for what was good and solid, honesty in the expression of materials and functions and the craft mentality were able to continue in force even when these new art forms had ceased to bloom. Enterprises such as the Vereinigte Werkstätten at Munich, the Werkstätte für Handwerkskunst at Dresden and above all the *Deutscher Werkbund founded in 1907, to which the most significant practitioners of Art Nouveau belonged, carried on the

Karl Friedrich Schinkel. Playhouse. Berlin, 1818–31

message. Parting from Art Nouveau proved the easier since no German architect had fulfilled the intentions of the new style as had Victor *Horta in Brussels, *Mackintosh in Glasgow, *Gaudí in Barcelona or even *Guimard in Paris. August *Endell's buildings, the wittiest creations of German Art Nouveau in architecture, remained examples of decorative art, two-dimensional surfaces attached to three-dimensional buildings. The Belgian Henry van de Velde built too late in Germany to exert a significant influence on architectural developments there.

August Endell. Buntes Theater. Berlin, 1901

Max Berg. Centenary Hall. Breslau, 1912–13

The Werkbund Exhibition at Cologne in 1914, where van de Velde erected a theatre in the generous flowing lines of the latest Art Nouveau, featured two buildings that anticipated the future: Bruno *Taut's pavilion for the German glass industry and the model factory by Walter *Gropius. A new building material, *glass, and a new building assignment, the factory, had led to a new aesthetic. Both buildings exhibit the close connection between function and expressive form which lasted until well into the twenties. Peter Behrens's turbine factory in Berlin (1908–9) with its heavy roof and Hans *Poelzig's chemical factory in Luban (1911–12) with its decorative masonry and carefully proportioned fenestration are not the monuments of a purely objective architecture which they have been made out to be. Nearly all important architects who played a significant rôle in the twenties have gone through an Expressionist phase: *Mendelsohn, Poelzig, the brothers *Taut and *Luckhardt, *Scharoun, Mies van der Rohe with his glasstower visions and the memorial to Karl Liebknecht and Rosa Luxemburg (1926) and Gropius with the sharply thrusting architectural sculpture of his War Memorial (Weimar, 1922).

The Bauhaus at Weimar and later at Dessau became the high school of 'Neues Bauen' (a name coined by Hugo *Häring). If the educational foundations were laid here, and the Dessau school buildings themselves were examples of the most avant-garde type of architecture, the real testing of the new architecture took place in the big cities. Berlin was the centre. Ever since Martin Mächler's new zonal plan of 1920, a kind of creative activity prevailed here, which did not confine itself to individual buildings but pursued a town planning concept. The 'white towns', Berlin's urban estates amid green settings, bear witness to this even today. The Weissenhof estate at Stuttgart, 1927, was largely built by Berlin architects, who moreover—despite stylistic differences—had joined together in an association, the *Ring. The new ideas radiated from Berlin. Bruno Taut, who was city architect in Magdeburg

for a time, Ernst *May, who built excellent
housing estates at Frankfurt, Richard
Döcker in Stuttgart, Otto Haesler in Celle
and Kassel were in the forefront. Contacts
with Holland and France strengthened the
avant-garde. Mies van der Rohe's German
pavilion at the Barcelona International
Exhibition of 1929, a subtle composition
of space-creating planes, proved that this
type of architecture was recognized by the
government too as representative of the
new republic. Northern Germany, where
Fritz Schumacher in Hamburg laid the
foundations for a type of country planning
that reached beyond the limits of civic
design, was the home of an architecture
which rested on the local tradition of
building in brick and kept its expressive
character somewhat longer.

The advent of National Socialism called a
sudden halt to the 'New Architecture'. The
Bauhaus was dissolved and architects such
as Gropius, *Hilberseimer, *Breuer, *Wagner, Mies, Mendelsohn, May and Hannes
*Meyer emigrated. In contrast to Fascism,
National Socialism tolerated no modern
architecture within the State. The official
style was a monumental, sterile, *neoclassicism. For residential buildings, a
Biedermeier-like native style supervened,
which had already gained ground shortly
after the turn of the century and had put
up a considerable proportion of all buildings even during the heroic period of the
modern movement. Only industrial buildings continued to permit functionally justified and aesthetically pleasing designs to be
carried out; it amounted to a kind of internal emigration.

The tabula rasa after 1945 was complete.
The character of German architecture in
the twenties had been largely formed by
the pioneer work carried out before the
First World War; that after the Second
World War stood alone. The task was immense. The demand for homes in the
Federal Republic was estimated at 6.5
millions in 1948. Even at the end of 1960
the deficit was still estimated at 1.3 millions,
to which another 1.5 millions must be
added, to replace condemned property. Of
the present 14 million living units less than
half include a bath!

550,000 new homes a year is an achievement. But it has not brought with it a new
way of living. There is nothing equivalent
to the English New Town movement or

Hans Scharoun. Siemensstadt housing estate.
Berlin, 1930

Mies van der Rohe. German pavilion at the
International Exhibition. Barcelona, 1929

*Le Corbusier's *Unités d'Habitation*. German architects had to build before they had time to think. The costly relief measures that have been devised for nearly all the larger cities nowadays to prevent their centres from becoming completely choked are more concerned with traffic restrictions than town planning. Only in individual cases such as Hanover have planning measures proved more far-sighted. Hamburg is considering building a second centre. New satellites like Sennestadt near Bielefeld by Bernhard Reichow (where there are no traffic crossings), the Neue Vahr near Bremen or the planned Nordweststadt near Frankfurt offer more pleasing prospects. In the Hansa district of Berlin, a central area in a parkland setting, major international architects have left their mark. But this enterprise which was opened in 1957 as the Interbau-Exhibition has remained a medley of remarkable individual buildings; no town planning principle can be deduced from the layout, rudely bisected as it is by a tarffic artery. Even the much publicized *Haupstadt Berlin* competition has remained without visible effect.

If any force towards integration in urban or country settings has hitherto been lacking, the isolated achievements of individual architects are admirable. Individual projects rate differently. High points are the prestige buildings of industry or communities: administrative buildings like the three-slab point block of the Phoenix-Rheinrohr at Düsseldorf by Hentrich and Petschnigg (1957–60) whose elevational treatment does not come up to the standard of the splendidly articulated massing; cultural buildings such as the municipal theatre at Münster (1954–6) whose team of architects have intelligently incorporated a neoclassic ruin into the building complex; or the municipal theatre at Gelsenkirchen (1958–9) with its transparent theatre mechanism. Extensive re-thinking on the subject of concert halls has gone into the Stuttgart Liederhalle (by Abel and Gutbrod, 1955–6) with its somewhat over-lavish décor, and especially into Scharoun's Berlin Philharmonic, with the audience orientated towards the centrally placed orchestra (under construction). Church buildings are on a high level with designs by Dominikus *Böhm, *Bartning, Baumgarten, Lehmbrock and Oesterlen; the churches of the archdiocese of Cologne stand out by their special quality. This is where Rudolf *Schwarz built many of his churches, three-dimensional images of an incontestably timeless quality.

Modern German architecture has no claim on any of its great masters any more. Gropius has built one private house and a block of flats for the Interbau in Berlin since the last war. Mies did not get his first German commission until 1960, an office block for Krupp's of Essen. But his influence above all can be felt in Germany either directly or indirectly in the way that his ideas have been treated by American architects such as *Skidmore, Owings and Merrill. The rectangular cube, the dissolution into glass, the narrow profile and the separation into load-bearing members and infill areas are features which are met with in many of the buildings by Friedrich Wilhelm *Kraemer, Johannes Krahn,

Helmut Hentrich and Herbert Petschnigg. Phoenix-Rheinrohr skyscraper. Düsseldorf, 1957–60

Gerhard Weber and Otto Apel. In this middle generation, which was young in the twenties and today occupies chairs at the colleges and academies, Egon *Eiermann and Hans Scharoun represent extreme positions: Eiermann who is concerned with the lucidity and perspicuous arrangement of the formal image and with elegance of design; Scharoun who works on each assignment as though the planning problem it exemplifies had never occurred before.

In the youngest generation freedom of conception, psychological command and originality of design are manifestly gaining ground. Wolske with his Beethovenhalle in Bonn (1959) has built a vast festival hall in the spirit of Scharoun. The Berlin Academy by Düttmann (1959–60) is a lively organism free from chilly reserve. Blocks of flats and houses by Oswald Mathias Ungers or houses by Reinhard Gieselmann seem to provide a parallel to international *neoplasticism or *Brutalism, but in actual fact they should be regarded rather as playing with plastic forms in the course of fulfilling the building programme.

Buildings by engineer-architects often determine the aspect of an extensive environment more strongly than architecture, in its narrower sense, is able to. Amongst television towers, the one in Stuttgart by Fritz Leonhardt (1954–6) has remained unequalled in its slender grace. The Nord bridge in Düsseldorf and the Severin bridge in Cologne are bold, suspended structures, the one at Cologne having been suspended asymmetrically from a single pier, out of planning consideration for the nearby Cathedral towers. Despite their international renown, Frei *Otto's tent roofs have not yet assumed the position in Germany that they may one day occupy, since they have been labelled as exhibition architecture. It would not be the first time that structural innovations had left their stamp on a new style.

Bibliography: Hermann Beenken, *Schöpferische Bauideen der deutschen Romantik*, Mainz 1952; Fritz Schumacher, *Strömungen in deutscher Baukunst seit 1800*, Leipzig 1935; G. Hatje, H. Hoffmann, K. Kaspar, *New German Architecture*, London 1956; *Planen und Bauen im neuen Deutschland*, Cologne 1960; U. Conrads and W. Marschall, *Modern Architecture in Germany*, London 1962.

WOLFGANG PEHNT

Rudolf Schwarz. St Anne's Church, Düren, 1951–6

Siegfried Wolske. Beethovenhalle. Bonn, 1959

Friedrich Wilhelm Kraemer. Technical and Evening College. Dortmund, 1956–9

Frederick Gibberd. Metropolitan Cathedral of Christ the King, Liverpool. Under construction. Model

Gibberd, Frederick, b. Coventry 1908. Studied at Birmingham School of Architecture; in private practice since 1930. Planning consultant to several borough councils and, since 1947, architect planner of Harlow New Town. Gibberd has designed a wide range of buildings, including flats, housing schemes and hospitals: Scunthorpe steelworks and power house, 1947–9; London Airport, 1955; National Dock Labour Board Offices,

London, 1956; Hinkley Point Atomic Power Station, Somerset, 1957; Ulster Hospital, N. Ireland, 1953–62; technical colleges at Hull, Kidderminster and Stourbridge. His prize-winning design for the Roman Catholic Cathedral at Liverpool shows the influence of *Niemeyer's Brasilia Cathedral. Gibberd has written a popular history of English architecture (1938), and a definitive work on town design (1953).

HAROLD MEEK

Gibson, Sir Donald Evelyn Edward, b. Manchester 1908. Studied at Manchester University School of Architecture. He was City Architect of Coventry (1939–55) when it was devastated by German air raids in the Second World War, and his powerful feeling for urban form and unswerving professional integrity succeeded in recreating a city centre there in which fewer opportunities have been missed than in any other city of *Great Britain, whose reconstruction of blitzed areas has generally attained a mediocre standard. From 1955 to 1958 he was County Architect of Nottinghamshire where the *CLASP system of prefabrication for schools was initiated under his auspices. In 1958 he became Director-General of Works in the War Department, where he brought CLASP construction into use for buildings of various types, including the Army's Computer Headquarters at Worthy Down. Since 1962 he has been Director-General of Research and Development in the Ministry of Public Building and Works.

HAROLD MEEK

D. E. E. Gibson. Broadgate House. Coventry, 1953

Gill, Irving John, b. Syracuse, New York 1870, d. 1936. First worked in the office of *Adler and *Sullivan in Chicago; after 1896 in San Diego on his own. His early buildings are in the 'Schindel' style, followed since about 1906 by work in which simple geometric elements assume importance: 'the straight line, the arc, the cube and the circle, the mightiest of all lines' (Wilson Acton Hotel at La Jolla, 1908; Dodge House, Los Angeles, 1916). His whitewashed, flat-roofed asymmetrically disposed *reinforced concrete buildings, which often display no mouldings of any kind, were inspired by Spanish mission stations in California and are markedly similar to the Cubist architecture of Adolf *Loos.

Burton and Turner. Palm House. Kew, 1844

Towards the middle of the 19th century the glass industry entered a period of intensive development; the end of the century saw the introduction of the first mechanized processes, backed by a systematic investigation of the physics and chemistry of glass. Hand manufacture and mouth-blowing are only employed today for special products and *objets d'art*.

The remarkable progress made by the glass and iron industries afforded new techniques for confronting the architectural problems of the early 19th century. The Galérie d'Orléans by Fontaine (Paris, 1829) is the prototype of all large pedestrian galleries, and is probably the first example of a large area with opaque walls covered by a glazed, translucent vault. A number of large greenhouses erected in France and England between 1830 and 1850 (at the Jardin des Plantes, Paris, by Rouhault, 1833; Chatsworth Conservatory by *Paxton, 1838; Palm House at Kew by Burton and Turner, 1844) exhibited a strictly functional character while reaching hitherto unfamiliar dimensions. Such structures became popular and were sometimes transformed into places of public resort (Jardin d'Hiver, on the Champs Elysées). With the Crystal Palace in London (1851) Joseph Paxton, by transferring the structural principles of the great greenhouses to the first exhibition pavilion, demonstrated the high degree of perfection that had been achieved in the manufacture and

Victor Horta. Maison du Peuple. Brussels, 1896–9. Detail of façade

Glass. Glass production has its origins in remote antiquity. The Phoenicians and Egyptians already made objects from molten glass; the Romans had a glass industry capable of producing precious objects, and the introduction of glassblowing is probably due to them. On the fall of Rome, Byzantium took over the leading rôle in the sphere of glass production. With the end of the eastern empire Byzantine artists in glass transferred to Venice, which soon became one of the most important centres of production. The German glass industry developed during the Middle Ages; from the 15th century Bohemian products began to acquire importance. Between the 17th and 18th centuries glass manufacture spread throughout France, Belgium, England, Spain and Russia; by the beginning of the 19th century it had reached North America as well.

Ludwig Mies van der Rohe. Office block,
Friedrichstrasse, Berlin, 1919. Project (first
version)

Bruno Taut. Glass pavilion at the Werkbund
Exhibition. Cologne, 1914

application of glass. The skill with which he
designed in new materials, without harking
back to academic tradition, was the result
of his habit as a greenhouse designer of
pursuing functional ends rather than those
of formal prestige.

The large glazed gallery became a basic
architectural feature of Paris International
Exhibitions in the second half of the
19th century, reaching in Dutert and
Contamin's Machinery Hall (1889) the most
complete expression of synthesis between
a great and original steel structure and its
transparent covering. In 1853, Baltard
built les Halles Centrales at Paris, roofed
partly in glass on an iron framework. After
1850 the use of huge transparent roofs
became common in railway stations
(Paddington Station, London, by Brunel
and Wyatt, 1854; Lime Street Station,
Liverpool, by Turner). In 1876 Boileau and
*Eiffel covered the 'Bon Marché' stores in
Paris with a complete glass roof. Large
glass roofs were adopted by *Berlage for
the Amsterdam Stock Exchange (1898–
1903) and by Otto *Wagner for the Savings
Bank in Vienna (1905) to give top lighting
to areas of major importance or prestige.
In less than a century the large glass roof
had become a definite part of the architect's
structural technique and repertory of
expression.

'The history of architecture shows that
down the centuries an unremitting battle
has been joined on behalf of light against
the obstacles imposed by the laws of
gravity: the history of windows' (*Le
Corbusier). Before the introduction of
modern structural systems the sizes of
vertical load-bearing elements in buildings
(especially multi-storey ones) of the traditional type were necessarily so large as to
confer on elevations more the character of
pierced walls than of surfaces with integrated fenestration.

The process of development whereby the
window ultimately extended its dimensions
to occupy practically the whole façade
began about the middle of the 19th century,
when cast-iron, which had already been in
use for half a century for internal construction, began to take the place of solid
walling on external elevations too (Harper
and Brothers' Building, New York, by

Page 131. Frank Lloyd Wright. Laboratory tower
for S. C. Johnson & Son. Racine, Wis., 1949

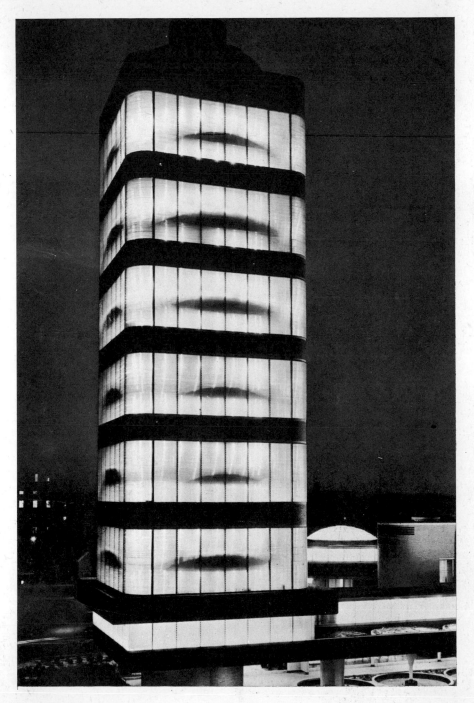

*Bogardus, 1854; riverfront buildings at St Louis, by unknown architects, 1850–80). The tendency to increase the ratio of glass to the total surface area was facilitated by the introduction and perfecting of completely framed buildings, firstly in cast-iron and later in steel, by William Le Baron *Jenney and other architects of the *Chicago School, thus answering the demand for as much natural light as possible for every room in those first large office blocks. With the Reliance Building of *Burnham and *Root (1890–4) and *Sullivan's Carson, Pirie and Scott department store (1899), the façade assumes a modular texture, with continuous rows of closely spaced but ample windows. The so-called 'Chicago window' is rectangular in shape, running horizontally, and features several lights with a large central pane.

*Horta, in his Maison du Peuple, Brussels, 1897, and *Behrens in his AEG works, Berlin, 1909, adopted continuous glass surfaces for almost the whole façade. Le Corbusier in the Pavillon Suisse, University City, Paris, 1930–2, reduced the formal importance of the steelwork, making it

Le Corbusier. Notre-Dame du Haut. Ronchamp, 1950–4. Detail of the south wall from inside

seem in the fully glazed wall simply the basic frame for a single great window.

Thus in addition to its traditional functions of providing daylight and view, glass began to be used for all the requirements of separation and insulation between interior and exterior. The window was extended to become the window wall. In the examples cited this is still contained within a single mesh of the structural grid, but elsewhere the continuity of the window units was developed until a continuous glass screen runs in front of the horizontal members (Fagus factory at Alfeld by *Gropius, 1911; Maison Clarté, Geneva, by Le Corbusier, 1932); or in front of the vertical members (model factory at the Werkbund Exhibition, Cologne, by Gropius, 1914; Salvation Army Hostel, Paris, by Le Corbusier, 1932); or in front of the whole structural grid of the façade (Hallidie Building, San Francisco, by *Polk, 1918; Bauhaus, Dessau, by Gropius, 1926; UN Secretariat, New York, by *Harrison and others, 1947–50).

While the window was becoming a glass façade, *Mies van der Rohe was investigating the theoretical bases for skyscrapers completely clad in glass with his projects for a skyscraper at Friedrichstrasse Station, Berlin, 1919, and a tower of glass and steel, 1921. These came to represent a typical manifestation of modern architecture, as defined in particular by two design features: simple volumes and glass surfaces. Outstanding examples of this type became numerous both in North America and Europe: Lake Shore Drive Apartments, Chicago, 1951 and the Seagram Building, New York, 1956, both by Mies van der Rohe; Lever House, New York, 1952, and Carbide Building, New York, 1960, by *Skidmore, Owings and Merrill; Torre Galfa, Milan, by Bega, 1959; Mannesmann Building, Düsseldorf by Schneider-Esleben, 1960.

Meanwhile developments were taking place in the design of structural frames; sometimes these were co-planar with the enclosing walls, at others they were set back, with the walls cantilevered out. This was the source of further compositional research on windows. Le Corbusier's 'Five points for a new architecture' (c. 1920), Mies van der Rohe's scheme for an office block in reinforced concrete (1922) and other projects led to the introduction and

Ludwig Mies van der Rohe, Seagram Building.
New York, 1958

widespread use of strip windows (Kiefhoek Estate, Rotterdam by *Oud, 1925; Van Nelle tobacco factory, Rotterdam, by *Brinkman and van der *Vlugt, 1928–30; Schocken department stores, Chemnitz, by *Mendelsohn, 1928; tobacco factory at Linz, by Behrens and Popp, 1930–5) and windows freely shaped and set in elevations (Lovell House, Los Angeles, by *Neutra, 1927; open-air school, Amsterdam, by *Duiker, 1930–2).

The possibility of obtaining ever greater areas of glass, the adoption of slender modern structures with large spans, the boldness with which traditional materials were being used in a new spirit, and the tendency to emphasize spatial continuity between adjacent rooms and between interior and exterior led to the emergence of completely transparent glazed walls with the structural frame reduced to a minimum (Tugendhat House, Brno, by Mies van der Rohe, 1930; pavilion at the Stockholm exhibition, 1930 by *Asplund; Villa Savoye, Poissy, by Le Corbusier, 1929–30). Commercial buildings with special need for transparency (windows of shops and large stores) and the incidence of particular requirements for spatial continuity (par-

tition between the reading room and stacks in the Bibliothèque Nationale, Paris, by Labrouste, 1858–68) had initiated this process already in the 19th century. Modern architectural theory and the new types of glass available have brought this development to its culmination.

The vocabulary of current architectural expression has also been enriched by the unusual, and sometimes fanciful use that has been made of special products of the glass industry: thick slabs of glass for the treads of top-lit stairs (Brewster Apartments, Chicago, by Turnock, c. 1890; Maison Clarté, Geneva, by Le Corbusier, 1932); glass bricks for walls and roofs; rows of glass tubing making up walls and ceilings (Johnson Wax offices, 1936, and laboratory tower, 1949, Racine, Wis., by *Wright); polarized glass for heat protection (Van Leer works, Amsterdam, by *Breuer, 1957–8); blown glass polyhedra for spatial compositions (Veneto Pavilion at the 'Italia '61' Exhibition, Turin, by Scarpa, 1961).

A new interpretation has similarly arisen of the ancient tradition of decorative glass, whose forms have been adapted to modern structural and architectural requirements (Steel Church, Cologne by *Bartning, 1928; Cathedral of St Michael, Coventry, by *Spence, 1954–62). Cartoons for stained glass windows were designed by outstanding modern artists (Chapel at Vence by Matisse, 1947), and new techniques for treating the glass (Notre-Dame du Haut, Ronchamp, by Le Corbusier, 1954) or binding the component parts of the design together (Church at Audincourt, by Novarina, Léger and Barillet, 1950–1; Church at Athis-Val by Laurence and Rocher, 1954) were explored. Finally, the task of directly expressing the decorative significance of the glass has been transferred to the design of the framework itself (Robie House, Chicago, by Wright, 1909; Church of Notre Dame, Le Raincy, 1923, and Ste Thérèse, Montmagny, 1926, by *Perret; glasswork in the Italian Pavilion at the Brussels International Exhibition, by *Gardella, 1958).

Bibliography: F. Franceschini, Il vetro, Milan 1955; R. McGrath and A. C. Frost, Glass in Architecture and Decoration, London 1961.

GIUSEPPE VARALDO
GIAN PIO ZUCCOTTI

Goff, Bruce, b. Alton, Kansas 1904. Designer of houses which clearly show their derivation from Frank Lloyd *Wright. Goff drives poetic impulse to formal caprice (circular and spiral buildings with continuous flowing space; house made up of cubic units).
Bibliography: Progressive Architecture, Dec. 1962.

Gollins, Melvin, Ward and Partners. Frank Gollins, James Melvin, Edmund Fisher Ward. Extensive practice distinguished for ability to handle large masses and exploit the results of careful research. Works include Castrol House, London (with *Casson and Conder), Cleveland Technical College, Redcar, and developments at the Western Bank area of Sheffield University, for which they have designed a library to hold a million books.

Sir Owen Williams. Boots' Factory. Beeston, near Nottingham, 1930–2

Great Britain. Modern architecture developed in France and Central Europe in the first three decades of the century, but it was late in coming to England. It is true that English domestic architecture seen in the work of Philip *Webb, Norman *Shaw, and C. F. A. *Voysey in the late 19th and early 20th centuries eloquently demonstrated designing that was logically and tastefully in answer to needs, and that this had a great influence in Europe, but the task of further development along such lines over a bigger field of building continued first in Germany, Austria, and to a lesser extent in France. Except for rare, isolated, examples it was not until the thirties that development along vigorous functionalist lines, in the broadest sense, was again manifest in England. Among the few exceptions was the Royal Horticultural Hall in London, designed by J. Murray Easton and Howard Robertson in 1923. This hall is constructed of *reinforced concrete parabolic arches, which hold together a step structure with four tiers of windows. It is a functional and expressive use of reinforced concrete and makes a beautiful and impressive interior.

Among the most important, slightly later, examples of modern architecture in England are the early works of a structural engineer, Sir Owen *Williams, of which the most notable are the large factory for Boots the Chemists at Beeston, near Nottingham, completed in 1932, the Empire Swimming Pool at Wembley (1934), and the Peckham Health Centre (1936). All these works are in reinforced concrete, the structure of which largely determines the appearance of the buildings. The Boots factory shows the influence of the *Bauhaus at Dessau, designed by Walter *Gropius. It is a large building and consists of reinforced concrete mushroom columns supporting concrete floors, the whole enclosed in glass walls, the only break in the glass being the edges of the concrete floors. By this simple mushroom-slab construction and the glass walls this building marked a big step forward in factory design in England and it was increasingly imitated. The Swimming Pool at Wembley was, at the time of its completion, the largest covered bath in the world. It was built on the reinforced concrete frame principle on a horizontal grid and vertical unit, which permitted the extensive employment of standardized parts. The roof is constructed of a series of three hinged arches held by vertical concrete shafts, which project above the plane of the low-pitched roof and perform a similar function to that of buttresses in a Gothic church. The Peckham Health Centre was a pioneer venture of two doctors, and Sir Owen Williams provided them with a modern three-storey structure of reinforced concrete with glass screens for external walls, thus admitting the maximum of light. Design is determined by purpose, and here the newest methods of construction are devised to satisfy that purpose as efficiently as possible. So as to enhance the enjoyment of sunlight and the surroundings the wall on the south-west side becomes in the two upper storeys a series of bay windows. Following similar lines, with extensive use of glass walls, is the Royal Corinthian Yacht Club building at Burnham-on-Crouch designed by Joseph Emberton in 1930. With its long balconies in front of glass walls, giving horizontal emphasis, it harmonizes with its position by the sea.

Some of the most notable contributions to modern architecture in the thirties in England are to be found in individually designed houses, and the torch of Webb, Voysey and Shaw seems to have been recovered by architects like Amyas Connell, Basil Ward and Maxwell *Fry, although the torch burns a somewhat different flame. What they have in common are plans and sequence of rooms, determined by convenience, ignoring any preconceived ideas of balance and symmetry. They are mostly built of reinforced concrete, with irregular plans, large windows towards the sun and flat roofs. The first of these houses was the famous 'High and Over' at Amersham, Buckinghamshire, designed by Amyas Connell in 1929. The house has three storeys, consisting of three arms radiating from a central octagonal hall which extends the whole height of the house. Another house built at Grayswood in 1933 by Connell in association with Basil R. Ward has a very irregular plan rather like an irregular triangle, but a perfect orientation is secured with the three principal ground-floor rooms—living-room, study, and dining-room—and the three bedrooms on the front floor all facing south. The irregular plan is reflected in the general appearance which composes

Tecton. Finsbury Health Centre. London, 1938–9

into a very agreeable relation of masses. This was one of the most ingeniously designed modern houses in Europe. It was followed by several other houses by the same architects, and these, and the stimulus given to English architects by the migration of famous German architects to England between 1933 and 1936, including Walter Gropius, Marcel *Breuer, and Erich *Mendelsohn, led several architects to design houses in a similar progressive manner. Among them was Maxwell Fry, who was Gropius's partner for a few years. After Gropius left for America, Fry built several houses on the most modern lines, one of the most effective being a house in Frognal, Hampstead (1938), which has a glass wall on the first floor opening on to a balcony. Fry was also responsible for a working-class housing scheme in Ladbroke Grove, London, which was, from the standpoint of light, good planning and spacing, the most advanced scheme of its kind in London at the time of its erection. Other architects who produced good modern work in which the new methods of construction were employed expressively were the *Tecton Group, who built the Highpoint block of flats at Highgate and the Finsbury Health Centre, both works in the modern idiom, but who became known chiefly for their constructions for the London Zoo: the Gorilla House and the Penguin Pool, where concrete has been used with good effect in a sculptural manner to show off the comic antics of the penguins. Mention should also be made of the Peter Jones Department Store in Sloane Square, London, designed by William Crabtree in association with Slater and Moberley and C. H. Reilly. Here the main supports of the building are set back from screen walls and the whole has a very light appearance.

In the early post-war period a great deal of experiment was conducted with new methods of house construction, but only a few of the many types survived and led to further developments. Probably the most outstanding post-war architecture in which the resources of modern building were used most intelligently was in schools, particularly those built in Hertfordshire. In these early post-war days materials were difficult to obtain in adequate quantities, and there was a shortage of skilled labour. Techniques were therefore adopted that permitted a fair degree of prefabrication and standardization which would contribute to speedy building. By these methods and designing that aimed at good lighting, large windows and cross-ventilation, some excellent school buildings were erected rapidly.

A notable and typical example of the Hertfordshire schools is the Hampden Secondary School for which the County Architect, C. H. *Aslin, was responsible with W. A. Henderson as the architect in charge. It was built in 1949–51 to accommodate 450 children, with a grouping of buildings according to the functions of general teaching, assembly, crafts and science, physical training and administration. The buildings are mainly two-storey, thus representing a departure from the previous post-war one-storey school building; yet the standard steel-frame structure employed in the latter was used in the Hampden School with cladding of concrete blocks. The irregular yet functional grouping and the long horizontal rectangular massing composes well with the landscape. Other

Tecton. Penguin Pool, London Zoo, 1938

William Crabtree, Slater and Moberley and C. H. Reilly. Peter Jones Department Store. London, 1938

C. H. Aslin. Junior School. Croxley Green, Hertfordshire, 1947–9 notable post-war schools in Great Britain are the secondary school at Hunstanton in Norfolk, completed to the design of Alison and Peter *Smithson in 1954, another functional grouping where the assembly and administration are on the ground floor and classrooms on the upper floor, mostly with glass walls. A notable example in London of a well-planned school characterized by lightness and large glazed areas is the Bousfield Primary School, Old Brompton Road, designed by *Chamberlain, Powell and Bon.

In 1951 three notable concert halls were built: the Royal Festival Hall in London, the Colston Hall in Bristol, and the Free Trade Hall in Manchester, the last two being rebuildings. In all these halls very special attention was paid to acoustics. In the Festival Hall designed by Robert *Matthew, the architect of the London County Council, a large area of slate is incorporated in the floor between the steeply raked auditorium and the orchestra so as to reflect sound. Vision is extremely good from every seat, and the whole building is an excellent design for its function, with a clever use of materials, while the large glass walls of the landings and rear corridors afford views over London and its river.

Some of the best large-scale housing in Britain is to be seen in certain blocks of flats in London and the vicinity, and in some of the two- and three-storey blocks in the new towns, such as Stevenage, Harlow, Basildon and Crawley near London, in Peterlee, Durham and the Scottish new towns of East Kilbride, Glenrothes and Cumbernauld.

The LCC Roehampton estate is one of the largest and most impressive of local authority developments. It accommodates nearly 10,000 persons, and consists of ten-storey tower blocks, six-storey slab blocks, four-storey maisonette blocks, and rows of two- and three-storey dwellings. The estate is situated in wooded undulating country, and the diverse buildings group pleasantly and look well in the landscape. The treatment of the slab blocks with their open ground floors is influenced by the work of *Le Corbusier, but they are marred by gallery access. Other notable housing estates in London are the Spa Green Flats in Finsbury by Tecton (1946–50); Churchill Gardens by *Powell and Moya (1947–53);

Robert H. Matthew. Royal Festival Hall. London, 1951

and the Golden Lane estate in the City of London by Chamberlin, Powell and Bon (1953–7). The dominating buildings in all these groups are tall slab blocks, seven to ten storeys, and they all succeed in being aesthetically pleasing because of well-designed patterns made by the windows and balconies, and by the relation of the blocks to the spaces between. Although they are all low-cost housing there is an agreeable effect of spaciousness between the blocks, while at the same time an effect of intimacy is occasionally obtained as in a group of shops and public house within the Churchill Gardens development.

Two interesting schemes with very different purposes have a strong architectural kinship: a tower block with four wings of small low-cost flats in Bethnal Green (1959) and a block of luxury flats in St James's Place, overlooking Green Park (1961), both by Denys Lasdun & Partners. The architectural idiom is similar in both: large glazed areas related to plain flat rectangular shapes of walls and balconies. The effect is particularly felicitous in the views of the St James's Place flats from various points in Green Park.

The best low-cost two- and three-storey housing during the fifties is undoubtedly in the new towns; one of the reasons for this is that many of the new town development corporations have commissioned well-known architects to design for them. Examples typical of the best are some parts

Denys Lasdun and Partners. Cluster Block.
Bethnal Green, London, 1958-60

of Basildon which, in the layout, are
adaptations of the Radburn planning of
residential areas. In these, by rear access
of vehicles to houses, some degree of
segregation of vehicular traffic and pedestrians is secured. Three areas: Barstable
planned by the development corporation
architect Anthony B. Davis; Vange by
Sir Basil *Spence; and Kingswood by
William Crabtree are examples where this
segregation has been achieved with some
varied and attractive housing. In Peterlee
new town some very compact housing
was designed by two development corporation architects, Peter Daniel and
Frank Dixon in collaboration with the
painter Victor Pasmore. Some of the
patterns of the rectangular façades are
reminiscent of Pasmore's abstract pictures.
As a whole industrial architecture of the
fifties shows a decided improvement on
that of the thirties where the custom of
having a symmetrically designed Georgian
office in front of a series of sheds was all
too common. In the fifties there has been a
more marked tendency to integrate the
various parts into a satisfactory architectural ensemble; some of the best examples
can be seen in the spacious industrial areas
of the new towns, four of the most notable

being at Stevenage, Hemel Hempstead and
Crawley round London, and East Kilbride
near Glasgow.

Perhaps the most original industrial architecture of the post-war period is seen in
power stations, in both the conventional
stations using coal or oil and the nuclear
power stations, a type of building of which
Britain has been a pioneer. In the early
thirties most power stations were built
with heavy walls of brick, but this was felt
to be unnecessarily substantial, and the
tendency has been towards a much lighter
cladding of glass, aluminium, asbestos and
other thin, light materials. Some well-
designed power stations have resulted, a
number of which are by *Farmer and Dark.
A good example is the Marchwood Power
Station on the Hampshire coast near
Southampton. This building in which
aluminium *curtain walling is employed
forms a long horizontal mass by the sea
with two tall chimneys. With nuclear
power stations different problems of design are presented because they include
immense reactor buildings which have to
be of very sturdy construction. All the
massive nuclear power stations so far built
—those at Berkeley and Hinkley Point
near the Bristol Channel are examples—
are different in design. The most recent,
that at Sizewell in Suffolk, designed by
Frederick *Gibberd, has something of the
massive character of a medieval fortress or
defensive castle. Instead of the nuclear
power stations spoiling scenic beauty, as
was feared, they have become interesting
features in the landscape.

A main development in British architecture during the fifties can be seen in
office and apartment blocks. Consent is
now given for higher buildings in certain
circumstances, and this has resulted in
many office blocks in London being built
well above the previously permitted 100
feet (generally about nine or ten storeys)
to fifteen, twenty, thirty storeys or even
more. The chief distinguishing architectural feature of office blocks since about
1952 is the curtain wall, and a tower block
of about fifteen or twenty storeys rising
from a lower block of about two or three
storeys. Notable buildings of this kind in
London are Castrol House, designed by
*Gollins, Melvin Ward & Partners; Thorn
House, designed by Sir Basil Spence; and
the Vickers Building, designed by Ronald

Ward & Partners, which is the highest office block built in London, having thirty-four storeys. There is a danger that the pattern of tower and low podium block if not designed with some originality may become monotonous, and thus architects, alive to this, are introducing more varied treatment such as the curved façade of the Vickers tower, and the Y plan of the new multi-storey Hilton Hotel in Park Lane. This plan serves the function of giving a maximum number of bedrooms views over Hyde Park. With parts of the building of various heights combined with a tower block, the architecture of office buildings is becoming a matter of the large-scale relation of masses, while in the treatment of curtain walls and end walls architecture is moving closer to the art of the painter with effects that depend on the abstract pattern of colours and textures.

Bibliography: J. M. Richards, *An Introduction to Modern Architecture*, 1st edition, London 1940, 3rd edition, London 1961; Edward D. Mills, *The New Architecture in Great Britain 1946–1953*, London 1953; John Summerson, *Ten Years of British Architecture*, London 1956; Trevor Dannatt, *Modern Architecture in Britain*, London 1959.

ARNOLD WHITTICK

Greene, Charles Sumner and Henry Mather. Charles Sumner, b. St Louis 1868, d. Carmel 1957. Henry Mather, b. Cincinnati, Oreg. 1870, d. Altadena, Calif. 1954. Studied at Massachusetts Institute of Technology, Cambridge. The Greenes' houses are among the best examples of Californian regionalism at the turn of the century, with their interpenetration of internal and external space, projecting roofs, flat gables and warm materials (timber, shingled walls, coloured windows). Blacker House (1907) and Gamble House (1908–9) at Pasadena, Calif.

Gropius, Walter, b. Berlin 1883. One of the outstanding architects and teachers of the 20th century, Walter Gropius is the son of an architect who occupied an important official position in Berlin. It is not without significance that his great-uncle, Martin Gropius (1824–80) was an architect of some reputation who designed, among other notable buildings, the great hall of the new Gewandhaus at Leipzig, and who

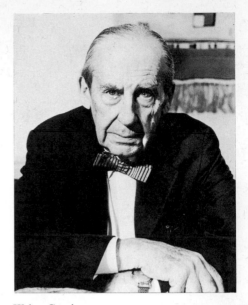

Walter Gropius

was also Principal of the Arts and Crafts School in Berlin and Director of Art Education in Prussia.

Walter Gropius received his training in architecture first at Munich from 1903 to 1905 and then in Berlin to 1907, when he entered the office of Peter *Behrens where so many young architects later to become famous had also worked, among them Mies van der Rohe and *Le Corbusier, who, however, stayed only for a short time. In 1910, after three years in Behrens's office, Gropius started on his own as an industrial designer and architect. His designing covered a wide range and included interior decoration schemes, wall fabrics, models for mass-produced furniture, motor-car bodies, and a diesel locomotive. His first important building was the Fagus shoelace factory at Alfeld-an-der-Leine, built in 1911 in collaboration with Adolf *Meyer. This building marked a step forward in steel and glass construction. It is three-storeyed, the steel frame supports the floors, and the walls have become glass screens, the non-structural character of which is emphasized by the absence of vertical supports at the corners. At the famous *Deutsche Werkbund Exhibition at Cologne in 1914 Gropius and

Walter Gropius and Adolf Meyer. Fagus factory. Alfeld-an-der-Leine, 1911

Meyer designed the Administrative Office Building which proved to be a very notable contribution to modern architecture. The building is symmetrical, the central portion of the front façade is faced with brick, and at the ends are spiral staircases enclosed for two storeys by glass towers. The glass screen held by a very light steel framework continues on the first floor along the narrow sides and for the whole length of the rear of the block, thus imparting the character of unusual lightness. The circular glass towers enclosing the staircases represent the first use of an architectural motif that was to become an important feature in many modern buildings, especially departmental stores. It was often used by Erich *Mendelsohn with fine effect. Gropius and Meyer also designed the hall of machinery and open garages at

Walter Gropius and Adolf Meyer. Model factory at the Werkbund Exhibition. Cologne, 1914

Walter Gropius. Bauhaus. Dessau, 1925–6

the back of the office block. The former had a slightly pitched roof with steel stanchions curving from the walls.

From 1914 to 1918 came the break of the First World War when Gropius served in the German Army. In 1915 he was given the position by the Grand Duke of Saxe-Weimar of Director of the Grossherzog-liche-Sächsische Kunstgewerbeschule and the Grossherzogliche-Sächsische Hoch-schule für Bildende Kunst at Weimar, and after the cessation of hostilities in 1919 he combined the two under the name of Das Staatliche *Bauhaus, Weimar, because Gropius believed in the unity of design and craft, of art and technics. He was Director first at Weimar from 1919 to 1925 and then at Dessau from 1925 to 1928 when he resigned because he wished to devote his energies more wholeheartedly to archi-tecture untrammelled by official duties.

While at the Bauhaus, however, he was the architect of several buildings and the designer of several projects, his most important building during this period being the world-famous group of buildings for the Bauhaus at Dessau, which was completed towards the end of 1926. Among other works was the rebuilding of the Municipal Theatre at Jena in 1923, designed in collaboration with Meyer, and two very interesting projects, one a build-ing for an international academy of philo-sophical studies and the other a 'Total Theatre'. The former, designed for a site near the University of Erlangen, belongs

to 1924 and shows the tendencies in his planning that two years later resulted in the Bauhaus building. The 'Total Theatre' design was made in 1927 in collaboration with Erwin Piscator, the Berlin theatrical producer. The purpose was to design a theatre that could be changed to accord with the type of play, changed, that is, from the Greek theatre with the semicircular orchestra, to the circus with the central arena and to the modern picture-frame stage. The theatre was so designed that the tiers of seats could be revolved in sections to enable the change from one form to another to be effected quickly. A model

Walter Gropius. Siemensstadt housing estate. Berlin, 1929

was exhibited at the 1930 Paris Exhibition, but it was never built. The movement towards building theatres of flexible construction, however, has grown considerably during the century, and Gropius's project has been a significant contribution towards the feasibility of the idea.

Gropius was not only an architect and industrial designer, but a sociologist who wanted to build on the basis of a rational interpretation of the needs of people. During the latter part of his directorship at the Bauhaus he studied the problem of obtaining the best living conditions in cities while preserving their urban character. He aimed to produce city dwellings in which the inhabitants obtained as much sunlight, space, and air and trees and lawns as possible at very much the same density as then existed. To achieve this he evolved the tall slab-like apartment block of about ten storeys, arranged, not parallel with the street but transversely with it, orientated according to the sun, with cross-ventilation and with broad stretches of garden between the blocks and open at both ends. He showed that with higher blocks housing people at the same density there is far more space and the angle of light is less.

Gropius was able partially to realize his ideas in the Dammerstock housing scheme near Karlsruhe in 1927–8, where he not only designed some of the five-storey blocks but acted as a co-ordinator for eight other architects. In this scheme several blocks are arranged in parallel lanes transversely with the streets. A more ambitious realization was in the large Siemensstadt estate near Berlin, in which Gropius was the supervising architect with several others collaborating, while he was himself responsible for two of the blocks. The general layout consists of long five-storey blocks, orientated north–south so as to get the maximum sunlight, widely spaced with stretches of grass and tall trees with light, delicate foliage between. The blocks have pale plain walls with large windows, and they are planned with two flats per landing. These Siemensstadt flats have exerted a wide influence and have been much imitated.

With the accession to power of the National Socialists in 1933 conditions became difficult for liberal and modern minded architects, so in 1934 Gropius left Germany for England. He settled in London and entered into partnership with E. Maxwell *Fry, one of the most successful of the younger British architects. Together they designed several interesting schemes, the work actually completed including the film laboratories for London Film Production at Denham (1936); two houses, one in Sussex (1936) and one in Old Church Street, Chelsea (1935); and Impington Village College, Cambridgeshire (1936), one of four village colleges erected by the County Council. This was Gropius's most important contribution to architecture in England. It is a one-storey building with single depth classrooms, fan-shaped hall, and club amenities, all very happily sited amongst lawns and trees to serve the dual purpose of a secondary school and community centre for adults.

Early in 1937 Gropius accepted an invitation to become Senior Professor of Architecture at Harvard University, USA, and the following year he became Chairman of the Department of Architecture. He very quickly demonstrated his practical ability as an architect by building his own house, which was completed in the year of his arrival. It has much of the classic restraint of the houses that he had designed for himself and the Bauhaus leaders in 1926. This was followed by a large number of private residences that he designed in collaboration with other architects in America. In the year of his arrival he entered into partnership with the Hungarian architect, Marcel *Breuer, who had been a student and master at the Bauhaus. In the years of their partnership in addition to several houses, including one for Breuer himself, they designed the Pennsylvania Pavilion, New York World's Fair in 1939, and an interesting housing scheme at New Kensington near Pittsburgh in 1941, in which year the partnership with Breuer terminated. The New Kensington housing was for the workers in an aluminium factory, and the houses were built on the slopes of the hills above the factory. They were irregularly sited and in accordance with the best orientation, following the contours of the hills; they were reached by winding paths.

Page 143. The Architects Collaborative. Harvard Graduate Center. Cambridge, Mass., 1949–50

When in Germany, in 1932, Gropius had begun experiments with standardized building elements for mass-produced housing, and he resumed these experiments during the war years 1943–5. The earlier ideas were concerned with copper-sheet houses, but these later developments were with timber panels based on a module both horizontally and vertically of 40 inches. After experiments made in collaboration with Konrad *Wachsmann in Long Island, these houses were erected on a considerable scale in California.

In 1945 Gropius went into partnership with several architects of the younger generation forming a team of eight under the name of 'The Architects Collaborative' (*TAC). In this enterprise Gropius was the guide and leading spirit. That he was able to enter with enthusiasm into so large a group demonstrates his great belief in the value of team-work which he had always felt to be necessary in modern building. The team was responsible for much interesting work which made a noteworthy contribution to mid-20th-century American architecture. It includes several private residences, all of which are worthy of study for their planning and siting; the Junior High School, Attleboro, Mass. (1948); the Harvard University Graduate Center, Cambridge, Mass. (1949–50), which consisted of a group of seven dormitory blocks in relation to the social centre; and the Harkness Commons, a grouping in which the open spaces between the buildings were very carefully related to function. In 1953 the team built the McCormick Office Building. In 1961 Gropius was invited to London to design a building for the Monico site in Piccadilly Circus, the former scheme for which had been rejected by the authorities as not being of sufficient architectural merit for this important site. Gropius's buildings are distinguished by an adventurous use of the modern materials of steel, concrete and glass, while he may be regarded as perhaps the principal innovator in the utilization of the complete

Walter Gropius and Wils Ebert. Block of flats. Interbau Exhibition. Berlin, 1957

The Architects Collaborative. US Embassy. Athens, 1961

The Architects Collaborative. Bagdad University, 1960. Project

glass screen in forming the outer shell of a building, thus admitting the maximum of light. Architecturally his work is always distinguished by a classic restraint and excellence of proportion of which the houses for the staff at the Bauhaus at Dessau are an example. But important as Gropius is as an architect, he is possibly even more important as a teacher and an influence. He was a great believer in the intelligent application of standardization and prefabrication, but above all he wanted a building to be the product of team-work in which each member of the team appreciated fully the relation of his contribution to the whole design. Gropius regarded this as a symbol of community living and the intelligent integration of society.
Bibliography: Sigfried Giedion, *Walter Gropius*, Paris 1931; Sigfried Giedion, *Walter Gropius: Work and Teamwork*, Stuttgart, Paris, New York and London 1954; J. M. Fitch, *Walter Gropius*, New York 1960. See also Bauhaus.

ARNOLD WHITTICK

Gruen, Victor, b. Vienna 1903. Studied under Peter *Behrens. Emigrated to the United States in 1938. Mainly town and country planning (e.g. Fort Worth, Texas). His conception of 'shopping centres' was epoch-making, sited out of town and catering for the needs of modern street traffic (Northland Shopping Centre, Detroit, 1952).

gruppo 7. Architectural co-operative of seven (predominantly Milanese) architects, Luigi *Figini, Guido Frette, Sebastiano Larco, Adalberto Libera, Gino *Pollini, Carlo Enrico Rava and Giuseppe *Terragni. The group, founded in 1926, appeared publicly in 1927 with an exhibition at the Biennale in Monza and was invited in the same year to the Werkbund Exhibition at Stuttgart. It stood for an architecture founded on the regional analysis of building functions and attempted to create an Italian tradition in modern building. 'The desire for sincerity, order, logic and clarity above all, these are the true qualities of the new way of thinking.' (Series of articles in *La Rassegna Italiana*, December 1926 to May 1927.)

Guimard, Hector, b. Paris 1867, d. New York 1942. Studied at the École des Arts Décoratifs and at the École des Beaux-Arts in Paris, where he later taught. Guimard was influenced by Victor *Horta, the most gifted and eminent architect of the French *Art Nouveau. His main work consists of the Castel Béranger, Paris (1897–8), the imaginative entrances to the Paris Métro, reminiscent of the organic forms of nature (1900), and the Humbert de Romans Building, Paris (1902), a large auditorium with a steel frame.

Hankar, Paul, b. Frameries 1859, d. Brussels 1901. The architect Paul Hankar was one of the moving figures in Belgian *Art Nouveau, together with Victor *Horta and Henry van de *Velde. He learnt his profession in the office and on the building sites of the architect Henri Beyaert from 1879 to 1894, when Beyaert died. During this period Hankar was personally responsible for the restoration and interior

Paul Hankar. Maison Kleyer. Brussels, 1898

decoration of the Church at Everberg in Brabant.

Hankar took over from his master certain elements of his style, such as the harmonious blending of white stone, blue stone and brick, but introduced modernist details into this traditional type of structure: wrought-iron grilles, consoles, handrails and balconies, and sgraffito murals. A number of medieval and oriental reminiscences are incorporated in his work, too: openings set asymmetrically, stilted arches, battlements, penthouses, broad cornices and heavy modillions, which conspire to produce a picturesque effect. He conceived of architecture as a synthesis of the plastic arts and designed the interior decoration and furniture for most of the private houses he built. He originated an Art Nouveau type of shop-front and fittings which gained rapid acceptance in Europe. He died before being able to carry out a major project, the *Cité des Artistes*, for which he had drawn up the plans.

Bibliography: Charles de Maeyer, *Paul Hankar*, Brussels 1962.

ROBERT L. DELEVOY

Häring, Hugo, b. Biberach 1882, d. Biberach 1958. Häring advocated in his writings and buildings a theory of organic building which differs from the *organic architecture of Frank Lloyd *Wright.

Häring studied at Stuttgart Technical College (under Theodor *Fischer) and at Dresden. In 1912 he established his own architectural practice in Berlin. In 1924 the *Zehnerring* was founded to fight the tendencies propagated by the then city architect Ludwig Hoffmann, and this group was later enlarged to become *Der *Ring*. The *élite* of the modern architects of Germany belonged to it, and Häring, as its secretary, was the leader of the association. In 1933 the *Ring* was dissolved by the Nazis. Though *Gropius and *Mies van der Rohe emigrated, Häring remained in Germany; he was the head of a private art school. In 1943 he returned to his native town of Biberach, where he died in 1958 after a long, painful illness.

Häring was responsible for a number of important works, of which the Garkau farm buildings (1923) have become particularly famous; his real importance, however, lies in the theoretical field. He expounded his views on organic building

Hugo Häring. Farm buildings at Garkau, near Lübeck, 1923

in numerous articles and lectures. He maintained that the work of rejuvenating architecture had to proceed in two stages. The first is concerned with research into changing needs, and aims at fitness for purpose and the 'organism'; the second, on the other hand, deals with 'design'. While other contemporary trends in the twenties (*Le Corbusier, for example) determined what shape fitness for purpose would take by using geometric forms accepted as *a priori* beautiful, Häring attempted to develop the design from its fitness for purpose without preconceived ideas of shape. 'We want to search for things and let them unfold their own design. It goes against the grain . . . to determine their shape from the outside, to subject them to a set of derived laws' ('Wege zur Form'). Häring emphasized that organic building did not mean copying the forms of nature but that—as in nature—shape arose from function.

The thesis sometimes propagated by his followers, that organic building demanded curved shapes, not based on orthogonal principles, was rejected by Häring. 'The identity of an object must determine the type of form appropriate to the individual building' ('Geometrie und Organik'). The decisive criterion in organic building is the determination of form from an object's identity. A building derives its shape from the function which it has to discharge as the tool (or 'organ' as Häring called it) of man. The house as the tool of its inhabitants is the starting point of his thinking.

Häring's ideas, which in the twenties were limited to a small circle, became increasingly important with the new phase of modern architecture that started about 1930. Today, architects as distinct as Alvar *Aalto, Louis *Kahn and Hans *Scharoun hold similar views.

Bibliography: Hugo Häring, 'Wege zur Form', in *Die Form*, No. 1, 1925; Hugo Häring, 'Geometrie und Organik', in *Baukunst und Werkform*, No. 9, 1951; Heinrich Lauterbach and Jürgen Joedicke (editors), *Organhaftes Bauen* (= Dokumente der Modernen Architektur 4), Zurich and Stuttgart in preparation.

JÜRGEN JOEDICKE

Harrison, Wallace Kirkman, b. Worcester, Mass. 1895. Studied at the École des Beaux-Arts, Paris. Worked on the Rockefeller Centre (1931–47). Partnership first with *Hood then with Fouilhoux and Max *Abramovitz. Harrison and Abramovitz are among the greatest American architectural firms and have specialized in office buildings. Storey-high units of aluminium or steel were used for the *curtain walls of such buildings as the Alcoa Building in Pittsburgh (1953) and the Socony Mobil Building in New York (1956). Harrison, who possesses excellent organizational ability, was principal architect for the United Nations Buildings, New York (1947–50, esquisse by Le Corbusier). As coordinator he is directing the construction of the Lincoln Center, a cultural project in New York (building in progress).

Haussmann, Georges-Eugène, b. Paris 1809, d. Paris 1891. As prefect of the Seine department under Napoleon III, Haussmann carried out a series of town-planning schemes in Paris that determined the present face of the city: construction of bridges and prestige buildings, opening up of streets and boulevards to meet military, ceremonial, hygienic and traffic requirements.

Havliček, Josef, b. Prague 1899, d. 1962. Studied at the College of Technology and the Academy of Fine Arts at Prague (1916–26). Housing, offices, hospitals, large-scale urban works. His 1930 buildings, white blocks with continuous horizontal strips of windows, are amongst the most disciplined examples of the *International Style.

Hilberseimer, Ludwig, b. Karlsruhe 1885. Worked in Berlin till 1928, then at the *Bauhaus in Dessau; since 1938 at the Illinois Institute of Technology in Chicago. Town-planning work of fundamental significance.

Bibliography: Ludwig Hilberseimer, *Grossstadt-Architektur*, Stuttgart 1927.

Hoffmann, Josef, b. Pirnitz, Moravia 1870, d. Vienna 1956. Hoffmann studied architecture in Vienna under Otto *Wagner, whose most faithful and convinced disciple he became. The rationalistic theories that underlay Wagner's teaching had a decisive influence on the course steered by Hoffmann, but the latter's famous elegance and refinement of taste was far removed from the severity of *Loos. He did not, in fact, despise ornament and this led him to show particular interest in the production of craft objects. He taught at the School of Applied Arts from 1899 onwards, and together with Koloman Moser set up a group of studios and workshops, which under the name of *Wiener Werkstätte* enjoyed widespread success and fame for thirty years.

In 1897 he joined with other young artists, including Joseph *Olbrich in founding the Wiener Sezession. Under the influence of the Glasgow School and of Belgian and French *Art Nouveau, its aims were more radically modernist than those of Wagner's school. Ten years later, he moved towards a new cultural avant-garde that centred round the painter Gustav Klimt, with whom Hoffmann founded the *Kunstschau* called 'the Secession from the Secession'. Meanwhile Hoffmann's first works of architecture gave him a European celebrity, which was confirmed by the commission he received to build a large house in Brussels for the Stoclet family. In the opening years of the century he had designed exhibition pavilions, schemes for internal decoration and four houses (Moser, Moll, Henneberg and Spitzer). With the Purkersdorf Sanatorium (1903) he became one of

Josef Hoffmann. Palais Stoclet. Brussels, 1905

the foremost exponents of the new style in architecture. His Palais Stoclet (1905) is an architectural masterpiece that evokes the exquisite poetry of Post-Impressionism and Symbolism. Although completely based on rationalist theories it is rich and refined to the point of decadence, a monument of the last bourgeois age which represents a milestone in Hoffmann's own career, and in the history of European architecture, at the moment when it was turning towards the new century.

In the years that followed, up to the eve of the First World War, Hoffmann built dozens of villas in Vienna with only a few basic variations. At the 1914 *Deutscher Werkbund Exhibition in Cologne, for which he designed the Austrian Pavilion in an elegant style of vaguely neoclassic derivation, he encountered in the work of *Gropius a new and more vigorous form of architectural modernity: one which was to mark, inevitably, the decline of his own, with its exquisite refinements of 'taste'.

In 1912 he began the construction of a villa colony at Vienna-Kaasgraben, which was interrupted by the war; his architectural work was only resumed in 1920, though the activity of the *Wiener Werkstätte* had continued. In 1920, too, he was appointed city architect of Vienna. But with the rise in Europe of De *Stijl, the *Bauhaus and *Le Corbusier's *Esprit Nouveau*, something a little anachronistic in Hoffmann's work was to leave it henceforth slightly on the margin of modern architecture, whose social content was also radically new. Hoffmann himself was aware of this. The housing schemes he carried out in 1924 and 1925 for the City of Vienna, and his terrace houses in particular for the 'Internationale Werkbundsiedlung' of 1932, are built in a style of extreme architectural purity that recalls the houses of *Neutra, Loos, *Rietveld and *Lurçat. They are the last proofs of Hoffmann's conscious and

Josef Hoffmann. Design for an auditorium. 1922

deliberate 'presence' in the process of total revolution through which architecture was passing in those years of unmitigated controversy. The next year, 1933, he decided to close down the famous *Wiener Werkstätte* for good. He designed the Austrian Pavilion for the 1934 Venice Biennale, and, after the last war, some blocks of workers' housing. He died in Vienna in 1956, while a large exhibition devoted to his work was on show in Brussels.

Bibliography: Ludwig Hevesi, *Acht Jahre Sezession*, Vienna 1907; Leopold Kleiner, *Josef Hoffmann*, Berlin, Leipzig and Vienna 1927; Armand Weiser, *Josef Hoffmann*, Geneva 1930; L. W. Rochowanski, *Josef Hoffmann*, Vienna 1950; Giulia Veronesi, *Josef Hoffmann*, Milan 1956.

GIULIA VERONESI

Holabird, William, b. Amenia Union, N.Y. 1854, d. Evanston, Ill. 1923. Trained in the office of William Le Baron *Jenney, later in partnership with Martin Roche. The Tacoma Building (Chicago, 1889) by Holabird and Roche is the aesthetic consequence of the introduction of steel frames for tall buildings; an extensive dissolution of the façade into glass, punctuated by projecting bays, and the abandonment of historical ornamentation.

Holford, Sir William, b. S. Africa 1907. Studied at Liverpool University School of Architecture. Rome Scholar, 1930. Professor of Civic Design at Liverpool, 1937; Professor of Town Planning, University College, London, 1948. Houses, factories, public buildings. Planning proposals for the County of Cambridge, 1950. Report on St Paul's precinct, 1956; three-level plan for Piccadilly. His fourteen-storey block of flats at Kensal (1958) has been called the first large-scale *modular building. President of the RIBA, 1960–2.

Holzmeister, Clemens, b. Tirol 1886. Churches, residential and public buildings. Worked in Turkey (Ministry of War, Summer Palace for Kemal Pasha). New Salzburg Festival Theatre (1960).

Hood, Raymond M., b. Pawtucket, R.I. 1881, d. Stamford, Conn. 1934. Gained first prize in the competition for the Chicago Tribune Building (1923–5, a neo-Gothic design); *c.* 1930 in collaboration with a partner he built the McGraw-Hill Building, New York, no longer revivalist in style, and the Daily News Building (1930) which anticipates the marked vertical stress of the Rockefeller Center.

Horta, Victor, b. Ghent 1861, d. Brussels 1947. A keen disciple of *Viollet-le-Duc, Horta was a leading figure of continental *Art Nouveau and the creator of an original vocabulary of ornament. He helped to open up new paths to 20th-century architecture by doing away with the traditional plan of the private house and providing an architectural expression for the new building programmes set in train by the social and cultural developments of his time. He was also instrumental in devising a number of subtle structural forms that drew on the resources of iron and glass.

Horta began his architectural studies at Ghent Academy (1876) and continued them at the Académie des Beaux-Arts at Brussels. After spending some time in the office of Balat, a neoclassic architect of repute, he built a group of three little houses in the Rue des Douze Chambres at Ghent (1886), where his great architectural ability is already obvious despite the modest scale

Victor Horta. Hôtel Tassel. Brussels, 1892–3

of the project. This first design of his, honest, straightforward and economical, gave little indication of a work that was to appear six years later, whose astonishing architectural and decorative richness revealed its author as someone of great creative maturity, albeit still young (thirty-one): the Hôtel Tassel, built between 1892 and 1893 at 6 Rue P. E. Janson, Brussels. This house, a veritable manifesto of Art Nouveau, is revolutionary in form and structure and is regarded today as one of the classic monuments in the history of architecture. It is the product of an expanding bourgeois economy, strong craft traditions and a country that has achieved a high degree of industrialization; but above all, the Hôtel Tassel is remarkable for the novelty of its plan: instead of the corridor usual in Belgium, Horta substituted an octagonal hall, from which a broad staircase leads off, giving access to the various rooms at different levels. This arrangement breaks with the practice of uniform layout floor by floor, foreshadowing the 'plan of volumes' conceived by *Loos in 1910 and *Le Corbusier's two-storey system of 1930.

Victor Horta. Hôtel Solvay. Brussels, 1895–1900

The Hôtel Tassel is also remarkable as being the first private house to make use of iron, both as a structural material (a huge winter garden on the ground floor is carried on an exposed iron frame, while an elegant iron column supports the staircase) and to supply decorative elements in a flexible linear style, exemplified by the wrought-iron handrails of the staircase and balconies. It is in this building, too, that an impressive repertoire of two-dimensional forms was initiated, based on a close study of plants and flowers: the 'whiplash line' or 'Horta line' literally covers the floors, walls and ceilings; it lashes out everywhere, coiling, interlacing, flying loose, climbing across glazing bars, encircling the feet of furniture, branching out in chandeliers and outstripping, often to excess, every structural requirement.

In the Hôtel Solvay (224 Avenue Louise, Brussels), built between 1895 and 1900, Art Nouveau can be seen in its maturity: it is an astonishing symbiosis, of Baroque and classical, sentiment and reason, craftsmanship and industry, colour and form, with aesthetics dominating technology. This building, wholly fitted out and furnished by Horta, is undoubtedly the most significant and complete example of its period. Horta built numerous houses in Brussels before the First World War in the same style (Autrique, 1893; Winssinger, 1895–6; Van Eetvelde, 1897–1900; Aubecq, 1900). The Maison du Peuple he designed for the Brussels branch of the Workers' Party (1896–9), and the department stores 'A l'Innovation' (Brussels, 1901) and 'Grand Bazar' (Frankfurt, 1903) all employ the structural resources of iron in the service of a new programme. The large glazed façades of these three buildings prefigure the light transparent envelopes that have led to the disappearance of the load-bearing wall.

In 1912 Horta was appointed a professor at the Académie des Beaux-Arts, whose head he eventually became (1927–31). After a stay in the United States (1916–19), his architecture assumed an austere, classical direction; the picturesque and calligraphic tendencies of Art Nouveau were conclusively superseded by the straight line. The Palais des Beaux-Arts in Brussels (1922–8) is the principal work of this period; well laid-out and designed in concrete, it was the first cultural centre of

Victor Horta. Maison du Peuple. Brussels, 1896–9

a type that was to gain wider diffusion after the Second World War.
Bibliography: Robert L. Delevoy, *Victor Horta*, Brussels 1958.

ROBERT L. DELEVOY

Howard, Ebenezer, b. London 1850, d. Welwyn Garden City 1928. In his book *Tomorrow: A peaceful path to reform* (London 1898) Howard advocates garden cities to counter flight from the land and the overpopulation of towns. His idea of an economically independent garden city surrounded by an agricultural belt and numbering approximately 30,000 inhabitants led to the foundation of the Garden Cities Association. First garden city: Letchworth near London (1903).

Howe, George, b. Worcester, Mass. 1886, d. Cambridge, Mass. 1955. Studied at the École des Beaux-Arts in Paris. Partner in the firm of Mellor, Meigs and Howe (residential buildings). Architect of the Philadelphia Savings Fund Society Building (1932), together with William *Lescaze.

Howell, Killick, Partridge and Amis. William Gough Howell, John Alexander Wentzel Killick, John Albert Partridge, Stanley Frederick Amis. Practice with a style characterized by a powerful striving after plastic originality. Their project for the Department of Commerce and Social Science at Birmingham University features *Gaudí-like façades of precast concrete balcony units; a redevelopment plan for St Anne's College, Oxford, consists of a series of curved blocks with highly modelled surface treatment, set in a wide oval round the college garden.

International Style. The term International Style, although recurrently under attack since it was first introduced a generation ago in the book of that name (New York 1932), has become—in considerable part by default—perhaps the most useful name for the dominant architectural current of the second quarter of the 20th century. Within the broad historical range of modern architecture, from the European and American modes of such men as *Voysey, *Horta and *Sullivan in the 1890s to the present 1960s, it defines a type of architectural design which came into existence in the early 1920s, developed at the hands of a few leaders to classic expression by 1930, and from that time on found wider and wider acceptance throughout the world.

Foreshadowed by the domestic building of Adolf *Loos, the early industrial constructions of *Perret, *Behrens and *Gropius, much work by engineers, European and American, and even the Futurist visions of *Sant'Elia, the new architecture of the pioneers among the second generation of modern architects, particularly the French-Swiss *Le Corbusier, the German Gropius and *Mies van der Rohe, and the Dutch *Oud and *Rietveld, representing a convergence of social and aesthetic aspirations characteristic of the second decade of the century, found early expression, mostly in projects, in the years 1919–23 immediately after the First World War. The large-scale projects of Mies (his glazed towers of 1919 and 1921), the Chicago Tribune Tower design of Gropius and Meyer (1922), and the spaced cruciform skyscrapers of Le Corbusier's 'City of Three Million', also projected in 1922, indicated a generic debt to American achievement in building, and by the mid century the International Style would even come to seem to many a characteristically American style. But for all the debt of

Walter Gropius and Adolf Meyer. Chicago Tribune Tower. 1922. Project

Le Corbusier. Second Citrohan House. 1922. Model

younger architects outside America to *Wright, especially in Holland and Germany in the fifteen years following 1910, the initiation of the new style—if style it be—was Western European, even specifically French, Dutch, and German; and it did not even begin to be accepted in other European countries—England, Sweden, Denmark, Finland, Russia and Italy—or in the New World until the late 1920s. As it spread internationally in the 1930s, however, political reaction and economic stagnation interrupted further development in several countries of Europe, notably Germany, Russia and France. On the other hand, by the late thirties, notable work was under way from Helsinki to

Ludwig Mies van der Rohe. Block of flats on the Weissenhof Estate. Stuttgart, 1927

Rio de Janeiro; and when building revived in the late 1940s after the Second World War the International Style had come to be almost universally accepted throughout the whole non-Communist world wherever modern technological advances were already an accomplished fact or even a relatively new importation.

As late as 1952 it was possible to claim (see the article 'The International Style Twenty Years After' in the *Architectural Record*) that, despite all the modulations, reactions and divagations up to that time, the International Style was still the essential core of international architectural practice. A decade later, now that the stylistic divergences of the last thirty years have become more strikingly apparent, the International Style probably still remains the basis of further architectural development since it was, very definitely, the discipline under which almost all architects under sixty were formed. To offer historical parallels not too pretentiously disparate in their chronological range, the divergent aspirations and achievements of the later 1930s, 40s, and 50s bear somewhat the same relation to the classic stage of the International Styles of the 1920s as the modu-

lations that followed the High Gothic in the mid and late 13th century or those that followed the High Renaissance in the mid and late 16th century. On these analogies the International Style, as the 'high' phase of modern architecture, may indeed continue to provide the basis of architectural developments for several generations—and even centuries—to come.

Returning to the book of 1932 which attempted at the end of the classic phase to formulate the International Style which had come into being through the preceding decade since 1922, certain quotations may still be relevant: 'The unconscious and halting developments of the 19th century, the confused and contradictory experimentation of the beginning of the 20th have been succeeded by a diverted evolution. There is now a single body of discipline, fixed enough to integrate contemporary style as a reality and yet elastic enough to permit individual interpretation and to encourage general growth. . . . The idea of style as the frame of potential growth, rather than a crushing mould, has developed with the recognition of principles such as archaeologists discern in the great styles of the past: . . . There is, first,

Alvar Aalto. Building for the newspaper Turun
Sanomat. Turku, 1928–30

Eero Saarinen. General Motors Technical Center.
Warren, Mich., completed 1955

a new conception of architecture as volume
rather than as mass. Secondly, regularity
rather than axial symmetry serves as the
chief means of ordering design. These two
principles, with a third proscribing arbitrary applied decoration, mark the productions of the International Style. This new
style is not international in the sense that
the production of one country is just like
that of another. Nor is it so rigid that the
work of various leaders is not clearly distinguishable. . . . In stating the general
principles of the contemporary style, in
analysing their derivation from structure
and their modification by function, the
appearance of a certain dogmatism can
hardly be avoided. (But) the international
style already exists in the present; it is not
merely something the future may hold in
store. Architecture is always "a set of
actual monuments, not a vague *corpus* of
theory".'

Some of those actual monuments may well
be named, in addition to the skyscraper
projects mentioned earlier. These, however, it should be noted, have proved
especially premonitory of what may be
considered the 'American' phase of the
International Style of the 1950s, which
could now be illustrated with monuments
as far apart geographically as the Edifico
Polar in Caracas, Venezuela, by Vegas and
Galia and the SAS building in Copenhagen, Denmark, by Arne *Jacobsen, not
to speak of prominent examples in countries
such as England, Germany, Italy, Belgium
and South Africa.

Perhaps the first modest realization of the ideals of the still unformulated International Style was a jewellery shop of 1921 in the Kalverstraat in Amsterdam by G. T. Rietveld inspired by the Dutch *neoplasticism. Parallel with this came the unrealized projects of Le Corbusier for 'Citrohan' houses (1919–21) and those by Mies van der Rohe for a brick country house and for a concrete office building (1922). Major works of the mature International Style followed, with Gropius's *Bauhaus at Dessau (1925–6), Le Corbusier's Cook and Stein houses (1926 and 1927), Oud's low-cost housing at the Hook of Holland (1926–7), Gropius's housing at Törten, Siemensstadt and Dammerstock (1928 and 1929), not to speak of his Dessau Employment Office (1928), perhaps his most perfect work; and finally Mies's German Pavilion at the Barcelona Exposition (1929) and his Tugendhat house in Brno, Czechoslovakia, and the Savoye house at Poissy outside Paris by Le Corbusier (both 1930).

Immediately after 1930 definite modulations began to appear away from some of the austerities of the classic phase, particularly in Le Corbusier's Swiss Hostel (1931–3) at the Cité Universitaire in Paris with its rubble rear wall of irregular curvature and its somewhat sculptural *pilotis* of rough concrete. Thus in the very years of the early 1930s, when the new style was spreading most rapidly throughout the world on the way to its almost universal acceptance after the Second World War, one at least of the founders was still in the lead in moving away from the rigid machinolatry implicit in the most advanced aspirations of the 1920s. But this should not be overemphasized. In the very years of the early 1950s, when Le Corbusier in his Church of Notre-Dame du Haut at Ronchamp in France and his High Courts of Justice at Chandigarh in India was reaching the extreme point of his reaction against the International Style, Mies van der Rohe in his Lake Shore Drive apartments was providing a new model of the tall building, based on his projects of the 1920s, destined to be enormously influential internationally; while Eero *Saarinen, whose early death in 1961 deprived the post-war world of one of its most typically versatile and divergent designers, was still faithful to the Miesian version of the International Style in his first major work, the General Motors Technical Center at Warren, Mich.

It still seems just, therefore, to return to the initial paragraph of this article and to state once more that the International Style was the dominant architectural development of the second quarter of this century, and that its core of tradition, at least, as well as its continued employment in vulgarized modes—to which the term is by some derogatorily restricted—is still the basis of the world's architecture even in the 1960s and may well remain so for many decades.

HENRY-RUSSELL HITCHCOCK

Iron. *Steel.

Italy. 'Since the 18th century there has been no architecture': it is with these words that *Sant'Elia opened his Manifesto of 1914. It would have been truer to say that since the 18th century Italy had produced no great architect, no new directions in architecture and no great school. Nevertheless, there has not been any substantial change from 1914 to the present day, despite Sant'Elia and despite *Nervi: for two centuries now, Italian architects, when they have not built like the ancient Romans, have trodden in the steps of foreigners; only *Terragni has dared to strive for independence. The few interesting architects of the *Stile Liberty* (the Italian *Art Nouveau), *Basile, D'*Aronco and *Sommaruga looked to the Belgians and French; while Vienna provided the models for Sant'Elia himself (influenced by the school of Otto *Wagner) and the Lombard rationalists prior to 1927, who were followers of *Loos and *Hoffmann. After 1927 the young 'Europeanists' of the modern movement reorientated themselves to *Le Corbusier, *Mies van der Rohe or *Gropius. This generation, which is now fifty or sixty years old, still represents the best in Italian architecture today.

Naturally, in the work of each of them, from Basile to *Albini, and from Sant'Elia to Nervi, the personal imprint is stronger than the foreign one; but it has not been as determinative either of the essential content or the original form as the foreign sources have; it is the latter, revived and worked over again, that one sees reflected there. One original element, in the years between the wars however, intervened amid the various foreign influences, as a dangerously suggestive constant: the *Novecento Italiano*, the only cultural movement that was typically Fascist (hence the 'Italiano'), recruited from the 'reactionaries of the modern revolution' (as one of its founders wrote), or rather from the 'revolutionaries of the Fascist reaction' as its critics saw it. But unlike the revolutionary architects of *Germany and the *Netherlands, the protagonists of the *Novecento Italiano* did not start from scratch. They carried out a modernist reform based on the principles of neo-classical architecture and the aesthetics of *valori plastici*, modified in the light of Cubism, or its Italian derivative, *Futurism. Giuseppe Terragni revivified this

Raimondo d'Aronco. Main Building at the Applied Art Exhibition. Turin, 1902

Matté Trucco. Fiat Works. Turin, 1927. Car ramp

movement by the support of his artistic genius; he was its most important architect, not only by reason of the absolute value of his works, and of the Casa del Fascio (Como, 1936) in particular, but above all because of the complexity of the problems he set himself in attempting to break down the 'national' barriers to his lively historical feeling for architecture; and by historical we mean European. Luciano *Baldessari worked with similar aims, building the fine Press Pavilion at the Vth Milan Triennale (1933).

The ferment of new ideas came to the boil in 1927, in particular with the work of the seven young architects united under the banner of *gruppo 7, who formulated their ideas in a number of publications and helped to promote the foundation of the *Movimento Italiano per l'Architettura Razionale*. But as architecture, more than any other art, was tied up with politics, the ambiguous attitude of the *Novecento Italiano* was passed on to the new movement. The subsequent confusion was great, since both opposing trends, the 'modern' and the 'ancient Roman' (whose leader was Piacentini) declared for Fascism. In reality the interests and claims of both sides were equally demagogic, and periods of inauspicious alliance were not lacking either. The journal *Quadrante*, edited by P. M. Bardi, supported the Fascist version of rationalism. Meanwhile, some architecture of note did get built: the Fiat Works by Matté Trucco (1927) and Pagano's Casa Gualino, both at Turin; some houses by Lingeri on Lake Como; and Terragni's Novecomum at Como.

The position was soon clarified, however, by Edoardo Persico, a young critic who since 1929 had been the editor of Giuseppe Pagano's *Casabella*. He showed that rationalist architecture was essentially anti-nationalist, according to the tenets of the *Bauhaus, itself the most rigorous expression of it. Persico had to fight within the editorial board itself of *Casabella* against Pagano's Fascist illusions and his own noble errors, for which he ultimately paid with his life, dying at Mauthausen in 1943.

In 1933 Gio *Ponti took over the direction of the Vth Triennale. Ponti was of modernistic neoclassical provenance, but anti-monumental, and never taking his standpoint to extremes; this made him the

favourite architect of the Milanese bour-
geoisie. In a spirit of free experimentation,
and without any polemical intent, he
invited the 'rationalist' group of architects
to take a large part in the Triennale, and
published their work in his journal *Domus*,
thus paving the way to success for them.
Their contribution to the Triennale, a
series of villas and small houses erected in
the park, was of a splendid precision and
uniformity; but on the moral plane, though
they were not aware of it, the compromise
was grave. It was only with the war and
the end of Fascism that nearly everybody,
starting with Pagano, understood the cause
that Persico had defended: they understood,
that is to say, that a revolutionary architecture is incompatible with a reactionary
government, which is always willing to
exploit alliances and compromises. But by
that time, Piacentini, the leader of Fascist
architecture, and certain Novecentists like
him, such as Muzio in Milan, had already
sown their colonnades, lictoral towers and
'Roman' arches up and down the length of
Italy. It was the same with town planning:
Mussolini founded new cities, only one of
which had any architectural feeling:
Sabaudia (by Cancellotti, Montuori, Piccinato and Scalpelli); and it was only
Adriano Olivetti who called in some bright
young architects—*Figini and *Pollini—
to draw up a plan for the Val d'Aosta.
After the war, the reconstruction drive was
beginning to bear fruit, when Bruno Zevi,
back in Rome after many years' residence
in America (where he had not seen Italy's
difficulties and problems), thought he
recognized an error in the general align-
ment of Italian architects, victorious at last,
along the front of 'rationalist' aesthetics.
But although he performed a task of cultural value in spreading, with polemical
ardour, a knowledge of Frank Lloyd
*Wright and his campaign for 'natural', i.e.
*organic as opposed to 'rational' architec-
ture, he nevertheless helped to confuse
once more the ideas of Italian architects
who had only recently managed to sort
them out, and who in any case found
rationalism in architecture congenial.
Zevi had the greatest effect on the School
of Rome, which counted some of the best
architects in Italy amongst its members,
including Piccinato, Quaroni (who built
some experimental villages at Matera),
Montuori, the designer of the new station

Gian Antonio Bernasconi, Annibale Fiocchi and
Marcello Nizzoli. Palazzo Olivetti. Milan, 1954

in Rome (1950, with Calini and others),
the whimsical Ridolfi, Moretti, Monaco and
Luccichenti. But above all, the architects
of Milan were disorientated. They had been
induced to re-think their architecture from
scratch, sometimes altering their whole
style, and it was this lack of ideological
clarity that later gave rise to the strange
form of the Torre Velasca (1957) and the
rising tide of 'neo-Liberty' (Art Nouveau
revival) which has almost drowned some
young architects and stirred up a scandal

Eugenio Montuori, Leo Calini, Massimo
Castellazzi, Vasco Fadigati, Achille Pintonello
and Annibale Vitellozzi. Main Railway Station.
Rome, 1950. Booking Hall

Pier Luigi Nervi and Annibale Vitellozzi. Palazzetto dello Sport. Rome, 1956–7

abroad out of proportion to the episode's size and significance.

In and around Milan however, innumerable buildings have arisen: workers' flats, factories, houses, office blocks, churches and a number of skyscrapers (the Pirelli Building by Gio Ponti; the much discussed Torre Velasca by *BBPR; the Torre Galfa by Bega; and the Torre al Parco by Magistretti). In addition to the architects of the first rationalist school, such as *Albini, Figini, Pollini, Sartoris, Lingeri, Belgioioso, Banfi (who died in a concentration camp), Peressutti, Rogers, *Gardella, Bottoni, Mollino, Astengo, Zavanella and *Nizzoli, may be named the younger generation of *Zanuso, Pagani, Castiglioni, Caccia Dominioni, Latis, *Fiocchi, Bernasconi, Morandi, Bassi, *Viganò and Mangiarotti (known for his 'glass church' at Baranzate) among others. But every city and every region is a centre where interesting architects are at work: Cocchia at Cosenza (Naples); Samonà at Minchilli (Bari); Michelucci, designer of the fine station in Florence (1936, in collaboration); the builders of the Market at Pescia in Tuscany (1951); *Scarpa in Venice, where the best school of architecture is situated; and Albini, himself a Milanese, in Genoa, where he has built the two splendid museums of the Palazzo Bianco (1951) and San Lorenzo (1954–6). Works of great interest may often be found in small towns, such as Terragni's Casa del Fascio at Como (1936), Gardella's buildings at Alessandria, those of Baldessari at Rovereto, Gellner's at Cortina, D'Olivio's at Trieste, Nervi's at Chianciano and Bologna, and those by Nizzoli, Fiocchi, Gardella, Figini and Pollini at Ivrea.

The nerve centre of the new Italian architecture is Milan, with its journals, its Triennali, its recently founded Museum of

Architecture, and the economic opportunities afforded by its industries. It was in Milan that culminated the activity of that generous and intelligent patron of modern Italian architecture, Adriano Olivetti; it is being continued by his son Roberto today. On the cultural plane, Rome competes for primacy; it is the home of the *Istituto Nazionale di Architettura*, headed by Bruno Zevi, who also edits *L'Architettura*, published in Rome. Architectural criticism, too, is very active in Italy, backed by an intelligent editorial policy (Argan and Zevi in Rome, Ragghianti in Florence, and Dorfles and Veronesi in Milan). Our general panorama may conclude on a positive note with the name of the greatest and best known amongst living Italian designers, the engineer Pier Luigi Nervi whose superb structures, which for the last thirty years have been rising throughout Italy and the world, have won for him universal renown.

Bibliography: Paolo Nestler, *Neues Bauen in Italien*, Munich 1954; Piero Bottoni, *Edifici Moderni in Milano*, Milan 1954; G. E. Kidder Smith, *Italy Builds*, London 1955; Carlo Pagani, *Italy's Architecture Today*, Milan 1955; Agnoldomenico Pica, *Architettura Italiana Recente*, Milan 1959.

GIULIA VERONESI

BBPR. Torre Velasca. Milan, 1957

Luigi Figini and Gino Pollini. Church of the Madonna dei Poveri. Milan, 1952–6

Jacobsen, Arne, b. Copenhagen 1902. Arne Jacobsen is an architect who has been to a notable degree open to new impulses without losing his attachment to the Danish tradition. The same sense for order, modular rhythms and natural proportions, which developed first in Danish half-timbered construction and later in the brick buildings of the classical revival, characterizes Jacobsen's architecture. Artistic discipline, together with an avoidance of sentimentality and theatric effects, led to a restraint which, combined with a sense for precision in detail and excellence in workmanship, pervades all Arne Jacobsen's later building.

Jacobsen grew up with *Functionalism. When he was a student *neoclassicism

Arne Jacobsen. Bellavista Housing Estate near Copenhagen, 1933

still dominated Denmark and the architecture of about 1800 was greatly admired, in particular that of the architect Nicolaj Abildgård. But his encounter with the architecture of *Le Corbusier and *Mies van der Rohe in exhibitions at Paris (1925) and Berlin (1927–8) was important both for Jacobsen himself and for the whole development of Danish architecture.

Jacobsen was trained in the architectural school of the Academy of Arts, from which he graduated in 1928. He had already attracted notice with the first of a long series of single houses, reminiscent externally of Abildgård and his period, with yellow bricks and a tiled roof. The ease and flexibility of his talent enabled him at the same time to try his hand at Functionalism's cubist style. Together with Flemming Lassen he created a sensation at an exhibition in 1929 with a circular 'house of the future' with helicopter landing-place on the roof.

In his earliest Le Corbusier-inspired villas the smooth whitewashed walls concealed technical faults which followed from the over-hasty adoption of the new style. In 1930–5 he created a harmonious group of buildings in the Bellevue area near Copenhagen, beginning with the baths, whose cabins and kiosks were designed with elegance. These were followed by the three-storey Bellavista housing blocks, whose staggered perspectives gave all flats an equal share of sun and view. Finally

came the Bellevue Theatre, which was thought of primarily as a summer theatre and therefore given a sliding ceiling which could make the night sky serve as a roof. Unfortunately both the theatre and the adjoining restaurant have been altered beyond recognition.

It was through his friendship with the Swedish architect Gunnar *Asplund that Jacobsen reached maturity as an artist. From Asplund he learned what it is to *work* at a building, both technically and architecturally, and to respect detail. Asplund's influence shows clearly in Stelling House in Copenhagen (1937–8) and the town halls of Århus (1937) and Søllerød (1940–2), designed in collaboration with Erik Møller and Flemming Lassen respectively. Gradually Jacobsen was able to free himself from Asplund's imprint without forgetting the lessons he had learned from him.

Wartime isolation and the conditions prevailing until 1950 allowed Denmark no opportunity to make use of the new impulses arriving from abroad. Then with the Søholm housing scheme Jacobsen won back his position among the leaders of Danish architecture. In Munksgård's School (1952–6), a single-storey construction with numerous bays and courtyards, he combined a sense for total unity of design and quality with an atmosphere of intimacy. In a series of new offices and administrative buildings he tried to introduce the largely American-developed principle of construction with internal supporting columns and *curtain-wall façades. He appreciated the fact that the aesthetic qualities of so simple, almost anonymous, an architecture must be based on proportions and detail, and designed accordingly [Jespersen's Building in Copenhagen (1955); Rødovre town hall (1955); the SAS Building in Copenhagen (1959)].

Since the war Jacobsen has also constructed a series of handsome private houses, which show to a marked degree his ability to fit buildings into the landscape, such as the houses for C. A. Møller (1951) and Ruthwen Jürgensen (1956), lying in attractive surroundings near the Sound. Exclusive residences were constructed in Jægersborg and Gentofte and blocks of flats in Rødovre (1951). On the industrial side mention should be made of Odden Smokehouse (1943), built with traditional materials, the Massey Harris exhibition and works building (1952), which was awarded the grand prix in São Paulo, Brazil, and Tom's Factories (1961). Arne Jacobsen does not wish to be a specialist. Not only does he range over the entire field of architecture, but he is just as willing to plan silverware, gardens, furniture, and fabric patterns.

Jacobsen has been invited to take part in a number of international competitions [town halls of Marl (1957) and Cologne (1959), World Health Organization's building in Geneva (1960)]. He has received first prize in many Danish and Swedish competitions, including Denmark's National Bank (1961) and Landskrona town hall and sports hall (1957). Since 1959 he has been engaged on St Catherine's College, Oxford. He has been Professor of Architecture at Copenhagen Academy of Arts since 1956.

Bibliography: J. Pedersen, *Arkitekten Arne Jacobsen*, Copenhagen 1954.

TOBIAS FABER

Japan. It was in the year 1868 that a decisive new era dawned for Japan under the rule of Emperor Meiji, putting an end to the long feudal age of the Tokugawa Shogunates which had lasted for 260 years. The isolation policy of the Shogunates was abandoned and the country opened its doors to the world, absorbing Western civilization with eagerness.

Arne Jacobsen. Housing. Søholm, 1950–5

Arne Jacobsen. Jespersen Offices. Copenhagen, 1955

Tetsuo Yoshida. General Post Office. Tokyo, 1931

In Japan wood had always been the main building material. After the restoration the Japanese invited architects from Germany, England, Italy and the United States to help them build Western style architecture of stone and bricks. Japanese architects then copied these examples and soon began to give birth to a Japanese-European style, introducing elements of Renaissance, Gothic and Italian into the traditional native architecture.

Japan is naturally very receptive and liberal in adopting foreign cultures and has been much influenced by them. But she also

Hideo Kosaka. Post Office Savings Bank. Kyoto, 1954

values and preserves her own age-old culture and blends it harmoniously with imported cultures, though the process of assimilation often takes a long time. The rapid introduction of Western architecture at the beginning of the Meiji period was a challenge to Japan's architectural circles. Scholars such as Professor Chuta Ito and Professor Tei Sekino turned their attention not only to the study of Western architecture but also to the traditions of their own country and other Asiatic lands.

Towards the end of the 19th century steel-framed structure and *reinforced concrete were introduced, bringing a rapid development in the Japanese building industry. Together with this innovation in building technique came the influence of modern movements in Europe such as *Art Nouveau and the Wiener Sezession. In 1920, under the prosperous conditions following the end of the war and with a call for humanism, the Japanese group Secession was formed by a number of younger architects, including Sutemi Horiguchi, Makoto Takizawa, Mamoru Yamada, Kikuji Ishimoto. In 1922 Japan's modern architecture was presented by this group at the Peace Exposition, Tokyo, for the first time. Of its members Mamoru Yamada designed the Central Telephone Office, Tokyo (1926); Kikuji Ishimoto, the Tokyo Asahi News Press Building (1927), and the Shirokiya Department Store, Tokyo (1929). Sutemi Horiguchi devoted his time to a re-examination of the traditions of Japanese architecture and received a doctor's degree for his thesis on Kundaikan-Sochoki, which is an historical document concerning interior decoration in 15th-century Japan.

Japanese modern style is best represented in works built for the Communications Services. Mamoru Yamada was first in this field. He was followed by Tetsuo Yoshida, *Functionalist in the best sense of the word, who designed the Tokyo General Post Office (1931); and later by Hideo Kosaka (Post Office Savings Bank, Kyoto, 1954). The *International Style found its way into Japan through contacts made by her younger architects and critics with modern groups in Europe. Kenji Imai, a professor at the Waseda University, went to Europe in 1926 to study modern architecture and became personally acquainted with *Gropius, *Le Corbusier, *Mies van der Rohe,

and others. On his return he published
reports on their activities. Kunio *Maekawa
went to Paris to work under Le Corbusier;
Iwao Yamawaki and Takehiko Mizutani
studied at the *Bauhaus in Dessau. About
this time two foreign architects visited
Japan who had a great influence on her
modern movement. One of them was
Frank Lloyd *Wright, whose famous
Imperial Hotel (1915–22) had very much
impressed Japan's architectural circles. The
other was a German architect, Bruno
*Taut, who travelled all over Japan, seek-
ing out the wonderful treasures of her
architectural tradition.

At this stage of their development Japanese
architects were confronted with many
difficult problems. They were not only
concerned with the basic principles of
modern building; they were also trying to
find answers to the demands of modern
living in a new age. In 1937 they founded
the *Kosaku Bunka Renmai* (Japanese Werkbund) and issued a publication, *Kosaku
Bunka*, in which they outlined their proposals and described the experiments they
had made. Hideo Kishida, Shinji Koike,
Sutemi Horiguchi, Yoshiro Taniguchi,
Takeo Sato, Kunio Maekawa were the
leading members of the group. But soon

Kunio Maekawa. Harumi Flats. Tokyo, 1957

Kenzo Tange. Sogetsu Hall. Tokyo, 1960

Kiyonori Kikutake. Sky House. Tokyo, 1958

the time became unfavourable to the growth of such a movement; with the rise of Fascism in Europe, militaristic nationalism took the lead in Japan, and finally the outbreak of war brought the activities of the Japanese Werkbund to an end. Their only chance lay in the rationalization which was necessitated during the war because of the shortage of material and labour.

After the signing of the San Francisco Peace Treaty in 1951 architecture began to develop again under the new democratic constitution. First came the construction of quarters for the occupation forces, then gradually the work of reconstruction in general. The leading architects were Mamoru Yamada, Kunio Maekawa, Kameki Tsuchiura, Kenzo *Tange, and Yoshiro Taniguchi, who had all formerly been connected with the Japanese Werkbund. Examples of their work are the Welfare Hospital by Mamoru Yamada (1953), the International House by Maekawa, Sakakura and Yoshimura (1955), the Peace Centre in Hiroshima by Kenzo Tange, and the Nagasaki Cultural Centre by Takeo Sato (1955). Isoya Yoshida, who remained deeply attached to the traditional styles of Japanese architecture, attempted a modern interpretation of these traditions in his building for the Japanese Academy of Art and several private houses. Kenzo Tange adopted a new curtain-wall technique for the Metropolitan Government Office in Tokyo. He also approached a traditional Jomon style in his use of reinforced concrete for the Sogetsu Hall and Kagawa Prefectural Office.

One of the most important problems for Japanese architects today is rationalization. They are encouraged by large-scale housing projects under the sponsorship of public corporations. Sky House, Kikutake's own house (1958), is an experiment pointing in the right direction for the future.

It is in the last ten years that Japan has given serious thought to the problems of her own cultural heritage. Younger architects such as Kiyonori Kikutake, Masato Otaka, Yoshinobu Ashihara are making great efforts to re-examine and revive Japanese architectural tradition and the Japanese way of living in terms of modern technology. The Kirishima Kogen Hotel, designed by Masachika Murata, is an attempt to achieve a harmony between the building and its natural environment, and the interior is perfectly in keeping with the traditional way of living (chopsticks and kimonos).

Bibliography: Shinji Koike, *Contemporary Architecture of Japan*, Tokyo 1953; Shinji Koike and Ryuichi Hamaguchi, *Japan's New Architecture*, Tokyo 1956; Udo Kultermann, *New Japanese Architecture*, London 1960.

SHINJI KOIKE

Jenney, William Le Baron, b. Fairhaven, Mass. 1832, d. Los Angeles 1907. Studied in Paris. He introduced the use of the steel frame in multi-storey buildings with his Home Insurance Building (Chicago, 1883–5), but the lavish mouldings of his masonry show no aesthetic consequences of his innovation. First Leiter Building (1879), second Leiter Building (1889–90), both in Chicago.

Johansen, John MacL., b. New York 1916. Studied at Harvard University under Walter *Gropius and Marcel *Breuer and worked in the offices of Breuer and *Skidmore, Owings and Merrill. Johansen is keenly interested in structural experiments: designs for a holiday house with a *reinforced concrete shell and a 'streamlined house' with walls of sprayed reinforced concrete. His design for the US Embassy in Dublin, a rotunda with circular courtyard and a façade of prefabricated, reinforced concrete frames, is based on the Irish round-tower tradition.

Philip Johnson. Johnson House. New Canaan, Conn., 1949

Johnson, Philip, b. Cleveland, Ohio 1906. Philip Johnson, the American architect, was the son of a prominent lawyer. In 1927, while studying classics at Harvard, he read an article on the modern movement in architecture by Henry-Russell Hitchcock which directed him towards his career: initially, in the thirties, as the first director of the pioneering architectural department of the Museum of Modern Art in New York; then, before the end of the forties, as a practitioner. During the period of his curatorship he distinguished himself as a propagandist and historian of the modern movement. In connection with the exhibition of modern architecture at the Museum in 1933, besides an influential catalogue, he wrote *The International Style* (1932) in collaboration with Hitchcock. It attempted an overall description of the aesthetic qualities of European modernism—and, incidentally, baptized the style with its generally accepted name (the suggestion of Alfred Barr, then Director of the Museum). Johnson's catalogue *Machine Art* (1934) was also influential, and the Museum's displays of industrial design under his aegis (while not exactly unprecedented in American museums) did much to stimulate museum interest in the exhibition of mass-produced objects. His catalogue for an exhibition of the work of *Mies van der Rohe (first edition, 1947; enlarged, 1953) was the first work on this architect. Johnson's work as a propagandist for modern architecture whetted his appetite

to become a practitioner. In the early forties, he left the Museum for Harvard, where he was strongly attracted by the teaching of Marcel *Breuer. But Mies, whom he had met in Europe in 1930, was his true mentor and he soon came to be known as Mies's most faithful disciple. His own 'Glass House' in New Canaan, Connecticut (1949) was derived from Mies's similar scheme for the Edith Farnsworth House in Fox River, Illinois (1950, but designed in 1946), and, more specifically, from the metal skeletal treatment of the buildings for the Illinois Institute of Technology. Despite these influences, the Glass House is a work of marked originality which instantly gained international recognition as among the masterpieces of the immediate post-war period. Unlike the austerely self-contained refinement of Mies's Farnsworth House, Johnson's Glass House possesses a romantic feeling for park-like landscape and a wealth of historical allusion (*Schinkel, *Suprematism, the diagram of the Acropolis from Choisy, for example). These qualities give an 18th-century quality of urbanity and wit to the play of the simple shapes on the terraced greensward: glass box, brick box and saucer pool diagonally opposed to one another around the axial vertical of Jacques Lipschitz's totemic *Figure*. In a series of commissions for suburban houses Johnson elaborated the themes of the Glass House in various ways, and complicated them by the introduction of

Philip Johnson. Boissonas House. New Canaan, Conn., 1956

courts. Notable among these early houses are the Hodgson and Wiley Houses in New Canaan (1951 and 1953 respectively), the Davis House in Wyzata, Minnesota (1954), and the Rockefeller Guest House in New York (now the property of the Museum of Modern Art, 1950). Meanwhile, Johnson's appreciation of both the architectonic and landscape values of the court led to what may well be the finest urban space designed during the decade and a half following the Second World War, the garden of the Museum of Modern Art (1953).

With his Temple Kneses Tifereth Israel at Port Chester, New York (1954–5), Johnson began to throw off his spiritual apprenticeship to Mies for more personal statements, although he was to collaborate with Mies on the Seagram Building (1957–), where his contributions are especially evident in the interior. In the Temple, the exposed Miesian metal skeleton is infilled with precast concrete slabs slotted with stained glass. The Ledoux-like ovoid entrance structure outside and the *Soane-like hung plaster vaulting within testify to his continued interest in bringing sophisticated historical allusions to bear on modern expression. Johnson's tentative use of precast concrete as a mural infilling in the Temple presages his increasing use of masonry in his recent buildings. In precast concrete or hand-carved masonry, he has reintroduced the classicist ideals of the portico and colonnade. His Sheldon Art

Gallery for the University of Nebraska in Lincoln (under construction) and the New York State Theater for the Lincoln Center (under construction) are major examples of this neoclassicism. Curvatures introduced at the juncture of column and 'entablature' of the Nebraska building are, by his own admission, also influenced by Gothic architecture. In his *béton brut* chapel for the Benedictine Priory in Washington, D.C. (designed in 1961), the relative weight of this combined classical/neo-Gothic inspiration shifts. If buttresses and vault are obviously medieval in feeling, the columnar character of supports alternating with the buttressing, together with the contained simplicity of the overall mass, are less evidently classicist. On the other hand, the specific design of the members is unimaginable without reinforced concrete construction.

Among the most convinced (and convincing) of modern 'traditionalists' (as Johnson has sometimes termed himself), his eclectic evocation of past architecture in his own work is far-ranging. For example, the domical forms of a nuclear reactor building for Israel (1960) and a shrine at New Harmony, Indiana (1960)—the first a gently gored shape in poured concrete, the second a bent wood and plywood structure thatched in wooden shakes—recall similar undulating domes in such a late Imperial Roman work as Hadrian's Villa or in Borromini's Baroque churches. But there are subsidiary recollections of Egyptian temple complexes in the one, of Indian *stupas* and Norwegian stave churches in the other. Meanwhile, both recall the austere containment of Ledoux's massing. Johnson's early interest in the steel skeleton appears in his campus complex for the University of St Thomas in Houston, Texas (two sections completed in 1959). He based the complex on Thomas Jefferson's scheme at the University of Virginia for an arrangement of separate buildings around a rectangular green, all linked by a covered colonnade. This interweaving of elemental building masses and covered colonnades with landscape also appears in his pavilion buildings, where the basic pavilion (supports and a roof) is repeated in plan as an irregular checkerboard. The Boissonas House in New Canaan (1956) and a garden pavilion for the Glass House (designed in 1961) variously call up classical, Islamic, and possibly Japanese prototypes, without specific reference to any of these.

Philip Johnson. Theater of the Dance, Lincoln Center. New York, under construction. Project (first version)

The catholicity of his historical allusion notwithstanding, certain qualities generally characterize Johnson's urbane architecture: severely elemental massing, meticulous detailing and finish, a formal elegance of planning which disciplines even the casual environment, and, finally, a sensitivity to landscape values ranging from the well-manicured park to the planted terrace. As a teacher and critic he has magnified the influence of his buildings.

Bibliography: John Jacobus, *Philip Johnson*, New York 1962; 'Glass House', *Architectural Forum*, *91*, New York November 1949; Henry-Russell Hitchcock, 'Philip Johnson', *Architectural Review*, *117*, London April 1955; Philip Johnson, 'The Seven Crutches of Modern Architecture', *Perspecta 3*, Yale Architectural Journal; William H. Jordy, 'The Mies-less Johnson', *Architectural Forum*, *111*, New York, September 1959; Ian McCallum, *Architecture USA*, London, New York 1959; Philip Johnson, *Perspecta 7*, pp. 3–8; Sibyl Moholy-Nagy, pp. 68–71; H.-R. Hitchcock, *Zodiac 8*, Milan 1961.

WILLIAM H. JORDY

Kahn, Albert, b. Rhaunen, Westphalia 1869, d. Detroit, Mich. 1942. Emigrated to America in 1881; 1928–32 in Russia (industrial building programme). Kahn's industrial buildings anticipated at an early date the precise and slender cubic shapes of the fifties (*Mies van der Rohe, Eero *Saarinen). Ohio Steel Foundry Company at Limy, Ohio (1939); automobile works in Detroit.

Kahn, Louis I., b. Island of Osel, Estonia (Russia) 1901. Kahn came to the USA while young and received a traditional *Beaux-Arts* architectural education at the University of Pennsylvania, graduating in 1924. After various jobs and travel in Europe, he worked with an academic architect, Paul Cret, and during the depression did a project for the Philadelphia City Planning Commission. In 1941 he began an association with George *Howe, a pioneer in modern design in the USA who had created the earliest *International Style skyscraper outside Europe in the Philadelphia Savings Fund Society Building (with William *Lescaze) in 1932. Kahn's first work to attract any attention was the Carver Court War Housing Project, Coatsville, Pennsylvania (1942–3), in partnership with Howe and Oscar Stonorov. His independent practice dates from 1947. In 1950–1 he was resident architect of the American Academy in Rome, and subsequently became design critic at Yale. In 1955 he was named Professor of Architecture at the University of Pennsylvania.

Louis I. Kahn. Building constructed from three-dimensional units. 1954. Project

Partly for lack of opportunity, partly because of an apparent reticence, Kahn did not emerge as a major creative figure until the mid 1950s. However, since that date he has been one of the most consistently discussed and admired of contemporary architects. Like all the undisputed masters of the 20th century, Kahn's mature style is the result of a dense fusion of many, sometimes contradictory, ideas and tendencies, all of which are brought together in a unique personal idiom. Unlike Philip *Johnson, Gordon *Bunshaft, and Eero *Saarinen, all of whom were drawing upon the industrial classicism of *Mies van der Rohe as a literal source for their designs of the early 1950s, Kahn, in his Yale Art Gallery, New Haven (1952–4), was already more self-reliant. The Miesian aspect of his first major building was not so much a matter of details and vocabulary as it was a question of creating large universal spaces for the gallery interiors (spaces which could be temporarily subdivided

according to need) and a simple cubic mass for the exterior. As for the details, the concrete frame and the tetrahedrons of the ceiling structure were a vigorous formal statement coming at a time when elegance and polished perfection were the fashion. Even the exterior, though aggressively simple in its contrast of brick and glass, avoided the classicizing smoothness of the then-popular Miesian envelope.

When the mid-20th-century wave of *neo-classicism and academicism at last overtook Kahn's design in the 1956 Trenton Bath Houses, his taste had already departed from the refined norms of Americanized modernism. At Trenton, the regular cross-axial plan with five square spaces, all but the central one being covered by pyramidal hipped roofs, revealed Kahn's early formed attachment to the plan-types favoured by the *beaux-arts* tradition, a tradition which, around 1895, had helped to focus the early development of *Wright, and which slightly later performed the same service in the orientation of *Le Corbusier's very different style.

This academicism, which was a literal aspect of Kahn's modest yet monumental Trenton building, aided in the creation of the more personally expressive Richards Medical Research Building, University of Pennsylvania (1958–60). Widely heralded by critics and architects as an unusually new departure in an age largely given over to imitations of the recent past, chic variations of historical styles, or irresponsible personal adventures, Kahn's Towers are equally, perhaps even more important as a major reinterpretation of several of the canonical aspects of the modern movement. Indeed, familiarity with this cluster of concrete and brick forms only underscores Kahn's reflexive utilization of his immediate roots, a utilization which is in no sense eclectic or narrowly cerebral. Some critics have noted that Kahn's perceptible separation of 'served' and 'servant' spaces parallels specific theorems in Wright's early work, notably the Larkin Building, Buffalo (1904); others are struck by similar instances of abrupt formal juxtaposition (caused by functional differentiation) that occur in works by Le Corbusier; while perhaps the most penetrating observation of all is that Kahn has, in this picturesque, red-brick conglomeration, found a road back to mid-19th-century

Louis I. Kahn. Richards Medical Research Building, University of Pennsylvania. Philadelphia, 1958–60

Victorian design principles, without, at the same time, sacrificing the gains of the modern movement. On the basis of this single building, Kahn has obtained a unique place in the annals of contemporary architecture, one which will certainly grow in the light of new constructions which have already begun to issue from his office.

JOHN M. JACOBUS, JR

Klerk, Michael de, b. Amsterdam 1884, d. Amsterdam 1923. Leading exponent of the generation of architects deriving from *Berlage, and centred round the journal *Wendingen* (*Netherlands). Residential buildings, especially in the suburbs of Amsterdam (*Expressionism).

Klint, Peter Vilhelm Jensen, b. near Skelskør 1853, d. 1930. Worked first as an engineer, then as a painter, and after 1896 as an architect. His best-known church is the Grundtvig Church in Copenhagen (1920–40), with its organ-shaped façade.

Kraemer, Friedrich Wilhelm, b. Halberstadt 1907. Studied at the Technical Colleges of Brunswick and Vienna. Private practice since 1935. Residential buildings, offices, schools, department stores, industrial buildings. Since 1946 he has been professor at Brunswick Technical College (Germany).

Labrouste, Henri, b. Paris 1801, d. Fontainebleau 1875. Trained at the *École des Beaux-Arts (Rome Scholar) which he later opposed with increasing vehemence. His epoch-making libraries employed steel frames encased in masonry. (Bibliothèque Ste Geneviève, Paris, 1843–50; Bibliothèque Nationale, Paris, 1858–68.)

Le Corbusier, b. La Chaux-de-Fonds, Switzerland 1887. Like few others of his generation, Le Corbusier (Charles-Edouard Jeanneret, called LC) had the opportunity while still studying of familiarizing himself with all the endeavours that led to the emergence of the new style. At his art school in La Chaux-de-Fonds reverberations reached him of Art Nouveau (in particular from the École de Nancy) and its search for organic, ornamental forms.

Le Corbusier

Le Corbusier. Dom-Ino system of construction.
1914

Then, in quick succession, he met nearly all the architects who had anything to give him: *Hoffmann in Vienna in 1907, *Garnier at Lyons and *Perret in Paris in 1908, and *Behrens in Berlin in 1910. He worked for a few months for both Perret and Behrens. In addition to his architectural and town planning studies, he was occupied from 1911 to 1912 with questions of mass-production and standardization in the circles of the *Deutscher Werkbund, which he had already been able to investigate under Perret, as far as they concerned the building trade. On extensive trips throughout Europe Le Corbusier, pencil in hand, analysed all possible architectural shapes and their settings from the Parthenon to a farmhouse, and from a Turkish summer house on the Bosphorus to Chartres Cathedral. After eventually settling down in Paris in 1917, he had his decisive encounter with Cubism. If we add that he

was occupied already before 1920 with the industrialization of building not only theoretically but practically, and that he exhibited a complete mastery of his profession in at least one executed design (Villa at La Chaux-de-Fonds, 1916), we shall come to the conclusion that the so-called amateur disposed of a knowledge and experience which no university training could have given him.

His preoccupation with painting, which he has never given up, and the founding, with Ozenfant, of Purism (*Après le Cubisme*, 1918) are far more than a mere episode. In attempting to determine the position of creative thought in the light of Cubism, Le Corbusier developed a theory of aesthetics which he published in the journal *L'Esprit Nouveau* in the form of 'Warnings to Architects'. In these articles, which appeared in 1923 in book form under the title *Vers une architecture*, followed in 1925 by *L'Art décoratif d'aujourd'hui*, *Urbanisme*, Le Corbusier has given the pithiest account of his architectural ideas. He himself demonstrated what he meant, first by models and drawings (Citrohan houses, 1920–2; 'A contemporary city of three million inhabitants', 1922), then by a series of houses (for Ozenfant, Jeanneret, La Roche, Cook, the Bordeaux-Pessac housing estate, 1922–6; Pavillon de l'Esprit Nouveau, 1925; Maison Stein at Garches, two houses at the Weissenhof Exhibition, Stuttgart, Villa Savoye at Poissy, 1927–31). These buildings, projects and writings are of threefold importance:

1. Every stylistic reminiscence is now rigorously removed from the vocabulary of

Le Corbusier. City of 3 million inhabitants. 1922. Project

Le Corbusier. Immeuble-Villa. 1922. Project

form. In the uncompromising reduction of all buildings to the basic geometrical shapes of rectangle, plane surface, cube and cylinder may be recognized a transposition of purist pictorial composition. The architectural means employed are *pilotis* (free-standing columns at ground floor level), continuous strips of fenestration, glass walls, and flat roofs. The polychrome effects which Le Corbusier introduced at Pessac as a town-planning feature can also be traced back to insights gained when painting.

2. These distinctly provocative designs are meant to make clear the radically functional renovation of the house as an instrument of living; as is well known, Le Corbusier speaks of 'machines for living in'. After early studies of a more theoretical nature (Dom-Ino Houses, 1914; Monol Houses), Le Corbusier's investigations resulted in a prototype as early as 1922 (Second Citrohan House), which proved important for later developments. The living area available is newly distributed according to the way that domestic functions are grouped. The living-room runs through two storeys, and all parts of the dwelling are arranged *en suite*. The

house is enlarged by the open space which results from the flat roof garden and the *pilotis* (built at Stuttgart, 1927). Already in the same year, 1922, his project for Immeubles-Villas (multi-storey villas) illustrates the possibility of retaining meaningful living units in the only type of collective dwelling acceptable from the town planning point of view. The argument was supplemented by a full-scale model of such a living cell shown in the Pavillon de l'Esprit Nouveau in 1925. Instead of the ordinary type of furniture, use was made partly of built-in units, partly of standard industrial products chosen for their purist shape.

3. The multi-storey villas belong to that class of novel town planning device by which the structure of present-day metropolitan areas might be adapted to the requirements of modern life. The plan for a 'contemporary city of three million inhabitants' certainly springs from Garnier's *Cité Industrielle* and is also in many ways reminiscent of *Sant'Elia's drawings for the *Città Nuova*, but in essential points differs from both of them. Garnier had thought of a town limited to 35,000 inhabitants, all engaged in industry; Sant' Elia had only sketched highly suggestive but isolated views of the town of tomorrow. Le Corbusier, however, from the outset steered towards the problem of the 'change-over town', as he called it later, a metropolis with diverse functions, which must be

Le Corbusier. Maison Stein. Garches, 1929

Le Corbusier. Maison Suisse. Cité Universitaire. Paris, 1930–2

disentangled. The Plan Voisin for Paris (1925) applies these theoretical studies to the particular case of Paris.

Le Corbusier is mainly concerned in the first instance to establish an orderly relationship between traffic lanes on the one hand and living and working zones on the other. Traffic must be classified, i.e. graded as to whether it is pedestrian or vehicular, through or delivery traffic. The tremendous loss of time occasioned by the incoherence of the present system may be reduced in this way. But 'traffic should not be allowed to develop'—the best way is to reduce distances to a minimum. If a metropolis is to be prevented from spreading out indefinitely, however, it must be built high: for residential areas multi-storey villas set in open parkland, instead of space-consuming, street-extending private houses; super-skyscrapers 1,300 feet apart,

surrounded by gardens, for business districts. This is the only way to unravel the present-day mix-up of traffic, work and living functions and to reduce the metropolis to human dimensions.

Owing to the economic crisis of the thirties, commissions by rich patrons of the arts, who were the main clients of modern architecture in France, were drastically reduced in number. Up to the outbreak of the Second World War, Le Corbusier devoted himself mainly to town planning projects (for Algiers, Nemours (Algeria), Barcelona, Buenos Aires, Montevideo, São Paulo, Zlín, Hellocourt, 'Paris 1937', 'Paris Ilot insalubre no. 6') and to refining the methods which he had only roughly defined: classified traffic lanes (the '7V' system), living units (design for the International Exhibition of 1937) and 'Cartesian' skyscrapers (design for Algiers, 1938). From the start (1927) Le Corbusier took an active part in the work of *CIAM. The *Athens Charter is entirely his idea and was also drawn up by him. His research, limited at first to restoring the urban body to health, was extended to country planning from 1934 onwards. In particular he interested himself in the renewal of production centres, agricultural ('radiating farm' and collective village, 1934) and industrial ('green factory', 1939–40). The synthesis of these ideas he ultimately summarized in 1945 in *Les Trois Etablissements Humains*, a book whose influence is still growing.

In the thirties, Le Corbusier also worked on his projects for monumental, large-scale buildings; in these he demonstrates his mastery in the organization and three-dimensional design of complex building programmes: competition design for the League of Nations Building in Geneva, 1927; plans for a museum with unlimited possibilities for extension (ultimately built in 1952–6 at Ahmedabad and Tokyo); the pensions office at Zurich; the Museum of Modern Art in Paris; a stadium and pageant arena for 100,000 spectators, etc. The only projects actually built were the Centrosoyus in Moscow, 1930; the Salvation Army Hostel and the Maison Suisse at the Cité Universitaire, Paris, 1931–2; and the Ministry of Education at Rio de Janeiro (in collaboration with *Costa, *Niemeyer and others, 1936–45). The ascetic geometry of his vocabulary of form which typified his

Le Corbusier. Unité d'Habitation. Marseilles, 1947–52

early work is enriched by new elements in these buildings and projects. White stucco gives way to an untreated finish (concrete or even stone in the Villa at Les Mathes, 1935). The abstract planary nature of the outer walls is superseded by a sculptural treatment, whose characteristic element is the 'brise-soleil' screen shading the glass wall (Ministry at Rio). This change is also noticeable on the 1938 model of a skyscraper.

Le Corbusier suggested 'Housing and Homes' as a theme for the 1937 International Exhibition, and as the main exhibit a completely furnished living unit, which could be let at the end of the exhibition. The idea to which he had constantly recurred since his multi-storey villas of 1922 was now ready for execution. This was how, after the war, the Unités d'Habitation at Marseilles (1947–52), Nantes-Rezé (1952–7), Berlin (1957) and Briey-la-Forêt (1960) came into existence. Here Le Corbusier's philosophy of domestic architecture seems to have found its final expression: vertical garden cities, which afford every family a maximum of privacy and independence (but also of communal services) combined with the utmost exploitation of space. These monumental structures, subtly proportioned on Le Corbusier's *Modulor system, function impeccably as 'machines for living in' and belong, without any doubt, to the grandest architectural creations of the century. That they have found no imitator so far can only be explained, apart from the prejudice that still continues, by the unadmitted feeling that only Le Corbusier can play with such vast masses (350 flats in eight double-storeys) without being crushed by them.

Le Corbusier. Supreme Court. Chandigarh, 1950–6

Le Corbusier. Project for Algiers Heights, 1942

Le Corbusier. Notre-Dame du Haut. Ronchamp, 1950–4

Le Corbusier. Monastery of La Tourette. Eveux, near Lyons, 1957

The other main projects of the fifties are as monumental as the 'Unités' and as likely to discourage any possible imitators. The capitol of Chandigarh (from 1950) is an approximately lyrical enhancement for the new metropolis of the State of Punjab of the idea for a community centre which Le Corbusier had worked out for the small town of St Dié in 1945–6. The symbolic significance of the composition, stressed by the dramatic treatment of the individual buildings, has been combined with astonishing ease into a harmonious whole with the practical functions that the law courts and the ministries have to fulfil, while making use of whatever local building resources were available. In the development and circulation plans for the city itself, Le Corbusier was able for the first time to realize his theories on zoning and traffic separation, practically without restriction. The grid-type layout, which some critics beforehand had called inhuman, has in practice proved excellent.

The pilgrimage church of Notre-Dame du Haut at Ronchamp (1950–4) strikes one at first as a wilful piece of sculpture, as

Le Corbusier. Maisons Jaoul. Neuilly, 1954–6

unsuitable for the fulfilment of any function as for instance F. L. *Wright's spiral shape for the Guggenheim Museum, built at roughly the same time. On closer examination, however, it proves to be an organism which (as previously with the living unit, the museum, the multi-storey offices, or even the farm) had been newly thought out in all its details and consequently completely altered in outward appearance. That the curved surfaces of Ronchamp were not just an impulse to which Le Corbusier had succumbed when he was confronted for the first time with a religious theme, has been proved by the Dominican novitiate monastery of La Tourette, at Eveux near Lyons (1957). The rectangle to which Le Corbusier had dedicated the 'Poème de l'angle droit' in 1955, is now only reserved for what Le Corbusier calls 'phénomènes d'espace indicible', 'phenomena of ineffable space', which he regards as the highest perfection in architecture. Such ideas, in which his work has always abounded, give even his secular buildings of the fifties an unforgettable, special note,

whether they are 'Unités', museums, the Brazilian House at the Paris Cité Universitaire or smaller intimate buildings such as the Textile Industry Club, Shodhan House at Ahmedabad, and the Maisons Jaoul at Neuilly, or projects in which Le Corbusier's rich experience of architectural space has proved itself on difficult subjects such as the model for a multi-storey hotel at the Gare d'Orsay, Paris, or the design for a college building at Harvard (1961).

However diverse the shapes may be that Le Corbusier has employed—whether in the possibly most perfect example from his first creative period, the Villa Savoye at Poissy, or later at Ronchamp or Chandigarh, his architectural work nevertheless displays an amazing unity. It can only be called 'classical', if this is taken to mean not a repertoire of forms and massing, but a sense of the right form. The traditional modules and orders represented a harmonious link between the human body and the dimensions of ancient buildings and articles of use. In our contemporary civilization, however, whose towns, machines and equipment create completely new dimensions of space and time, they are no longer adequate. Their endless repetition is stifling, their extension emphatic and false. By a completely new, all-embracing system of measurement, by abandoning the scale imposed through dividing an elevation into storeys, but even more by an unprecedently sure instinct for proportion Le Corbusier has made his buildings examples of classical massing which contrasts sharply with the inhuman disorder of so many pseudo-modern buildings. Le Corbusier is the purest exponent of the French tradition in building, in whose noblest creations logic and lyric become one in the service of mankind.

Bibliography: Le Corbusier, *Oeuvre complète*, 1910–57, at present 6 volumes, Zurich 1929 ff.; Le Corbusier, *Mon Oeuvre*, Paris 1960; Maximilien Gauthier, *Le Corbusier*, New York 1945; Stamo Papadaki, *Le Corbusier*, New York 1948; J. Alazard, *Le Corbusier*, Florence and Paris 1950; Anton Henze, *Le Corbusier*, Berlin 1957; Françoise Choay, *Le Corbusier*, New York 1958; Boesiger/Girsberger (editors), *Le Corbusier, 1910–60*, Zurich and Stuttgart 1960.

MAURICE BESSET

Lescaze, William, b. Geneva 1896. Pupil of Karl *Moser. Architect of the Philadelphia Savings Fund Society Building (1932) in collaboration with George *Howe.

Lewerentz, Sigurd, b. Bjärträ near Sundsvall, Sweden 1885. After graduating from Göteborg Technical College (1908), he lived in Germany. Residential buildings and housing estates. Crematorium at Malmö (1943), church at Skarpnäck near Stockholm (1960).

Lissitzky, Eliezer (El) Markovich, b. Polshinotz near Smolensk 1890, d. Moscow 1941 (or 1947). Studied at Darmstadt Technical College, 1909–14. Teacher at Moscow Academy, 1921. Emigrated to Germany and Switzerland, back in Russia 1928. Collaborated with the avant-garde of Central European architects (van *Doesburg, *Mies van der Rohe) and was a co-founder of *Constructivism. At the same time as *Tatlin's Memorial to the Third International, Lissitzky's office designed a speaker's platform (1920) in the form of a sloping steel structure of great expressiveness. In 1924, together with Mart Stam, he designed the 'Cloud Props' project, an extensively cantilevered office block on immense piers.

Lods, Marcel, b. Paris 1891. Collaborated with Eugène *Beaudouin. Designed buildings for the French Ministries of Education and War. Housing estate at Marly-le-Roi near Paris (with Honegger and Beuté), buildings in Guinea.

Loos, Adolf, b. Brno 1870, d. Vienna 1933. A keen admirer both of vernacular and Roman architecture, Adolf Loos was a great pioneer of the modern movement in Europe, and, at the beginning of the 20th century, one of the first architects to react against the decorative trends of *Art Nouveau.
Loos was the son of a stone-cutter. He attended classes at Reichenberg Polytechnic before studying architecture at Dresden technical college. On the conclusion of his studies he was anxious to broaden his outlook and in 1893 made a journey to the United States; he remained in America for three years, working by turn as a mason, a floor-layer and even as a dish-washer. During this time he was able to observe the innovations made by the young School of *Chicago: the expressive steel-frame structures Le Baron *Jenney introduced for office buildings, the austere blocks of *Burnham and *Root, and the uncompromising severity which *Sullivan was displaying in his famous Guaranty Building (Buffalo, 1894–5). Sullivan it was who, after providing American architecture with an original and personal style of floral surface decoration, wrote in 1892 in an article entitled 'Ornament in Architecture': 'It would be greatly for our esthetic good if we should refrain entirely from the use of ornament for a period of years, in order that our thought might concentrate acutely upon the production of buildings well formed and comely in the nude.'
This attitude was to provide Loos with a conception of major significance for his work. On his return to Europe in 1896, he settled in Vienna, a cosmopolitan centre with a culture typified by elegance of thought and sophisticated manners. In this milieu, Loos showed himself forthwith an

Adolf Loos. Kärntner Bar. Vienna, 1907

ardent and aggressive doctrinarian. In a first series of articles published chiefly in the *Neue Freie Presse* between 1897 and 1898, he took up arms against the stylistic and aestheticizing tendencies preached by the painter Klimt and the architects *Olbrich and *Hoffmann to the Wiener Sezession, which they had founded in 1897. Basing himself partly on Sullivan's purist argument, and partly on the functionalist doctrine which Otto *Wagner had expounded to the Vienna Academy in 1894, Loos set out to show that the type of ornament inculcated by Art Nouveau is unworthy of our culture; that a work divested of ornament is symbolic of pure and lucid thought and a high degree of civilization; that good form must find its beauty in the degree of usefulness it expresses, and in the indissoluble unity of its parts; and that consequently all ornamentation must be systematically rejected.

Loos was to resume and develop this thesis in a major essay published in 1908 entitled 'Ornament und Verbrechen' ('Ornament and Crime'). To spread his theories, he had founded a Free School of Architecture in 1906. His rationalist philosophy underlies his rare and very puritanical architectural works: the Villa Karma (Montreux, 1904); Steiner house (Vienna, 1910), one of the first private houses to be built in reinforced concrete, and a turning point in the history of modern architecture (reshaping of plan, new method of condensing and articulating internal space, purity of the straight line, flat roof, horizontal fenestration, dominance of solids, cubic style); the imposing Goldman commercial block on the Michaelerplatz (Vienna, 1910), where the arrangement of levels foretells the complete expression of the 'plan of volumes' achieved by the Rufer house (Vienna, 1922).

From 1920 to 1922 Loos was in charge of municipal housing in Vienna, where he drew up some bold development schemes, such as the Heuberg model estate. In 1923 he settled in Paris, where he established contact with the leading figures of the *Esprit Nouveau*. He frequented Dadaïst circles and built a house for Tristan Tzara (1926). Returning to Vienna in 1928, he built the Moller house at Pötzleinsdorf; the Khuner house at Payerbach (1930); and also in 1930, his finest work, the Müller house in Prague.

Adolf Loos. Maison Tristan Tzara. Paris, 1926

Bibliography: Adolf Loos, *Ins Leere gesprochen, 1897–1900*, Paris 1921; 2nd edition, Innsbruck 1932; Adolf Loos, *Trotzdem, 1900–1930*, Innsbruck 1931; Heinrich Kulka, *Adolf Loos*, Vienna 1931; Franz Glück, *Adolf Loos*, Paris 1931; Ludwig Münz, *Adolf Loos*, Milan 1956.

                                    ROBERT L. DELEVOY

Luckhardt, Hans and Wassili. Wassili Luckhardt b. Berlin 1889. Hans Luckhardt b. Berlin 1890, d. Bad Wiessee 1954. Their first designs were in the Berlin *Expressionist style, characterized by the precision of their rectangles (Schorlemer Allee experimental estate, Berlin, 1927; private houses at Rupenhorn, Berlin, 1928) or dynamically curved blocks divided up by continuous strips of fenestration (projects for the new layout of the Alexanderplatz, Berlin, 1929). Berlin Pavilion at the Constructa Exhibition, Hanover (1951); Regional Government Offices, Munich (1957).

Bibliography: Udo Kultermann, *Wassili und Hans Luckhardt, Bauten und Entwürfe*, Tübingen 1958.

Lundy, Victor A., b. Los Angeles 1921. Studied at Harvard under *Gropius. Timber churches with large curved roofs (First Unitarian Church at Westport, Connecticut, 1961), Motel with reinforced concrete awnings at different heights (Warm Mineral Springs Inn at Venice, Fla., 1958). Exhibition pavilion of the US Atomic Energy Commission, a 'pneumatic' structure (1962).

Lurçat, André, b. Paris 1892. His houses typify the style of the late twenties and early thirties in France (Villa Hefferlin at Ville D'Avray, 1931–2). School at Villejuif (1931–3).
Bibliography: André Lurçat, *Oeuvres Récentes I*, Paris 1961.

Lyons, Eric Alfred, b. 1912. Architect whose schemes have set a new standard for private-enterprise housing in *Great Britain, where he controls the planning and landscaping of entire estates. His layouts feature simple buildings that display an eye for textures, and the highly repetitive use of structural elements and equipment in dispositions which largely avoid streets by creating courtyards and varying patterns of 'external enclosures'; this he considers to be the secret of urbanity. Flats at Ham Common, near Richmond; at Blackheath; and West Hill, Highgate (for the Soviet Trade Delegation). Houses, flats and maisonettes at Cambridge; housing for old people at Bognor Regis, with certain shared accommodation.

Lyons, Israel and Ellis. Edward Douglas Lyons, Lawrence Israel, Thomas Bickerstaff Harper Ellis. Partnership that has developed a powerful and expressive style in reinforced concrete: Peckham Comprehensive School (reinforced concrete frame); Wolfson Institute, London University; theatre workshops for the Old Vic Company, with constant expression of function by exposed reinforced concrete frame, inside and out; Trescobeas Secondary Modern School, Falmouth; Finchley Town Hall.

Mackintosh, Charles Rennie, b. Glasgow 1868, d. London 1928. Mackintosh, a resolute adversary of historic revivalism, was one of the most brilliant precursors of 20th-century rationalist architecture. As leader of the *Art Nouveau movement in Great Britain this Scottish architect made, a contribution of fundamental importance in reappraising the rôle of function in building, expressed via a style based on ancient Celtic ornament and the cultural traditions of Japan.

When he was barely sixteen, Mackintosh entered John Hutchinson's office as an articled pupil; from 1885 he attended evening classes at the Glasgow School of Art. In 1889 he was engaged as a draughtsman in the building firm of J. Honeyman and Keppie, where he met the architect J. Herbert McNair, his future brother-in-law. He stayed with the firm until 1913, having become a partner in 1904. In 1890 he was awarded a scholarship which enabled him to make a study-tour in France and Italy. His first executed work, the corner tower of the Glasgow Herald Building (1894), reveals Mackintosh as about to emancipate himself from academic trammels. He participated (December 1895) in the opening exhibition of the Maison de l'Art Nouveau in Paris with a number of posters which already clearly displayed the linear symbolic style of the Glasgow School. In 1897, at the age of twenty-nine, he won the competition for an extension to the Glasgow School of Art. These buildings were erected between 1898 and 1909 and made a profound impression on the Continent at the time. In 1898 he drew up a bold scheme for a concert hall on a circular plan, covered by a parabolic dome, which was not however premiated at the Glasgow Exhibition of 1901.

At the same time Mackintosh was interested in the decorative arts and in furniture. The pieces he designed are notable for their character, which is at once exquisite and austere, slender and taut, based on the straight line and the right angle, and set off in light tones (ivory). The upswing of their slim parallels elongates their forms beyond any functional requirement, as Mackintosh's aesthetic fancy turns to mannerism. This is the style he adopted when commissioned in 1897 to design the furniture and decorations for Cranston's chain of tea-rooms. The Buchanan Street Tea-room (1897–8) illustrates the curvilinear style of this first period (1894–1900) most completely: the walls are dominated by two-dimensional figures, tall and graceful, enclosed within a network of vertical

Charles Rennie Mackintosh. Library of the
Glasgow School of Art, 1907–9. Reading room

Charles Rennie Mackintosh. Library of the
Glasgow School of Art, 1907–9

lines and entwined by circular waves that
evoke the manner of Klimt. This style first
became known on the Continent through
the illustrations published in 1897 by *The
Studio*, followed the year after by the
showing of a suite of furniture at Munich,
and in particular by the contribution
Mackintosh sent to the annual exhibition
of the Wiener Sezession in 1900. The
furniture and panels he showed at Vienna
emphasize the close links between the
Scottish trends and the Viennese School.
In the same year Mackintosh had married
a former student of the Glasgow School of
Art, Margaret Macdonald, an interior
decorator and metalworker, whose sister
Frances had married the architect Herbert
McNair in 1899. These ties helped to knit
together more closely a little group united
since 1890 by similar professional and
aesthetic interests, which had already won
an international reputation under the name
of The Four. It was as the leader of this
group that Mackintosh entered a competition in 1901, organized under the auspices of the *Zeitschrift für Innendekoration*
of Darmstadt by its editor, A. Koch. The
subject was a house for a connoisseur,
including its interior decoration. Mackintosh was awarded second prize. His scheme
envisaged a revolutionary use of space, with
an arrangement of large, simple volumes
distinctly cubic in appearance, stripped, in
elevation, of any kind of ornament or
moulding, and marked by an asymmetrical
predominance of solids over voids: it
was a harbinger of the purist style of
*Loos.
If the country houses Mackintosh built in
the environs of Glasgow (Windy Hill at
Kilmacolm, 1899–1901; Hill House at
Helensburgh, 1902–3) still show external
stylistic affinities with the Scottish baronial
tradition (angle towers with conical caps,

huge double-pitch roofs, massive chimneys), their internal layouts evince great boldness in the handling of space. The hall of Hill House (1903) is a masterpiece where light, colour, openwork partitions, cage-type lamps and light furniture combine in a spatio-dynamic composition that anticipates Russian *Constructivism and Dutch *Stijl.

The superb library which Mackintosh built as an addition to the Glasgow School of Art (1907–9) shows similar stylistic trends. The straight line reigns supreme, and the subtle arrangement of horizontal beams and rectangular pillars which support the galleries punctuate space in a manner hitherto unknown, raising architecture to the level of poetic abstraction. Similar principles are at work, with equal effect, in Mackintosh's last masterpiece, the Cranston Tea-room in Ingram Street (1907–11). Apart from this, in his short architectural career, the Scottish Pavilion

Charles Rennie Mackintosh. Glasgow School of Art, 1898–1909

at the Turin Exhibition of 1902 may be noted, which Mackintosh built and furnished.

He moved to London in 1913, where his activities were limited to designing furniture and printed fabrics. In 1920 he retired to Port-Vendres to devote himself exclusively to water-colour painting.

Bibliography: Hermann Muthesius, *Haus eines Kunstfreundes*, Darmstadt 1902; Nikolaus Pevsner, *Ch. R. Mackintosh*, Milan 1950; Thomas Howarth, *Charles Rennie Mackintosh and the Modern Movement*, London 1952.

ROBERT L. DELEVOY

Maekawa, Kunio, b. Niigata-shi, Japan 1905. Studied at Tokyo University; worked for *Le Corbusier; on his own since 1935. Maekawa's investigations into the structural possibilities of reinforced concrete (stimulated by Pier Luigi *Nervi) led to buildings in a sculptural idiom: Town Hall at Fukushima (1958), Community Centre at Setagaya (1959). His Harumi flats in Tokyo (1957) carry over Japanese domestic traditions into the dimensions of a modern skyscraper. Maekawa has had a considerable influence on the younger Japanese architects; Kenzo *Tange joined him on finishing his studies.

Maillart, Robert, b. Berne 1872, d. Geneva 1940. After studying from 1890 to 1894 at Zurich Technical College (ETH), where he graduated as structural engineer, Maillart worked in various engineering offices until he became an independent partner in the building firm of Maillart and Co., Zurich, in 1902. In 1911 he was appointed a lecturer at Zurich Technical College. In 1912 he left Switzerland to build in Russia, whence he returned penniless after the Revolution. In 1919 he started an engineering office in Geneva followed in 1924 by others in Berne and Zurich. Maillart has not only built bridges but has also designed the structural details for a large number of multi-storey buildings. The intrinsic character of his constructions shows up particularly clearly, however, in his bridges: these are the outcome of his ability to think through a problem in its entirety and to look for the specific solution to each specific instance, based on his own specially developed methods of construction. In 1901, Maillart built the first of his forty or so reinforced concrete bridges at Zuoz in the Engadine. It already displays some of the essential features of that concept of his which does away with the old principle of separation between the functions of bearing and loading. All parts of a bridge are integrated in their structural function; the roadway is no longer a load carried by the bridge vaults but is incorporated as a structure element. Economy of means, structural strength and harmonious balance make Maillart's bridges works of art to the extent that anything may be considered as art which is perfect of its kind.

Maillart's most important bridges are those built according to the principle he developed of the triply articulated box girder; they include the Rhine bridge at Tavanasa (1905, destroyed 1927) and the Salginatobel bridge near Schiers (1929–30, 295 feet long), both in Graubünden; the Rossgraben bridge near Schwarzenburg in the Canton of Berne (1932, 269 feet long); the Arve bridge near Versey, Geneva (1936); and the overpass between Altendorf and Lachen, Canton Schwyz (1940), the last project personally supervised by Maillart.

Robert Maillart. Bridge over the river Thur at Felsegg, 1933

Robert Maillart and Hans Leuzinger. Cement Pavilion at the Swiss Provinces Exhibition. Zurich, 1939

Another of his structural systems was the so-called stiffened bar arch which he used among others on the following: the Val Tschiel bridge (1925), and the curved Landquart railway bridge at Klosters (1930), both also in Graubünden; the Schwandbach bridge between Hinterfultigen and Schönentannen in the Canton of Berne (1933), also on a curve; and finally the Aire bridge at Lancy, Geneva, with an arch-span of 167 feet, designed in 1938 and built 1952–4. A number of his boldest bridge designs were never carried out.

Among the multi-storey buildings for whose architectural form Maillart's contribution was essentially responsible, the following may be mentioned: the entrance hall of a warehouse at Chiasso (1924–5) and the barrel-vaulted Cement Pavilion at the Swiss Provinces Exhibition, Zurich, 1939, a show building of the Swiss cement industry. His most important invention in the field of high structures was made in 1908 with mushroom slab construction, which he used for the first time on a large scale in 1910. In this method, columns, beams and floors are no longer treated as separate units as in timber or steel structures, but the

column passes organically into the beamless floor slab. Here again, a structural system that is economical in the use of materials permits flexibility in application and helps to ensure a light and elegant appearance.
Bibliography: Max Bill, *Robert Maillart*, Zurich 1949; 3rd edition 1962.

MARGIT STABER

Malevich, Kasimir, b. Kiev 1878, d. Leningrad 1935. In his early days, he was strongly influenced by the paintings of the Post-Impressionists, the Fauves, and later the Cubists. Transition to geometric (*Suprematist) painting between 1913 and 1915. His 'suprematist architectures' are architectural sculptures made of wood, in which he investigates the interrelationship of simple cubes. Visited the *Bauhaus (1927).

Mallet-Stevens, Robert, b. Paris 1886, d. 1945. Exponent of French avant-garde architecture in the late twenties and early thirties. His buildings, in particular private houses, are often characterized by over-emphasis of cubic form.

Markelius, Sven, b. Stockholm 1889. Graduated in 1913 from Stockholm Technical College and from the Academy of Fine Arts in 1915. Influenced by *Le Corbusier. Flats and offices, concert hall at Hälsingborg (1932). First won international recognition with his Swedish Pavilion at the World Fair in New York (1939). Responsible for the establishment of the satellite town of Vällingby near Stockholm (commenced 1953) in his capacity as head of the town-planning department.

Matthew, Robert Hogg, b. Edinburgh 1906. Studied at Edinburgh College of Art School of Architecture. From 1946 to 1953, he was architect to the London County Council, during which period his department emerged as one of the most progressive forces in the architecture of *Great Britain, and his Royal Festival Hall (1950) was acclaimed as the first modern building to achieve a feeling of monumentality. Appointed Professor of Architecture at Edinburgh University, 1953; in private practice with Stirrat Johnson-Marshall since 1957. University buildings for Dundee, Aberdeen and Edinburgh; Turnhouse Airport, Edinburgh, 1956; New Zealand

House, Haymarket, London; seventeen-storey flats in the Gorbals, Glasgow; power station at Killin; Commonwealth Institute in Holland Park, London, with an ingeniously planned exhibition layout under a hyperbolic paraboloid roof. Far-reaching town- and country-planning proposals for the Government of Northern Ireland, 1963.

May, Ernst, b. Frankfurt 1886. Studied at Munich Technical College under Thiersch and *Fischer. Was City Architect at Frankfurt am Main between 1925 and 1930 (suburban development with extensive rationalization of building processes). In Russia (1930–4), later practised in East Africa. After the war served as town planner for several German towns.
Bibliography: J. Bueckschmitt, *Ernst May, Bauten und Planungen*, Stuttgart, in preparation.

Maybeck, Bernard Ralph, b. New York 1862, d. Berkeley, Calif. 1957. Studied at the École des Beaux-Arts in Paris. Was much impressed by the restoration work of *Viollet-le-Duc. Eclectic, especially Far Eastern motifs, which always played an important part on the west coast of America, were combined by him with structural experiments such as the employment of prefabricated units (Christian Science Church, Berkeley, 1910). Private houses, clubs. Fine Arts Building, San Francisco (1915) in neoclassic style with romantic trappings.

Mendelsohn, Erich, b. Allenstein, East Prussia 1887, d. San Francisco 1953. Among the architects of the 20th century who have used the new methods of construction made possible by steel and concrete with originality and imagination and have been successful in imparting to their buildings the quality of organic unity Erich Mendelsohn must hold a notable place. He received his architectural training at Berlin and Munich. In 1912 he started practice and for the first two years was engaged chiefly in stage designing, painting, and on projects for various buildings. During this period he became interested in the *Expressionist movement, and its influence can be seen in some of his early work. During the First World War he served in the German army, first on the Russian front and later on the Western front.

Erich Mendelsohn. Synagogue. Cleveland, Ohio, 1946–52. Project

Shortly after the war he held an exhibition in Berlin of architectural sketches which attracted considerable attention. They were designs of a wide variety of buildings: factories, grain elevators, observatories, religious buildings, in which steel and concrete were used expressively and in which the purpose of the building was suggested by the symbolism of its forms, thereby showing the influence of Expressionism.

One of his first buildings was the Einstein Observatory at Potsdam (1920) which caused a sensation. This was followed by a very large number of buildings that he designed during the twenties, including several departmental stores such as the Petersdorff Store at Breslau (1927), and the Schocken Stores at Stuttgart (1927) and Chemnitz (1928); a group of buildings adjoining Kurfürstendamm which included a cinema with a dramatic interior with horizontal emphasis (1928); and the Columbus House (1931), a large block of offices and shops in the Potsdamerplatz, which together with the Schocken Store at Chemnitz represent Mendelsohn's best work in Germany. The façades of both have long bands of fenestration alternating with opaque bands, and the whole effect is one of lightness combined with grandeur, the effect of lightness being achieved by a cantilevering of the walls beyond the structural supports.

Owing to the racial persecution which accompanied the rise to power of the

Erich Mendelsohn. Schocken Department Store. Stuttgart, 1927. Project

National Socialist Party, Mendelsohn left his native land in March 1933 and went first to Brussels, and then to London, where he began practice in partnership with Serge Chermayeff in the summer of that year. For the next six years Mendelsohn divided his practice between England and Palestine. His principal work in England was the now famous De la Warr Pavilion, Bexhill (1934). His work in Palestine was more considerable and included two large hospitals, that at Haifa (1937) and the University Medical Centre on Mount Scopus, Jerusalem (1937–9); the Palestine Bank, Jerusalem (1938); several large houses, a college and library.

In 1941 Mendelsohn went to America, and after the war he started practice in 1945 in San Francisco. His principal work in America was the Maimonides Hospital in San Francisco (1946) and a series of large synagogues and community centres, some of which remained only projects. Those completed are at St Louis, Missouri (1946–50); Cleveland, Ohio (1946–52), which includes a large dome 100 feet in

Erich Mendelsohn. Schocken, later Merkur, Department Store. Stuttgart, 1927

Erich Mendelsohn. Columbus House. Berlin, 1931

diameter; Grand Rapids, Michigan (1948–52); and St Paul, Minnesota (1950–4).

Mendelsohn's work was characterized by a sympathetic and original use of materials, steel, concrete and glass, and by an expression of purpose through the forms of his building, seen in such works as the Observatory at Potsdam, the departmental stores in Germany, the Bexhill Pavilion, and the hospitals in Palestine. His designs were always actuated by the principles of organic unity, so that each part by its character denotes its relation to the whole, and each building is closely wedded to its site. The synagogue at Cleveland, where the forms of the building harmonize so well with the contours of the undulating site, is a notable example.

Bibliography: Mario Federico Roggero, *Il contributo di Mendelsohn alla evoluzione dell'architettura moderna*, Milan 1952; Bruno Zevi, 'Eric Mendelsohn', in *Metron*, Nos. 49–50, Rome 1954; Arnold Whittick, *Eric Mendelsohn*, London 1956, New York 1956, Bologna 1960.

ARNOLD WHITTICK

Messel, Alfred, b. Darmstadt 1853, d. Berlin 1909. Flats and commercial buildings, in particular department stores (Wertheim department store in Berlin, 1896), with extensive use of glass on façades and basically functional design.

Erich Mendelsohn. De la Warr Pavilion. Bexhill, 1934

Erich Mendelsohn. House on Pacific Heights. San Francisco, 1950–1

Enrique del Moral. 'La Merced' Market Hall. Mexico City, 1957

Pedro Ramírez Vázquez and Rafael Mijares. Ministry of Labour and Social Welfare. Mexico City, 1953

Mexico. Mexico was the first of the Latin-American countries to come to terms with the claims of the *International Style. The revolt against the senseless imitation of inherited building forms in the mid-twenties, i.e. a decade before the building of the Ministry of Education at Rio de Janeiro, found expression first in the teaching of the architect José *Villagrán García and in his early works and those of his pupils Legorreta, *O'Gorman, de la Mora and Yáñez. The hospitals, houses and schools designed by this group took the Functionalism of *Le Corbusier's *Vers une architecture* literally, and thus presented the starkest contrast to the popular love of decoration. During the two subsequent decades, modern architecture made uninterrupted progress in Mexico. The economic advantages of the purism that went hand in hand with the new structural methods, account for only a part of its rapid success. In the main it was due to the fact that the

Juan O'Gorman, Gustavo Saavedra and Juan Martínez de Velasco. University Library. Mexico City, 1952

government held the modern style to be an adequate expression of its progressive administration and social building programme, and used it for numerous buildings, thus helping it to secure general approval. At the beginning of the fifties this development reached its peak in the building of the University City (to a layout by Mario Pani and Enrique del Moral) for 20,000 students, a number which has doubled in ten years. With the collaboration of approximately one hundred young architects and engineers, the extensive complex was finished in three years.

Mexico's building tradition, which in contrast to the *USA has strong roots in the centuries before and after its conquest by Europeans, has left its mark on the modern architecture of the country. In the University City this influence is immediately obvious in the extraordinary dimensions of its open spaces and in the ever-recurring passion for decoration. In the name of integrating art and architecture, the restraint of the last twenty years was abandoned and all available surfaces were covered with murals, mosaics and reliefs in an idiosyncratic social-realist style. In some cases, as for instance the main library (Juan O'Gorman) and the stadium (Diego Rivera), this kind of façade decoration may be considered successful. But its unfettered use, as for example on the Ministry of Transport

building, has reduced this tendency to the absurd.

In the capital today, offices and hotels with *curtain walls reign supreme in the North American manner (architects: Alvarez, Marcos, Kaspé, Sordo Madaleno, Villagrán García and others). State-backed housing schemes are currently being promoted in increasing measure, and large, integrated complexes—whole districts even of apartment houses—are being built (architects: Felix Sánchez, Alejandro Prieto, Mario Pani). Private houses have a more distinctive personality, especially those in the new suburb of Pedregal, built on a foundation of lava in the southern part of Mexico City (architects: Barragán, Cetto, Greenham, Artigas, Attolini Lack, Rosen, Castañedo and others).

Mexico's contribution of the greatest significance to modern architecture lies in the most recent development of shell vaulting by *Candela. Often, in collaboration with other architects, he has built factories, warehouses, filling-stations, market halls, pavilions, restaurants and churches in free organic shapes, from which a new sculptural quality emerges. It was with similar intentions, based however not so much on structure as on a mannerist attempt to broaden the frontiers of architecture, that the sculptor Goeritz fashioned his 'emotional' casing for the Eco nightclub (1953) and the group of non-functional towers at the entrance to a satellite town under construction (1958). The painter-architect

Juan O'Gorman. O'Gorman House. San Angel, 1956

Juan O'Gorman peopled his fantastic dream cave inside and out with creations made of coloured stones and seashells.

The school building programme of the present government, which will take till 1970 to complete, deserves the international regard which was given it at the XII Triennale at Milan. Its essential core is a school unit made up of prefabricated parts by the architect Ramírez Vázquez and his collaborators, which solves the urgent problem of Mexican village schools both economically and functionally.

Bibliography: I. E. Myers, *Mexico's Modern Architecture*, New York 1952; Henry-Russell Hitchcock, *Latin-American Architecture since 1945*, New York 1955; Max Cetto, *Moderne Architektur in Mexico*, Stuttgart 1960.

MAX CETTO

Meyer, Adolf, b. Mechernich, Eifel 1881, d. on the island of Baltrum, in the North Sea 1929. Trained as a cabinet-maker. Attended the Art School at Düsseldorf and worked as an architect with *Behrens and Bruno Paul. He taught at the *Bauhaus from 1919 to 1925 and worked as city architect in Frankfurt from 1926 to 1929. Meyer was a collaborator of *Gropius (Fagus Works at Alfeld, 1911, and Jena Municipal Theatre, 1925), then flats, schools, the planetarium of the Zeiss Works in Jena (1925–6), and municipal buildings in Frankfurt.

Meyer, Hannes, b. Basle 1889, d. Crocifisso di Savosa, Switzerland 1954. Appointed lecturer and studio master at the *Bauhaus, Dessau, and succeeded *Gropius as director (1928–30). Competed (with Hans Wittwer) for the League of Nations Building, Geneva (1927); German Trades Union School at Bernau (1928–30), a school laid out in separate blocks. Worked in the Soviet Union from 1930 to 1936, then in Switzerland; from 1939 to 1949 in Mexico. Meyer rejected architecture that depended on aesthetic principles of form: 'Architecture is not the individual, emotional activity of an artist. Building is a collective activity.'

Michelucci, Giovanni, b. Pistoia 1891. Took his architect's diploma at Florence in 1914. Joint architect of the S. Maria Novella Station at Florence (1933–6). Savings Bank, Florence (1953).

Hannes Meyer and Hans Wittwer. League of Nations Building, Geneva, 1927. Project

Mies van der Rohe, Ludwig, b. Aachen (Aix-la-Chapelle) 1886. Ludwig Mies van der Rohe, German-American architect, is generally acknowledged as one of the four most influential architects working during the first half of the 20th century—the others being Frank Lloyd *Wright, *Le Corbusier, and Walter *Gropius. He was born Ludwig Mies, later compounding his surname with that of his mother. Without formal training as an architect, his initiation into building and the superb craftsmanship for which his architecture is famous, came initially from his father, who was a master mason and the proprietor of a stone-cutting shop. Mies learned to draw as a designer for stucco decoration. In 1905 he went to Berlin where he worked briefly for a minor architect who specialized in wooden structures. Better to master this material, he apprenticed himself for two years to Bruno Paul, a leading furniture designer. In 1907 Mies set up briefly on his own as an architect, but the following year he joined Peter *Behrens, at the time the most creative architect in Germany. While Mies worked in the office, Walter Gropius was among the chief designers, and Le Corbusier passed a few months there.

The three years which Mies spent with Behrens (until 1911) provided his most valuable training. In a sense Behrens's career anticipates Mies's. On the one hand, as the designer for the Allgemeine Elektricitäts Gesellschaft (AEG), Behrens not only designed the factory buildings of the German electrical combine but its products as well. More than any other architect of his generation, he therefore anticipated the ideal of the architect as a comprehensive designer for the modern industrial society. Behrens's product design in metal reinforced the training which Mies had received in cabinet making from Paul, while both contributed to Mies's achievement in furniture design. Moreover, Behrens's Turbine Factory in Berlin (1909), with its bold exposure of the metal structural frame infilled with glass, is astonishingly prophetic of Mies's much later development of an architecture austerely dependent on the naked metal skeleton. But Behrens's factory production represented one aspect only of his *œuvre*. He also brought the neoclassicism of Karl

Ludwig Mies van der Rohe

Mies van der Rohe. Kröller House. The Hague, 1912. Project

Mies van der Rohe. Glass skyscraper. 1920–1.
Project

Friedrich *Schinkel to his architecture—
especially to his monumental and domestic
commissions, although Schinkelesque neoclassicism occasionally appears in the
severe masonry piers and simplified pedi-
ments of some of his factories as well. To
create a modern architecture with a neoclassical severity of means, purity of form,
perfection of proportions, elegance of detail
and dignity of expression is the underlying
preoccupation of Mies's career. For this
ideal he owed much to the imperfect
synthesis of industrialism and neoclassicism in Behrens's work.

Initially, Mies was more overtly influenced
by the neoclassical rather than by the
industrial aspects of Behrens's work, in
large part perhaps because he had served
as the supervisor of construction for one
of Behrens's most monumentally neoclassical edifices, the German Embassy in
St Petersburg (1911–12). Leaving Behrens
in 1911, Mies designed several houses in
a neo-Schinkelesque style akin to Behrens's
work. The most notable design of the
group (and superior to the neoclassicism
of his mentor) was a projected house and

gallery for Mme H. E. L. J. Kröller (1912),
the owner of the famed Kröller-Müller
Collection. This went as far as a full-scale
mock-up of the house in canvas and wood,
built on the site at The Hague. For the
Kröller commission, Mies went to Holland.
There he came to know the work and
philosophy of Hendrik Petrus *Berlage,
who was the Dutch counterpart to Behrens.
Where Behrens was primarily concerned
with form, however, Berlage derived his
architectural philosophy from the 19th-
century moralistic theory of the 'honest'
expression of structure and materials,
which was Gothic rather than neoclassical
in inspiration. Taken together, Behrens's
emphasis on neoclassical form, Berlage's
on revealed structure and materials, and
their joint desire for a new architecture
somehow expressive of modern conditions,
might be said to stake out the territory
which Mies would explore.

His romantic neoclassicism continued up
to the war. After this interruption to his

Mies van der Rohe. Reinforced concrete office
building. 1922. Project

career, there was, in 1919, one last post-
war project in the Schinkelesque vein.
Whereupon Mies's career in modern architecture was abruptly launched in a series of
projects from 1919 to 1924 which are
astonishingly varied and original. They
reflect the sense of liberation in post-war
Berlin which suddenly felt the impact of
native *Expressionism, of De *Stijl from
Holland, of *Constructivism and *Suprematism from Russia. Mies was active in
this ferment, not only as a designer, but as
a propagandist too. He was among the

Mies van der Rohe. Memorial to Karl Liebknecht and Rosa Luxemburg. Berlin, 1926

founders of the magazine *G* (for *Gestaltung*, or creative force) which was devoted to modern art. He joined the *Novembergruppe*. Founded in 1918, and named after the month of the Republican Revolution, this organization too publicized the modern movement. Mies directed the architectural section from 1921 until 1925. It was principally in the annual exhibitions of the *Novembergruppe* that his early modern projects appeared.

In two glass skyscrapers, the first (1919) of triangular forms, the second (1920–1) of curved free forms, Mies sought to dramatize the reflective qualities of glass in

Mies van der Rohe. Wolf House. Guben, 1926

faceted shapes. In fact, the free form curvature of the second of these skyscrapers was specifically determined by the shape which produced the greatest play of light over the building. A project for a reinforced concrete office building (1922) was even more prophetic. Cantilevered slabs closed by a parapet permitted continuous inset window bands with the lightest of metal mullions. Although not widely known until much later, this project, among the first ribbon window designs, uses the ribbon motif so logically and purely that, as a consummate expression of what became a familiar element in modern architecture, it has remained unsurpassed. The initial series of projects is concluded by two houses. One, that of 1923 for a brick country house, uses De Stijl principles. Brick panels in slab, L and T shapes, infilled where necessary with floor-to-roof window panels, modulate a spatial continuity through their arrangement in a tense asymmetrical equilibrium in space. For the first time in architecture, the wall by its placement and shape actually generates the plan. Although the design is schematic only, it nevertheless represents the first truly architectural achievement employing De Stijl principles of composition, since earlier ventures had arbitrarily intermixed De Stijl with Cubist elements. The second project for a country house, this time for a concrete structure, is a spreading structure in a pinwheel composition around a multi-terraced site. Both the horizontality of the house and the determination of the irregular mass in accordance with the major elements of the plan run counter to the compact *prisme pur* enclosure of space which dominated the *International Style at the time. Mies's concrete country house in this respect looks rather ahead to later developments of the International Style after 1930. On the whole these five projects are among the most creative architectural conceptions of the early twenties, and remain among the least dated.

The latter half of the twenties finally sees a few (very few) executed buildings in Mies's modern style. Notable among them are the Monument to Karl Liebknecht and Rosa Luxemburg in Berlin (1926, and demolished by the Nazis). A textured brick slab, faceted with horizontal, box-like projecting and receding elements and emblazoned at one end by the hammer and sickle with a flagstaff, it is among the few significant memorials erected in the 20th century. Two brick houses—the Wolf House in Guben (1926) and the Hermann Lange House in Krefeld (1928)—reveal how far Mies had come from his pre-war neo-Schinkelism, and how much his early neoclassicism continued to influence his work. Both possess a solidity and rootedness at variance with current practice in the International Style. Their elegance of detail and proportioning are such as Schinkel himself would have admired. The Wolf House is especially fine in the extension of the beautiful precision of the brick walls (a material which Mies had come to appreciate during his interlude in Holland) and in an abstract arrangement of brick terracing reminiscent of the Liebknecht-Luxemburg Monument. Meanwhile, during the late twenties, too, Mies continued to be interested in the glass office building, and he projected no less than four different schemes, none of which came to fruition. His early work in planning the exhibitions of the *Novembergruppe* prepared him to design several such exhibitions in which products are displayed with a restrained elegance that enhances their visual qualities.

His work at this time, however, is climaxed by two major works. One, the Weissenhofsiedlung in Stuttgart (1927), was a large-scale outdoor exhibition of housing of various types with designs by most of the leading modern European architects. Sponsored by the *Deutscher Werkbund and directed by Mies, this outdoor exhibition contained no less than twenty-one permanent buildings, ranging from one-family villas to Mies's dominating apartment structure, together with an adjunct of temporary exhibits. The most comprehensive group endeavour of the International Style, it clearly revealed the unifying characteristics of European modernism, An even more impressive work qualitatively, and indeed among the masterpieces of modern architecture, was Mies's German Pavilion for the International Exhibition in Barcelona (1929). It continues the De Stijl experiment of Mies's project for a country house of 1922, but with a simplification of elements and a breadth of treatment far surpassing the complications of the earlier design. Over a portion of a

Mies van der Rohe. German Pavilion at the International Exhibition. Barcelona, 1929

raised podium, Mies lightly supported a reinforced concrete slab on cross-shaped, chrome-plated steel columns. He placed vertical slabs of travertine and panels of glass of various kinds well under the spreading slab of the roof. Partially enclosing the roofed area, and partially sliding from under it, these panels in their right-angled asymmetrical arrangement loosely, but firmly, ordered the space while preserving its continuity. Two pools completed the complex: the larger on the open terrace; the smaller at right angles to it at the opposite end of the podium. The smaller is enclosed in a semi-court created by the slide of the travertine panels from under the slab of the roof. The sculpture of a female figure by Georg Kolbe placed in the water serves as a tenuous point of destination within this scrupulously chaste pavilion, otherwise occupied (so far as the standard photographs tell us) only by some of Mies's furniture. It was in this pavilion that he displayed his famous 'Barcelona Chair'. Among the classics in modern furniture design, this was the culminating piece in a series of distinguished designs which Mies realized during the late twenties. Although relatively little noted during the summer of its existence, the photographic record of the modest structure—truly 'almost nothing' in Mies's own aphorism on his architecture—has made it

Mies van der Rohe. Tugendhat House. Brno, 1930

among the most influential buildings of the 20th century.

Immediately after the Barcelona Pavilion, Mies designed the most important house of his European career, the concrete-surfaced Tugendhat House at Brno, Czechoslovakia (1930). Built on a gentle slope, the house presented a closed one-storey front to the street, with two storeys to the rear. The continuous space of the lower living floor with its chrome-plated columns and free-standing panels (one a semicircle of Macassar ebony) recalled the treatment of the Barcelona Pavilion. Here an even richer display of Mies's furniture completed an elegance, every detail of which (down to the curtain tracks) was meticulously custom-designed.

The Tugendhat House was Mies's last important executed building in Europe. Among the projects of the early and mid thirties the designs for houses within walled courts are the most interesting. Although the surrounding brick walls occasionally opened on to a distant view, for the most part these houses were wholly bounded by their rectangular frame, while in one instance several houses of various sizes, walled from one another, shared the same enframement. Inside the enclosure there was the usual Miesian spatial continuity interrupted here and there by carefully placed glass walls and solid panels, partially roofed (again slabs on metal supports), and partially open overhead. Indoors and out, ceiling and sky, solid and transparency are brought into intimate play with one another in these characteristically dynamic but serene spaces which are here adapted to a type of residence ideal for urban living.

On Gropius's recommendation Mies succeeded him as the Director of the *Bauhaus in 1930. Immediately thereafter, however, Nazi pressure forced Mies to move the school from Dessau to Berlin. There it had a tenuous existence, until Mies finally decided to close it in 1933. The hostile political environment made it increasingly impossible to work in Germany and, in the summer of 1937, when just past fifty, he emigrated to the United States. There, in 1944, he became an American citizen.

Whereas Mies had built relatively little in Europe and his work was known to a discriminating few, his practice and influence grew rapidly in the United States. It

Mies van der Rohe. Farnsworth House, Fox River, Ill., 1946–50

was here, precisely a decade after his arrival, that Mies had his first large retrospective exhibition at the Museum of Modern Art in New York. For this exhibition his principal disciple, Philip *Johnson, published the first book on Mies's work— at a time when, as he notes in the preface, only two articles wholly devoted to Mies's work had appeared. This publicity and the importance of his American commissions established Mies's popular fame. In 1938 he had been called to teach at the Illinois Institute of Technology (then known as the Armour Institute) in Chicago, as Gropius had been somewhat earlier called to Harvard. His first major American commission, a campus plan (1940) and buildings (the first in 1942–3) for IIT, immediately established the central theme of his American work: the exposed metal frame as it reticulated neutral rectangular volumes. He viewed the cleared site, which consisted of a number of city blocks in a scrubby area of the Chicago South Side,

as an idealized space, much like the podium of the Barcelona Pavilion. On this he arranged rectangular and slab-shaped blocks in accord with a modular grid for the entire project, such that semi-courts and corridors of space were created in a manner analogous to (but more formal than) his conditioning of interior space by slabs from the Barcelona Pavilion onward.

The revealed metal frame in his American buildings is rarely the structure itself, since fire regulations demand that most steel must be covered. Hence the visible 'structure' is more often symbolic of the reality beneath, much as pilasters symbolized columns in Renaissance buildings— except that Mies's pseudo-structure more convincingly resembles and more intimately relates to the real thing within. From the standard alphabet of the steelmaker's catalogue (the I-shaped beams, the H's, L's, the plates, and channels), he welds mouldings as the metallurgical equivalent of the carved mouldings of the past. The careful proportioning of his frame, the gradation of components from heavy to light, the firm elegance of his profiling and the subtleties of transitions where corners occur or one material butts another: this intensity of effort and artistry expended on the image of the structure has been unexcelled and all but unmatched by his numerous followers, most of whom have taken his image as a mere convenience for prefabrication.

Even as the first buildings were going up on the IIT campus, Mies designed (1946, completed 1950) a glass and metal house for Dr Edith Farnsworth in Fox River, Illinois. Three floating slabs—a terrace slab, and behind it floor and roof slabs—are all lifted from the ground on metal I-beam supports. The welding of the supports to the sides of the slabs, as though magnetism kept the frame intact, enhances the floating quality of the spreading slabs. Smaller slabs, also seemingly floated, serve as stairs, from the ground to the terrace and from the terrace to the entrance porch of the rectangular glass-box living area. It is so apparently simple that the subtleties of this extraordinarily elegant frame are readily missed on casual inspection, as are the subtleties of a composition in which the evident asymmetry is countered by hidden symmetries.

In his American work especially Mies has

Mies van der Rohe. Crown Hall, Illinois Institute of Technology. Chicago, 1952–6. Staircase

repeatedly taken a basic building type—in this instance the open pavilion lightly supported around the perimeter—and worked variations on the theme. Thus he enlarged the pavilion theme of the Farnsworth House by suspending the roof slab from exposed girders in a series of projects which was eventually realized in Crown Hall for the School of Architecture and Design at IIT (1952). Again the floating stair slabs rise to the floating terrace, and more stairs rise to the floor slab, which is lifted a few feet above the ground much as that of the Farnsworth House. Despite appearances, however, the Crown Hall floor slab is conventionally supported from the basement beneath. Where the earlier glass box was completely open beneath its floor slab, this is glazed, so that Design can be crowded into the basement, while Architecture reigns in the all but uninterrupted space of the glass box above. Again, the openness of this space is enhanced by the suspended nature of the two slabs hanging or abutting (rather than resting) on their supports. In so far as Mies has been concerned with space at all in his American work, it has tended towards the universal box of Crown Hall and not towards the further development of the subtly modulated spaces of his European work after the Barcelona Pavilion.

Enlarged again, the pavilion becomes the project for a convention hall on the Chicago lake-front (1953). The roof slab of this unbuilt pavilion is a three-dimensional structure of interwoven trusses built on a cubic module of 30 feet in each direction and 30 feet deep. Mies designed this heroic structural slab to span 720 feet (or roughly two city blocks) so as to provide a column-free interior space with a height of 112 feet for a capacity audience of 50,000. Diagonal bracing extended from the outside edges of the three-dimensional ceiling trusses makes a two-dimensional truss of the exterior walls. This bracing brings the entire structure down on low reinforced concrete columns spaced 120 feet apart, with the area between available for entrances wherever needed. Finally, a pattern of triangles in light and dark metal panels not only dramatizes the triangulation of the structure, but also provides a compelling visual

Page 197. Mies van der Rohe. Crown Hall, Illinois Institute of Technology. Chicago, 1952–6

entity for what Arthur Drexler in 1960 termed 'the most monumental image 20th-century architecture has yet produced'.

As the basic pavilion could be proliferated into a series of buildings, so could the skeletal skyscraper. Mies's two classic skyscrapers, 860 Lake Shore Apartments (1957) and the Seagram Building in New York (1958) are in a sense exactly the same building creating different experiences, much as the Greek Temple of Poseidon at Paestum and the Parthenon are at once the same building and different buildings. Relative to one another, the Paestum-like severity of Lake Shore contrasts with the Parthenaic refinement of the Seagram. In the Lake Shore Apartments, vertical blocks are set at right angles to one another across a narrow interval of space in such a manner that their static shapes are always in tension with one another. As we circle the complex, we find that it possesses neither a true 'front' nor a true 'back'. We always see the narrow side of one block against the broad side of the other in a constantly changing relationship. The I-beam projections from the walls appear to close over the windows seen obliquely and open over those seen head-on, while in moving so as to open those which closed we automatically close those which were open. The Seagram Building, on the other hand, reconciles the Lake Shore paradox of static elements in perpetual disequilibrium. The bronze building rises like a dense, dark cliff behind the absolute void of its entrance *plaza*. The axis of the *plaza* culminates in the formal grandeur of the entrance with its two-storey stilts each backed by the pylons of the elevator shafts. Where, in the window grid of the Lake Shore Apartments, horizontals constantly challenge the verticals, this tension too is reconciled in the Seagram by the clear affirmation of verticality. In the Lake Shore, then, a perpetual tension; in the Seagram, the reconciliation of tension in a formal climax. To cite Mies's famous axiom, 'Less is more.' As he has extracted architecture from the 'almost nothing' of the brick or the I-beam considered as ultimate 'things in themselves', so he has used elemental building types to squeeze different buildings from the same one. His approach is

Mies van der Rohe. Seagram Building. New York, 1958

Mies van der Rohe. Convention Hall. Chicago, 1953. Model

Mies van der Rohe. Lake Shore Apartments. Chicago, 1957

narrow, and his austerity can lead to dryness where the problem has already been so substantially resolved that only refinement is left. But the narrowness of approach permits his passionate integrity and purifying artistry to come to focus. In his greatest works, the 'almost nothing' contains the paradoxical plentitude of an elemental demonstration.

Bibliography: Philip Johnson, *Mies van der Rohe*, 2nd edition, New York 1953; Ludwig Hilbersheimer, *Mies van der Rohe*, Chicago 1956; Arthur Drexler, *Mies van der Rohe*, New York 1960; Peter Blake, *Masters of Modern Architecture*, New York 1960; Ian McCallum, *Architecture USA*, London, New York 1959; 'Farnsworth House', *Architectural Forum*, *95*, October 1951; Arthur Drexler, 'Seagram Building', *Architectural Record*, *124*, July 1958; Lewis Mumford, 'Skyline: the Lesson of the Master', *New Yorker*, *33*, 13 September 1958; William H. Jordy, 'Seagram Assessed', *Architectural Review*, *124*, London December 1958; William H. Jordy, *Zodiac 8*, Milan 1960.

WILLIAM H. JORDY

Mills, Edward David, b. 1915. Studied at Polytechnic School of Architecture, London. In private practice since 1937; churches, schools, industrial buildings, research centres, flats and houses. Designed the British Industries Pavilion and the Britannia Inn at the Brussels International Exhibition, 1958.

Modular Coordination. It is, perhaps, unfortunate that the words 'module' and 'modular' were adopted by the pioneers of modular coordination and given a restricted sense after having been current in a wider meaning for several thousand years. 'Module' is the English, or French, form of the Latin *modulus*, which meant a small unit of measure, being the diminutive of *modus*. In classical architecture the modulus is half the diameter of the column at its base and is the unit for proportioning the classic order of column and entablature. Its actual size is not determined in advance, but prescribed for each particular design.

In modular coordination the module is not a unit of proportion, but a predetermined standard size used for coordinating the dimensions of components for building (doors, windows, panels, beams) with the dimensions of the spaces in a projected building into which they are intended to fit. The modular size (or basic size) of the component is expressed in the same whole number of modules as the size of its space in the building. The actual size of the component, the size found by measuring it, will be less than the modular size, by an allowance for the width of joint and for tolerances (manufacturing and positional). The confusion between 'module' as a unit of standardization and its ancient use as one of architectural proportion persists, for example, in a misunderstanding of the use of Le Corbusier's 'Le Modulor'. This is, in fact, a method of applying the Golden Section proportion and has nothing to do with modular coordination. Modulor has nothing in common with Modular.

The module in modular coordination is sometimes referred to as the 'Basic Module', to distinguish it from its multiples which are used as 'Planning Modules', 'Derived Modules', 'Design Modules' and so on. The best usage, however, is to confine the term 'module' to the Basic Module and to find other expressions, such as

'Planning Grid' for its multiples. This is because the size of the Basic Module has been fixed internationally as 10 centimetres for metric countries and 4 inches for countries using inches and feet, after a long process of debate and experiment. The logic behind the choice of this size as the Basic Module does not, by analogy, support the use of any other size, larger or smaller, repetitively as a module. In short, there is only one module (10 centimetres or 4 inches).

The international 10 centimetres/4 inches module is the resultant of two forces pulling against each other: the pull from manufacturers was to make it as large as possible in the interests of simplification and mass-production; that from architects was for it to be as small as possible for the greatest freedom of aesthetic and functional design. That this resultant should have been the same in all parts of the world, where the problem has been tackled, is a significant reassurance of its validity. National standards have been published for modular coordination in the following countries, on the 10 centimetres module unless otherwise stated:

1942 France	1954 USSR
1945 USA (4 in.)	1955 Chile
1948 Belgium	1955 Poland
1949 Italy	1956 Portugal
1951 Germany (10	1956 Roumania
cm. and 12.5 cm.)	1957 Austria
1951 Norway	1958 Denmark
1951 Hungary	1958 India
1952 Sweden	1959 Canada (4 in.)
1953 Argentine	

The promulgation of a national standard for modular coordination does not by itself achieve the savings in cost and in construction-time that are expected to derive from the use of the modular method. Much development work is required, by manufacturers in the choice of modular sizes for particular sets of components, and by architects in the application of the method to building design so as to incorporate standard modular components to the best advantage. In this process of development a vicious circle has constantly to be broken: manufacturers are reluctant to change their production to modular sizes until there is a clear demand for them from architects, whilst architects maintain that it is of no use to design modular buildings until ample ranges of modular components are available on the market. This vicious circle even appears in the 'planned economy' of Socialist countries, as is reported by a contributor from Poland to *The Modular Quarterly* (1963/1, p. 16).

In most of the countries named above, and in others, e.g. New Zealand and the Central American Republics, where modular coordination is under study but where a standard has not yet been issued, the development of modular method is entrusted to the Standards institutions or other agencies of government. In some, however, the initiative has been taken by private organizations.

In the USA there is the Modular Building Standards Association, Washington, D.C.; in Australia there is the Australian Modular Society, based at Sydney with branches in other states; and, in the United Kingdom, the Modular Society, London. Besides these three national societies (though the UK Modular Society has many overseas members) there is the International Modular Group, with its headquarters at the housing ministry in Copenhagen.

Finally, a few words on the situation in the United Kingdom at the time of writing (February 1963). It has not yet been possible to get the unanimous support from all sections of the building industry that is required for the issue of a British standard for modular coordination. Nevertheless, the Ministry of Public Building and Works has published a first statement on 'Dimensional Coordination for Industrialized Building', which in effect adopts the 4-inch module and the modular method for the whole of the government building programme, although for tactical reasons it adopts a somewhat off-beat terminology. This statement is expected to break the vicious circle and to create the demand from architects that will fill the *Modular Catalogue* of the Modular Society with ample ranges of modular components.

Bibliography: Modular Coordination— Second Report, EPA Project 174, OEEC., HMSO, London 1961; E. Corker and A. Diprose, 'The Modular Primer' in *Architects' Journal* 1.8.62 (reprinted by Modular Society); *Scandinavian Modular Coordination in Building*, Ministry of Housing, Copenhagen 1960; *The Modular Quarterly* (journal), London.

MARK HARTLAND THOMAS

Le Corbusier. Modulor

Modulor. A scale of proportions laid down by *Le Corbusier and his colleagues, 'which makes the bad difficult and the good easy' (Albert Einstein). The Modulor is based on two lines, arrived at via the Golden Section and related to the proportions of the human body. The initial dimension is 7 ft 5 in. (226 cm.) (an upright man with his hand raised) and half that, viz. 3 ft 9 in. (113 cm.). A man's height is taken as 6 ft (183 cm.).

Bibliography: Le Corbusier, *The Modulor: A harmonious measure to the human scale, universally applicable to architecture and mechanics*, London 1954. Continued in: Le Corbusier, *Modulor 2, 1955 (Let the user speak next)*, London 1958.

Morris, William, b. Walthamstow 1834, d. Kelmscott, Oxfordshire 1896. In 1861, together with artists from the Pre-Raphaelite Brotherhood, he founded the Morris Company whose products (furniture, textiles, metalwork, stained glass and wallpapers) sought to convey honesty and decency in the crafts. This attitude and the example set by the Red House at Bexley Heath, Kent, which Philip *Webb built for him, exerted a strong influence on the architecture of the times. Morris, who had trained under the architect G. E. Street, never built anything himself.

Moser, Karl, b. Baden, Switzerland 1860, d. Zurich 1936. Studied at Zurich College of Technology and later at the École des Beaux-Arts, Paris; 1887–1915 architect at Karlsruhe, 1915–28 taught at Zurich. Moser, whose reinforced concrete Church of St Anthony, Basle (1926–7) was the counterpart to *Perret's Church at Le Raincy (1922–3), taught many modern Swiss architects.

Muthesius, Hermann, b. Gross-Neuhausen 1861, d. Berlin 1927. Studied at Berlin Technical College; worked in Wallot's office. Period in Japan; attaché at the German Embassy in London (1896–1903), with a brief to study English architecture and design. His book *Das englische Haus* (Berlin 1904–5) by spreading a knowledge of the works of *Voysey and his contemporaries stimulated a renaissance in domestic architecture on the Continent. Founder-member of the *Deutscher Werkbund.

Nash, John, b. London 1752, d. East Cowes 1835. After a varied career, he worked as an architect in London from 1796. Built partly in classic, partly in Gothic style. His friendship with the Prince of Wales, later King George IV, led to many important commissions: town planning, public buildings, landscaping, country estates, churches, buildings and designs for the Royal House, including the eccentric Brighton Pavilion (1815–23). *Bibliography:* Terence Davis, *The Architecture of John Nash*, London 1960.

Nelson, George, b. Hartford, Connecticut 1908. Designer (in particular furniture and advertising) and architect who faces the problems of modern industry in his architectural designs. Factories, private houses. The model of his experimental house (1957) incorporates a flexible arrangement of square room units.
Bibliography: George Nelson, *Problems of Design*, New York 1957.

Neoclassicism. In the German-speaking countries of Europe the new architecture of the 20th century was born under the sign of the Doric Column, which appears in *Behrens's Mannesmann Building, Düsseldorf, in *Mies van der Rohe's Perls House, Berlin, and in Adolf *Loos's 'Looshaus' in Vienna. At the same time, Loos, like Hermann *Muthesius and others, was acclaiming K. F. *Schinkel as 'the last great architect'. In the same years Julien Guadet, professor at the *École des Beaux-Arts in Paris, taught a system of architecture that had hardly changed from that taught eighty years earlier by J. N. L. Durand and contrived to impose its concepts even on students as radical as Auguste *Perret and Tony *Garnier. Thus, all the fathers of the modern movement in architecture were soundly grounded in neoclassicism, and—even while they protested their disgust at the academies—they took over into their own work the academic neoclassical apparatus of trabeated structure, the preference for simple geometrical forms and smooth surfaces, and the concept of 'elementary composition', i.e. design, as the assembly of a number of disparate volumes, each dedicated to a single identifiable function.

In this way a durable neoclassical tradition was built into modern architecture from the beginning and was the basis for most concepts of 'order' and 'discipline' current in the first thirty years of the century. Since technology was also seen as one of the enemies of disorder, the mechanistic enthusiasms of the Futurists were early assimilated to the neoclassical tradition—in the writings and designs of Antonio *Sant'Elia in 1914, the rhetoric of a Marinetti is allied to an architectural vision more classically pure than even that of Loos. In *Le Corbusier's *Vers une Architecture*, nine years later, parallels between machinery and classical architecture are openly drawn, and the author equates Phidias with the designer of modern sports cars.

Le Corbusier. The Parthenon. 1911. Sketch

By about 1930, however, a new generation of critics and historians who had attached themselves to modern architecture as its mouthpieces (e.g. Sigfried Giedion) began to offer an account of modern architecture that relied exclusively on a supposed *'Functionalist' origin, and by 1936 another historian, Nikolaus Pevsner, could offer an account of the rise of modern architecture in which the academic and neoclassical contributions were not discussed at all. Rapidly, and especially after the disastrous competition for the League of Nations headquarters in Geneva, classicism came to be regarded as the enemy of modern architecture. But this was classicism in the superficial and debased sense of 'ornamented with Greek and Roman detail', for the planning of Le Corbusier's unsuccessful entry in the competition was fully as academic and neoclassical as that of the preferred designs. Similarly one finds, in Italian modern architecture, *Terragni praised for his 'rationalism' and Piacentini damned for his classicism—though a comparison of the façade of Terragni's Casa del Fascio at Como reveals it to be fully as classicist as Piacentini's arcading at EUR42 (Terza Roma) which is fully as rational as Terragni's space-games.

This facile and purely stylistic opposition between modern and classical, this growing ignorance among modern architects of the origins of their own design techniques, was to lead to profound intellectual confusions in the years after the Second World War. On the one hand, Bruno Zevi was to point out, with justice, how neoclassicism was the outstanding weakness of much second-rate modern architecture, but at the same time many Anglo-Saxon critics failed to see that the supposed modernism

Mies van der Rohe. Perls House. Berlin. 1911

Mies van der Rohe. Crown Hall, Illinois
Institute of Technology. Chicago, 1952–6

list Llewelyn Davies read Mies's repetitive
façades at the Illinois Institute of Technology as 'endless' and believed that their
complex corners implied the continuation
of the planes of the façades beyond the
ends of the buildings. But a younger
generation of English writers (e.g. Colin
Rowe) rendered consciously classicist by
the influential writings of Rudolf Wittkower (such as his book, *Architectural
Principles in the Age of Humanism*) preferred
to read the façades as closed, symmetrical
compositions, and the complex corners as
emphatic visual terminations, comparable
to the doubling of pilasters at the corners
of buildings, such as had been regular
classical practice since the time of
Bramante.

Among the intellectuals of Anglo-Saxon
architecture the rediscovery of the roots of
the classical tradition through the works
of scholars like Wittkower had a profound
influence and was seized upon as a welcome
source of order in a modern architecture
that, deprived of its classical origins, had
lost its way in the formless currents of
Functionalism. Under such names as
neo-Palladianism or the New Formalism,
it visibly affected the design of monuments
as diverse as Marchwood II power station
(England), designed by John Voelcker (of
*Farmer and Dark), the Goodyear House
in Connecticut, designed by John *Johansen, and even the first major building of the
*Brutalist movement: Hunstanton School,
by Alison and Peter *Smithson. But here
the Anglo-Saxon stream of development
divides; in *Great Britain the native preference for a functionalist solution, aided, no

of the Italian buildings then in vogue was
little more than a frank exhibition of a
neoclassicism that they no longer recognized as their own, an error that left them
entirely unprepared for the abandonment
of the moral and functional imperatives of
modern architecture by the *neo-Liberty
faction in Northern Italy.

A similar confusion can be seen in the
various valuations placed upon the architecture of Mies van der Rohe in the years
after 1950. The English radical functiona-

Philip Johnson. Sheldon Art Gallery. Lincoln, Neb., under construction

Alison and Peter Smithson. Hunstanton School. Norfolk, 1954

doubt, by the example of the anti-classicism of Ronchamp and the absence of a strong *beaux-arts* tradition, produced a situation in which neoclassicism was absorbed back into a kind of rational functionalism, and became little more than a modular discipline for the design of structures (e.g. *CLASP schools).

But in the *USA neo-Palladianism rapidly struck root in a *beaux-arts* tradition that had been only thinly buried by the dominance of *Gropius, *Sert, *Breuer and Mies. Philip *Johnson progressed rapidly from the Miesian classicism of his own house at New Canaan to the revival of the vault-forms of Sir John *Soane in the adjoining guest-pavilion, and from there to the vaulting and axial planning of the Port Chester Synagogue, the clearest and most justifiable example of the neoclassical revival in the USA. A more subtle and guarded neoclassicism is seen in the work of Louis *Kahn: the concealed axiality of the Yale Art Centre (1955); the use of elementary composition in the planning of the Philadelphia laboratories; the Laugier-esque primitivism of the Trenton bath-house (1955); and the pure *Prix-de-Rome* planning of the Torrey Pines Biological Institute.

This reawakening to the neoclassical roots of modern architecture coincided with a general relaxation of functionalist discipline, with rising standards of affluence and the retirement of Gropius from Harvard. The result, on the east coast at least, has been a slow recrudescence of *beaux-arts* academicism, with contrived symmetrical plans and even Doric columns such as could be seen in a number of designs that received awards from the magazine *Progressive Architecture* in 1962. In countries other than the USA, however, neoclassicism seems not to have proceeded any further than various forms of Miesian symmetry and rectangularity. But it does seem to be firmly entrenched as an essential part of the mental substructure of modern architectural design-practice, a geometrical discipline common to both classicizing formalists and prefabricating functionalists.

REYNER BANHAM

Louis I. Kahn. Baths. Trenton, N.J., 1956. Plan

Neo-Liberty. Reversion of post-war Italian architects to *Art Nouveau (Italian: Stile Liberty) forms, in particular to its last geometrical phase, as practised in Vienna and Scotland. Attempts to justify this movement have sparked off heated controversies between English and Italian architectural writers.

Neoplasticism. Piet Mondrian's term for his own painting, developed from Cubist prototypes. The artists and architects of De *Stijl were the protagonists of neoplasticism's clear, geometric order and transferred its concepts to architecture.

Nervi, Pier Luigi, b. Sondrio, Lombardy 1891. Nervi graduated in engineering at Bologna in 1913. He lives in Rome and since 1946 has lectured on structural engineering in the Faculty of Architecture at Rome University. He was awarded an honorary degree by the University of Buenos Aires in 1950.

This great builder ranks with *Freyssinet and *Maillart in his prodigious ability to derive beauty from the results of calculations, and form from the nature of his materials and techniques, which he has made the instruments of his vision. He takes his place in the history of architecture above all for the absolute aesthetic value of some of his buildings, where technology and aesthetics combine to determine dimensions and proportions, based on the same structural rationale that presided at the birth of the pyramid and the column. He himself, on the other hand, has many times laid down the principle in his writings, which he firmly believes in, that the process of creating form is identical, whether it is the work of technicians or of artists: the principle, that is, whereby the beauty of a structure, for example, is not just the outcome of calculations, but of an intuition as to what calculations to use, or with which it is to be identified. This perfect identification has clearly not been achieved in all his works, but where it has the architecture of the 20th century is ideally symbolized.

The material Nervi has adopted is reinforced concrete, which he moulds and works with an understanding of its possibilities which allows his imagination free rein. His first structures (for a theatre in Naples) date from 1927, the year in which

Pier Luigi Nervi. Communal Stadium. Florence, 1930–2

the *Movimento Italiano per l'Architettura Razionale* was founded, and the Weissenhof estate built at Stuttgart. The idea was gaining ground (the source of much subsequent misunderstanding) that 'form follows function', and it was this idea that brought the engineer Nervi into architecture forthwith. His first important work, the Communal Stadium at Florence (1930–2), consisting of nothing but exposed structural elements, was published straightaway in the most controversial journals as an example of modern architecture, which could be compared, in its dramatic exploitation of structure, with certain designs of *Le Corbusier and strikingly highlighted the expressive possibilities of the raw material, concrete.

Projects followed for viaducts, bridges, silos, tanks and even small revolving houses on a circular plan, which were never built. In 1935, however, Nervi designed a military hangar (of which versions were built, from 1936 to 1941, at Orvieto, Orbetello, and Torre del Lago) which started him on the study of roofs built up from a network of loadbearing joists. These were to prove the object of constant and even deeper research on his part, in an infinite variety prompted by his taste for creation and experiment. In the hangars which he built (now destroyed) Nervi achieved a great step forward in the process of lightening his structures, at which he has been aiming all his life, for aesthetic as much as for technical reasons.

In the same period, around the year 1940, he brought to a successful conclusion the studies and experiments he had been carrying out to obtain 'strength through form' in buildings, i.e. strength in surfaces alone; this is at once the most technically interesting and the most aesthetically satisfying of his achievements. He went on to design a series of immense roofs for warehouses, factories, aircraft hangars, stations and pavilions of various kinds. In 1947 he built the swimming baths at Leghorn, and in 1948–9 the fantastic roof of the great hall of the Exhibition Building in Turin, which remains one of his masterpieces, although due to a misunderstanding on the part of those responsible for the actual erection an important internal detail was altered, thus depriving it of the perfection which Nervi's design had attained. The enormous building consists in effect of a single roof structure, made up of undulating prefabricated units; Kidder Smith has called it the finest exhibition building in Europe since *Paxton's Crystal Palace, and ranks it with Le Corbusier's Unité d'Habitation at Marseilles as the two most important buildings in post-war Europe.

A number of smaller buildings followed, based on the same principle of roofing in reinforced concrete which leaves the space below completely free; some are on a circular plan, such as the halls at Rome Lido and Chianciano Terme (1950–2). Sometimes Nervi works in conjunction with architects, but not always. In 1953 he planned a huge Sports Palace for Vienna on a circular plan, which carried his experience at Turin a stage further; it was not built, however, nor was a smaller, but equally impressive design for a hangar at Buenos Aires.

At the same time as the above works, Nervi was carrying out research on improved systems of reinforced concrete prefabrication, using small ferroconcrete moulds for on-site manufacture, in conjunction with a movable type of staging patented by

Pier Luigi Nervi. Aircraft hangar. 1935

Pier Luigi Nervi. Exhibition hall. Turin, 1948–9

Pier Luigi Nervi. Main Railway Station. Naples, 1954. Project

himself, Bartoli and Angeli. This device permitted a great variety of designs based on a ribbed structure, making de *Baudot's boldest and most utopian designs now seem capable of realization. Another important invention of Nervi's in the technical field is his system for the hydraulic pre-stressing of reinforced concrete. But none of these researches is an end in itself. The ever greater liberty which these technical improvements bestow, by making work simpler and quicker, has led Pier Luigi Nervi to deeper researches of another kind, e.g. on rhythm as an element of beauty, as may be seen in his design for the concourse building of the new Main Railway Station in Naples (1954), in the Palazzetto dello Sport in Rome (1957), and above all in the conference hall of the Unesco Building in Paris (1953–7, jointly with Breuer and Zehrfuss).

With its overtones of barbaric monumentality reminiscent of some ancient temple, combined with extreme technical and aesthetic modernity, the Unesco Building is one of Nervi's most interesting

structures, one of the most interesting examples, in fact, of recent European architecture generally. The system of 'strength through form' has contributed to produce this splendid result. Strength was in fact achieved by corrugating the surfaces, and Nervi has studied the principle on the corrugated surfaces of shellfish, insects and flower calixes; the magical perfection of infinite smallness in nature seems to be transferred with the same qualities of strength and beauty to his own works.

In the construction of the Pirelli Skyscraper in Milan (1958, with Gio *Ponti and the architects of his office), the principle on which its strength is based is derived from nature too, viz. from the example of a tree. This is the prototype of the building's sectional development, with its four main stanchions growing ever more slender towards the top, as might have been seen more clearly if a lighter cladding had been used. Nervi's creative mastery of structure may also be seen in the most recent projects for which he has acted as the engineer: in the sail-like roof of the exhibition hall for the Centre National des Industries in Paris (1955), in the circular exhibition building in Caracas (1956), and in the enormous columns, shaped like palm trees, of the Palazzo del Lavoro at Turin (1961).

Bibliography: Pier Luigi Nervi, Arte o scienza del construire?, Rome 1954; Pier Luigi Nervi, El lenguaje arquitectonico, Buenos Aires 1950; Pier Luigi Nervi, Costruire correttamente, Milan 1954; G. C. Argan, Pier Luigi Nervi, Milan 1955;

Pier Luigi Nervi and Annibale Vitellozzi. Palazzetto dello Sport. Rome, 1956–7

Jürgen Joedicke, *The Works of Pier Luigi Nervi*, London 1957; Ada Louise Huxtable, *Pier Luigi Nervi*, New York 1960; Ravensburg 1961; Pier Luigi Nervi, *Neue Struckturen*, Stuttgart 1963.

GIULIA VERONESI

Netherlands. Modern architecture in the Netherlands undoubtedly begins with H. P. *Berlage, whose classic work is the Amsterdam Stock Exchange, completed in 1903. His immediate predecessor and contemporary was P. J. H. *Cuijpers, who as a follower of the romantic school was an enthusiastic adherent of *Viollet-le-Duc. His numerous works, including the Rijksmuseum (1885) and main railway station (1889) in Amsterdam, mark the close of eclecticism, and the neo-Gothic phase in particular, in the Netherlands. Despite his predilection for this style and the French neo-Renaissance, Cuijpers too, like Berlage, helped to promote the trend back to an architecture based on craft traditions. Nearly all the Dutch practitioners of arts and crafts around the year 1900 were graduates from Cuijpers's studio. From that time onwards, we can speak of a 'school of Berlage' also often referred to at the time as the Amsterdam School.

For the younger generation, Berlage was the leading personality of his time in the fields of art, architecture and handicrafts. His many lectures and articles exerted great influence. Breaking completely free from the eclecticism of the 19th century, he took as his starting point a consideration of the demands of reason and logic in the use of materials and in structure. As reinforced concrete was virtually unknown as an architectural medium at this time, he chose to work in brick. In his later works, however, he made an equally 'logical and honest' use of concrete.

Around 1910, a diametrically opposite movement began in Dutch architecture; its leading figure became Michael de *Klerk (1884–1923) together with P. L. Kramer and M. van der Mey. The best known example of this new *Amsterdam School is the Marine Terminus Building in Amsterdam (1914). This trend was basically anti-Berlage: individual artistic design was seen as the highest goal, and personal idiosyncrasies of detail were

P. J. H. Cuijpers. Rijksmuseum. Amsterdam, 1885

Hendrik Petrus Berlage. Stock Exchange. Amsterdam, 1897–1903

Michael de Klerk. Eigen Haard flats.
Amsterdam, 1921

realized, where necessary, at the cost of logical construction and the right use of materials.

This period, which lasted from about 1912 to 1926, is characterized by a form of *Expressionism, comparable to that which was developing in *Germany; international interest was drawn to Dutch architecture, and to the new housing in Amsterdam in particular. A typical Expressionist façade-architecture developed at this time, which left the real problems of modern mass-housing untouched. The new estates in South

Willen Marinus Dudok. Town Hall.
Hilversum, 1928–30

Amsterdam built in the years around 1922 all exhibit the influence of this romantic school, which has become identified today with the name of de Klerk, undoubtedly an architect of great gifts. The influence spread into the provinces, where it was long active, leaving its mark on numberless second- and third-rate buildings. Even Berlage was not wholly immune from it as his flats on the Mercatorplein in West Amsterdam show.

A new tendency emerged with the founding of De *Stijl, which set itself against both the unaffected outlook of Berlage and the romantic architecture of de Klerk and his circle. A violent struggle ensued, which led to the ultimate defeat of the romantic cause. In addition to J. J. P. *Oud, De Stijl attracted to its side such figures as Robert van't Hoff, Jan Wils and Gerrit Thomas *Rietveld. It was chiefly concerned with basic problems of space and colour. In principle, colour has no 'additional' decorative function, but acts rather as a space-moulding element. In practice, however, it turned out that spatial and decorative functions often overlapped.

After his break with van *Doesburg, Oud went his own way, while still adhering to De Stijl ideology, and became a leading figure in West European *Functionalism. His circle included J. B. van Loghem, J. A. and L. C. van der *Vlugt, B. Bijvoet, J. *Duiker, Cor van *Eesteren, B. Merkelbach, Ch. J. F. Karsten, Rietveld, Mart Stam, J. G. Wiebinga, Jan Wils and B. Groenewegen. This powerful upsurge of functionalism again focused the attention of the architectural world on Holland, while simultaneously marking the end of the romantic Amsterdam School. The platform for functionalism was provided by the controversial journal *De 8 en Opbouw*, in whose pages the advanced spirits of Amsterdam and Rotterdam made common cause. It stood in opposition to the ethically and aesthetically orientated journal *Wendingen*. The fact that, since 1912, every new building in Holland required the official approval of a 'vetting' committee, explains why it took till 1930–2 for a pioneer building such as Duiker's open-air school in the Cliostraat, Amsterdam to get built, and then only in the face of numerous protests from the experts.

A completely independent part was played by Willem Marinus *Dudok. Though showing himself an admirer of Berlage in his early works, he gradually developed an extremely personal style, of which Hilversum Town Hall (1928–30) is a typical example. The 'Dudok Style' found many imitators in Holland up to about 1935, especially in the provinces.

Another turning point in Dutch architecture was reached in 1925, with the appointment of Professor G. M. Granpré Molière to Delft Technical College. His philosophy and system of aesthetics, based on the Roman Catholic religion, made a strong appeal to many students. The first building to appear which bore his stamp was the Town Hall at Enschede (1933) by his pupil G. Friedhoff; it also shows Scandinavian influence. With the professor from Delft, Dutch architecture became subject to ever more philosophical considerations. Granpré Molière was opposed to a so-called technical and materialistic outlook. He was against the undermining of religion, and against functionalism and humanism, which he considered the common denominator of everything Oud and his circle stood

for. In the pre-war atmosphere of political unrest and increasing malaise towards the tendencies of modern culture and technology, the Delft theories fell upon fertile ground.

The School of Delft, which was historically orientated, especially in regard to church building and town planning, seemed to dominate Dutch architecture until about 1955. Architects and town planners from this group were entrusted with the reconstruction of bombed cities during and after the Second World War. Functionalism and De Stijl seemed to be played out. Granpré Molière exerted particular influence on the development of Dutch church architecture, and not only amongst his fellow-Catholics, but on Protestant architects, too. The character of the Delft School was chiefly determined by the real or supposed tradition of Dutch building, and the maintenance and romantic perpetuation of craftwork in the manner of Berlage. This led to the evocation of great interest in comparable architectural trends in the Scandinavian countries and Germany (Tessenow, *Muthesius). Four years of German occupation also naturally left their mark.

Johannes Andreas Brinkmann and L. C. van der Vlugt. Van Nelle tobacco factory. Rotterdam, 1928–9

J. H. van den Broek and Jacob B. Bakema.
Lijnbaan pedestrian precinct. Rotterdam, 1953

The situation changed around 1950. It
was in particular the badly damaged city
of Rotterdam that led the way. The
traditional type of reconstruction scheme
that had been originally planned was
abandoned and a new one adopted.
Rotterdam became a centre of architectural and town-planning activity,
thanks chiefly to the work of van den
*Broek and *Bakema. The former was
appointed professor at Delft Technical
College in 1948. He and Bakema chal-
lenged the concepts of the Delft School,
and in this they were supported by Oud

Aldo van Eijck. Municipal Orphanage.
Amsterdam, 1955

and a small group of fellow spirits.
Functionalism began to develop again,
but it was of a clearly different type from
that which had flourished from 1925 to 1935.
In Amsterdam itself however, few buildings of note have been erected, save for
the large town extension schemes in West
Amsterdam. A scheme for a new town
hall by the architects Berghoef and
Vegter encountered stiff opposition both
from the profession and the public. The
two architects were convinced disciples
of Granpré Molière.
The general impression made by Dutch
architecture a few years after the Second
World War was chiefly one of diversity
and vigour. The works of architects in
Sweden, Italy and North and South
America (*Breuer, *Gropius, *Mies van
der Rohe) were making their influence
felt, as was the ever-increasing number of
publications. The *CIAM idea was
revived, and its meaning for our time was
critically reassessed. The desperate housing shortage focused particular interest
on this sphere of building. The well-nigh
impregnable bastion of the romantic
Delft School was being progressively
undermined in practice. After c. 1955
even its most zealous adherents became
converted—some hesitantly, others out
and out—to a new and in many respects
modern form of functionalism. A comparison of the highly ornate Provincial
Authority Headquarters at Arnhem
(1955) with the Town Hall at Groningen
(1961), both by J. J. M. Vegter, illustrates
this change. Delft School concepts held
out longest in the sphere of Catholic
church building, especially in the predominantly Catholic provinces of North
Brabant and Limburg, in the south,
where the so-called 'Hertogenbosch
School' clung on to the North Italian type
of Early Christian basilica. But here too,
in Catholic lay and architectural circles,
loud protests have been voiced against
this trend, and attempts are being made
to exploit new methods, as in Protestant
church architecture, where reinforced
concrete is no longer rejected out of hand
as an ignoble material.
By the side of good contemporary design,
a vast amount of building has gone up in
what is no more or less than bread-and-
butter modern. This is especially the case
with housing. The few notable figures

include van den Broek, Bakema and later, Aldo van *Eijck; Rietveld's work is greatly admired by most of the younger generation. Dissatisfaction with CIAM's doctrinaire outlook led to the setting up of Team X, whose views have been appearing in the Dutch press since 1959, especially in the journal *Forum*, and have given rise to sharp controversy. 'Architecture is the three-dimensional expression of human behaviour' (Bakema).

An attempt to carry some new ideas into effect may be seen in the Municipal Orphanage, Amsterdam (1955), by Aldo van Eijck. The transitions from exterior to interior, and the spatial relationships of this building make it one of the most important of its time. Van Eijck and his circle have been able to realize their theories to a certain extent in planning for the village of Nagele, in the south-east Polder. Van den Broek and Bakema's proposals for the Kennemerland region of Noord-Holland also herald some new developments in the field of town planning. The same architects' design for a civic centre at Marl, currently under construction, will no doubt give ample expression to the new theories of the *Forum* group.

Bibliography: J. P. Mieras and F. R. Yerbury, *Dutch Architecture in the 20th Century*, London 1926; J. J. Vriend, *Nieuvere Architectuur* Amsterdam 1957; J. J. Vriend, *Reflexen*, Amsterdam 1958; J. J. Vriend, *Algemeen Overzicht Architectuur van deze eeuw*, Amsterdam 1959; G. M. Granpré Molière, *Woorden en Werken*, 1949; H. L. C. Jaffé, *De Stijl 1917–31. The Dutch Contribution to Modern Art*, Armsterdam 1956; R. Blijstra, *Netherlands Architecture since 1900*, Amsterdam 1960.

                    J. J. VRIEND

Neutra, Richard Joseph, b. Vienna 1892. Neutra was trained at the Technische Hochschule, Vienna, receiving his diploma in 1917. He met Adolf *Loos in 1910 and was influenced by the elder architect's work (e.g. the Steiner House, 1910), by his strictures against the use of ornament in architecture and by his admiration for American design (which Loos knew at first hand from a stay in the USA in 1893–6). Neutra was also impressed with the novel character of Otto *Wagner's Vienna subway entrances, dating from before 1900.

Richard Neutra. Lovell House. Los Angeles, 1927–9

Richard Neutra. Sidney Kahn House. San Francisco, 1940

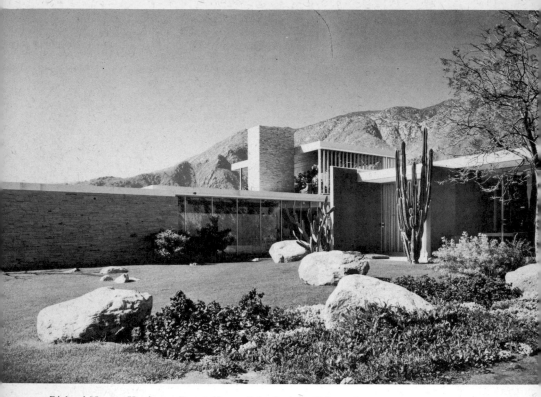

Richard Neutra. Kaufmann Desert House. Palm Springs, Cal., 1946–7

In 1911 his interest in American architecture was broadened through the discovery of the work of Frank Lloyd *Wright
which had just been extensively published
in Europe. Many of the motifs that dominate Neutra's architecture today, a half-
century later, can be traced to this familiar
and influential source.

Immediately after the First World War
Neutra worked in Switzerland, gaining
experience in the fields of landscape and
city planning. Employed in the Municipal
Building Office, Lukenwalde, Germany, in
1921, he subsequently became associated
with Erich *Mendelsohn in 1922. The
following year Mendelsohn and Neutra
were awarded a First Prize for a Business
Centre in Haifa. Neutra moved to the
USA in 1923, and for the next few years
he worked alternately in Chicago, with the
large commercial firm of *Holabird and
Roche, and at Taliesin, Spring Green,

Wisconsin, with Frank Lloyd Wright. In
1926 he settled in Los Angeles, beginning
his practice in the office of another Vienna-
born architect, Rudolph *Schindler.
Schindler had been an assistant of Wright
in the construction of several houses in
Los Angeles in the early 1920s, and in
1926 was building the concrete-framed
Lovell House, Newport Beach, in a
striking, liberated style reflecting his
origins, both in the proto-*International
Style of Central Europe and in the more
romantic architecture of Wright. In 1927
Schindler and Neutra collaborated in a
project for the League of Nations competition.
Under these several influences Neutra's
personal style rapidly came into focus in
the late 1920s. The key work in his early
maturity was the rambling, quasi-pictur-
esque Lovell House (1927–9) built for
Schindler's former client on a steep,

challenging Los Angeles hillside site. A contemporary (albeit geographically isolated) of *Le Corbusier's noted Villa Stein, Garches, France, and *Mies van der Rohe's Barcelona Pavilion, Neutra's steel-framed Lovell House, with its slabs and balconies supported from above by steel cables, differs in certain structural details from these European masterworks, but is stylistically identical in terms of its thin, weightless forms which only partly enclose a series of fluidly juxtaposed interior spaces. Neutra developed and expanded this International Style into a more pronounced personal idiom throughout the 1930s in such houses as the one built for Josef von Sternberg, San Fernando Valley (1936), and these simple forms were often realized in novel or unusual materials. Always interested in large-scale planning, with implications of social welfare, Neutra found a wartime opportunity in the Channel Heights Housing Project, San Pedro, California (1942–4), where out of necessity redwood was substituted for the more familiar materials of the machine age. At the same time he worked on numerous projects for schools and health centres in Puerto Rico.

The apogee of Neutra's career occurs in the immediate post-war era with the construction of the Kaufmann Desert House, Palm Springs (1946–7), and the Tremaine House, Santa Barbara (1947–8). Here the elegant restatements of the by now traditional International Style themes reach a degree of elegance and precision that is not present in the earlier work, and these features are further enhanced by sensitive siting and landscaping. In 1949, with an expanding practice, he formed a partnership with Robert E. Alexander. Since that time domestic work has had to vie with more sizeable projects in Neutra's *œuvre*. While his houses of the 1950s have almost invariably maintained the suavity of those of the 1940s, the designs have tended towards the rhetorical in their repetition of earlier motifs. In general, in the most recent phase of his career, Neutra's customarily sensitive works have appeared to have less and less relevance with the constantly changing direction and interest that is to be found in the main stream of building design in the late 1950s and early 1960s.
Bibliography: Richard Neutra, *Survival through Design*, New York 1954; W.

Boesiger, *Richard Neutra, 1950–60, Buildings and Projects*, Zurich 1959; Esther McCoy, *Richard Neutra*, Ravensburg 1962.
JOHN M. JACOBUS, JR

Niemeyer, Oscar, b. Rio de Janeiro 1907. The leading exponent of modern architecture in Brazil, by virtue of the extent, the scope and the character of his work, Oscar Niemeyer Soares Filho, as his name is written in full, has had a rich and varied career. He graduated in 1934 from the National School of Fine Arts, Rio, and a few years later stepped into a position of effective leadership when he succeeded Lúcio *Costa as the head of the design team for the new building of the Ministry of Education and Health. Since then he has always been in the front line of architectural development in Brazil, setting trends and opening up new avenues of plastic expression, as well as influencing students and fellow architects to a very noticeable degree.

Niemeyer himself was decisively influenced by *Le Corbusier, with whom he worked on the design for the Ministry of Education and Health during the master's short stay in Brazil, in 1936. He began by applying Le Corbusier's basic ideas, as in the Day Nursery, Rio de Janeiro (1937). Very soon, however, he branched out in a personal direction, adding to such ideas an element of adaptation to local conditions, an imaginative and creative exuberance, and a typical lightness of touch, which to this day distinguishes all his work, even when it is apparently massive or heavier than usual.

Disregarding the tenets of orthodox *Functionalism whenever they seemed to him to run counter to the ideal of architecture as a great art of expression and of social purport, Niemeyer has consistently striven for beauty and harmony, grace and elegance in an enriched formal vocabulary as the legitimate goals of architectural creation in opposition to merely technical and functional refinements. Unafraid of the curved line, for which he found good precedent in Brazilian Baroque architecture, Niemeyer has used it with an instinctive lyrical touch and an uninhibited spontaneity throughout his career—free-flowing and seemingly arbitrary in the earlier phases, subtly distilled and sophisticated in his later work, where conciseness of expression is equally

Oscar Niemeyer. Yacht Club. Pampulha, 1943

stressed in the straight and in the curved lines of the composition. This use of the curved line, however, is but one aspect of Niemeyer's most characteristic contribution to modern architecture, his genuine inventiveness, always blossoming in beautifully expressive new forms, or in the revitalized use of consecrated ones. In this connection, his collaboration with numerous structural designers must be mentioned, starting with Emilio Baumgart in the early days and reaching supreme fulfilment with Joaquim Cardoso, from Pampulha to Brasilia.

Oscar Niemeyer, Zenon Lotufo, Helio Uchôa and Eduardo Kneese de Mello. Palace of Industry, Ibirapuéra Park, São Paulo, 1951–4

The extent and variety of Niemeyer's significant work, both the executed jobs and the relatively fewer unrealized projects, defeat any attempt to shorten their list. If four larger ones may be thought to highlight Niemeyer's career—Pampulha (1942), São José dos Campos (1947), Ibirapuéra (1950–4), and Brasilia (1956–61)—a great many others have to be taken into account in the intermediate periods. Prior to Pampulha, besides the Brazilian Pavilion at the New York World's Fair in 1939, with Lúcio Costa, three others must be noted: the Hotel Ouro Preto (1940); the architect's own house in Rio (1942); and his competition design for the National Stadium (1941); the first for its fusion of old and new in the traditional setting of the colonial town, the second for its open interior plan, on three levels, and its pioneering use of an inside ramp, the third as a first example of large-scale planning. The Pampulha group of buildings, famous for its display of new forms, different yet kindred, its gay interplay of light and shade and its deliberate integration of architecture with painting and sculpture—the Casino with the ovoid prism well joined to the crisply rectangular block, the circular Dance Hall with its freely flowing marquee, the Yacht Club with its inverted double slope roof, and the St Francis Chapel with its several parabolic domes— also marks the beginning of the close collaboration between Niemeyer and Juscelino

Kubitschek, then Mayor of the City, later Governor of the State of Minas Gerais, and finally, as President of the Republic, the creator of Brasilia.

The period from 1942 to 1947, to which belong the Boavista Bank, Rio (1946), distinguished by its unassuming openness and its light undulating glass-brick wall in the main banking hall, the Municipal Theatre in Belo Horizonte and the Cataguazes Academy for Boys (1946), as well as the Peixoto residence (1943), is important because of a number of projects which, though never carried out, led Niemeyer into an intensive study of residential architecture. He discovered new possibilities in the interplay of volumes, planes and levels, and better relationships with the site and the view. These conceptions were realized in the Staff Housing units for the São José dos Campos Aeronautical Technical Centre (1947), built as part of an overall scheme which had won first prize in a competition. Later in 1947 Niemeyer joined the international team entrusted with the design of the United Nations' Headquarters in New York, strongly influencing the final scheme, derived from Le Corbusier's and Niemeyer's proposed solutions.

Oscar Niemeyer. Sul America Nursing Home. Rio de Janeiro, 1953

Then follow a series of projects exploring the use of reinforced concrete in the development of complex curved surfaces, such as the twin-theatre Annexe for the Ministry of Education and Health esplanade (1948), the proposed shell-like dome for a monument to Rui Barbosa (1949), or

Oscar Niemeyer. President's Palace. Brasilia, completed 1959 the Duchen Factory (1950, with Helio Uchôa), a 300-metre-long block dramatized by a row of double-span curved rigid frames, spaced 10 metres apart, carrying a roof slab designed to improve the distribution of light; and several equally important jobs emphasizing the possibilities of long straight lines, in wide overhangs or in variously designed sloping supports, as in both the Club and the School at Diamantina (1951), or in the Governor Kubitschek Building in Belo Horizonte (1951), a huge apartment unit complex of two tall simple towers contrasting with the flowing lines of the supporting single storey, which covers almost two city blocks.

All this led to the Parque Ibirapuéra exhibition buildings for the Fourth Centennial of the City of São Paulo, a rare instance of integrated planning of a group of permanent fair buildings over a wide area. Niemeyer unified the scheme by the spreading irregular marquee which links the various blocks to each other; two low ones, 140 metres long, Palace of Nations and Palace of States, with their tilted concrete brackets; the three-storey Palace of Industry, 250 metres long, with its various interior levels capriciously silhouetted by the outline of the mezzanine slab; and the dome-like Palace of the Arts, with its spectacular and almost surrealist interior. All these were designed in 1951 (with Zenon Lotufo, Helio Uchôa and Eduardo Kneese de Mello as associate architects, Gauss Estellita and Carlos Lemos as collaborators).

The sweep and imaginativeness of the Ibirapuéra job, dramatizing and stressing the simplicity of the scheme and of the general concept, in contrast to the hodge-podge usually found in exhibition grounds, seems an appropriate stepping-stone for Niemeyer's crowning achievement, the design of the main public buildings of Brasilia (1950–60). In the intervening

Oscar Niemeyer. Museum with Congress Building in the background. Brasilia, completed 1960 period he is working on the Sul America Hospital (1953); his own house at Gavea (1953), a leaf-like slab inserted in a gorgeous sub-tropical site; the High School at Belo Horizonte (1954), with its striking eye-like auditorium; a project for a museum at Caracas in the form of an inverted pyramid (1954); and an apartment building in the Hansa district of Berlin (1955).

In Brasilia, however, where he was given the task of designing all the main public buildings, Niemeyer was able not only to express the symbolic content of each job and of the whole, implicit in Lúcio Costa's sophisticated general plan, but also to achieve it within a restrained vocabulary, in which poetic flights of imagination, severely disciplined, only highlight, where the artist considers necessary, the particular significance of one or another element in the general context: for example, the beautiful colonnade of the Palace of Dawn, an original theme whose variations may be found in the Supreme Court Building or in the Highland Palace; the startling flower-like design for the Cathedral; the concave and convex dome of the Congress Building in contrast to the soaring twin towers and the horizontal expanse of the base block; farther away, the truncated pyramid of the Opera House; all of them unforgettable accents underlining, against the backdrop of Brasilia's wide horizon, the essential quietness, the coherent simplicity and dignity of all the other architectural elements.

Bibliography: Oscar Niemeyer, *Minha Experiencia em Brasilia*, Rio de Janeiro 1961; Stamo Papadaki, *The Work of Oscar Niemeyer*, New York 1950; Stamo Papadaki, *Oscar Niemeyer—Works in Progress*, New York 1956; Stamo Papadaki, *Oscar Niemeyer*, Ravensburg 1962. Also most of the issues of *Modulo*, which document Niemeyer's later work, especially with regard to Brasilia.

HENRIQUE E. MINDLIN

Nizzoli, Marcello, b. Boretto, Reggio Emilia 1895. Architect, painter and designer. Housing at Ivrea (together with Annibale *Fiocchi and Mario Oliveri), Palazzo Olivetti in Milan (together with Gian Antonio Bernasconi and Annibale Fiocchi, 1954).

Nowicki, Matthew, b. 1910, d. 1949 in a plane crash on the way from India to the United States. He was the architect of the arena at Raleigh, N.C. (1952–3), together with William H. *Deitrick and Severud. Together with Albert Mayer, he produced the first town plan for the new capital of the Punjab, Chandigarh, but this was not executed.

Noyes, Eliot, b. Boston 1910. Architect and designer. Studied at Harvard Graduate School of Architecture, latterly under *Gropius and *Breuer. Sometime director of the Department of International Design at the Museum of Modern Art. His balloon house at Hobe Sound, Florida, was made by spraying concrete on an immense inflated balloon, to produce a hemispherical shell.

O'Gorman, Juan, b. Coyoacán, Mexico 1905. Pupil of José *Villagrán García. His private houses at San Angel (1929–30) are amongst *Mexico's first buildings in the *International Style. Mosaics on the University Library, Mexico, 1952. O'Gorman's own house, a fantastic dream castle in a mannered style, takes advantage of a natural grotto in the rocks.

Olbrich, Joseph Maria, b. Troppau 1867, d. Düsseldorf 1908. Architecture, arts and crafts, book design. Pupil of Otto *Wagner,

Joseph Maria Olbrich. Hochzeitsturm. Darmstadt, 1907

co-founder of the Vienna Sezession, whose exhibition building he designed in 1898–9. Olbrich was the architect of nearly all the buildings for the exhibitions on the Mathildenhöhe in Darmstadt. His Hochzeitsturm ('Wedding Tower') at Darmstadt (1907) is one of the most distinguished pieces of civic adornment in modern architecture.

Organic Architecture. That architecture should in its appearance have a character similar to a natural organism and give the same impression of unity has actuated the work of some of the most important architects of the age, of whom Henry van de *Velde and Erich *Mendelsohn are notable examples in Europe and Louis *Sullivan and Frank Lloyd *Wright in America.

Different theories of organic architecture have been advanced and there is some confused thinking on the subject. It is therefore important to try to dispel this confusion. Some writers have confused the idea of organic architecture with functional building according to social needs, so that if a house is designed in stages according to changing needs, rooms being added as the family grows, that is regarded as organic. It might be regarded as organic building for social needs, but it is too simple and elemental an idea to cover the meaning of organic architecture as conceived by the famous architects mentioned and by others who have been influenced by the idea.

The theory derives from ancient Greek and Roman architecture, and was further developed during the Renaissance. The Greeks based the proportions that should determine the design of temples on the proportions of the human figure. This is recorded and developed by Vitruvius, and many artists of the Renaissance inevitably adopted the theory. Vasari remarked that architecture must appear organic like the body, and Michelangelo held that a knowledge of the human figure led to a comprehension of architecture. Later writers have

Alvar Aalto. Aalto House. Helsinki, 1935–6

Erich Mendelsohn. Synagogue. Cleveland, O., 1946–1952. Model

Frank Lloyd Wright. Jacobs House. Middleton, Wis., 1948

seen in the theory of *Einfühlung*, whereby bodily feelings are projected into the forms of a building, the basis of a modern theory of organic architecture. Although there is a kinship between the two they are not identical. One is the recognition that our bodily existence and bodily feelings must be the measure of the world around us, the other is the application of the principles of that organic life to design.

The nature of organic structure indicates these principles. We find in all natural organisms a certain harmony of parts in relation to the whole which appears to be conditioned by the work the organism is designed to perform, and we find in nature that the plan of an organism influences the character of the subordinate organisms. Transferred to a building this means the integration of the parts with the whole, so that the design of the whole controls the design of the subordinate parts. In addition it would appear to mean that the forms of a building integrated into an harmonious whole shall express a purpose similar to the conditioning of the forms of an organism by the work it is created to perform. This purpose may be to express the structure, such as emphasis on the lines of stress, of thrust and support, and in this there is again the link with *Einfühlung*. The application could not legitimately be extended further to include the social purpose of the building, for this enters the realms of symbolism and departs from the physical context of organic architecture.

We find the theory controlling the work of many modern architects. It was a consistent aim with van de Velde and Mendelsohn, and the latter was pleased when Einstein remarked of his Observatory building at Potsdam that it was Organic. Most architects who are guided by the theory of organic unity do not limit it to the building but insist that the building should be a unity with its surroundings, especially with the site, with the earth on which it stands. Frank Lloyd Wright was especially insistent on this, and he said that a building should not be *on* a hill, but *of* a hill, that it should appear to grow out of the earth. With domestic architecture he said that house and garden should be one, and that it should be difficult to discern where the house ends and the garden begins, a characteristic found in much Japanese architecture. Mendelsohn in many of his buildings let the contours of the ground control the design of his buildings. In brief, organic architecture is not only the complete harmony of the parts of a building with the whole but an integration of the building with its site and surroundings. In a theory of organic architecture, building and town planning should conform to the unity, to the integration of parts, found in the natural world.

Bibliography: Walter Curt Behrendt, *Modern Building*, London 1937; Frank Lloyd Wright, *An Organic Architecture— The Architecture of Democracy*, London 1939; Bruno Zevi, *Towards an Organic Architecture*, London 1950.

ARNOLD WHITTICK

Otto, Frei, b. Siegmar near Chemnitz 1925. Designs for suspended roofs and inflated plastic structures. Marquees at the Federal Flower Shows in Kassel (1955) and Cologne (1957).
Bibliography: Frei Otto, *Über zugbeanspruchte Konstruktionen*, Berlin 1962.

Oud, Jacobus Johannes Pieter, b. Purmerend 1890, d. 1963. Oud received his education at the Quellinus School, the State School of Draughtsmanship in Amsterdam, and Delft Technical College, which awarded him an honorary doctorate after the Second World War. He worked for the architects Jan Stuijt and Theodor *Fischer in Munich for a time, and

Jacobus Johannes Pieter Oud. Workers' housing estate. Hook of Holland, 1924

Jacobus Johannes Pieter Oud. Shell Building.
The Hague, 1938

became City Architect of Rotterdam in 1918, where he was responsible for the Spangen and Tussendijken housing estates (1920). Oud played a leading part in the development of *Functionalism in Western Europe, from the stage of *Neue Sachlichkeit* to the emergence of the *International Style.

Round about the year 1916, Oud came into contact with Theo van *Doesburg, and was an active participant in the new De *Stijl movement. Like most of his generation, Oud was a great admirer of

Jacobus Johannes Pieter Oud. Bio-Children's Convalescent Home near Arnhem, 1952–60

*Berlage, as his early works clearly show. Berlage's honest handling of materials and structure was to influence Oud's functionalist architecture strongly, despite its complete difference of form. Oud was faced with the difficult task of translating De Stijl's often all too theoretical ideas into practical building terms. Examples of his De-Stijl-type architecture include the Café de Unie in Rotterdam (1924–5, destroyed 1940), a project for terraced housing on the promenade at Scheveningen (1917), and a design for a factory at Purmerend (1919). After a few years, Oud broke with van Doesburg, who laid too much stress on the rôle of abstract painting in modern architecture. The housing schemes at Oud-Mathenesse (1922), Hook of Holland (1924–7) and Kiefhoek, Rotterdam (1925–7) demonstrate the transition to *Neue Sachlichkeit*. From about 1935 onwards, Oud renounced the strictly functionalist style (Shell Building, The Hague, 1938, and several post-war office blocks in Rotterdam). This defection drew on him some sharp criticism, which still affects the estimation of his *oeuvre*. His competition design for the South Holland Local Government offices at the Hague (1952, not premiated), and more recent buildings such as the Bio-Children's Convalescent Home near Arnhem (1952–60), demonstrate, however, that the Shell Building belongs to a transitional period influenced by the general tension in Europe on the eve of the Second World War. The same malaise in orthodox Functionalism, albeit differently manifested, is clearly implied in the developments of the last ten years (*CIAM, Otterlo, 1959).

In his book *Mijn Weg in De Stijl* (1961) Oud wrote: 'The desire for abstraction requires melody. Pure abstraction is like religion without humanity. Humanity means living in the flowing continuum of daily existence. The flow and rhythm of daily existence demand melody from architecture.'

Bibliography: J. J. P. Oud, *Holländische Architektur* (Bauhausbücher 10), Munich 1926; J. J. Pieter Oud, *Mijn Weg in De Stijl*, Rotterdam 1961; Henry-Russell Hitchcock, *J. J. P. Oud*, Paris 1931; Giulia Veronesi, *J. J. Pieter Oud*, Milan 1953.

J. J. VRIEND

Paxton, Joseph, b. Milton-Bryant, Bedfordshire 1803, d. Sydenham 1865. A farmer's son, Paxton was trained as a gardener and became head gardener to the Sixth Duke of Devonshire at Chatsworth, Derbyshire, in 1826. Subsequently he became the Duke's land-agent, business adviser and friend. Paxton had no training as an engineer or architect, but had a gift for shrewd observation and deduction; he proceeded empirically in all his ventures, which stemmed from his own knowledge of natural phenomena.

Paxton had started experimenting with horticultural building at Chatsworth in 1828, and in 1831 hit upon the idea of the 'ridge and furrow' roof. This was refined in detail to become a sloping glass roof without rafters, with very light sash-bars and with the Paxton gutter, which collected both internal and external moisture as well as being a structural member. This roofing was entirely of wood and glass, the wooden parts being produced by machinery which Paxton himself had designed. Hollow cast-iron columns were introduced to support longer spans, serving also for drainage of the roofs. This principle was followed in the curvilinear Great Conservatory at Chatsworth (1836–40), the curved members being of laminated wood, the house being 277 feet long, 123 feet wide and 67 feet high. From curved roofs Paxton moved to a flat roofing system, still with ridges and furrows, for the Lily House of 1849. This was essentially the same system —except for a necessarily larger iron framework—as that used by Paxton in his design for the Great Exhibition Building of 1851, erected in concert with the contractors, Fox and Henderson, and the glass-maker R. L. Chance. This, the largest building ever erected up to that date, was a completely prefabricated structure of standardized, mass-produced parts, based on a module of 24 feet, covering a ground area of over 770,000 square feet. The materials were used afterwards in the erection of the Crystal Palace at Sydenham (1852–4, destroyed by fire 1936), a more elaborate design with three arched transepts and a vaulted nave. Amongst other designs by Paxton for glass buildings were the projects for Crystal Palaces in New York and Paris, the latter being as long as the 1851 building but with three great circular domes in front.

Joseph Paxton, Crystal Palace. London, 1851

At the same time as he was developing his glass structures, Paxton was building conventional masonry houses in accepted styles, including the mansions of Mentmore, Buckinghamshire; Ferrières, near Paris; and Lismore Castle in Ireland. As a landscape architect he designed the grounds of the Crystal Palace, modified the gardens at Chatsworth and laid out a number of public parks, notably that at Birkenhead. He experimented successfully with hydraulic engineering, constructing the highest fountain jet in the world at Chatsworth,

Joseph Paxton. Crystal Palace. Sydenham, 1852–4

and in heating and ventilating. His interests as a railway promoter, contractor and Member of Parliament led him to advocate important town-planning schemes, of which the most important were the Thames Embankment (1864–70) and his project for the Great Victorian Way (1855). The latter was to be an eleven-mile-long 'girdle' around central London, to solve its traffic problems, combining a glass-roofed road lined by houses, shops and public buildings with railways on upper tiers.
Bibliography: Violet Markham, *Paxton and the Bachelor Duke*, London 1935; G. F. Chadwick, *The Works of Sir Joseph Paxton*, Architectural Press, London 1961.

G. F. CHADWICK

Pei, Ioh Ming, b. Canton, China 1917. Studied at the Massachusetts Institute of Technology and at Harvard. Office blocks, department stores, town planning projects. The Mile High Center at Denver, Col. (1956) has an attractive façade design featuring two intersecting systems: columns and beams with dark cast-aluminium cladding; the air conditioning ducts are sited

Auguste Perret. Apartment Block, Rue Franklin. Paris, 1903

behind strips of bright enamelling. Has worked on the development plans of Washington, Chicago and Philadelphia.

Perret, Auguste, b. Brussels 1874, d. Paris 1954. Perret had his first architectural training at the Paris *École des Beaux-Arts, which he left, however, before sitting his finals. He entered his family's building firm, which had early specialized in reinforced concrete construction; the first building he himself designed dates already from the year 1890.

Perret is frequently reproached with having, on the one hand, applied reinforced concrete methods that were still in their infancy at the time of his first sensational buildings (apartment house in the Rue Franklin, Paris, 1903; Garage Ponthieu, Paris, 1906; Théâtre des Champs-Elysées, Paris, 1910–13) to a system of columns and beams taken over from carpentry, hence depriving architecture for decades to come of freedom in employing the new material. On the other hand it is said that in his old age he grafted neoclassic features onto this monolithic material which were in no ways a logical outcome of its use (Mobilier National, Paris, 1931; Musée des Travaux Publics, 1937; atomic research station, Saclay, 1947; reconstruction of Le Havre). The reproach of neo-Academic formalism is justified as regards Perret's late work. His talent for structurally lucid design peters out into empty trifling. It can hardly be claimed, however, that Perret's early intervention in the history of reinforced concrete construction has had negative consequences. Not only did Perret make it possible to use *reinforced concrete in architecture, which none of his contemporaries succeeded in doing to the same extent, he was also the only one among the pioneers of modern architecture who did not simply preach 'honest building' but practised it as well. His system of columns and beams, the essence of the whole method of framed structures, accords exactly with the demand for economy of formwork. The fruit of his mature years displays a perfection of craftsmanship which is only to be encountered elsewhere in *Mies van der Rohe, who, incidentally, has not a little in common with Perret. But Perret was not just a consummate structural designer who paved the way to architecture for reinforced concrete. His consistent use of the material resulted in a number of buildings still considered exemplary today, among them that masterpiece of 20th-century architecture, the Church of Notre-Dame at Le Raincy (1922–23). There the neoclassicist Perret has paradoxically been successful—uniquely in his time—in reviving the Gothic church lunette. His numerous villas and studio-houses of the next decade are characterized by precision and delicacy of proportion and detailing. The sharp distinction made between framework and infill is raised to the point of dogma and leads to a new conception of form reminiscent of the purest creations of a Gabriel or *Schinkel. Thus both traditions of French rationalism are perpetuated in Perret's reinforced concrete style, that of the neo-Gothic, as significantly formulated by *Viollet-le-Duc, and that represented by the classicism of Perret's teacher Guadet.

The freest expression of Perret's structural genius is to be found in his industrial commissions where he is relieved of the frustrating task of achieving monumentality (warehouses at Casablanca, 1915; clothes factory and scene painting studio, Paris, 1919; workshops for steel or aluminium rolling mills at Montataire, 1920 and Issoire, 1939; watch factory at Besançon, 1939; aircraft hangar at Marseilles, 1950). Unhampered by decorative details, these purely functional buildings however lack those amazing effects achieved by *Maillart, *Nervi, or *Freyssinet through the use of novel structural shapes. And yet they have an elegance and dignity, attained by their unparalleled lucidity of construction and harmony of rhythm and proportion. Perret's industrial buildings, from the Garage Ponthieu to the marine laboratories on the Boulevard Victor, Paris (1928), like those by Saarinen and Mies, rank amongst the most important architectural efforts to stress the 'nobility of the industrial age'.

Finally, Perret's research into the standardization and industrialization of building components should be mentioned, which apart from anything else was not without influence on his sometime pupil *Le Corbusier.

Bibliography: Auguste Perret, Contribution à une Théorie de l'Architecture, Paris 1952; P. Jamot, A. et G. Perret et l'Architecture du Béton Armé, Paris and Brussels 1927; Ernesto N. Rogers, Auguste Perret, Milan

Auguste Perret. Notre-Dame. Le Raincy, 1922–3

1955; Bernard Champigneulle, Auguste Perret, Paris 1959; Peter Collins, Concrete —The Vision of a New Architecture, London 1959.

MAURICE BESSET

Auguste Perret. Place de l'Hôtel de Ville. Le Havre, commenced 1947

Hans Poelzig. Grosses Schauspielhaus. Berlin, 1919

Gio Ponti. Pirelli Building. Milan, 1958

Poelzig, Hans, b. Berlin 1869, d. Berlin 1936. Poelzig exerted great influence in Germany both as an architect and as a teacher (Professor at the Charlottenburg Technical College). His office building, Breslau 1911, anticipates the favourite motive of the twenties, fenestration in horizontal strips. Industrial buildings such as the Luban chemical factory near Posen (1911–12) and the water tower at Posen (1911) are the forerunners of Poelzig's Expressionist phase. His designs just after the First World War (Project for the Salzburg Festival Theatre, 1920–1) are of visionary imagination. The rebuilding of the Schumann Circus into Max Reinhardt's Grosses Schauspielhaus was based on these designs (Berlin 1919): a 'space-cave' masked by stalactite-shapes, which made acting on an arena stage feasible. Towards the end of the twenties, Poelzig went over to buildings of a monumental straightforwardness. (Administrative block for IG-Farben, Frankfort on the Main, 1928–31).
Bibliography: Theodor Heuss, *Hans Poelzig, Lebensbild eines deutschen Baumeisters,* Tübingen 1955.

Polk, Willis Jefferson, b. near Frankfort, Kentucky 1867, d. San Mateo, Calif. 1924. Pupil of *Maybeck. The Hallidie Building (San Francisco, 1918) by Polk and Co. is one of the first buildings with a fully glazed, non-loadbearing outer wall (*curtain wall).

Pollini, Gino, b. Rovereto, Trentino 1903. Graduated Milan 1927. Founder-member of *gruppo 7. Works in collaboration with Luigi *Figini.

Ponti, Gio, b. Milan 1891. Ponti is the best known Italian architect today. He graduated in Milan in 1921, and already had some professional experience when the foundation of the *Movimento Italiano per l'Architettura Razionale* in 1927 presented Italian architects with radically new problems and new responsibilities, at a period when the *Novecento Italiano's* neoclassic revivalism was triumphant.
In this current, which saw the end of *Futurism, Gio Ponti practised an elegant 'modernism', derived partly from the Viennese style of the time, mixed with neoclassic motifs and rationalist lucidity. In

Gio Ponti. Italian Institute. Stockholm, 1959

contrast to the other architects of his generation, who relied on the classical effects of arches and columns and took no account of the new developments in building technology, Ponti adhered in general to the tenets of the rationalist and functionalist school; but he stayed clear of the controversies, perilously conducted by Persico and Pagano, nor did he join the revolt of the younger architects (banded together as *gruppo* 7) against revivalism, the historic styles and the abuse of decoration.

Ponti founded the journal *Domus* in 1928. Now the most widely read publication in the field of interior decoration, it proved a very effective instrument at the time in improving the taste of the Italian middle classes. In 1933, before he had discarded his neoclassicist leanings, Ponti was appointed to the executive committee of the V Milan Triennale, then known as 'Ponti's Triennale'. Its great merit was that it opened the doors of this famous international exhibition to the young 'rationalists' of the Milanese avant-garde, who had now become the most representative archi-

tects of the modern movement. During these years Ponti did a good deal of work in the field of industrial design, to new criteria; built flats, churches and factories; and wrote articles and books (e.g. *La casa all'Italiana*, 1933) in which he put forward the viewpoint that architecture must always preserve some national characteristics.

Ponti's long series of buildings began in 1923. In 1934 he designed the Institute of Mathematics for the University of Rome; but it was only in 1936, with his scheme for the Catholic Press Exhibition in Vatican City, one of his happiest creations, that he gave up the strict symmetry and conventions of neoclassicism. Again in 1936 he designed the first office block for the Montecatini Company in Milan (the second dates from 1951), in which he combined *Novecento* elements (e.g. maximum plastic evidence of volumes) with others of the rationalist system of aesthetics. This imposing building remains one of his most important and lasting works. After a series of projects carried out in every part of the world save in Italy, from São Paulo to Caracas, and from Paris to Stockholm, he achieved his masterpiece in 1958 with the Pirelli Skyscraper in Milan (with *Nervi as structural engineer), whose outline is now universally familiar. This building, with its hexagonal plan and its sides tapered like a ship's bows, has affected the town planning layout of the whole surrounding zone, itself partly designed by the same architect.

Among the buildings he has currently under construction may be mentioned a new hospital for Milan, with an interesting surface treatment; two churches; offices for the Bagdad Planning Board; and eight ministry buildings for Islamabad, the new capital of Pakistan. Since 1936 Gio Ponti has lectured in the faculty of architecture at Milan Polytechnic, and has held courses in the Universities of São Paulo, Paris, Delft, Istanbul, Barcelona, Caracas, Zurich, Stockholm, Madrid and Gothenburg. He was the first president of the International Museum of Modern Architecture, founded in Milan in 1961.

Bibliography: Gio Ponti, *Amate l'Architettura*, Milan 1957; Edoardo Persico, 'Giovanni Ponti', in *L'Italia Letteraria 29*, April 1934; James S. Plaut, *Espressione di Gio Ponti*, Milan 1954.

GIULIA VERONESI

Joseph Paxton. Crystal Palace. London, 1851. Assembling prefabricated units

Powell and Moya. Philip Powell and John Hidalgo Moya. Studied at the Architectural Association School of Architecture, London, and founded their partnership in 1946, two years after graduating, to carry out the Pimlico Housing Scheme, London, which they had won in competition against sixty-four entrants with a design that proved a significant landmark in the attempt to establish a post-war vernacular. Vertical feature ('Skylon') at the South Bank Exhibition, London, 1951; Mayfield Comprehensive School, Putney, 1956, 'subtle, elegant, humane' (Ian Nairn); Princess Margaret Hospital, Swindon; undergraduates' rooms at Brasenose College, Oxford; hexagonal theatre with an arena stage, Chichester, 1962.

Prefabrication. Prefabrication is the attempt of modern building technology to increase building productivity. Many variations of this idea and its realization are feasible and are already being developed today. Even traditional building consists of a large number of parts previously fabricated in factories, but they rarely exhibit common principles of design, structure or manufacture. Besides raising productivity by the use of rationalization on the building site, the logical aim of prefabrication must be the factory-made building, turned out by industrial production techniques. The method still in use today of craft prefabrication is imperfect and must be supplemented by the complete interposition of industrial manufacturing processes. Entire dispensation with site work, however, is only possible in the case of smaller private houses (prefabricated houses). That is why the greatest efforts are being concentrated on turning out this type of building in factories.

These attempts to produce a prefabricated or even an industrially manufactured house have so far not evinced any conclusive results. Many prototypes and some production models of certain series are available, however. Examples—some already of historical interest—include the Acorn House, the Dymaxion House (*Fuller), the General Panel House (*Gropius, *Wachsmann), the Lustron House and the TVA-Trailer, to mention but a few. Another large field of application that has opened up is that of filler units, internal and external wall panels, and roof and floor slabs; other typical products include *curtain walls, infill panels and movable partitions.

The various materials and the industrial processes connected with them have rendered novel structural methods possible and a number of countries have already turned out some excellent products. Fundamentally light structural systems, light forms of building with light or even heavy materials show the greatest progress as compared with traditional building. Integral structures, *space frames and *suspended roofs are particularly progressive developments of this method of building. Other branches of industry, such as aircraft and vehicle production, have strongly influenced the ideas of architects and structural engineers.

The hazards of prefabrication and the industrial manufacture of buildings lie on the sociological plane. Heavy structural systems are particularly unsuitable as they lack adaptability to the multifarious natural patterns of population and their ways of living. That is why adaptability in building

Pier Luigi Nervi. Exhibition hall, Turin, 1948–9. Erecting prefabricated reinforced concrete units from a mobile staging

Below left. Richard Buckminster Fuller. Dymaxion House, 1927. Elevation and isometric view

Walter Gropius. Type series house, with various methods of combining the individual components. 1923. Project is given special consideration when pre-fabricated structures and components are designed: hence the emergence of 'building block' systems that can be combined to meet different circumstances, together with the reduction of the total number of building types, effected by standardization. Modular coordination, which has long been recognized as a prerequisite for rational manufacture and planning, has been introduced in many countries and is proving an indispensable rule in the design of these new building products.

The achievements of individual countries have been helped by the conscious co-operation of industry, government departments and large planning and construction teams. In the *United States, the mass-production of family houses has made great headway, while *curtain walling in

Kaija and Heikki Siren. Terraced housing on the Tapiola estate, 1954–5. Erecting a prefabricated façade unit

particular has been developed for multi-storey buildings. In *Great Britain, after the Second World War, a systematic development of various methods of light pre-fabricated construction for school buildings has taken place, which have not only quickly solved a technological problem but have also made an indirect contribution to education for free and contemporary living. In *France, Scandinavia and the USSR likewise since the Second World War numerous prefabricated heavy structural systems, based on concrete units, have been devised for multi-storey blocks of flats. Examples, however, which are functional and economic in their countries of origin are not necessarily suitable for export elsewhere without modification. Another interesting development towards complete prefabrication has taken place, again in the United States. In 1960, for example, twice as many caravans, i.e. mobile houses, have been manufactured as prefabricated stationary houses. Thus for the first time we have a building completely prefabricated in the factory, from raw material to final assembly.

With the introduction of prefabrication and the aim of industrial manufacture the demands on architects, planners and engineers have risen. The traditional methods of architectural design are no longer sufficient. These new requirements and the increased responsibility that goes with them make it essential today to transfer the methods of applied science and industrial engineering to architecture. Architecture is thus becoming more and more of an applied science.

Bibliography: Buckminster Fuller, *Brief Building Construction*; Robert W. Marks, *The Dymaxion World of R. Buckminster Fuller*, New York 1960; Konrad Wachsmann, *Wendepunkt im Bauen*, Wiesbaden 1959.

HERBERT OHL

Prouvé, Jean, b. Nancy 1901. What Jean Prouvé, constructor in light metal, has in common with the great ironwork engineers of the 19th century, apart from a sure feeling for his material and a wealth of technical and design ideas, is a dynamic conception of the interplay of the different components and functions of a structure, regardless of whether he is designing a prefabricated façade element, a living unit, a school or a desk. Jean Prouvé is a son of the painter Victor Prouvé, who played a leading part in the École de Nancy, one of the most important centres of Art Nouveau. A trained art-metalworker, Prouvé tackles the formal problems of construction in the 'organic' spirit of this school. For him, form can develop only from a synthesis of all structural and functional components, which in their turn must be considered as parts of a unique constellation. At the same time he is fully aware that the road to the architecture of the future inevitably leads via the thoroughgoing industrialization of building methods, and that industrialization without sweeping standardization of forms is unthinkable.

Prouvé escapes this dilemma by an empirical attitude which abolishes all formalism. As early as 1934 he developed *curtain walling, which he employed in 1936 for a club house at Buc airport and in 1937–9 at the Maison du Peuple at Clichy (architects *Beaudouin and *Lods). But while this type of structure often becomes a purely graphic pattern, Prouvé has created a number of variants that constitute a series of very acceptable formal innovations, conceived from a need to achieve the best possible adaptation to particular technical and functional requirements: Building Industry Association Headquarters, Paris, 1950 (with Lopez); Exhibition Hall, Lille (with Herbé); CNIT Exhibition Hall, Paris (with *Zehrfuss, Camelot and de Mailly) and the French Pavilion at Brussels (with Gillet), 1958; block of flats, Paris, 1954 (with Mirabaud); hall for the *100 Years of Aluminium* exhibition in Paris, 1954; Technical College, Lyons (INSA with Perrin-Fayolle); Central Research Institute of Grenoble University, 1959. Prouvé considers that all building components, from roof slabs to built-in cupboards, and from the columns to the essential services (kitchen, bath, w.c.) can be factory-made, ready for assembly in the same way as façade units, and put into service structurally as well as functionally at the same time. As a result of decades of research, which led to the extensive redesigning of all these elements, Prouvé began to mass-produce prefabricated buildings of all types (houses, schools, offices, canteens, workshops, laboratories, holiday camps), among which the shell type houses (estate at Meudon, 1949), the Abbé Pierre

Jean and Henri Prouvé, André Sive. Experimental houses. Meudon, 1954

House, the isothermal living quarters for Sahara conditions and the schools deserve special mention.

Despite the extreme economy of their method of production and their standardization, these buildings possess an almost luxurious character and retain a high degree of individuality. This is in contrast to the usual dreary monotony found in prefabricated buildings and recalls instead the affluent architecture of *Mies van der Rohe.

Jean Prouvé and Maurice Novarina. Refreshment room. Evian, completed 1957

Jean Prouvé, Belmont and Silvy. Point block of flats for lecturers, Cité Universitaire. Nancy. Project

The reason is not so much the precise finish and the carefully planned equipment but the feeling of freedom bestowed by the elegance of proportions and forms and the generous distribution of space. In some buildings (villas at Nancy and on the Côte d'Azur, school at Villejuif, refreshment room at Evian) Prouvé's artistry in structure reaches a point of perfection, where the building seems to be weightless. Although the shell of such buildings is exclusively of glass, they do not appear to be mere glass boxes. Tensile stresses which infuse the structural forms with a lively excitement, hinged stanchions with asymmetrically cantilevered arms, intersections which are not rectangular but acute or quite gradual, even with curved transitions, and finally a spatial flow which is never unnecessarily interrupted, all these combine to lend his buildings a clear, gay character which is unique in the architecture of today. These designs, which originated in the laboratory and the factory, have nothing artificial or schematic about them; on the contrary, they are alive and unfold with a surprising spontaneity, like organisms friendly to man.

Bibliography: Special issue of the journal *Architecture*, Nos. 11/12, Brussels 1954; Françoise Choay, 'Jean Prouvé' in *L'Oeil*, Vol. X, No. 46, Paris 1958; G. Gassiot-Talabot, 'Jean Prouvé' in *Cimaise*, Vols. VII-VIII, No. 54, Paris 1961.

MAURICE BESSET

Rainer, Roland, b. Klagenfurt 1910. Trained at the Vienna Technical College. Began teaching 1953; professor at the Vienna Academy of Fine Arts (1956). Since 1958 town planner at Vienna. Schools, housing (prefabricated housing estate for Vienna XIII, together with Auböck, 1954), municipal halls for Vienna (1954–8), and Bremen (under construction).

Reidy, Affonso Eduardo, b. Paris 1909. Reidy graduated at the Escola Nacional de Belas Artes, Rio, in 1930. Before joining the design team of the Ministry of Education Building, he had already produced a significant straightforward job in the 'Home of Good Will', a charitable institution for old people (1931–2), and when Lúcio *Costa appointed *Warchavchik Professor of Architectural Design at the School of Fine Arts (1931) had served as his assistant. Subsequently, his work developed in a subtly personal manner, characterized not only by the apparent casualness with which he embarked upon the most daring formal or structural scheme but also by a pioneering research into new architectural and technical solutions, noticeable, to a greater or lesser degree, in all his projects and finished work. Among others, in the designs for the City Transport Service

Affonso Eduardo Reidy. Pedregulho Estate. Rio de Janeiro, commenced 1947

Offices and Workshops, Rio (1939), with double saw-tooth roofs over the workshops area; for a pumping station in Rio (1949), a service installation transformed into an attractive spot in a park by the sculptural integration of all the elements of the programme; the design for a Museum of Visual Arts, São Paulo (1951), a clean-cut triangular prism sitting on an expressive base structure, on a highly irregular site; or for a Student Theatre, Rio (1955), with the structural supports of the auditorium roof almost floating in mid-air, cantilevered from the massive stage block. And again, in such finished work as the 'Pedregulho' Housing Development, Rio (begun in 1947), with its 260-metre-long apartment block, following the winding contour of the hillside, and its imaginatively designed school, gymnasium, clinic, laundry and

Affonso Eduardo Reidy. Museum of Modern Art. Rio de Janeiro, commenced 1954. Sketch market; or the Marechal Hermes Community Theatre, Rio (1950), a precise and pleasant application of the inverted double slope roof; or the private houses built for Miss Carmen Portinho (1952–4) or Dr Couto e Silva (1955) as well as his latest country house near Petropolis. These same qualities find expression in several important projects still under construction: the 'Gavea' Housing Development, in Rio (1954–), an extension of the principles first applied in the 'Pedregulho' project; the Experimental School in Asuncion, Paraguay (1953–), and the Museum of Modern Art of Rio de Janeiro (1954–), two limpid groupings of various different volumes, underlined by serene rows of concrete ribs enclosing and supporting roof and floor slab, and characterized by freely flowing wide spaces as well as by the novel ways in which natural daylight is combined with artificial lighting; the headquarters for the Rio City Employees Insurance Fund (1957–), with its striking *brise-soleil* façade arrangement.

Reidy's superb plan for the development of Santo Antônio Hill, in the centre of Rio (1948), still under way, has unfortunately suffered the impact of bureaucratic antagonism in many important respects.

Bibliography: K. Franck, *The Works of Affonso Eduardo Reidy*, London 1960.

                                        HENRIQUE E. MINDLIN

Reinforced Concrete. In 1895, François Hennebique completed the Charles VI Mill at Tourcoing. Its loadbearing structure in reinforced concrete was clearly expressed in the elevations; designed without any straining after decorative effects, it fulfilled the functional and technical requirements of its industrial programme admirably, achieving a formal equilibrium and a new vocabulary of style without recourse to traditional solutions. Two years later, Anatole de *Baudot, with the technical collaboration of Contamin, finished building the Church of St Jean-de-Montmartre, Paris—the first conscious exploitation of the new material for architectural and compositional ends as compared with purely technical ones.

It was in this way, at the end of the 19th century, that the design possibilities of a new material were demonstrated in the first buildings to use it, though it had been discovered, experimented with and its basic technical properties established over the course of the previous fifty years. Reinforced concrete is an artificial monolithic material, derived from the union of steel and concrete, when the latter hardens after the mix has been poured in a fluid state into specially prepared shuttering. The concrete itself is obtained from mixing cement, water and aggregate (sand and gravel) in proportions that vary with the technical results required. The steel reinforcement consists of a cage of steel bars, normally round, though other special sections are sometimes used to increase the degree to which the reinforcement is anchored in the concrete. The size and disposition of the bars is determined in accordance with the particular static and technical requirements involved. The shuttering which holds the mix in its liquid state until it has set, determines the shape of the concrete. Shuttering, or form-work as it is sometimes called, is made up of timber boards, metal panels or units of other material; structural, economic, architectural and decorative factors influence the choice. The two components of reinforced concrete perform the static functions appropriate to their respective properties: basically, the concrete takes up the compressive stresses, and the steel absorbs those of tension.

The idea of assigning different but complementary stress-resistant functions to different materials within the same static system, was first developed and applied many centuries ago; examples may be found in the use of chains for tying in vaults in Byzantine, Islamic, Italian Gothic, Renaissance and Baroque architecture, for which iron, and more anciently wood, was employed. Working to different formal standards, static systems were also evolved, especially after the Late Renaissance, in which the device for resisting tensile stress (chain or hoop) was masked. In Paris, from the 17th century onwards, stressed reinforcements were incorporated and interposed between single elements of the same masonry structure (colonnade at the Louvre by Claude Perrault, 1665–80; portico of the Church of Ste Geneviève (later the Panthéon) by Germain Soufflot, 1757–90). At the Panthéon in particular, the iron ribs, disposed in a more complex manner than hitherto, specifically absorb the forces of tension and shear, thus achieving empirically the typical layout of the bars in reinforced concrete and anticipating intuitively the results that were to be reached a hundred years later by the processes of scientific calculation.

The first instances of the employment of iron in conjunction with concrete, however, only go back to the first half of the 19th century: these consist of wrought-iron I-section floors with thin curved metal plates running between the girders, filled in on top with concrete; the engineer William Fairbairn built an eight-storey refinery at Manchester in 1845 using such a system, patented in 1844. A number of basic experiments were carried out between 1849 and 1878: in 1849–50 the French gardener Joseph Monier made some concrete tubs for orange-trees in which he embedded a mesh of iron rods; J. L. Lambot exhibited a boat in concrete on a frame of iron flats at the 1855 Paris Exposition; in 1861, the French builder François Coignet improved the strength of his concrete structures by inserting a metal mesh in them; a British immigrant to America, Thaddeus Hyatt, outlined the theory of reinforced concrete in 1877 on the basis of tests with beams, made for him at a laboratory in London. Between 1867 and 1878 Monier took out a series of patents for various applications, showing a clear appreciation of the different stress-resistant properties of iron and concrete respectively. Theoretical and experimental research carried out chiefly by Wayss, Bauschinger, Contamin, Bordenave, Hennebique, E. Coignet and De Tedesco succeeded between 1880 and 1900 in fully establishing the main characteristics and the static behaviour of the new material, and the theoretical bases for calculating structures in it. The use of reinforced concrete began to spread at the beginning of the 20th century in projects of ever-increasing importance; official standards and codes of practice were called for, and these were published in various countries in the first decades of the century.

The young French architect Tony *Garnier in his scheme for a *Cité Industrielle* (1901–4) made sytematic use of reinforced concrete and other modern materials, adopting the unadorned grid system even for housing and offices, which Hennebique had employed for the first time in 1895 for the Charles VI Mill. He thus anticipated

Hennebique's reinforced concrete system, 1892

by almost twenty years an architectural idiom that was first to become widespread only in the period of the *International Style.

At the same epoch, Auguste *Perret, at the beginning of his career as an architect and builder, erected a house in the Rue Franklin,

Anatole de Baudot and Contamin. Church of St Jean-de-Montmartre. Paris, 1894–7

Tony Garnier. Town Hall. Cité Industrielle. 1901–4. Project

Paris, in which he exploited the technical possibilities of a reinforced concrete-framed structure (smaller size of stanchions and greater freedom of manoeuvre with them) to resolve a difficult planning problem, basing the architectural treatment of the façade on the contrast between the loadbearing frame and the infill panels. Meanwhile, in the villa he built himself at Bourg-la-Reine in 1904, Hennebique demonstrated the static possibilities of reinforced concrete in controversial fashion with such structural novelties as an octagonal tower carried on 13-foot cantilevers. The architectural idiom employed is still traditional and eclectic, but Hennebique, perhaps unconsciously, opened up new prospects of three-dimensional design.

The first, almost contemporary, works of the Swiss engineer Robert *Maillart, on the other hand, are the result of a far-reaching attempt to achieve absolute stylistic purity by deliberately aiming at unity of form and static behaviour in his structures. In his bridge over the Rhine at Tavanasa (1905) carriageway and structural framework are intimately fused to produce a structural and plastic unity. The first example of mushroom slab construction occurs in a warehouse he built in 1910 at Zurich,

where beams are eliminated and the floor slab itself is designed in such a way as to take over their static functions.

The problem of large-span roofs, hitherto dealt with by using steel-frame structures, was now finally tackled and solved in reinforced concrete. In his Centenary Hall at Breslau (1912–13), Max *Berg roofed the central area of the assembly hall with a dome made up of huge concrete ribs 213 feet in diameter. Eugène *Freyssinet covered his two airship hangars at Orly (1916–24) with a barrel vault consisting of a thin membrane of reinforced concrete, pleated to give the necessary rigidity, and parabolic in overall section to reduce tensile stresses to a minimum.

The employment of reinforced concrete for large industrial complexes became a regular practice. In 1915, the engineer Matté Trucco began building the Fiat-Lingotto works at Turin, with an area of over a hundred acres. He adopted reinforced concrete for every type of structure, solving technical problems of great difficulty in the automobile testing track he sited on the roof of a five-storey factory, and the access ramp that leads up to it.

It was during these years, too, that *Le Corbusier, not yet thirty, was working out the premises of his architectural manner. Reinforced concrete seemed to him to be the most appropriate medium for realizing them in. With his project for the Dom-Ino houses (1914), based on a modular grid in reinforced concrete, he set forth the theoretical preconditions for designing a free plan. America, too, whose architecture had developed during the 19th century via the habitual adoption of the steel frame, began to accept the use of reinforced concrete (albeit not without controversy), especially for large-scale industrial buildings (warehouse for Montgomery, Ward & Co., Chicago, by Schmidt, Garden and Martin, 1908; silos at Fort William, c. 1900). *Gropius published these buildings in 1913 in the Annual of the *Deutscher Werkbund, acknowledging them as creations of modern architecture.

The commission to design the Einstein Observatory-Tower at Potsdam in 1920 gave Erich *Mendelsohn his first opportunity of bringing to actual realization the architectural vision which had been maturing in his sketches from 1914 to 1919

Max Berg. Centenary Hall. Breslau, 1912–13

Auguste Perret. Garage Ponthieu. Paris, 1906

(*Expressionism). Reinforced concrete is the material theoretically best adapted for modelling a form that has to be rendered as a fluid, homogeneous and continuous mass, and for creative works of architecture freed from the traditional schematism of horizontal and vertical lines. It was impossible to make use of the new material, however, because no curved shuttering was available: the tower had to be built in brick and rendered over. The full exploitation of the plastic possibilities of concrete was achieved shortly afterwards, in the German Expressionist manner, with the War Memorial at Weimar by Gropius (1921) and the Goetheanum at Dornach by Rudolf Steiner (1925–8).

Inspired by the climate of research and experiment of the early post-war years, *Mies van der Rohe prepared a scheme for the Novembergruppe Exhibition in 1922 for a reinforced concrete office block in which the stanchions are set back from the façades and support the floors, which project out all round, by a cantilever arrangement. The external walls assume the character of a series of horizontal strips, one on top of the other. In the years that followed, this architectural idiom became the common property of the rationalist movement, and may be met with in the works of many architects before the Second World War, modified to accord with personal styles (Boots' Factory at Beeston, by Sir E. Owen *Williams, 1932; Open-Air School, Amsterdam, by J. *Duiker, 1930–2; tobacco factory at Linz, by P. *Behrens, 1930–5).

Perret, meanwhile, had carried his architectural use of reinforced concrete further. In the Church of Notre-Dame, Le Raincy (1922–3), a limited budget favoured the elimination of many of the frills usual in ecclesiastical work. The reinforced concrete frame supports a system of vaults and forms the bell-tower. The walls are perforated concrete panels set with coloured glass. The decorative result is indubitably rich, despite the poverty of materials and the rough appearance of the concrete left completely exposed. Karl *Moser's Church of St Antony, Basle (1926–7) is an organic structure in frankly exposed reinforced concrete which derives its inspiration from the contemporary works of Perret.

Walter Gropius adopted reinforced concrete construction in 1925–6 for all the buildings of the Bauhaus. The individual

Le Corbusier. Unité d'Habitation. Nantes-Rezé, 1952–7

character of the various structural elements, however, was not stressed by underlining their physical consistency and technical properties, but static and formal design was rigorously conditioned by architectural and functional requirements. Henceforth reinforced concrete became a structural element of great versatility, capable of responding to all the demands made on it by the compositional freedom of modern architecture, without having to assume major status as a source of expression. In Le Corbusier's Pavillon Suisse (1930–2) the reinforced concrete substructure, consisting of six huge piers over which the steel frame of the upper storeys is cantilevered, provides an airy and welcoming portico that is imposing in appearance while effecting a happy transition between the external surroundings and the inside of the building. The surface of the concrete is left in the state it was when the shuttering was struck, the irregular impressions made by the timber creating a kind of decorative effect.

Thus began a long series of works in which Le Corbusier was to interpret with extraordinary freedom the technical, architectural and decorative possibilities of reinforced concrete, thereby setting a trend that found many followers amongst the practitioners of modern architecture in Europe and beyond (Ministry of Education, Rio de Janeiro, by *Costa, *Niemeyer, *Reidy and Vasconcellos, 1936–43; consultant architect: Le Corbusier). In the Unité d'Habitation at Marseilles (1947–52), reinforced concrete is systematically employed for the main framework of the building, cladding on the façades and 'interior roads', sun-breaks and emergency stairs. In the Church of Notre-Dame du Haut, at Ronchamp (1950–4), the inventive plan for Chandigarh (1950 onwards) and the Dominican Convent of La Tourette (1957) Le Corbusier has finally freed himself of rigid geometrical schemes, relying on reinforced concrete for a type of three-dimensional creation that is not limited to single elements but comprises the total scope of the architectural organism.

Frank Lloyd *Wright, too, has employed a strongly personal and at times unprecedented style in the projection of bold, if

Page 239. Pier Luigi Nervi. Exhibition Hall. Turin, 1948–9

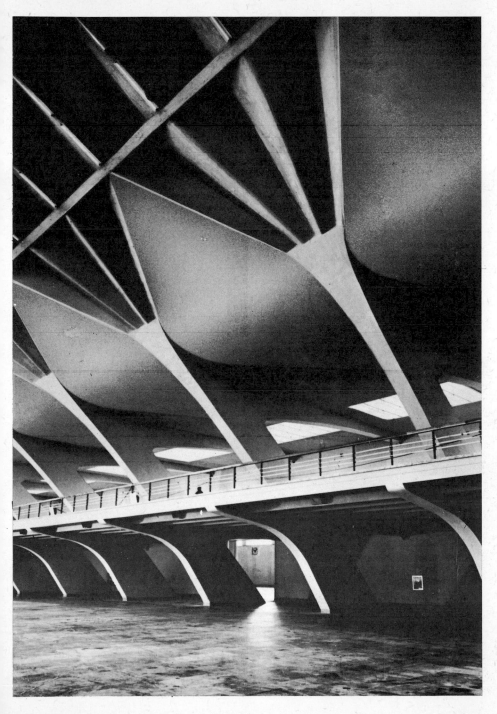

not always strictly pertinent, structural schemes in the field of residential and commercial building. Notable examples of his use of reinforced concrete include the Imperial Hotel, Tokyo (1916–22), an earthquake-proof design with projecting floor slabs; 'Falling Water' House at Bear Run, Pa. (1937–9) with its cantilevered balconies; the Johnson Wax Building, at Racine, Wis. (1936–9), featuring umbrella-type columns; the laboratory tower at the same site (1949), where the upper floors are cantilevered out from a central core; the Guggenheim Museum, New York (1956–9), based on a spiral ramp; and the Price Tower at Bartlesville, Okla. (1955).

The reconstruction of Le Havre (1947–54) gave Perret the opportunity at last for a great experiment in the employment of reinforced concrete on an urban scale, making extensive use of heavy *prefabrication. Methods like these had been successfully tried out in the inter-war period (Le Corbusier, at the Pavillon Suisse; *Beaudouin and *Lods at La Muette, 1933); they have since been developed further in *France and many other European countries, including the Soviet Union.

Besides these experiments in coordination aimed at industrializing the building trade in the service of vast housing projects, further refinements of technique were worked out and gained currency in the field of multi-storey structures. Pier Luigi *Nervi employed undulating prefabricated reinforced concrete units on a vast scale in his Exhibition Hall at Turin (1948–9), considerably reducing the self-weight of the structure while greatly increasing its elasticity and tensile strength. In the Unesco Building, Paris (1953–7, with *Breuer and *Zehrfuss), he stresses the correspondence between the way the structure is modelled and the development of bending moments by varying the depth and profile of the undulations in the roof of the Conference Hall.

Nervi's vaults; Maillart's bridges, and his barrel-vaulted pavilion for the cement industry at the Swiss Provinces Exhibition in Zurich (1939); the structures of Eduardo *Torroja and the recent emergence of *shell structures (*Candela), all show the current tendency in engineering to transcend the orthogonal system of beams and girders in order to attain a structural unity in the whole building. For their arena at Raleigh, N.C. (1952–3), *Deitrick, *Novicki and Severud adopted reinforced concrete for the anchorage structure of the tension cables of the *suspended roof. Opportunities for using reinforced concrete have been multiplied still further by the introduction of pre- and post-stressing, in which the steel reinforcement is placed in stress either before or after the concrete is poured.

Reinforced concrete is now being used for tower blocks of flats or offices, achieving parity of esteem in a sector which for many decades had been the exclusive prerogative of steel. In Mies van der Rohe's design for the Promontory Apartments, Chicago (1949) and *BBPR's scheme for the Torre Velasca, Milan (1957), two structural solutions were drawn up and compared, one using reinforced concrete, and the other steel. The choice fell in both cases to reinforced concrete, Mies keeping to the strict grid system he had envisaged for either solution, and BBPR, on the other hand, opting for a more continuous and unitary scheme which the choice allowed. The Pirelli Building by Gio *Ponti and others (1958) and the Torre Galfa by M. Bega (1959), both at Milan, make use of great reinforced concrete piers, sited orthogonally, as the bases of their support structures. In their departure from the usual grid pattern they open up new possibilities for attaining variety and freedom in design.

Bibliography: C. Cestelli-Guidi, *Cemento armato precompresso*, Milan 1960; R. Gabetti, *Origini del calcestruzzo armato*, Turin 1955; R. Morandi, *Strutture di cemento armato e di calcestruzzo precompresso*, Rome 1954; P. Collins, *Concrete: The Vision of a New Architecture*, London 1959.

GIUSEPPE VARALDO
GIAN PIO ZUCCOTTI

Revell, Viljo, b. Vaasa, Finland 1910. Revell studied at a time when Functionalism had its first flowering in *Finland. His studies, during which he also worked as an assistant to Alvar *Aalto, were completed in 1937. Already before then he had built the so-called 'Glass Palace' with two colleagues, Kokko and Riihimäki, a department store which introduced a bold piece of modern architecture into the then very conservative scene at Helsinki. For his diploma design, Revell characteristically chose a real subject: a building for a small manufacturer; and he dealt with the problem in a logical way, as a rationalist would. An eye for the practical solution, a propensity for systematic thought and a talent for organization fitted him for the directorship of the Reconstruction Office, founded by the Association of Finnish Architects during the war, and later for the chairmanship of the Finnish Standards Committee.

Revell's first important design was for an office block with a hotel, Teollisuuskeskus at Helsinki (1952, in collaboration with Keijo Petäjä). His studio had meanwhile become a kind of headquarters for the new Rationalism in Finland, and the way up for many of today's leading young architects led through Revell's office. Revell often confined himself to critical advice when training his assistants, who were allowed much freedom. An impressive number of competition prizes and completed buildings are the visible achievement of this constantly rejuvenated team (Meilahti Primary School, Helsinki, 1953, together with Osmo Sipari; experimental housing at Tapiola; luxurious private villas, terraced houses).

The clear layout, the externally simple but effective shape and the precise planning of the Kudeneule Textile Works at Hanko (1955) are immediately obvious. Revell does not stress the repetition of secondary elements but presents a unified formal theme. He prefers to work with large structures and wide spans. This conception is also apparent in some of his unbuilt competition designs (Sininen Nauha housing estate, planned for Helsinki, 1954; Tasa, planned for Tampere, 1953) in which Revell's ideal becomes obvious: wide open spaces, whose only boundary is the horizon.

Together with H. Castrén, B. Lundsten and S. Valjus, Revell won the competition for Toronto City Hall in 1958. The design arose out of an attempt to emphasize the significance of this public building by giving it a shape that would mark its difference from the commercial skyscrapers. At the same time, the building is an expression of Revell's striving after free form, which has also been apparent in other rationalists towards the end of the fifties. Revell's generalizing, international and industrially orientated outlook is in

Viljo Revell and Keijo Petäjä. Teollisuuskeskus Hotel and offices. Helsinki, 1952

Viljo Revell. Kindergarten. Tapiola, 1954

Viljo Revell. Toronto City Hall. 1958. Model

contrast with the rest of Finnish architecture, which mostly shows a preference for individual building on a small scale and in a style that tends to betray a craft approach. But it is exactly because contrasts are conducive to development that Revell's influence is so fruitful.

KYÖSTI ÅLANDER

Richardson, Henry Hobson, b. St James Parish, La., 1838, d. Boston 1886. Richardson studied at the École des Beaux-Arts, Paris and worked in the studio of Henri *Labrouste. Returned to the States in 1865. Housing, offices, churches and public buildings. Richardson, who commanded nation-wide respect, developed a characteristically heavy style with reminiscences of the Romanesque. His Marshall Field Warehouse in Chicago (1885–7), with massive masonry, has a slab-like unity despite its enormous arched windows. His taut monumentality long influenced the School of *Chicago.
Bibliography: Henry-Russell Hitchcock, *The Architecture of H. H. Richardson and his Times,* 2nd edition, Hamden, Conn. 1961.

Riemerschmid, Richard, b. Munich 1868, d. Munich 1957. Architect and designer. Riemerschmid, like many artists of the *Art Nouveau, progressed from painting to the applied arts. In 1897 he was a founder-member of the United Workshops for Art in Craft; 1901, interior decoration of the Munich Theatre; 1910, factories at Hellerau.

Rietveld, Gerrit Thomas, b. Utrecht 1888. Rietveld worked as an apprentice from 1899 to 1906 in his father's joinery shop, and then ran his own cabinetmaking business in Utrecht (1911–19). His first architectural studies were carried out under the architect P. J. C. Klaarhamer in Utrecht (1911–15); Rietveld was also an admirer of *Berlage. In 1918, chiefly through the agency of Robert van't Hoff, he came into contact with the founders of the *Stijl movement, of which he remained a member till 1931. His early furniture designs (from 1918) were primarily three-dimensional compositions. In 1921 he began collaborating with the interior decorator Tr. Schröder-Schräder (Rietveld-Schröder House, Utrecht, 1924). Work with van *Doesburg and van *Eesteren followed in 1923. Rietveld was one of the founders of *CIAM at La Sarraz in 1928. From then on he worked as an architect in the Netherlands (terraced housing, Utrecht, 1931–4; Vreeburg Cinema, Utrecht, 1936), Germany, Austria, Italy (Venice Biennale, 1953), Curaçao, France and Belgium.
After his difficult start, which brought him, however, international fame, the number of Rietveld's commissions began to dwindle (shops for the Wessels company, Utrecht 1923, now altered). From 1931 onwards, when *De Stijl* ceased publication and the group broke up, modern architecture passed through a difficult period in the *Netherlands, having to sustain a running battle with the historicizing 'national' style. This trend

Gerrit Thomas Rietveld. Schroeder House. Utrecht, 1924

received a particular fillip in the years 1945–55, and its practitioners considered Rietveld's work to be completely superseded. His reputation began to revive with the new interest shown in America, and later Europe, in the work of Mondrian and De Stijl. Since then Rietveld has received an increasing number of important commissions, and achieved complete recognition by the younger generation of architects (country houses; Soonsbeek Pavilion, near Arnhem, 1954, since demolished; De Ploeg Textile Works, Bergeijck, 1956; housing development, Hoograven, 1954–6, with other architects).

One of the main characteristics of Rietveld's work is his three-dimensional handling of space, which has developed from De Stijl practice without ever becoming fixed in rigid attitudes. This also explains his consistent interest in interior decoration and furniture design. Rietveld has always been receptive to anything new, whether in materials or methods, while making no concessions to the merely fashionable. His use of the primary colours red, blue and yellow still testifies to his close allegiance to De Stijl. But the natural colours of his materials have gained the upper hand, and together with a restrained palette of

Gerrit Thomas Rietveld. Zonnehof Museum. Amersfoort, 1959

white, grey and black, help to set off the ever-cubistic forms of his architecture.
Bibliography: Th. M. Brown, *The Work of G. Th. Rietveld*, Utrecht 1958.

                                    J. J. VRIEND

Ring, Der. Berlin architects' association founded in 1925. Among its members were such eminent German architects as *Bartning, *Behrens, Döcker, *Gropius, *Häring, Haesler, *Hilberseimer, the brothers *Luckhardt, *May, *Mendelsohn,

*Mies van der Rohe, *Poelzig, *Scharoun, and the brothers *Taut.

Rogers, Ernesto N., b. Trieste 1909. Graduated Milan 1932. Belongs to the architectural team *BBPR. Publisher of the architectural journal *Domus*, then (since 1954) of the architectural journal *Casabella Continuità*.
Bibliography: Ernesto N. Rogers, *Esperienza dell'Architettura*, Turin 1958.

Gerrit Thomas Rietveld. House. Ilpendam, 1959

Root, John Wellborn, b. Lumpkin *c.* 1850, d. Chicago 1891. Partner of Daniel Hudson *Burnham.

Rotterdam, School of. *Stijl, De.

Rudolph, Paul, b. Elkton, Ky. 1918. Studied at Harvard University under Gropius. Since 1958 Chairman of the Department of Architecture at Yale University, New Haven, Conn. Rudolph developed an astonishingly wide range of design features ('new freedom') in his search for an individuality appropriate to the function of each building: Cultural Centre with resemblance to the neighbouring older neo-Gothic buildings of Wellesley College, Mass. (1955–9); schools at Sarasota, Fla.; a scheme featuring closely interlocking blocks for a motel at Waverly, N.Y., and students' quarters at Yale University, New Haven (both started in 1960); an elegant cantilevered concrete structure for a multi-storey garage at New Haven (started 1959); a building radiating in many directions as a chapel at Tuskegee, Ala. (started in 1960).

Saarinen, Eero, b. Kirkkonummi, Finland 1910, d. Birmingham, USA 1961. Eero Saarinen was the son of the architect Eliel *Saarinen. He came to the USA with his family in 1923, and received his degree from Yale University in 1934. He travelled in Europe in 1934–6, and subsequently entered into partnership with his father at Cranbrook. Although Eero's influence is certainly to be seen in his father's work from the late 1930s onward, it was the

winning of the Jefferson Memorial Competition, St Louis, 1949 (which he had entered by himself), that established the younger man as a separate personality.

His first major work, the General Motors Technical Center, Warren, Michigan, completed in 1955, was for a client who had originally engaged his father for the task. Eero Saarinen and his associates responded to the demands of this remarkable challenge with considerable distinction. The numerous buildings of simple, cubic shape are spaced irregularly around a central lagoon in a manner reminiscent of the master plan of *Mies van der Rohe for the Illinois Institute of Technology, Chicago (1940). However, the shapes of the Saarinen buildings are more individualized in scale and surface modulation, and are more varied in colour than is the case with Mies's inveterately regularized 'industrial classicism'. Together with the contemporary works of Philip *Johnson and of *Skidmore, Owings and Merrill, Saarinen's General Motors designs determined the trends that would dominate American architecture until the late 1950s.

In the light of his subsequent development, and of the evolution of architecture that has taken place since then, this General Motors 'style' already seems at least superficially antiquated. Two 'central plan' edifices for the Massachusetts Institute of Technology, Cambridge, Mass., finished in 1955, the shell-domed Kresge Auditorium and the Chapel, indicate a multiple heritage as well as a diverse future for Saarinen's architecture. The simple domical form enclosed a complexly shaped

Eero Saarinen. General Motors Technical Center. Warren, Mich., completed 1955

Eero Saarinen. Yale Hockey Rink. Yale University, New Haven, Conn., completed 1958

auditorium with a single, sweeping curve in a way that provoked much criticism, especially from those who felt that the arbitrary-seeming form of the exterior was not suited to the varied requirements of the interior space. There is indeed a paradox in the outer forms and the interior workings of the Kresge Auditorium, and it tends to underscore one of the most challenging problems in recent architecture. The difficulty comes about from the recurring effort to reconcile a style appropriate to the exact programme of the building and the technological nature of modern construction with the desire to use forms of a pure, simplified character, indeed forms with pronounced classicizing overtones. In their late styles, both Mies van der Rohe and *Le Corbusier have found eminently successful personal means of reconciling the paradoxical demands of the machine age with their latent predilections for inventing shapes whose ancestry lies in classic or pre-classic Mediterranean architecture.

Eero Saarinen. Kresge Auditorium, Massachusetts Institute of Technology. Cambridge, Mass., completed 1955

Eero Saarinen. Yale Colleges, Yale University. New Haven, Conn., under construction. Project

Page 247. Eero Saarinen. Yale Hockey Rink, Yale University. New Haven, Conn., completed 1958

Saarinen's difficulty—and, for that matter, the difficulty encountered by many of his contemporaries—is that his reconciliation seems tentative and insecure. It is made to seem even more unconvincing in the Kresge Auditorium with the presence near by of the more romantic, subjective form of the Chapel, a work which seems to be a devout evocation of his father's stylistic conceptions. The lack of *rapport* between these two MIT structures, which, in itself, is thought-provoking, sounds a warning as to the shifting nature of Eero's later development until his untimely death in 1961. Subsequent designs for large interior spaces, such as the Ingalls Hockey Rink, Yale University, the TWA Terminal, Idlewild, New York, and the Dulles Airport, Washington, D.C., show a more comprehensible relationship between interior space and exterior form. However, while the spaces themselves seem to indicate a common spirit of dynamic coordination, the forms are heterogeneous. The spaces may be expressive or appropriate in a dramatic way, yet one wonders whether there is a justifiable relation between these inventions and the material demands of the programme and of structural technology.

Only the future will be in a position to bear out the validity of these designs, as well as such 'neo-academic' designs for government structures as the American Embassies in London and in Oslo, buildings which represent other efforts at creating distinctive and unique-seeming forms at the expense of allowing a more personal, idiomatic style to evolve. The London Embassy was intended to harmonize with the vernacular architecture of London, but failed to accomplish this aim. The residential colleges at Yale are yet another effort to harmonize with tradition, or, more exactly in this case, with the neo-traditionalism of 'collegiate Gothic', while at the same time maintaining the imprint of modernism. We cannot be sure that Eero Saarinen developed a new method for the design of contemporary buildings; indeed, it can almost be said that he did not produce an individual, consistent style. None the less, he produced a sequence of influential if not organically related buildings that have been much discussed, and which surely illuminate the direction taken by modernist architecture in the 1950s.

JOHN M. JACOBUS, JR

Saarinen, Eliel, b. Rantasalmi, Finland 1873, d. Michigan 1950. Saarinen studied painting at the University and architecture at the Polyteknisk Institut, Helsinki (1893–7). In 1896 he formed a partnership with Herman Gesellius and Armas Lindgren, and in 1899–1900 they received international recognition with the Finnish Pavilion at the Paris Exposition. Significantly, their somewhat neo-medieval design indicates a possible influence from American architects such as H. H. *Richardson and Louis *Sullivan, and at the same time reveals the spirit of the *Art Nouveau in certain decorative touches.

In 1902 Gesellius, Lindgren and Saarinen began work on a joint residence and studio, Hvitträsk, in the wooded countryside outside Helsinki. Certainly one of the most important examples of domestic architecture at the turn of the century, and, in spite of its somewhat indigenous appearance, worthy of comparison with contemporary houses in various parts of the world by *Wright, *Voysey, *Mackintosh and *Hoffmann, Hvitträsk also demonstrates that its architects were familiar with the new spirit in interior design that was then centred in Vienna and Glasgow. Equally, this studio-house reveals an awareness of the progressive domestic designs of such late-19th-century masters as Philip *Webb, Richard Norman *Shaw and Richardson. A similar awareness is to be found in the Saarinen design for the Helsinki Railway Station of 1904, constructed from 1910 to 1914. A typical eclectic monument of the period, its boldly articulated and simply detailed masonry masses sum up a variety of academic, romantic and rational influences that were common at the time. More important, however, is the individual character which Saarinen has wrought from these multiple inheritances of the early modern tradition, and the personal infusion which makes this design unique in the railway architecture of the period. Its creative spirit is equalled only in the more severe romanticism of *Bonatz's nearly contemporary Stuttgart Station.

The scope of Saarinen's architectural practice continued to expand during this decade with his involvement in a number of city planning schemes, one of which was a project for Canberra, Australia. His participation in the competition for the Chicago Tribune Tower, 1922 (for which

Eliel Saarinen. Main Station, Helsinki. Designed 1904, built 1910–14

he received a second prize), led to further work in the USA, to which he moved permanently in 1923. In 1925 he began work on what was destined to become a group of schools at Cranbrook, Michigan. In 1928 he built his own house in Cranbrook, a simple pale brick structure which seems closer in appearance to the bland 'collegiate Gothic' of 20th-century American architecture than to the more pronounced modelling and incisive detail of Saarinen's earlier and more overtly romantic style. Other features at Cranbrook are distantly suggestive of Wright's characteristic use of horizontals, with sheltered loggias, etc. By way of contrast the Cranbrook Academy design of 1940 possesses a dry, neoclassic solemnity, and although its plans and elevations are not perfunctory they are similar in appearance to the simplified, modernized academic tradi-

tionalism that was a feature of monumental architecture throughout the world in the 1930s. Comparison of the Cranbrook buildings of the 1920s and 1930s with the earlier Helsinki Station reveals little or no intensification or development of a personal style, but instead only an overall simplification or generalization of forms that are ultimately derivative.

In 1937 Eliel Saarinen formed a partnership with his son, Eero *Saarinen, and many of his last works must be considered as fundamentally collaborative designs. The Kleinhans Music Hall, Buffalo, New York (1938), clearly indicates an awareness of the new European architecture of the 1920s and early 1930s, which had blossomed after Saarinen's departure from Finland. Here and in a series of churches culminating in Christ Lutheran, Minneapolis, Minn. (1949–50), there is an effective blend of the half-century-old romantic, craftsman-like approach in both decoration and constructive elements, along with a new spirit of design that is more decisive in its geometric simplicity, bolder in the abstract handling of spatial and lighting elements, and even outwardly functional in the sense of the word as then understood. The first Saarinen projects for the General Motors Technical Center were done in 1945, but the definitive designs were not completed until after his death in 1950. The final result was a group of buildings in a severe, industrial, *Mies van der Rohe style that in certain ways is foreign to the more genteel, occasionally unobtrusive personal manner of Eliel Saarinen.

Bibliography: Eliel Saarinen, *Search for Form*, New York 1949; Albert Christ-Janer, *Eliel Saarinen*, Chicago 1949.

JOHN M. JACOBUS, JR

Sant'Elia, Antonio, b. Como 1880, d. Monfalcone 1916. Sant'Elia studied architecture at Milan and later at Bologna, where he graduated at the age of twenty-four. He then began to work for other architects, and to design for himself in the manner of Otto *Wagner's Vienna School. He was greatly attracted by many features of North American civilization, not those realistic and rational aspects of it which had impressed Adolf *Loos, but the romantic aspects of its technical development and the progressive expansion of an industrial metropolis. The new city, the city of the future, thus appeared to him a reality that could be achieved in Italy too, but an Italy shaken from her long sleep and aroused to life once more. He set himself to work out a grandiose project for a *Città Nuova*, both in general and in detail, which was shown in 1914 at the first exhibition in Milan by the *Nuove Tendenze* group, of which he was a member. Designs for 'Structures of a modern metropolis' were displayed at the same exhibition by Sant'Elia's fellow student, the architect Mario *Chiattone, who shared his ideals.

Eliel Saarinen. Cranbrook School for Boys. Bloomfield Hills, Mich., 1925

Eliel and Eero Saarinen. Christ Lutheran Church, Minneapolis, Minn., 1949–50

Antonio Sant'Elia. Città Nuova. 1914. Project

In the catalogue to this exhibition Sant' Elia published a diffuse manifesto on the need for breaking with the past in order to create in Italy too, where 'everything had to be revolutionized', a new architecture, as new as 'the state of mind' of the younger generation; this alone could give valid form to the city of men freed from the bonds of traditions and conventions. Thus, for Sant'Elia, it was eminently a case of historical necessity.

His text was published again a few months afterwards by Marinetti, who had modified it on a number of points. Henceforth one speaks of *Futurist architecture, and Sant' Elia himself is referred to as a Futurist. In reality Sant'Elia was a Socialist, who had joined Marinetti's movement without enthusiasm, for it was of an outspokenly nationalist character and ended up a few years later by going along with Fascism completely. Sant'Elia, however,

did not have much time to think out his position as an architect vis-à-vis Marinetti, for he was called up in 1915 on Italy's entry into the war and was killed a year later leading an assault.

Sant'Elia's architecture had very little affinity with the beginnings of the modern movement that was currently stirring in *Germany and *Austria; it remains an isolated phenomenon in Europe, although it introduced a number of motifs to Italian culture and a stylistic formula that had much in common with Russian *Constructivism. Its main influence was on the architecture of the great international exhibitions and their pavilions. But it is due to him that Italian culture, shaken by his words, looked for the first time at the problem of the new architecture as a problem, albeit a limited one, of a new life and new customs, in an age that witnessed the triumph of the petit-bourgeois mentality.

Antonio Sant'Elia. Skyscraper. 1914. Project

Hundreds of Sant'Elia's designs have come down to us; one of them was actually built posthumously at Como, although altered in too many details. A recurrent theme in them is the architecture of a metropolis, derived from a mechanical and industrialized civilization: towering buildings with external elevators, multi-level road bridges, enormous stations, and imaginary factories: monuments of the city of the future, seen through the vision of Sant'Elia, and raised by their unreal dimensions and perspectives to the level of symbols. A permanent exhibition of Sant'Elia's works has been opened at the Villa Olmo near Como.

Bibliography: Giulio C. Argan, 'Il pensiero critico di Antonio Sant'Elia', in *L'arte*, Rome September 1930; Alberto Sartoris, *Antonio Sant'Elia*, Milan 1930; Gherardo Dottori, *Sant'Elia e la nuova architettura*, Rome 1933; Francesco Tentori, 'Le origini liberty di Antonio Sant'Elia' in *L'architettura*, Rome July/August 1955 and January/February 1956; Umbro Apollonio, *Antonio Sant'Elia*, Milan 1958.

GIULIA VERONESI

Scarpa, Carlo, b. Venice 1906. Pavilions for the Biennales at Venice, new fittings and extensions of museums in Florence, Palermo, Possagno, Venice, Verona. Organic architecture in the manner of Frank Lloyd *Wright.

Scharoun, Hans, b. Bremen 1893. Scharoun grew up in Bremerhaven until he took his school certificate; he studied from 1912 to 1914 at Berlin Technical College, and during his military service worked as an architect on reconstruction in East Prussia, whence he established contact with Bruno *Taut and the circle of young architects round him in Berlin. In 1925 Scharoun accepted an appointment through Oskar Moll at Breslau Academy of Art and Crafts. Here he met Rading and they collaborated on schemes in Breslau and Berlin. For the WUWA (Home and Work Exhibition, Breslau, 1928) he built an apartment block with set-back floors, roof gardens and communal services on the ground floor; and a private house in 1927 on the Weissenhof estate of the *Deutscher Werkbund at Stuttgart, co-ordinated by *Mies van der Rohe.

As a member of the Berlin architectural association *Der *Ring*, Scharoun designed the layout of the large Siemensstadt estate. There in 1930 he built a number of blocks of flats, standing set back from the street, with living-rooms extending the entire depth of the block from wall to wall. In the twenties in Berlin, Scharoun participated in numerous town planning schemes and competitions under the leadership of Martin *Wagner. He built blocks of flats at the Kaiserdamm, Hohenzollerndamm and Flinsberger Platz in an attempt to keep the business of renting flats an economic proposition for private enterprise by carefully thought-out planning.

For the exhibition '*Sun, air and houses for all*' at the Berlin Funkturm in 1932, Scharoun built a 'growing house'. His design is based on the grid system to give the builders a precise synopsis of costs during the whole process of erection, together with the necessary extensions. In the same year, he built a house for an industrialist by the name of Schminke at Löbau in Saxony, a steel-frame structure that seems to be freely suspended amidst the scenery.

Under the Nazis, Scharoun was cut off entirely from all chance of executing major schemes. He was merely allowed to build private houses in and around Berlin. In these years of enforced inactivity, he worked on numerous drawings and designs whose ideas he drew on in later work. After the end of the war in 1945, he was appointed by Berlin Corporation head of the Department for Building and Housing. He prevented the complete demolition of many factories and offices in the shattered city and set up the planning group called the 'Berliner Kollektiv', which presented a revolutionary plan for the rebuilding of Berlin in 1946. This plan was an application and development of theoretical work by Miljutin and Soraja y Matyas, and a realization and continuation of Martin Mächler's theories: 'not a land-use plan but a dynamics plan' His work on the centre of Berlin was continued in 1958 in the *Metropolis Berlin* competition, 'the first design that deserves to be taken seriously in the rebuilding of the city centre'. While working on detailed plan analyses for the Havel area (Spandau, Potsdam) in his capacity as head of the Building Institute at the German Academy of Sciences from 1947 to 1950, he was also (until 1960) lecturer in town planning at Berlin Technical

University, of which he was one of the re-
founders in 1946.

In this post-war period, he carried out many
important competition designs: the rebuilding of the island of Heligoland, the
Liederhalle in Stuttgart, the American
Memorial Library and an old-people's
home in Berlin. Prize-winning and world
famous designs such as the theatre at
Kassel and the National Theatre at Mannheim were never built; they were based on
a far-reaching analysis of theatrical problems. An analysis of the principles affecting
the spatial problems of school buildings
led to a design for a primary school at
Darmstadt on the occasion of his Darmstadt lecture on 'Man and Space' in 1951.
Scharoun's design marks an important
advance in his work as well as in the
development of modern architecture. In
1955 he was commissioned to build the
Geschwister Scholl High School at Lünen,
Westphalia, completed in 1962. The classrooms in this girls' school have been
arranged as a 'flat', in order to humanize
the division between school and home in
modern education. 'Scharoun is the
guarantor of a continuity between post-
1918 and post-1945 Germany.' (*L'Architettura*).

This continuity is expressed particularly
in his residential buildings. In 1947
Scharoun designed a suburb south of the
Stalinallee, as it later became, his first
attempt to combine some ideas of Ludwig
*Hilberseimer's with the experience he had
gained on the Siemensstadt scheme in the
1930s, and to create a design team. In
1954 he submitted plans and models for
the rebuilding of the Hansa district, which
he was commissioned to do by the revived
Ring. He also built 'homesteads' in Charlottenburg-Nord (1955–61), a further
development from linear building in its
social aspect, as evaluated by the most
recent research. At Stuttgart, Scharoun
built Romeo and Juliet point blocks in
collaboration with Wilhelm Frank, whose
penthouses and studios must be understood as the completion of a design which
had hitherto featured only low buildings.
These blocks show a connection with the
idea that underlies the Breslau Exhibition
flats of 1928. They may similarly be associated with the concept of townscape, as
are the 'Salute' block at Stuttgart and the
concert hall for the Berlin Philharmonic

Hans Scharoun. Apartment house at the Home
and Work Exhibition. Breslau, 1928

Hans Scharoun. Schminke House. Löbau, 1932

Hans Scharoun. Charlottenburg-Nord housing estate. Berlin, 1955–61

Orchestra, both of which are currently under construction.

Scharoun was awarded the commission for building the new Berlin Philharmonic Concert Hall as a result of a prize-winning competition design which condenses the unity of music and space into three-dimensional form.

Bibliography: Margit Staber, 'Hans Scharoun. Ein Beitrag zum organischen Bauen', in *Zodiac 10*, Milan 1962.

KLAUS-JAKOB THIELE

Hans Scharoun. Concert Hall for the Berlin Philharmonic Orchestra. Berlin, under construction. Section

Schindler, Rudolph M., b. Vienna 1887, d. Los Angeles 1953. Studied at the Vienna Academy of Art, strongly influenced by Otto *Wagner; 1913 emigrated to Chicago; 1916–21 worked in Frank Lloyd *Wright's office. In Schindler's buildings the relationship of horizontal and vertical, solid and void appear as an American parallel to De *Stijl (Lovell Beach House, Newport Beach, 1926).

Schinkel, Karl Friedrich, b. Neuruppin 1781, d. Berlin 1841. Architect and painter. Pupil of David and Friedrich Gilly. Extensive journeys in Italy and France; worked in Berlin. Schinkel combined classical forms with a romantic spirit in his dignified designs: New Guard House, Unter den Linden (1815–16), Theatre (1818–31), Old Museum (1823–8), all at Berlin. Early Gothic Revival work in his Memorial to Queen Louise (1810) and his Werdersche Church in Berlin (1824–30). Schinkel influenced *Mies van der Rohe and through him 20th-century architecture with his designs for a shop (1829) whose façades consist of glass areas divided by masonry piers, and with his country-house projects. *Bibliography:* Paul Ortwin Rave, *Karl Friedrich Schinkel, Das Lebenswerk,* 1942–56.

Schwarz, Rudolf, b. Strasbourg 1897, d. Cologne 1961. Pupil of *Poelzig. His ecclesiastical buildings form an important contribution to modern Catholic church design. Schwarz sought to create with them 'high inhabitable pictures like life-size parables'. Fronleichnam Church, Aachen (in collaboration with Hans Schwippert, 1928), St Anne, Düren (1951–6), St Michael, Frankfurt (1953–4).
Bibliography: Rudolf Schwarz, *Kirchenbau,* Heidelberg 1960.

Seidler, Harry, b. Vienna 1923. Studied at Harvard University, Cambridge, Massachusetts, and Manitoba, Canada. Collaborated with *Breuer and *Niemeyer. Since 1942 independent practice in Sidney, Australia. Houses and offices; Olympic Stadium at Melbourne (1956), a suspended roof structure for 125,000 spectators.

Bibliography: Harry Seidler, *Houses, Interiors and Projects,* Sidney 1954.

Harry Seidler. Lend Lease House, Sydney

Semper, Gottfried, b. Hamburg 1803, d. Rome 1879. From 1834 in Dresden which he left for political reasons in 1849. Stayed in Paris and London. In Zurich (1855), Vienna (1871). His work is removed from the romantic classicism of *Schinkel, who was a friend of his. His adaptations of Romanesque, Gothic and Renaissance features are typical examples of 19th-century historicism. Semper's originality lies in his massing, where the building's function stands out sharply. (The projecting curvature of the auditorium in the Dresden Opera House, 1837–41, rebuilt in 1878 following the fire of 1871). Dresden Art Gallery (started 1847); Burgtheater in Vienna (rebuilt differently, 1874–88). His theoretical writings stress the influence of structure on style and recommend the use of colour in architecture.
Bibliography: Gottfried Semper, *Der Stil in den technischen und tektonischen Künsten,* Frankfurt 1860–3.

Sert, José Luis, b. Barcelona 1902. Studied at the Escuela Superior de Arquitectura in Barcelona; 1929–30 worked for *Le Corbusier and Pierre Jeanneret in Paris.

Walter Bauersfeld. Grid for the shell dome of the Planetarium in the Zoological Gardens. Berlin, 1926

Richard Norman Shaw. Old Swan House. London, 1876

Emigrated to the United States in 1939; 1947–56 President of *CIAM at whose instance he published among other writings *Can our Cities Survive?* (3rd edition, Cambridge, Mass. 1947). Since 1958 Dean of the Harvard Graduate School of Design. US Embassy, Bagdad (commenced 1955); Harvard University Health Center, Cambridge, Mass. (1957–61); Maeght Museum, St Paul-de-Vence (work still in progress). Extensive town-planning projects.

Shaw, Richard Norman, b. Edinburgh 1831, d. Hampstead 1912. Studied at the Royal Academy, London. Shaw, who synthesized numerous influences and styles in his own work, exercised a strong influence on his contemporaries with his churches, offices and in particular with his tasteful private houses. Among the latter, the Old Swan House, London, is especially distinguished by its delicate and slightly mannered proportions.

Shell structures. Support features formed from a singly or doubly curved surface and consisting of tension- and compression-resistant material (i.e. material resistant to bending) are called shell structures; the thickness of the shell is slight in relation to its surface area. The most important properties of a shell are that it is not straight but curved, and it is thin. Hence the designer also calls the shell a plane support structure. A girder on the other hand is called a beam-type support structure. In a plane support structure, two dimensions (length and width) are considerably greater than the third (thickness); in a beam-type support structure, however, two dimensions (depth and width of section) are decidedly smaller than the third (length).

Beam-type support structures and plane support structures are different with regard to their stresses. A girder which is loaded at right angles to its axis is acted on by bending moments and sheer stress, whereas an ideal shell has neither bending moments nor sheer stress, only normal stresses uniformly distributed over its thickness. A girder resists loading by its strength, a shell by its shape. A simple test will explain the structural properties of a shell. A piece of paper, spread out flat and held along its two edges, will bend. It cannot even carry its own weight, let alone additional loads. But if the same piece of paper is curved and held along its edges, it develops a surprising rigidity. In nature we find many forms comparable to our new shell structures. We may mention diatoms, single-cell creatures consisting of siliceous algae; eggs, sea-shells and snails. These shapes are built on the principle that a firm casing may be formed from the minimum of material. Their rigidity does not depend on the firmness of the material or its thickness, but on the casing's curved shape.

The engineers Walter Bauersfeld and Franz Dischinger deserve the credit for having established the theoretical and practical advantages of shell construction. It is true that early attempts to calculate similar structures can be found in the literature of the end of the 19th century and the beginning of the 20th, but no practical use was made of this theory. Bauersfeld and Dischinger in the early twenties were the first to tackle the problem both in theory and in practice and thus laid the foundations

Eduardo Torroja. Grandstand. Zarzuela race course, near Madrid, 1935

for one of the most interesting developments in the field of structural engineering. Since that time development has been rapid and constant. In the twenties the first barrel and dome shells were constructed by the Zeiss-Dywidag process, invented by Bauersfeld and Dischinger, (Dome shells: experimental structure near Jena, 1922; factory for Schott and Gen., 1923–4; Jena Planetarium, 1925. Barrel shells: roof of the exhibition halls at the GESOLEI, Düsseldorf, 1926; market hall, Frankfort on the Main, 1926–7. Intersecting barrel shells in the shape of cross-arched vaults: market hall, Leipzig, 1927–9; market hall, Basle, 1929). *Freyssinet built the market hall at Rheims in the shape of a barrel vault (1928–9) and the repair workshop at Bagneux as a conoidal one (1928–9). As early as 1934 G. Baroni built the first shell in Milan in the shape of a hyperbolic paraboloid (iron foundry at Milan) and in 1938 the first shell in the shape of an up-turned umbrella (warehouse at Ferrara). Bernard Lafaille has been working with shell structures since 1929. Between 1931 and 1933 different types of hall structures

Pier Luigi Nervi and Annibale Vitellozzi. Palazzetto dello Sport. Rome, 1956–7

were put up on a grid system, where the shell thickness for spans between 98 and 164 feet was a mere 2 to 2¾ inches. A little later, Konrad Hruban worked on similar structural shapes. After 1940 his shells developed in the form of hyperbolic paraboloids began to be used and are employed in many ways for industrial buildings. Eduardo *Torroja designed the roof of the market hall at Algeciras (1934), the racecourse at Zarzuela (1935) and the ball-games hall, Madrid (1935). Dischinger constructed a number of large-span aircraft hangars in the thirties (Bug/Rügen hangar 1936–7). *Maillart's Cement Hall for the Swiss Provinces Exhibition, Zurich, 1938–9, may be called a model instance of the structural and sculptural possibilities of shell construction.

It is at first amazing that up to the present time the knowledge of these structures and their application has remained confined to a small circle of architects. Neither *Le Corbusier, nor *Gropius, not *Breuer concerned themselves during the twenties or thirties with shell structures. It is only now, in a changing architectural world, that architects regard shell construction as a suitable means for realizing their ideas. Frequently, however, they restrict themselves to accepting shapes designed by structural engineers. The task that lies before architects of employing this form of construction as an architectural medium is only being achieved step by step.

The application of shell construction is now reaching every type of architecture. Among the most important examples are the airport reception buildings at St Louis, Mo. by Hellmuth, Leinweber and Yamasaki, engineers Roberts and Schaefer Co. (1953–5); exhibition hall of the Centre National des Industries et Techniques at Paris by Camelot, de Mailly and *Zehrfuss, engineer Esquillan (1957–8); Palazzetto dello Sport, Rome, by A. Vitellozzi, engineer *Nervi (1956–7); Palazzo dello Sport, Rome, by Piacentini, engineer Nervi (1958–60); TWA airport reception building at Idlewild, New York, by Eero *Saarinen and Associates (1961–2); Windward City Shopping Centre at Kaneohe, Hawaii by Wimberley and Cook, engineer Bradshaw (1957); buildings by Félix *Candela; market hall at Royan by Simon, Morisseau, engineer René Sarger (1955). *Bibliography:* Jürgen Joedicke, *Schalenbau* (= Dokumente der Modernen Architektur 2), Stuttgart 1962.

JÜRGEN JOEDICKE

Sheppard, Richard Herbert, b. 1910. Studied at the Architectural Association School of Architecture, London; in private practice since 1938, latterly with Geoffrey Robson and other partners. Wide range of buildings, especially educational ones; awarded RIBA Bronze Medal for Harrowfield Boys' School, Harold Hill, Essex (1954). Winner of the limited competition for Churchill College, Cambridge (1959) with a design featuring twenty courts grouped informally round a library and

Page 259. George Francis Hellmuth, Joseph William Leinweber and Minoru Yamasaki. Airport reception building. St Louis, Mo., 1953–5

clerestory-lit reading room in the centre. Students' hall of residence, Imperial College, London; pithead bath, Dudley Colliery, Northumberland.

Siren, Heikki and Kaija. Heikki Siren, b. Helsinki 1918, Kaija Siren, b. Kotka 1920. Studied at Helsinki Technical College. Since 1946 this married couple have had an office of their own. Schools, housing (in part prefabricated), office blocks. Small auditorium of the Finnish National Theatre, Helsinki (1954); Chapel, Otaniemi Technical College (1957).

Skidmore, Owings and Merrill (SOM) (Louis Skidmore, b. 1897, Nathaniel A. Owings, b. 1903, and John O. Merrill, b. 1896).

Skidmore, Owings and Merrill. Lever House. New York, 1952

Skidmore, Owings and Merrill. Connecticut General Life Insurance Building, Hartford, Conn., 1957

This American architectural firm was founded by Messrs Skidmore and Owings in 1935 and the partnership was expanded to include Mr Merrill in 1936. Although the two founders had been associated with the 'modernistic' designs of the Chicago 'Century of Progress' Exposition (1933), the impact of the firm upon the course of recent architecture was not significant until after the Second World War. Its leadership dates from the completion of the Lever Building, Park Avenue, New York City (1952), the design of Gordon *Bunshaft, a partner in the firm who has been largely responsible for the establishment and direction of the SOM style. The Lever design was one of the very first successful commercializations of the *Mies van der Rohe geometry of metal and glass; so successful that by the end of the 1950s imitations of this specific office block could be found in London, Copenhagen, Caracas and elsewhere.

Since that date SOM, with offices in Chicago, San Francisco and Portland, Oregon, as well as in New York, has proceeded to refine the original model in a series of increasingly simple yet elegant glass towers, notably those for Inland Steel, Chicago (1954), Pepsi Cola (1959), Union Carbide (1960), and Chase Manhattan Bank (1957–61), the last three in New York City. Their style has been imitated at one time or another, albeit usually in a coarsened form, by almost every large American architectural firm, irrespective of location or previous taste. This largely SOM-created image of expensive efficiency became, by the end of the 1950s, the most universally admired quality in large-scale architectural schemes. Their abstractly classicizing contemporary idiom, with all of its carefully proportioned urban restraint, was even applied in large-scale offices constructed in artfully landscaped rural sites, notably in the entirely glazed three-storey blocks of the Connecticut General Life Insurance Company, near Hartford, Conn. (1957). Similar elements were utilized on a vaster scale and in a more dramatic, mountainous setting in the Air Academy, Colorado Springs, Colo., finished 1959. This huge complex heralded the momentary establishment of the SOM modernist idiom as the semi-official architectural style of the day. However, at the exact moment of the

Skidmore, Owings and Merrill. John Hancock Building. San Francisco, 1960

greatest success of this mirror-like purist style, which was the ultimate and most academic manifestation of the taste established by the masters of the *International Style of the 1920s, new tendencies were to be discerned in other SOM projects and realizations. The John Hancock Building, San Francisco (1960), rather self-consciously rejected the glass *curtain wall in favour of a bay system of separate windows and load-bearing external walls. A vigorous, structurally expressive touch was provided by the flaring concrete piers which formed the Expressionistic 'order' of the ground floor and mezzanine. In other projects, such as the Banque Lambert, Brussels (1958), or in the Rare Book Library, Yale University, New Haven, Conn., still other design innovations appear, all of which represent divergences from the established orthodox modernism of the glass box. In the Yale design the rectangular cubic form of the building is carried upon a huge Vierendeel truss which is supported by four concrete pylons at the corners. Hence while the bulky mass is dramatically elevated from the ground, it

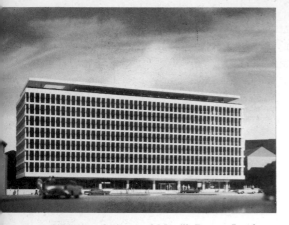

Skidmore, Owings and Merrill. Banque Lambert.
Brussels, 1958. Model

does not float gracefully or hover above
the site in the characteristically contemporary fashion of the Lever Building, nor
are its forms sheathed in the seemingly
weightless glass surfaces first employed by
the International Style. Instead the external surfaces are divided into emphatic grid
patterns by precast concrete elements of
a marble aggregate.
SOM is not the largest of American architectural firms; neither is it truly typical of
the building design industry in the USA, if
only because of its superior taste and
understanding of the stylistic requirements
of contemporary commercial and monumental architecture. However, its finest
work does represent in a particularly
elevated fashion the aspirations of a major
segment of today's architectural profession.
Bibliography: Ernst Danz, *SOM: Architecture of Skidmore, Owings and Merrill
1950–1962*, London 1963.

JOHN M. JACOBUS, JR

Smithson, Alison and Peter. Alison
Smithson, b. Sheffield 1928. Peter Smithson, b. Stockton-on-Tees 1923. The
Hunstanton School, Norfolk (1954), ranks
as the first example of *Brutalism. Their
design for the Berlin City competition
(third prize) provides for a closed pedestrian precinct on a second level. Economist
Building, London (started 1962).

Soane, Sir John, b. Goring-on-Thames
1753, d. London 1837. Appointed architect

to the Bank of England in 1788, for which
he carried out alterations and new addi-
tions from 1788 to 1833. Numerous
government commissions; from 1806 professor at the Royal Academy. Churches,
private houses, villas. His composition
with abstract shapes reminiscent of the
French revolutionary architects, the broad
disposition of his volumes and masses, as
well as the exposed cast-iron construction
of his cupolas have earned Soane the
reputation among modern architects of
being contemporary in feeling.
Bibliography: J. N. Summerson, *Sir John
Soane*, London 1952; Dorothy Stroud, *The
Architecture of Sir John Soane*, London 1961.

Soleri, Paolo, b. Italy 1920. Since 1947 in
the United States. Influenced by Frank
Lloyd *Wright for whom he worked.
Admirer of Antoni *Gaudí. Advanced
designs such as the tubular bridge (1947)
and the project for a 'town on a table
mountain' with two million inhabitants
(since 1959). Among his few executed
designs is the House in the Desert (Cave
Creek, Ariz., 1951, together with Mark
Mills) which is roofed by two movable
hemispheres, and a ceramics factory at
Vietri sul Mare near Salerno (1954), a
five-storey hall with spiral ramps.

Sommaruga, Giuseppe, b. Milan 1867,
d. Milan 1917. Studied architecture at the
Brera, Milan. He was the main exponent
of Italian *Art Nouveau, together with
D' *Aronco and *Basile. Sommaruga employed floral Art Nouveau details, particularly in his decorative friezes, which
contrast with the bare masonry. Palazzo
Castiglioni, Milan (1900–3), Mausoleum
Faccanoni, Sarnico (1907).

Space Frames. The development of space
frames is a challenging task for engineers
and architects. The traditional concept of
a linear progression of stresses in structures
has been extended by a system involving
the spatial dissolution of the stresses, with
all the load-bearing members working together. Thus structures could be devised
that are remarkable for stability and load-
bearing capacity despite their low weight.
A wealth of possibilities for the dissolution
of tensile and compressive stresses in space
grids has already been examined.
The different systems are principally distinguished by the geometric form of the

Paolo Soleri and Mark Mills. House in the Desert. Cave Creek, Ariz., 1951

Konrad Wachsmann. Structural system for halls. 1950–3. Model grid module they use, which often already constitutes a stable element. Further distinctions result from the uniform use of tension and compression members or surfaces, or by a clear differentiation between tension and compression members. The most extreme, efficient and fascinating structures are undoubtedly the continuous tension-compression systems made up of cables and struts by Buckminster *Fuller.

The natural requirement that buildings should afford protection from the elements leads to the development of closed surfaces. These surfaces are integrated into the space frame as tension or compression components and become an effective part of the structure. This method of construction affords further important advantages in that even plastics can be employed as structural building materials. In this instance, the low modulus of elasticity of these materials is of no effect due to the extraordinarily advantageous spatial distribution of stresses and the geometrical stability of the structure as a whole.

Space frames are particularly suitable for prefabrication, due to their multitude of modular components. That is why all space frame structures so far known are made of standardized prefabricated building components which can be quickly erected by simple methods such as the Unistrut, Mero and Space-Deck systems. Outstanding schemes made possible by this development include: the aircraft hangar built as early as 1946 by *Wachsmann and the different types of geodesic domes by *Fuller. Makowski and Le Ricolais have made further important advances towards a full theorectical and practical understanding of the distribution of stresses in these systems.

These structures will become ever more important in the future, as their current applications already indicate. The freedom of uninterrupted space and spans which they afford, even of the largest dimensions, and their almost unlimited adaptability to changing and diverse requirements, permit functional solutions of a completely new type.

The architectural expression of these structures is leading to a new aesthetic dimension. In a way that compares with the composition of matter itself, they provide direct spatial models of their theoretical content in their dematerialized multiformity.

Richard Buckminster Fuller. Geodesic Dome. 1954. Individual units of cardboard

Bibliography: Buckminster Fuller, *Brief Building Construction*; Z. S. Makowski, *Space Structures*; Konrad Wachsmann, *Wendepunkt im Bauen*, Wiesbaden 1959; Robert W. Marks, *The Dymaxion World of Buckminster Fuller*, New York 1960.

                                        HERBERT OHL

Spence, Sir Basil, b. India 1907. Studied at the Schools of Architecture of London and Edinburgh Universities. Assisted Lutyens on the Viceroy's House, New Delhi. In private practice since 1930. Won the competition for Coventry Cathedral (1951); Sea and Ships Pavilion, at the South Bank Exhibition, *Festival of Britain; university buildings at Durham, Exeter, Liverpool, Newcastle, Nottingham and Southampton. His design for Sussex University is a Piranesian fantasy of flat arches and barrel vaults. Housing estates at Dunbar, Selkirk and a premiated

Page 265. Basil Spence. Coventry Cathedral. 1954–62

scheme at Sunbury-on-Thames (1951); tall
blocks of flats in the Gorbals, Glasgow and
Basildon Town Centre. Churches, theatres,
factories and office buildings, including
Thorn House, St Martin's Lane, London
(1959). His most celebrated design, that
for Coventry Cathedral (1954–62), represents an attempt to express a traditional
layout in a contemporary idiom. As such
it may be considered to have achieved a
fair measure of success, though it does not
display any radical re-thinking from the
point of view of the liturgical movement,
or the modern movement in architecture.
Bibliography: B. Spence, *Coventry Phoenix*,
London 1962.

HAROLD MEEK

Steel. In the second half of the 18th century the first steps were taken in England
which opened up the way for the industrial
manufacture of iron products at Abraham
Darby's Coalbrookdale foundry: coke was
used in 1747 for smelting iron ore instead
of charcoal, and by 1750 they were able to
produce malleable pig-iron in bars. Up to
then iron had only been worked by the
elementary methods of artisan production,
and was used for two main purposes in
building: for structural members, mostly
in tensile stress (tie-rods, chains, tie-
bars for arches and vaults), and for wrought-
iron.
The first of the new manufactured products
used in building construction were cast-

Matthew Boulton and James Watt. Cotton Mill.
Salford, 1801

Eugène Emmanuèle Viollet-le-Duc. Assembly
Hall. 1863–72. Project

iron girders, beams and columns. The first
known use of cast-iron columns in England
is in St Anne's Church, Liverpool, by a
certain Dodd (1770–2). Matthew Boulton
and James Watt built a seven-storey cotton
mill in Salford (1801) with an internal
framework of cast-iron columns and inverted T-section beams with external walls
of solid masonry. In the following decades
this type of construction was frequently
adopted for factories and warehouses
(mills in Derbyshire and Lancashire; warehouses at St Katherine's Docks, London,
by Thomas Telford, 1824–8 and at Liverpool Docks by J. Hartley, 1824–45). In an
eight-storey refinery built in 1845, William
Fairbairn adopted an analogous system,
but for cast-iron beams substituted
wrought-iron I-sections, and instead of the
shallow brick arches running between
girders employed in the previous factories
he used thin curved metal plates, filled in
with concrete. Meanwhile John Cragg had
built three churches at Liverpool, St

George's, St Michael's and St Philip's (1813–16) to designs by Thomas Rickman, using cast-iron frames throughout.

Taking advantage of the ease with which different types of section could be obtained in cast-iron, Humphrey Repton designed a pheasant-house for the Royal Pavilion at Brighton in 1808, fanciful in its general lines and decorative details. The Pavilion itself was built by John Nash in 1818 in the 'Indian Style', and made use of cast-iron on a grand scale for the first time in a prestige building (columns, girders, dome structure, decorative elements).

In France, the roof of the Théâtre Français, Paris, was built on an iron frame to the designs of Victor Louis (1786), and Bélanger and Brunet rebuilt the dome of the Halles au Blé, destroyed by fire, in iron and copper (1811). This rapid and widespread recourse to iron is due to its properties of adaptability to complex profiles by means of casting, its fire-resistance, ease of use and ability to span large areas with slender members at distant centres.

Works involving particular technical difficulties were faced from the outset and solved. The earliest cast-iron bridge was built over the Severn at Coalbrookdale between 1775 and 1779. It spans 100 feet and consists of five ribs subdivided into two series of half-arches, each cast in a single piece by the Darby Foundry. An experiment of great boldness was completed in 1796 with the Sunderland Bridge, spanning 236 feet, erected by Rowland Bourdon over the Wear to a design of Tom Paine's. This structure was built up from ribs consisting of openwork cast-iron voussoirs and wrought-iron straps, laid upon timber centering. The same technique, derived from masonry construction, was proposed by Telford in 1801 for a bridge across the Thames with a span of 600 feet, which was never realized, however, due to difficulties in acquiring the land on either bank for the abutments. In France, too, iron was used in 1801–3 for a bridge that still exists and is in use: the Pont des Arts, Paris, a multiple arch structure by de Cessart and Dillon.

The technique of constructing suspension bridges had been developed from the end of the 18th century, firstly with chains and later with wire ropes (Conway Castle Bridge, by Telford, 1822–6; Rhône Bridge, by Séguin, 1824). In 1836, I. K. Brunel

James Bogardus. Cast-iron foundry. New York, 1848–9

commenced building the Clifton Suspension Bridge over the river Avon, at Bristol, which with its span of 700 feet is one of the masterpieces of 19th-century engineering. Brunel, a naval architect, pursued the experiments begun around the year 1825 on the application of iron to shipbuilding. In 1843, he launched the first screw steamer to cross the Atlantic; it had an iron hull, and initiated the technique of self-supporting riveted shell structures. Similar techniques were adopted for other major engineering projects, as instanced by Robert Stephenson's Britannia Bridge over the Menai Straits (1846–50) which features pairs of huge rectangular wrought-iron tubes which run between massive masonry towers.

Simultaneously with these developments improvements were being made in the technology of iron manufacture. The production of puddle iron entered the industrial stage in 1840; steel production with Bessemer converters began in 1856, followed by the open-hearth process in 1864 and the basic converter process in 1878. The *glass industry had made great strides, too, from the second half of the 18th century onwards, and the combination of glass and iron opened up new possibilities in architecture: galleries, conservatories, exhibition buildings such as Joseph *Paxton's Crystal Palace in London and

Gustave Eiffel and L. A. Boileau. Bon Marché
Department Store. Paris, 1876

Ste Geneviève (1843) and the Bibliothèque
Impériale (1855) using a system of cast-
iron columns and arches to give greater
space, though retaining eclectic or traditionally academic forms for the walls that
formed the outer shell and for the decoration. In his Bibliothèque Nationale (1858–
68), while employing the same structural
and decorative schemes as in the Bibliothèque Impériale for the reading room, he
adopted a system of stanchions, girders and
floor grilles for the book stacks that allowed
the daylight, coming in from above, to
filter down to the lower floors; the structural elements are exposed to view without
any decorative trimmings, and conspire to
produce novel spatial effects of a high
order. Another important contribution to
the handling of internal spaces was made
by the Bon Marché department store in
Paris (1876), by Boileau and Eiffel, who
achieved their effects by an airy system of
foot-bridges, supported by slender columns
and lit by the large glazed roof.

The years around the middle of the 19th
century saw the beginnings of framed construction as we know it now. A decisive
step in this direction was the replacement
of solid external walls by columns and
beams or arches in cast-iron. The first
evidence of the new technique may be seen
in the work of James *Bogardus, who is
considered the inventor of this method of
construction, on the basis of his designs
(New York World's Fair, 1853) and
executed projects (five-storey factory, New
York, 1848; Harper and Brothers Building,
New York, 1854). The system underwent
notable developments, including those in
quality, in the United States (riverfront
buildings at St Louis) and England
(commercial buildings in Liverpool). All
the formal elements of these cast-iron
façade structures, however, were taken
from the traditional repertory of 19th-
century historicism.

One of the first buildings to use a framed
construction throughout was the Chocolat
Menier factory built at Noisiel-sur-Marne,
near Paris by Jules Saulnier in 1871–2. The
iron frame, with diagonal struts clearly
showing on the façade rests on four hollow
iron girders supported by four masonry

buildings at the various Paris Exhibitions,
culminating in Dutert and Contamin's
Machinery Hall (1889), whose nave is
roofed via a series of three-hinge portals
with a span of c. 380 feet.

An important rôle in the gradual perfecting of structural methods and components
was played by Gustave *Eiffel; the designer
of many bridges, viaducts and the Eiffel
Tower, he pursued an architectural ideal
that sought to make the essential lines of a
structure correspond with its static functions. The architect Henri *Labrouste, who
founded a private school of architecture in
Paris with the aim of teaching strict
adherence to the demands of function and
structure, designed the Bibliothèque

Page 269. Ferdinand Dutert and Contamin.
Machinery Hall at the International Exhibition.
Paris, 1889

piers built up on the bed of the Marne. The reconstruction of Chicago, growing rapidly after the fire of 1871, provided the impulse for exploiting the possibilities of frame construction (hitherto only used for industrial buildings) in multi-storey commercial blocks, with their need for fireproofing and broad areas of glass. William Le Baron *Jenney, having used the by now usual internal structure with iron columns in his first Leiter Building (1879), employed a complete metal framework for the Home Insurance Building (1883–5), though the surrounding masonry wall shared part of its loadbearing functions. With the second Leiter, Manhattan and Fair Buildings, he refined his structural system, reducing the façades to a form of light cladding carried on a uniform metal frame, thus achieving the prototype of the modern office block. In the spirit of Le Baron Jenney, the architects of the *Chicago School perfected the system, and in the Loop district defined the original

Victor Horta. Hôtel Aubecq, Brussels, 1900. Dome over the stair well

Hans Poelzig. Water tower. Posen, 1911

architectural physiognomy of the first centre of the modern movement. Having passed through a phase of attempting to interpret the new structures by adapting traditional stylistic details, they began to derive their forms logically from the framed structure, and abandoned superimposed decoration (Marquette Building by *Holabird and Roche, 1894; Reliance Building by *Burnham and *Root, 1890–5; Carson, Pirie and Scott Building by *Sullivan, 1899). After the 1893 Columbian Exposition in Chicago, American architecture underwent a period of stylistic eclipse with the return of eclecticism and academicism. Meanwhile however, steel frame techniques for skyscrapers were making progress—sometimes sensationally so—throughout America (Woolworth Building [58 storeys] 1912; Empire State Building [85 storeys] 1931, both in New York).

The main exponents of progressive architecture in Europe at the turn of the century approached the use of steel without any preconceptions, and employed it freely in their schemes in conformity with their own styles and the possibilities they saw for applying it. Victor *Horta in the Hôtel

Otto Bartning. Steel Church. Cologne, 1928

Tassel (1893) and the Maison du Peuple (1896–9) in Brussels achieved a perfect unity between structure and decoration. H. P. *Berlage obtained unusual effects in his Amsterdam Stock Exchange (1897–1903) by exposing the structural elements. Otto *Wagner in the hall of the Post Office Savings Bank in Vienna (1904–6) aimed at unity of composition by reducing the individual structural elements to their simplest formal expression. Peter *Behrens in his AEG Works, Berlin (1908–9) revealed that steel, too, had a secret form of expression that lay within the material itself. Hans *Poelzig infused a unitary character into the variegated structures that went to make up his water tower at Posen (1911), derived from his *Expressionist type of sensibility.

The modern movement, in the period after the First World War, took the steel-frame structure for granted, as an indispensable instrument for achieving freedom and rationality in design. In the Weissenhof Estate at Stuttgart (1927) and in other more or less contemporary works, the masters of the modern movement (*Neutra, *Le Corbusier, *Mies van der

Rohe, *Mendelsohn) presented a substantially unified panorama to the public, in which a joint purpose and a broad measure of agreement were more in evidence than any personal differences. A common denominator was the principle of the pure expression of function by structural elements. Around 1930, modern architecture began to gain ground in America, and the *International Style was applied uncompromisingly to the skyscrapers, too, where the severity of the modern method brought a notable measure of lucidity to the traditional treatment (Philadelphia Savings Fund Society Building by *Howe and *Lescaze, 1932).

The outburst of building activity after the Second World War helped to perfect and spread the methods of steel frame construction to the most diverse of building types. The need to make savings in time, cost and upkeep led the industry to prefabricate various versions of *curtain walling, which afford numerous possibilities for architectural expression. Outstanding contributions in these fields of research have been made by Mies van der Rohe, whose theoretical studies go back to the year 1919.

Parallel to the work of perfecting the steel frame construction, other forms of structural technique have been studied and applied: *suspended roofs, hung from stressed steel cables; *shell structures in welded plate (water tower at General

Skidmore, Owings and Merrill. Manufacturers Trust Company. New York, 1953–4

Ludwig Mies van der Rohe. Crown Hall, Illinois Institute of Technology. Chicago, 1952–6. Steelwork in course of erection

Motors Technical Center, Detroit, by Eero *Saarinen, 1955); wide span cantilever roofs of ribbed flats on reinforced concrete piers (hangar at San Francisco airport, by Góldsmith, 1959; Palazzo del Lavoro, Turin, by *Nervi, 1961); reticulated *space frames of prefabricated modular units (geodesic domes by Buckminster *Fuller and studies by K. *Wachsmann). These new techniques, which provide the opportunity and means for bold architectural experiments, may be considered the bases for developing new forms of expression and design.

Bibliography: John Gloag and Derek Bridgwater, *A History of Cast Iron in Architecture*, London 1948; O. Johannsen, *Geschichte des Eisens*, Düsseldorf 1953; *Construire en acier, Bauen in Stahl*, Zurich 1956; V. Zignoli, *Costruzioni metalliche*, Turin 1956–7; *Ponti stradali in acciaio*, Milan 1958; Konrad Wachsmann, *Wendepunkt im Bauen*, Wiesbaden 1959; H. R. Hitchcock, *Early Victorian Architecture in Britain*, London 1954; T. K. Derry and T. I. Williams, *A Short History of Technology*, Oxford 1960.

GIUSEPPE VARALDO
GIAN PIO ZUCCOTTI

Stijl, De. A group of artists and architects, formed in Leiden in 1917, which published a journal of the same name; its members included Vilmos Huszar,

Antonie Kok, Piet Mondrian, Jacobus Johannes *Oud and Theo van *Doesburg. They were subsequently joined by the architects Robert van't Hoff, and Gerrit Thomas *Rietveld, the painter Bart van der Leck and the sculptor and painter Georges Vantongerloo.

The type of design associated with De Stijl was very much determined by the neoplasticism of the painters Piet Mondrian and Theo van Doesburg; it implied, in every respect, a break with tradition. Like neoplasticist painting, De Stijl architecture was influenced by Cubism, too. Right angles and smooth walls were almost exclusively the order of the day; the demand for unmistakably spotless surfaces excluded the use of bricks, which

Theo van Doesburg and Cor van Eesteren. Studies for a private house. 1923

gave too graduated and imprecise a colour-effect. The cube or parallelopiped served as the point of departure, but the cubic shape, as an elementary expression of space, was not felt as something static, but as part of an infinite environment, into which the internal walls continued. Hence every circumscribed definition of a building by front, side or rear elevations was rejected. The designed space, i.e. the room, opened out on all sides into the universal space, conceived of as a crystal.

New attitudes emerged with regard to the use of colour, both as regards external surfaces and interior decoration. Colour no longer served as an element of decoration, but helped to define space. Following Mondrian's example, the primary colours, red, blue and yellow, were used exclusively; white, black and grey were admitted as contrasting tones. All other colours were regarded as impure, in stark contrast to the picturesque brown tones that had prevailed in late-19th-century interiors. Typical examples include Rietveld's Schröder House in Utrecht (1924) and the Café de Unie in Rotterdam by Oud (1924–5, destroyed in the 1940 blitz).

Its cubistic design, simplicity and austerity of line are the reasons why the architecture of De Stijl is often confused with the concept of 'Neue Sachlichkeit', a term that was applied to German painting around 1925. De Stijl architecture certainly exerted great influence, and set the type for developments in the later twenties (*Functionalism, *International Style) with its new attitude to space.

Robert van't Hoff. Huis ter Heide. Utrecht, 1916

But despite the contrary asseverations of its supporters, De Stijl was to a great extent an aesthetic theory. In this respect it differed from later developments, since Functionalism and the International Style rejected all fixed notions of aesthetics, believing in the unity of form and function.

The translation of De Stijl's theories into architectural practice was not accomplished without a measure of conflict. After an initial period of collaboration, the partnership between Oud and van Doesburg broke up, since Oud's solid expertise in architecture was confronted by the brilliant dilettantism of a painter and theoretician, who, as an architect, was self-taught. Oud developed his

J. J. P. Oud. Factory at Purmerend. 1919. Project

architecture from the tentative essays of De Stijl, and went on to exert a leading influence on Functionalism in W. Europe. Reminiscences of De Stijl features are still discernible in Rietveld's buildings, especially in the décor; his work, and with it the significance of De Stijl, were rediscovered by the younger generation of architects after 1945.

Bibliography: De Stijl, International Maandblad voor de Nieuwe Kunst, Weten-schap en Kultuur, Leiden 1917–31; De Stijl, Catalogue 81 of the Stedelijk Museum, Amsterdam 1951; Bruno Zevi, Poetica dell' architettura neoplastica, Milan 1953; H. L. C. Jaffé, De Stijl 1917–1931, The Dutch Contribution to Modern Art, Amsterdam 1956.

J. J. VRIEND

Stillman and Eastwick-Field. John Cecil Stillman and John Charles Eastwick-Field. Miscellaneous practice including houses, hospitals and farm buildings. Point block of flats at Hide Place, Westminster, for the local authority, with extensive use of pre-cast concrete techniques. Authors of a valuable study on joinery practice.

Stirling and Gowan. James Stirling and James Gowan. Partnership producing work of distinctive plastic effect. Housing at Ham Common (1958) with imaginative use of untreated concrete detailing to give rich sculptural quality; rehousing scheme at Preston with powerful visual patterns of fenestration evoking *Constructivist imagery.

Hugh Stubbins. Congress Hall. Berlin, 1957

Stone, Edward Durell, b. Fayetteville, Ark. 1902. Stone, who was called 'a young man with a brilliant future' by Frank Lloyd *Wright, first built clearly defined square blocks with smooth white surfaces, punctuated by strips of fenestra-tion (Mandel House at Mount Kisco, New York, 1930; Museum of Modern Art, New York, 1939, together with Philip L. Good-win). Commissions abroad, especially in tropical and sub-tropical countries, may have led to his now characteristic screen walls, non-loadbearing partitions in front of or behind the real structural members. These pierced walls of tiles, profilated bricks or metal grilles, which provide shade and ventilation, and which Stone employs in all buildings, appear as huge, carpet-like patterned areas and often go together with classically symmetrical plans and façades: Medical Centre at Palo Alto, Calif. (1957–60); US Embassy at New Delhi (1958). Stone used them also for the circular US pavilion at the Brussels Exhibition of 1958, where the roof structure rested on a compression ring more than 328 ft in diameter.

Stubbins, Hugh, b. Powderly, Ala. 1912. Became Walter *Gropius's assistant at Harvard Graduate School of Design in 1939. Private houses, schools, office blocks, churches. The stage of the Loeb Theatre at Harvard (1957–60) can be changed from a proscenium type to an arena. The Congress Hall in Berlin, which was erected for the Interbau Exhibition, comprises auditorium, conference rooms, exhibition hall and theatre. Its saddle-shaped roof, whose weight is partly carried by walls and internal columns, partly by two anchors, is a bold feat of engineering.

Subtopia. Term coined by Ian Nairn to connote 'the world of universal low density mess . . . an even spread of abandoned aerodromes and fake rusticity, wire fences, traffic roundabouts, gratuitous notice-boards, car-parks and Things in Fields' extending out from suburbia to the country 'and back into the devitalized hearts of towns, so that the most sublime backgrounds, urban or rural, English or foreign, are now to be seen only over a foreground of casual and unconsidered equipment, litter and lettered admonition. . . . Within the town the agents of Subtopia

Louis H. Sullivan. Auditorium Building. Chicago, 1886-9

are demolition and decay, buildings replaced by bijou gardens, car-parks and
underscale structures, reduction of density
where it should be increased (and the)
reduction of vitality by false genteelism,
of which Municipal Rustic is the prime
agent.'

Bibliography: Ian Nairn, *Outrage*, London
1955; Ian Nairn, *Counter-attack against
Subtopia*, London 1957.

Sullivan, Louis H., b. Boston 1856, d.
Chicago 1924. Sullivan's fame is based

upon the refinements that he introduced in
the design of large metal-framed commercial buildings, and upon the development
of an organic theory of architecture. In
1873 he attended architectural classes at
the Massachusetts Institute of Technology
and subsequently worked for the Philadelphia architect, Frank *Furness. Afterwards he spent a few months at the *École
des Beaux-Arts, Paris (1874), and in 1875
went to Chicago to seek employment. After
several routine positions, he joined the staff
of Dankmar *Adler and rapidly displayed

his talents as a designer. Two years later, in 1881, the partnership of Adler and Sullivan was formed, Adler devoting his energies to technical and business problems while Sullivan carried the burden of responsibilities with respect to design. The early work of this partnership is outwardly utilitarian, though its style remains somewhat tentative. It is only with the design of the Auditorium Building, Chicago (1886–9) that Sullivan's talent comes into focus. The monumental, round-arched vocabulary which dominates the exterior sheath of the Auditorium Building (which was an hotel and office building as well as a theatre) derives from the example of *Richardson, notably his Marshall Field Warehouse,

Chicago (1885–7). On the other hand, the interior, and notably the proscenium of the auditorium, is one of the most original instances of planning and decoration in American architecture.

Office buildings—skyscrapers—were the stock-in-trade of the Chicago architectural profession, and Sullivan accommodated himself to such programmatic limitations during a decade (the 1890s) of extremely successful commercial design before a combination of personal and business problems deprived him of major commissions. After 1900, and the nominal close of the earlier portion of his career, most of his works were modest-sized edifices for clients in small mid-western farming communities.

Sullivan's Chicago skyscrapers of the 1890s reflect his sensitivity with respect to the adjustment of external detail to the rhythms and proportions of the building's structural core, the steel frame. Contrary to the implications of his oft-quoted epithet, 'Form follows function', Sullivan used the building's material and structural requirements as a point of departure for his creation, rather than conceiving of functional expression as a fixed, limited goal. The Wainwright Building, St Louis (1890–91) and the Guarantee Building, Buffalo (1894–5), represent the maturing of this attitude, which is well expressed by the title of an article by Sullivan of 1896, 'The Tall Office Building Artistically Considered'.

After the termination of Sullivan's partnership with Adler, he was sometimes engaged to design the façades of commercial buildings that were built by other architects, as in the Bayard Building, New York (1897–8), and the Gage Building, Chicago (1898–9). The adjustments of proportion and the expressive clarity of detailing in the cornices and vertical members of these two façades are not equalled by their general shape, over which Sullivan had no control; it is regrettable that he did not have an opportunity in this period to build the kind of free-standing skyscraper that is so common today. Not even the corner site of his Carson, Pirie & Scott Store, Chicago (1899), his last major commercial building, suggests what he would have done on an

Louis H. Sullivan. Wainwright Building. St Louis, 1890–1

Page 277. Louis H. Sullivan. Auditorium Building, Chicago, 1886–9. Stair well

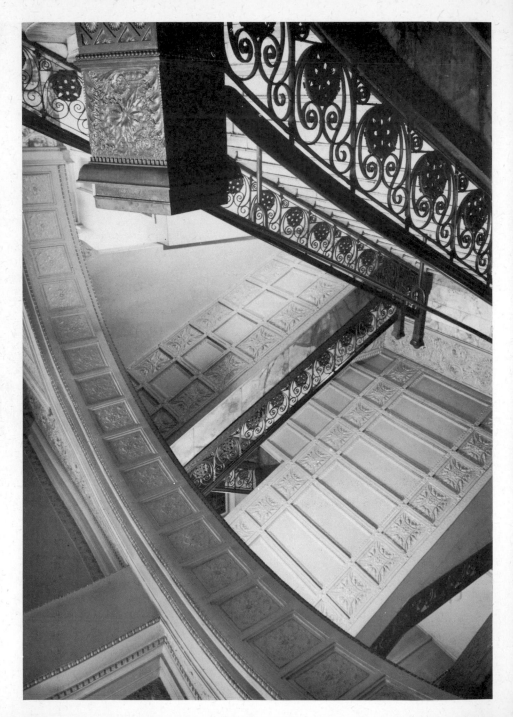

open site, since the client insisted upon the round corner element and the mass of the building was subsequently extended by D. H. *Burnham, albeit using Sullivan's elevation. Thus his genius is apparent here only in the adjustment of detail to the bay system imposed by the steel frame.

Under the circumstances it is understandable that Sullivan's gift for inventive ornament, ultimately of a quasi-Art Nouveau, organic quality, developed to such a remarkable extent. This interest almost dominates his formal, monumental work, notably the Wainwright Tomb, St Louis (1892), and the Transportation Building at the Chicago World's Columbian Exposition of 1893. This latent urge towards the fusion of elaborate ornament with rhetorical, monumental forms is developed in his late, post-1900 work, notably in the National Farmers Bank, Owatonna, Minn.

Louis H. Sullivan. Carson, Pirie and Scott. Chicago, 1899

(1907-8), and in the Farmers and Merchants Union Bank, Columbus, Wis. (1919). Critical appraisal of these buildings has tended towards condescension as they are supposed to represent a falling off of creative force and functional cogency. However, an objective consideration of these small but major designs amply demonstrates Sullivan's continued development and creative maturity, albeit in a direction that is not immediately related to the more revolutionary strains of contemporary architecture.

In contrast to these almost traditional buildings, Sullivan's writings, notably Kindergarten Chats (1901) and The Autobiography of an Idea (1922-3), contain flashes of wisdom and insight into the evolution of contemporary architecture. However, these thoughts, occasionally beautifully expressed, are buried in texts which are turgid and unnecessarily repetitious. Contrary to accepted opinion, the very best of Sullivan's late work is to be found consistently in his buildings, and only occasionally in his writings.

Bibliography: Hugh Morrison, Louis Sullivan, Prophet of Modern Architecture, New York 1952; Willard Connely, Louis Sullivan as he lived, New York 1960.

JOHN M. JACOBUS, JR

Suprematism. A term invented by Kasimir *Malevich for purely abstract art, of the kind he first exhibited in 1915. Suprematism meant for Malevich the 'Supremacy of pure sensation in the fine arts'. The simple elements of form in his paintings are also applied to abstract architectonic compositions.

Suspended Roofs. Suspended roofs originated from the discovery that a structure consisting of tensile members involves little self-weight yet is capable of supporting relatively great loads. Tents and suspension bridges are early examples. As distinguished from these is an essentially new principle which consists in providing complete rigidity of form by the use of saddle-shaped surfaces (especially hyperbolic paraboloidal planes or lattices). Any deformation of shape such as buckling, oscillation or vibration caused by wind force or by self-weight can thus be avoided. The hall at Raleigh by *Deitrick and *Nowicki (1952-3) is one of the first known

examples of this type of construction and the new kind of architecture to which it has given rise. It served as a pointer to the future of the new building method; apart from its logical use of stressed cable lattices, it also employs extremely light-weight prefabricated slab units for cladding purposes. Simultaneously with the new saddle-shaped suspended roofs, cable lattices or *shell vaults, methods of supporting compressive stresses via optimum stress arcs or modified thrust collars were developed. New shapes for roofs and halls and in particular a methodical system of foundations were developed by Le Ricolais, in theory and experimentally, as an extension of these principles. Inspired by the possibilities of traditional tent shapes and the new knowledge about suspended roofs, Frei *Otto has produced a wealth of forms in which he has used the roofing material itself as a structural component. Suspended roof systems have introduced new possibilities to modern architecture, which question the whole principle of the use of rectangular shapes, while considerably enriching the contemporary idiom at the same time.

Bibliography: Frei Otto, *Über Zugbean-spruchte Konstruktionen*, Berlin 1962.

HERBERT OHL

Sweden. Industrialism came rather late to Sweden. In the late 19th century the economy of the country was still mainly based on agriculture, mining and forestry. Architecture followed the general European development on rather a moderate scale. The tendency of the 1880s was a combination of stylistic eclecticism and realistic treatment of the materials. In the following decade a German-influenced neo-Baroque played an important part. This was the background for the rise of modern Swedish architecture.

Its key figure was Ferdinand Boberg (1860–1946). Under the influence of the American H. H. *Richardson he began about 1890 to design a series of buildings such as the fire station at Gävle and the old Stockholm electricity works, which are characterized by a functionalist grouping of massive, block-like volumes. In his subsequent work the cubic heaviness is developed, but set off against concentrated elegant ornaments, in which the inspiration of *Sullivan is evident. Towards the turn of the century the influence of *Art Nouveau was beginning to be felt in Sweden. It was, however, of rather a well-balanced and moderate character. An important part was played by the painter Carl Larsson, whose blond interiors from his own home greatly influenced interior architecture. In the bank buildings of Gustaf Wickman (1858–1916) neo-Baroque and Art Nouveau are skilfully mingled in sculpturally expressive forms. The desire to discard historical forms is especially evident in an interesting group

Matthew Nowicki, William H. Deitrick and Fred Severud. Arena, Raleigh, N.C., 1952–3

Other tendencies had by then become dominant. A group of architects had taken up Boberg's cubic forms and combined them with a new interest in materials of a rich, living texture, such as red brick or traditional Swedish timber. This 'national realism' derived partly from *Morris and his successors in England and the Nyrop circle in Denmark, but old Swedish architecture came to be of increasing importance as a source of inspiration. Nevertheless the character of the movement was not reactionary. The stress on traditional techniques and constructions was rather natural in a country where industrialism had not yet advanced very far. But what was modern was the social awareness of the leading architects. For perhaps the first time low-cost housing was seen as a task worthy of first-rate architectural treatment. The building which is generally regarded as the first work of this school is the one completed for the Medical Society in Stockholm in 1905 by Carl Westman (1866–1936). He used the traditional forms

Page 281. Erik Gunnar Asplund. Stockholm Exhibition. 1930

of office buildings in Stockholm designed by different architects. The façades all show a pronounced vertical treatment, often with very big glass areas between narrow pillars. Internally skeleton construction is used. Outstanding are a couple of buildings created by Ernst Stenhammar (1859–1927) and Erik Josephson (1864–1929).

Most important of the architects who tried to get away from the old forms were Carl Bergsten (1879–1935) and Georg A. Nilsson (1871–1949). The radical ideas of Bergsten reflect the influence of the Vienna Secessionists, but in his tendency to regard the building is made up of geometrical planes he is also strongly reminiscent of *Berlage and Frank Lloyd *Wright. This is shown in his remarkable competition project for the Stockholm City Hall of 1905. The Norrköping Exhibition of the following year and the Hjorthagen Church in Stockholm gave him opportunities to realize his ideas. Nilsson's production as a whole is much more moderate, but some of his works show an evident affinity with the Anglo-Saxon modernists. His finest work is the iron-skeleton office building in Stockholm, Regeringsgatan 9, the final culmination of this modern school.

Carl Bergsten. Liljevalch Gallery. Stockholm, completed 1916

in a realistic and rational way, as is shown especially in his Stockholm Law Courts Building ten years later. The functional ideals of the period were even more stressed in the work of Erik Hahr (1869–1944), for many years city architect of Västerås, where he carefully preserved the old character of the town but also added industrial buildings and workmen's houses; these are remarkably advanced for their day, but nevertheless clearly show the links with tradition. Hahr's work also illustrates a very important feature of the architecture of this time, namely the strong feeling of relationship between buildings and town planning.

The artistic possibilities of this architecture of volumes and materials were exploited to the full by Ragnar Ostberg (1866–1945), the supreme artist of the period. His greatest work, the Stockholm City Hall, was a source of inspiration to others during the long history of its design and erection, but by the time it was completed in 1923 other ideas had taken the lead. Romantic in a way, similar to Ostberg's buildings, but more freely modern in its details, was the Engelbrekt Church in Stockholm by Lars Israel Wahlman (1870–1952). Quite different is Wickman's great wooden church at Kiruna, a remarkably powerful synthesis of form and structure. These are the two most important works in the religious architecture of the period.

About 1910 the school of national realism had become dominant in Swedish architecture. But at the same time the first signs

Sven Markelius. Concert Hall, Hälsingborg, 1932

of a reaction began to appear among the younger architects. They started to look for geometrical precision, for the nuances of lines and shadows and for materials of a more abstract character. Instead of heavy blocks they wanted to create a lighter impression. It was natural that their interest began to turn towards classicism. The first of the leading architects to develop these tendencies was Ivar Teng-bom (b. 1878), who had been one of the foremost theorists among the national realists. Gradually he introduced a more restrained way of handling the materials and a simplification of forms—a typical example of the progressive, in no way revolutionary development towards a completely new architecture that has characterized so many Swedish architects.

But the greatest of the modernists, Carl Bergsten, saw clearly that classicism was only a stage in the search for pure new forms. In his Liljevalch Art Gallery in Stockholm, completed in 1916, he had covered quite a good bit of the way. The block character is gone, exterior and interior have been put in close relation to one another. One of the central ideas behind 20th-century architecture, the continuity of space, is appearing.

In the development of modern architecture as we see it today no generation has played a greater part than those born about the middle 1880s, the generation of *Gropius, *Le Corbusier, and *Mies van der Rohe. Three very important Swedish names belong to this group: Oswald *Almqvist Gunnar *Asplund and Sigurd *Lewerentz. They started within the bounds of national realism. When Lewerentz designed a group of holiday houses in the Stockholm archipelago in 1914, he used the forms of Swedish tradition, but in such a timelessly functional way that these little houses are extremely difficult to date. Through Kay *Fisker they came to exercise a considerable influence on Danish architecture. A couple of years later Almqvist created the 'Bergslagsbyn', a village for the workmen and employees of the Domnarvet iron works, where the red wooden houses and the carefully studied town plan make up a model housing scheme which must be counted as one of the best Swedish examples from this century. Asplund at the same time was developing a feeling for space which was fundamentally related to

Sven Bäckström and Leif Reinius. Gröndal Estate, Stockholm, 1944-5

modern international tendencies, only that he worked with more traditional forms. But it became increasingly clear that his classicism was only a superficial, artistic game and that his real development lay deeper. With the 1920s industrial architecture came to be of real importance. On the merits of his water-power stations Almqvist must be counted one of the great pioneers in the field, judged from an international point of view. The mighty Forshuvudforsen of 1921 still remains in the functional tradition, but with Hammarforsen and Krångforsen, both designed and built in 1925-8, he had cut all ties with the past. These buildings, extremely pure and simple, have nevertheless a very strong dynamic expression, conveying something of the idea of water-power. Chenderoh in Malaya, completed in 1930, is perhaps even finer in its bright, calm clarity.

Almqvist had developed into 'the first Swedish functionalist' practically independently of all influences from abroad. At about the same time, however, Le Corbusier's theories got an intelligent and the social consciousness which had for so

far-seeing interpreter in the person of Uno Åhrén (b. 1897). Of first-rate importance also was the founding in 1925 of the Co-operative Society's architects' office, with Eskil Sundahl (b. 1890) as chief architect. The factories, shops and other works sponsored by this office came to be known for a purist quality with strong social, and one might even say moral, aspects, which became of decisive importance for the whole Swedish architecture of the 1930s.

In 1930 Asplund was finally ready to discard the cloak of formalism under which he had been carrying out his studies of space problems and room relations during the whole of the 1920s. In the Stockholm Exhibition he exploited to the full the artistic possibilities of the 'new architecture' with a refinement and an elegance probably unsurpassed to this day. Within a very short time functionalism then became generally accepted in Sweden. The ground had been well prepared. The progressive political atmosphere favoured the social consciousness which had for so

long been part of the architectural programme; on the formal side, the more
abstract line in the classicism of the 1920s
had been gradually leading up to pure
*Functionalism. Of course there were dif-
ferences of opinion and heated debates,
but hardly worth mentioning if we compare
the situation in most other countries
where the new ideas had to fight hard
against official resistance. In this way
Sweden became the 'model country' of
modern architecture in the 1930s. But to
a considerable extent the real strength lay
on the side of the social programme. Much
of what was built seems in retrospect rather
dry and schematic. This concerns especially the town plans with their parallel
blocks, where a correct orientation was
valued higher than the creation of outdoor
rooms between buildings.

Nevertheless there were many buildings of
high artistic value. The leading name was
Asplund, who was now softening the
abstract character of the pioneer works by
his exquisite feeling for different materials.
The Gothenburg Concert Hall by Nils
Einar Eriksson (b. 1899) shows similar
qualities. Le Corbusier's influence is evident in the works of Sven *Markelius,
especially in his private houses. But the
strongest personal note is to be seen in
the very limited production of Lewerentz,
who shows a deep feeling for all the
technical and aesthetic aspects of building, accepting no ready-made solution
but working until the problems are mas-
tered. Thus, while Lewerentz's buildings
are always technically right, as independent
works of art they also stand on a level above
most contemporary architecture and show
a continuous personal development. In
1937 he built a remarkable private house at
Falsterbo; the landscaping of the Stockholm Forest Cemetery round Asplund's
crematorium is chiefly his work, and in
1943 he completed his own crematorium
in Malmö in the cemetery which he had
begun to plan already in 1920.

In the 1940s a reaction started against
international Functionalism. This was
partly caused by the war, which cut off
contacts with other countries and also
restricted the use of certain building
materials. Swedish architecture turned
provincial. The clarity of the 1930s gave
way to a superficial play with forms and
materials. This romanticism could, how-

Sven Backström and Leif Reinius. Town centre
with cinema and assembly rooms in background.
Satellite town of Vällingby, near Stockholm,
commenced 1953

Sigurd Lewerentz, Björkhagen Church, Skarpnäck
near Stockholm, 1960

ever, sometimes lead to fine results, as in the Karlskoga Town Hall and Hotel by Sune Lindström (b. 1906), where it was combined with strongly disciplined volumes. A new tradition in brick building was formed. A really positive contribution of the decade was the abandoning of the stereotyped housing schemes in favour of differentiated plans, where the architects sought to create more 'home-like' surroundings and the plans of the houses themselves were very thoroughly studied. The partners Sven Backström (b. 1903) and Leif Reinius (b. 1907) are the most important architects of such projects.

With the 1950s a new wave of international influences swept over Sweden. This time, however, it was less surely handled than in the 1930s. There was no artist of Asplund's calibre to take the lead. Perhaps the general level might be called quite good, but there were no highlights. The really important things still happened on the programme side, above all in civic planning, where such projects as the Vällingby scheme, with its much-studied social and commercial centre, saw the light. The rebuilding of the central parts of Stockholm is another gigantic project which has attracted much interest. But here again uncertainty in the treatment of volumes, materials and details has often been manifest.

A new reaction began to appear at the end of the 1950s. Interest in the truly three-dimensional aspects of architecture has awakened again, but it has not taken the form of any wild experimentation. The liking for the simple cube is coming back, combined with a tendency to strong individualization. Not seldom colourful materials such as bricks are used. There are certain parallels to the tendencies of about 1910. These ideas have come to light most vigorously in church architecture. The works of Peter Celsing (b. 1920) offer a good field for study. But most remarkable is Lewerentz's church at Skarpnäck near Stockholm, a group of low brick volumes that seem to be in some way naturally grown on their site. There is nothing radically new in such a way of building, but it has here been given the timeless quality of a great work of art. And continued progress has always been more popular than revolution in Sweden.

Bibliography: G. E. Kidder Smith, Sweden Builds, 2nd edition, New York 1957; New Swedish Architecture, Stockholm 1939; Swedish Housing of the 'Forties, Stockholm 1950; New Architecture in Sweden, Stockholm 1961 (all published by SAR, the National Association of Swedish Architects).

BJÖRN LINN

Switzerland. Long before the term modern architecture could be used with regard to Switzerland, Robert *Maillart (from 1901 onwards) constructed his reinforced concrete bridges which were as technically audacious as they were aesthetically perfect. Karl *Moser, whose Church of St Anthony at Basle (1926–7) was the first ecclesiastical building in Switzerland built entirely of reinforced concrete, taught the next generation of architects while he was professor (1915–28) at Zurich Technical College (ETH). At the same time, Hans Bernoulli by his writings awakened their

Karl Moser. Church of St Anthony, Basle, 1926–7

Paul Artaria, Hans Schmidt, Max E. Haefeli; Carl Hubacher, Rudolf Steiger, Werner M. Moser and Emil Roth, Neubühl Estate, Zurich, 1930-2

sense of responsibility for civic design and town planning; he, too, was a professor at the ETH (Chair of Civic Design, 1919-39). The younger generation gave their point of view in the journal *ABC* (1924, Hans Schmidt and Mart Stam). Moser's successors to the professorship were O. R. Salvisberg and Hans Hofmann. Above all, *Le Corbusier's ideas exerted great influence. The Weissenhof houses at Stuttgart (1927) and the developments in

Hermann Baur. School on the Bruderholz. Basle, 1938-9.

Holland were studied. The *Bauhaus, directed in 1928-9 by the Swiss architect Hannes *Meyer, after Gropius's resignation, made its effects felt in Switzerland, too. Meyer's Trade Union School at Bernau (1928) was one of the first examples of a purely functional building; his design for the League of Nations Building at Geneva (1927), awarded the third prize, was the antithesis to Le Corbusier's scheme, which came first. *CIAM was founded at La Sarraz in 1928 and the *élite* of the world's architects joined it. In the ideological struggle against 'vernacular style', the new buildings erected between 1930 and 1940 achieved the homogeneity of functional thought; precise, objective and unpretentious, adapted to the rich local tradition of burgher and peasant culture and to the variety yet compression of the landscape within the framework of a federally constituted democracy. A high standard of housing was achieved, backed by perfection of structure and workmanship. Switzerland built excellent housing estates, hospitals and schools; her theoretical contributions, publications and exhibitions were influential. Paul Artaria, Ernst F. Burckhardt, Karl Egender, Max Ernst Haefeli, Werner M. Moser, Emil and Alfred Roth, Hans Schmidt, Otto Senn and Rudolf Steiger began to work at this time; Max *Bill and Hans Fischli came from the Bauhaus.

The National Provinces Exhibition at Zurich in 1939 (chief architect Hans Hofmann) aimed at showing a cross section of all that had been built since 1914. One of its positive results was the foundation of the Swiss Town and Country Planning Association (1943). The next National Provinces Exhibition to be held in Lausanne in 1964 will itself be an example of modern planning, and will make a fundamental attempt to tackle the planning problems of our time (chief architect: A. Camenzind; divisional architects: Max Bill, Zurich; Frédéric Brugger, Lausanne; Tita Carloni, Lugano; Jean Duret, Geneva; Marc-J. Saugey, Geneva; Florian Fischer, Basle; Jakob Zweifel, Zurich).

The Neubühl estate by the Werkbund at Zurich (1930-2) became a prototype of its kind; it featured differentiation of living requirements, standardization of units, and provision of open spaces by arranging the blocks at angles to each other (Artaria and

Max Bill. College of Design (Hochschule für Gestaltung). Ulm, 1953–5

Schmidt; M. E. Haefeli; C. Hubacher; R. Steiger, W. M. Moser and E. Roth). The housing scheme for Prilly near Lausanne went even further (1947; M. E. Haefeli, W. M. Moser, R. Steiger, M. Hottinger—not built) in envisaging a mixed development, including point blocks. The Gellert district at Basle (general layout by H. Baur, 1956) adopted the same principle but different means of execution. The estate at Halen near Berne (1957; Atelier 5, Berne, and Niklaus Morgenthaler) is a group of detached houses set close together in the manner of a village and rationalized by the use of prefabricated concrete units.

Hospital and school buildings were freed from schematism. At the cantonal hospital, Zurich (started 1942; M. E. Haefeli, R. Steiger, W. M. Moser, H. Weideli, J. Schütz, H. Fietz) spatial unity has been achieved in accommodating the most modern therapeutic knowledge, with its facilities in a constant state of renewal and extension. The current level of this development may be seen in Zurich Dental Institute, by the same architects. The school on the Bruderholz at Basle by Hermann Baur (1938–9) gave the lead to this type of district school, freely laid out amidst greenery. There is a large number of excellent examples of this kind today everywhere in Switzerland. The school building programme of Zurich in particular is remarkable for its far-sighted planning for anticipated requirements under the direction of progressive architects. Larger

schools are best represented by the technical colleges: Zurich, Karl Egender, (1926–32); Berne, Hans Brechbühler, (1937–9); and Basle, H. and H. P. Baur, F. Bräuning and A. Dürig (1956–61). As an example of the organization of a complex group of buildings in a natural setting, on the basis of uniform elements, the College of Design (Hochschule für Gestaltung) at Ulm by Max Bill may be cited (1953–55). A similar problem arose at Zurich, where the Freudenberg cantonal school by Jacques Schader (1958–61) had to combine two types of schools on a limited site.

Rudolf and Peter Steiger. 'Cern' Laboratory. Geneva, 1954–60

Switzerland has started even later to let modern architecture in; but there Italian influence is unmistakable.

Bibliography: Max Bill, Moderne Schweizer Architektur 1925–1949, Basle 1949; G. E. Kidder Smith, Switzerland builds, London and New York 1950; Hans Volkart, Schweizer Architektur, Ravensburg 1951.
MARGIT STABER

TAC ('The Architects Collaborative), founded in 1946, an architectural association in which Walter *Gropius joined with architects of the younger generation (Norman Fletcher, John Harkness, Robert McMillan, Louis McMillen, and Benjamin Thompson). Gropius here realized his conception of 'teamwork by individualists' in such large TAC schemes as the Harvard Graduate Center (1949–50), the US Embassy in Athens (1961), and the project for Bagdad University.

Tange, Kenzo, b. Imabari City in Shikoku 1913. Tange spent his high school days at Hiroshima. Imabari and Hiroshima are both located facing the Inland Sea, which is said to be the Mediterranean Sea in Japan. Being fascinated since his early days by *Le Corbusier, whose works are based on Mediterranean traditions in Europe, Tange entered the Tokyo Imperial University and took architectural courses in the Department of Engineering from 1935 to 1938. Immediately after his graduation, he entered Kunio *Maekawa's architectural office, and later with Maekawa he joined the Japanese Werkbund. While he was working there, he was almost entirely responsible for the planning of the Kishi Memorial Gymnasium. Later, in 1941, he re-entered the Tokyo University and took a post-graduate course. In 1942 he was awarded first prize in a competition for the design of a Far East memorial building sponsored by the Japanese Architectural Institute. A year later he won a prize for the plan of a Japan-Thai cultural centre to be built in Bangkok. However, none of these projects were realized. His first building to be erected was a Pavilion of Local Products for the Kobe Industry and Trade Fair (1950), which was removed after the fair was over.

Page 289 Kenzo Tange. Town Hall of the Kagawa Prefecture, 1958

Since 1945, new buildings in Switzerland have assumed a multitude of shapes. Typical examples include the churches that followed Le Corbusier's experiment at Ronchamp. The multi-storey office building 'zur Palme' in Zurich by M. E. Haefeli, W. M. Moser, R. Steiger, O. Caretta and A. Studer (under construction) attempts a form of three-dimensional modelling inspired by Frank Lloyd *Wright. The terraced layouts at Zug by F. Stucky and R. Meuli (1957–60) and at Zurich-Witikon by C. Paillard and Peter Leemann (1959–60), with flats stacked above each other in self-contained living zones, are all distinguished by the utmost economy in the exploitation of the site. Large blocks of flats with a high standard of comfort have appeared, particularly in Geneva (Denis Honegger, Arthur Lozeron, Marc-J. Saugey). The construction of the 'Cern' Research Centre near Geneva by R. and P. Steiger (1954–60) successfully coped with spatial requirements of a hitherto unknown category for nuclear research. In French Switzerland modern architecture has made a late start, although the famous Swiss architect Le Corbusier, who has been living in Paris since 1917, came from this region. The Italian part of

Max E. Haefeli, Werner M. Moser, Rudolf Steiger, O. Caretta and André Studer. Multi-storey office block 'zur Palme', Zurich, under construction. Model

Kenzo Tange. Peace Centre. Hiroshima, 1955–6

From that time Tange's creative talent rapidly increased. He designed the Ehime Convention Hall and his own house in 1954 as well as the Shimizu Town Hall. The Kurayoshi Town Hall was built in 1956, and the Tokyo Metropolitan Government Office was completed in 1957. Other important buildings were the Peace Centre in Hiroshima, a library for children which reveals his originality in space vision, and the small but carefully planned Tsuda College Library in Tokyo.

Tange's aim has always been to integrate Japan's architectural traditions with the needs of modern society, and he sought an answer to this problem through the planning of a series of buildings for local communities; he reached a successful solution in the Kagawa Prefectural Office completed in 1958. The realization of the project owed a great deal to the influential

Kenzo Tange. Town Hall. Shimizu, 1954

governor, Kaneko, who appreciates Tange's work. The building marks a peak in his career. Versatility and creative power have characterized Tange's work from the time he participated in the prize competition up to the present with his design for the Sogetsu Hall in 1960. If he succeeds in establishing his architectural philosophy on a firmer foundation, he should be one of the leading architects of the future.

He has written an essay on the 'Relation between Regional Planning and Architectural Design in Big Cities', and received his doctor's degree. At present, he is a professor at the Tokyo University and gives lectures on City Planning in the Engineering Department.

Bibliography: Robin Boyd, *Kenzo Tange*, New York 1962.

SHINJI KOIKE

Tatlin, Vladimir E., b. Moscow 1885. Graduated 1910 from Moscow Academy. First Constructivist type of work 1913–15. His design for a memorial to the Third International (1920) was a leaning spiral made of steel and wire and anticipates the buildings and designs of *Constructivism; Tatlin imagined the memorial as a 1,300-ft-high structure with large rooms.

Taut, Bruno, b. Königsberg 1880, d. Ankara 1938. Pupil of Theodor *Fischer. Erected a 'Monument of Steel' at the Leipzig Building Exhibition of 1913, and a glass pavilion at the 1914 Cologne Exhibition, which demonstrated in a most imaginative way the potentialities of *glass as a building material. During the First World War produced designs for Utopian *Alpine Architecture* (published Hagen 1919). Worked as City Architect at Magdeburg. Housing estates in Berlin in the *International Style. Taut went to Moscow in 1932, to Japan in 1933, and to Istanbul in 1936.

Bibliography: Bruno Taut, *Die neue Baukunst*, Berlin 1929.

Taut, Max, b. Königsberg 1884. Private practice since 1911. Schools, housing and office buildings (in particular for trade unions; headquarters for the German Printers' Union, Berlin, 1928); 1945–53 Professor at the Berlin College of Fine Arts.

Tecton. Architectural team founded by Berthold Lubetkin, to which Anthony Chitty, Lindsey Drake, Michael Dugdale, Val Harding and Denys Lasdun belonged. Highpoint Flats, Highgate (1933), Finsbury Health Centre, London (1938–9). The work of this group received popular recognition with their buildings for the London Zoo, in which *reinforced concrete was used in an imaginative way.

Telford, Thomas, b. Westerkirk, Dumfriesshire 1757, d. London 1834. Scottish architect and engineer. Stone buildings with large areas punctuated by projecting planes, not by ornaments, with Romanesque touches (St Catharine's Dock, 1824–8). Bold designs for bridges making use of cast iron (design for a Thames bridge, London, 1801; Conway Castle Bridge, 1822–6).

Terragni, Giuseppe, b. Meda near Milan 1904, d. Como 1942. Terragni is one of the most complex and at the same time most consistent figures of the early modern movement in Italy. His work covers a period of only thirteen years, from his graduation in Milan in 1926 to the time of his call-up in 1939. He fought on the Greek and Russian fronts, was repatriated to Italy, and died of the after-effects of exhaustion in January 1942. In this short span he was responsible for some of the most significant buildings produced during the period, beset with so many difficulties and reverses, that brought Italian architecture from its neoclassical and eclectic backwaters to join the mainstream of the modern European style.

Terragni originally adhered to the *Novecento Italiano* group, which set out on a rationalist basis to restore plastic values and a sense of volume to modern architecture, in opposition to the new *International Style, which depended for effect on the manipulation of surfaces. In 1926 he helped to found the *Movimento Italiano per l'Architettura Razionale*, which unleashed the whole weight of the academic opposition against the young members of *gruppo 7* (Terragni, *Figini, *Pollini, Frette, Larco, Rava and Libera); he kept up the lively controversy which ensued to the very end of his life, writing his last article from the Russian front. The debate was a difficult and bitter one, since the protagonists on both sides were Fascists, and in consequence the movement's ideology ended in a hopeless impasse of opinions, tastes and interests.

Terragni's best arguments were his buildings, however. His first design to be carried out was a block of flats at Como (1927), called Novecomum, a typically 'novecentist' design which caused a considerable stir. A series of shops and interior decoration schemes followed, with various contributions to the Monza Biennali and the 1933 Milan Triennale. In 1932 he designed a hall for the Exhibition of the Fascist Revolution in Rome. In the same year he drew up plans for the Casa del Fascio at Como (completed in 1936), which remains the purest and most interesting monument of the *Novecento Italiano*, standing as it does on the verge of *Functionalism. The building is a cube devoid of any movement or ornament, in which solids and voids, by virtue of the violent contrasts they afford of light and shade, create a dramatically punctuated architectural dialogue. This austere and interesting building is the only

Giuseppe Terragni. Novecomum. Como, 1927

Giuseppe Terragni. Casa del Fascio. Como, 1936

one to have conferred a European validity
on that typically Italian phenomenon, the
Novecento. It was denounced however by
Giuseppe Pagano in the pages of *Casabella*
as an example of '17th-century affectation
applied to Functionalism', since he feared
that the younger generation of Italian
architects might be diverted by it from
their true objectives.

In his next work, however, a kindergarten
at Como (1937), Terragni abandoned the
Novecento line to create, within the framework of European Functionalism, the
most elegant and lucid of his projects.
Three houses dating from the same year
(Villa Bianca at Seveso, Villa Bianchi at
Rebbio and the Casa Pedraglio at Como)
restate the problem in strictly geometrical
terms, while pointing somehow to a
specifically 'spatial' type of solution. With
his last important work, the Casa Frigerio
at Como (1939), the volumetric cube is
broken up, although a freely articulated
plan is not achieved. Among his other
works may be mentioned four houses in
Milan (1935-6, in collaboration with
Pietro Lingeri) and the Casa del Fascio
at Lissone (1939, with Carminati).

Terragni left behind him a large number of
architectural and town-planning schemes;
also a collection of controversial writings
which reveal that intellectual honesty and
sensitivity which led him, on the eve of his
death, to renounce his great political error
in despair.

Bibliography: Giuseppe Pagano, 'Tre anni
di architettura in Italia', in *Casabella*,
February 1937; Mario Labò, *Giuseppe
Terragni*, Milan 1947; Attilio Podestà,
'Omaggio a Terragni' in *Emporium*, Vol.
CVII, No. 640, April 1948; Giulia Veronesi,
*Difficoltà politiche dell'architettura in Italia,
1920–1940*, Milan 1953.

GIULIA VERONESI

Torroja, Eduardo, b. Madrid 1899, d. 1961.
Studied civil engineering in Madrid. He was
director of the Instituto Técnico de la Construcción y del Cemento, and an honorary
doctor of numerous universities.

Torroja belongs to the great creators of
architectural form in the 20th century. As
his many works built in Europe, Africa and
America strikingly demonstrate, he possessed great imaginative powers, capable of
stating surprising problems and devising

unexpected solutions for them, together with an immense technical capacity for solving these problems and actually carrying out the solutions. His views may be found in essence in his book *Philosophy of Structures*, where we see how different he is from the usual mathematical type of engineer when he asserts from the outset the rights of the imagination and declares that calculations only serve to show whether what has been imagined will stand.

According to Torroja, there are three classes of structure: those which serve to contain a volume, those which carry loads and those which resist thrusts. The architectural problem centres round his system of four equations with four unknowns. The equations are those of ultimate purpose, static function, aesthetic qualities and economic conditions. The unknowns are the materials, the structural types, the critical shapes and sizes and the actual building process. In determining structural types, Torroja started by considering the conditions of stress. The networks set up by the systems of stress, namely the

lines of tension and compression, allowed him to emphasize the way each form works. As regards materials, recognizing the truth of *Wright's assertion that each one of them speaks its own language, he concentrated on exploiting the great properties of reinforced and pre-stressed concrete, which was his favourite means of expression.

In considering the question of aesthetic expression, Torroja believed that truth alone was not enough and that a psychological factor in the material supervened which might lead to the possibility of structural jests, surprising absurdities and a gratuitous playfulness. Notwithstanding this, he considered simplicity a virtue. In regard to the architectural forms of his times, he used to speak with a certain sadness about materialism, and about those who disclaim nature on anti-romantic grounds while assigning excessive value to rhythm. He accepted an essentially baroque principle in maintaining the idea that the eye is deceptive, and in preferring psychological phenomena to material reality. Although regular geometrical forms exist

Eduardo Torroja. Grandstand at Zarzuela race track, near Madrid, 1935

Eduardo Torroja. Church of the Ascension.
Xerralló, 1952. Sketch

in some of his works, such as the twelve-
sided concrete coal bunker he built for the
Instituto Técnico de la Construcción y del
Cemento (Madrid, 1951), most of his
designs employ folded, undulating or
warped shapes.
In 1928, *Freyssinet took out the first
patent for pre-stressed concrete. A year
later, Torroja was using it for the Tempul
bridge, where the longitudinal girders were
pre-stressed. His ribless roof for Algeciras
Market Hall (1933) was Torroja's response
to the ribwork of Basle Market Hall (1929).
For the Zarzuela race track near Madrid in
1935 he designed a system of fluted grandstand roofs with a very extensive cantilever,
counterbalanced by vertical tie rods behind
the stanchions. In the same year he built
the shell roof of the Frontón Recoletos,
whose form derives from the penetration
of two barrel vaults of different dimensions
running parallel to each other. The hyperboloid form of a reservoir for Madrid (1936)
was the forerunner of the great hyperboloid
dome of the water tower at Fedala,
Morocco (1956).
Torroja's Aldoz aqueduct (1939), with
X-shaped pipeline supports, broke new
ground in this type of structure. His
Martín Gil bridge over the Esla (1940) with
its 623-foot span, broke the world record
for a single arch. It is currently (1963) the
third largest in the world in absolute span,
and the second largest railway bridge. The
Torrejón de Ardoz hangars, with their
structural panache, were completed in

1942; in the following year, the great roof
over the entrance to the Campo de Les
Corts in Barcelona, with its sinuous outline, is the first of Torroja's major works
to feature organic asymmetry; its final
flowering is to be seen at the Táchira Club
at Caracas (1957).
Torroja's churches at Xerralló, Sant
Esperit and Pont de Suert (1952) are the
first examples of modern religious art to
be found south of the Pyrenees since the
Civil War.
Bibliography: Eduardo Torroja, *Philosophy
of Structures*, California 1958; Eduardo
Torroja, *The Structures of Eduardo Torroja*,
New York 1958; Fernando Cassinello,
'Eduardo Torroja' in *Cuadernos de Arqui-
tectura*, Barcelona 1961; Eduardo Torroja,
Logik der Form, Munich 1961.
                    ALEXANDRE CIRICI-PELLICER

Town planning is the preconcerted disposition of urban living-space. Already in
the tight society in the years prior to 1800,
consideration was given to the building of
cities in a manner which could be termed
planning. The planned layout of a town,
however, was such a self-evident part of
government that any special discipline concerned with the technical or economic
questions of town layout or planning was
simply not referred to.
Even the distinction between towns that
have grown and those that have been
planned was only invented by art historians
of the last century, attempting to demonstrate, for some of the historical towns at
least, an ideal conception of their time,
'growth from the free interplay of forces'.
Ungeometrical towns were said to have
'grown', in contrast to those with geometrical shapes. Today, however, we know
that towns of both basic shapes, regular and
irregular, have been planned at some time
or other, and that an act of foundation preceded the existence of each town. Most
town extensions, too, were planned or
comprised in an overall scheme. The common interest of all citizens in effective
defence by a system of fortifications made
it necessary to conform to a plan.
For a long time the irregularly shaped
town was thought to represent an earlier
stage of development, the regular shape a
later one. No single form, however, has
exclusively prevailed at any time. Aristotle,
who summarized the whole scientific

knowledge of antiquity and remained a
supreme authority throughout the Middle
Ages, declared that both methods had
their advantages and disadvantages, and
both might be used according to local conditions. The irregular shape is said to be
the more economical one. The necessity for
defence and the prevalence of emotional
tendencies certainly led to a predominance
of ungeometric shapes in the early periods
of town development, while the rational
and economic tendencies of later epochs
displayed a preference for geometric for-
mations. Changes in society have also
played their part in the differentiation of
town shapes.

After 1800, the last effective possibility of
controlling town growth in Central Europe
was lost. With the removal of fortifications and quick growth due to increased
prosperity as a consequence of industrialization, cities spread rapidly along their
main arteries, beyond their former limits.
Property speculators provided hastily
erected tenement houses, badly lighted and
cramped, for the mass of people streaming
into the towns from the country. Building
by-laws which permitted a shameless
exploitation of people and sites left their
mark on the appearance of these districts.
The grid-type layouts of the surveyors, the
unvaried street widths and heights, and
the squares dotted here and there without
rhyme or reason, were meant to be neutral,
so as to avoid obstructing the action of
economic forces. The fate of the town was
thus left to chance and speculation, and it
grew in unconnected single phases.

Around the year 1900, movements for
social reform attempted to remedy the
poor living conditions of the towns (E.
*Howard, H. George, Damaschke, Fritsch,
Eberstadt and others). The science of town
planning was gradually developed; with
the foundation of town planning associations the recognition emerged that town
and country must complement each other
and be subjected to a common plan (Unwin,
Schumacher). Traffic considerations came
first, closely followed by economic factors.
For a time, living conditions occupied the
focus of attention, then politico-sociological
aspects of the town and finally the demand
for green belts and landscaping. Only a
team consisting of every kind of specialist
(mining engineers, surveyors, architects,
economists, sociologists, doctors, lawyers

Georges-Eugène Haussmann. Boulevard
Richard-Lenoir. Paris, 1861–3. Remedial measures
are confined to cutting new streets through

and landscape architects) is in a position
to grasp such a complex problem as the
town of today, and to work out a plan that
does justice to all these aspects of development. Academies and associations such
as *CIAM (with its *Athens Charter) drew
up minimum requirements and optimum
conditions for the renewal or reconstruction
of cities. A recognition of the basic needs
a town has to provide for (work, living,
traffic, leisure) and their correct coordination with each other was a start.
Minimum health requirements for sunshine, daylight, dust and noise abatement,
green belts and open spaces, were formulated. The subdivision of the town into
organic units with service centres featuring
schools, churches, cultural buildings and
shops, separated from other such units by
belts of parkland, became a further
instrument of urban design. In this conjunction the problem arose of how to
ensure the best use of city sites. City
centres needed thinning out, while denser
development was called for on the peripheries; hence internationally valid speci-
fications for optimum land use were
involved.

The 'floorspace index' represents the ratio
of the total floor area of a building to the
area of its site, and may vary from 2.0 to
approximately 0.2 in areas with main
services (highest in business areas; City of
London currently 6.3!). These rules have
become necessary not only to ensure

sufficient ventilation, sunshine, daylight
and parkland; they are an essential consequence of the ever-increasing density
of traffic. For volume of building and
volume of traffic are interrelated: by reducing the volume of building, a reduction of
traffic density can be achieved. A floorspace index of 1.0, which may be regarded
as the upper limit for purely residential
areas, corresponds to a population density
of 200 inhabitants per net acre, and a
building density of about 60 dwelling units
per acre, while the cities of Central Europe
have maximum population densities of 400
an acre.

In urban residential districts supplied with
main services, FSI 0.2 should not be ex-
ceeded (giving a plot area of about 360 square
yards) as otherwise the town spreads out
uneconomically. No type of development
is more expensive than the type of 'suburban sprawl' generally encountered today,
with detached private houses on 1,200
square yard plots. While it is essential to
thin out the unsanitary and overcrowded
tenements that often survive in central
zones, a denser development of the out-
lying suburbs is currently aimed at by
planners. By adjusting both extremes,
towns with an average FSI of 0.4 would
not have to extend beyond the present
boundaries of their built-up areas. In
Berlin, the most densely populated district
of Kreuzberg has 480 dwelling units per
acre, while that of Zehlendorf has only 5.
If the regulations for distances between
buildings and the restrictions on density
are adhered to, the problem of correct
orientation for blocks of flats or rows of
houses is no longer a difficult one. The
most favourable disposition in the British
Isles is without doubt a south-west aspect,
but others are also possible and have
advantages for certain occupations or
members of the family. One thing must
however be avoided, living-rooms facing
north!

The type of building presents another
problem, whether multi-storey, medium-
high or low. Where no specific housing
tradition prevails, as it does in countries
such as England, the United States and
Holland where low structures are the
general rule, the type of building to be
erected is determined by considerations of
profitability to the landlord and ease of
running. Sociological and biological factors

Area of Tokio in 1880 and 1953. An increase in
radius from 5 to over 15 km.

should, however, be the criterion. Low
buildings are usually better for people with
children and dependents who feel united
as a family. Multi-storey blocks of flats are
more suitable for childless couples, un-
married people and families whose jobs
require them to move about. The medium-
high building has become almost meaning-
less, and simply serves to make the supply
of accommodation of various types appear
the more diverse. In cities and metropolitan areas, the number of people re-
quiring flats in multi-storey blocks may be
estimated at 20–30 per cent, naturally

higher than in medium-sized towns (5–20 per cent). In small towns the demand goes down virtually to zero, corresponding to the considerably larger number of people living in families. The method previously used of classification according to social strata and equivalent types of accommodation has all the disadvantages of a monolithic social system. Within a neighbourhood unit—preferably in a group of about 100 dwellings—every type of professional and family combination on the social scale should be included.

In the last century, industries were sited in the immediate neighbourhood of residential districts, as had been the custom of the old craft manufactories. It was not due to the resultant inconvenience but to the lack of space for extension that factories were moved to the outskirts and into industrial districts. With the introduction of electrical power, dust-extraction plants, and the sub-division of industry into smaller factory units, partial decentralization of industry becomes possible: either in the shape of small industrial plants attached to the neighbourhood units or by transference to the country. Only heavy industry, complex processes and offensive trades are tied to actual industrial districts. For the rest, industry can become the most flexible unit in the town, as its buildings usually have to be replaced after ten to twenty years.

Town planning measures are most easily realized nowadays in matters of traffic engineering, which everybody can understand. In the last thirty years enormous sums have been spent in the United States on the provision of highway facilities, but without remarkable success. The lesson to be learnt from this by European town planners is the need to avoid excess traffic by advance planning, thinning out congested areas and redirecting traffic sources and their destinations. Journeys to and from work make up 60–70 per cent of all the traffic in a town. Consideration of how living and working zones might be related to each other, and how change of work-place and removal from home could be coupled, is of such significance that it cannot be rejected by references to individual liberty. Shopping, school and leisure

J. H. van den Broek and Jacob B. Bakema. The Lijnbaan pedestrian street. Rotterdam, 1953

journeys can be reduced by planning (gardens surrounding houses, parks accessible on foot, shopping centres, schools and cultural facilities within the district). What essential traffic remains should be directed via differentiated lanes (motorway to residential street) so that its main stream makes contact with the town according to its nature. The town itself should be divided into traffic-free precincts, in which only pedestrians, cyclists and emergency traffic (doctors, police) are permitted. On the edge of the pedestrian precincts there should be adequate parking facilities.

Parks as recreational areas in the centre of a town have only been called for in our own times. It is the town planner's task today to link up incidental open spaces such as parks, cemeteries, the areas between buildings, allotments, sports grounds, and rivers and lakes with their banks into an interconnected green network. Like the traffic network, the green network should pass through each district so that each part of a town, and the countryside also, may be reached on foot via one of these links. These green belts should contain all secondary schools, sports facilities and baths, and any woodland in the town. Apart from them there are the green areas inside the individual districts, which accommodate playgrounds, primary schools and nursery schools. These constitute the actual centre of the district.

The vast extension in the size of towns means that the city centre forfeits its vitality. Hence the city must be decentralized, i.e., on the one hand it must be afforded increased ground space to accommodate ever-growing public and private services; on the other hand, all functions which have no definite central character can be moved into the suburbs. Satellites or New Towns are built to relieve the city's burden.

In Great Britain the New Town Act of 1946 provided for the development of a series of townships, each with populations of between 30,000 and 50,000. Apart from the usual apparatus of civic amenities, each town was designed to attract its own

Stockholm City Planning Office; Chief Architect: Sven Markelius. Satellite town of Vällingby, near Stockholm, commenced 1953. Site plan

Tony Garnier. Residential district. Cité Industrielle. 1901–4. Project

industries of various types, to prevent it from lapsing into a mere dormitory. Projects include Basildon, Stevenage, Harlow (chief planner: F. Gibberd), Hatfield (L. Brett), Peterlee, Newton Aycliffe and Corby in England; East Kilbride and Glenrothes in Scotland; and Cwmbran in South Wales. The standard of achievement varies, but the more successful express considerable urban distinction. Their example, and the progressive legislation which underlies them, have inspired other countries, Scandinavia in particular. Germany, too, has recently built a number of satellite towns in the neighbourhood of the larger cities.

A comprehensive advance in planning law is marked by the 1947 Town Planning Act, which lays an obligation on all planning authorities in Great Britain to produce a plan for their areas. This has given a great impetus to town planning practice, since many local authorities have had to set up planning departments for the first time. The development plans they are expected to work out, are based on a simple form of comprehensive survey, showing the future policy of land use in each area, and indicating where development or redevelopment is expected to take place; these plans are reviewed at five-yearly intervals. In addition, the 1947 Act provides for the safeguarding of trees and woodlands and the protection of buildings of historic interest, which it requires to be listed; it also embodies powers for the control of outdoor advertising.

Subsequent legislation includes the 1951 New Streets Act, which ensures that private developers do not leave their highways unadopted, and the 1952 Town Development Act, designed to facilitate the planned expansion of towns chosen to receive overspill populations.

Many schemes for the comprehensive redevelopment of central areas have been drawn up in recent years, frequently in collaboration with property companies.

Bibliography: Lewis Mumford, *The Culture of Cities*, New York 1938; Roland

Le Corbusier. Chandigarh, commenced 1950. Site plan

Rainer, *Städtebau und Wohnkultur*, Tübingen 1948; Frederick Gibberd, *Town Design*, London 1953; 4th edition 1962; Hans Bernhard Reichow, *Die autogerechte Stadt*, Ravensburg 1959; Fritz Jaspert, *Vom Städtebau der Welt*, Berlin 1961; Gordon Cullen, *Townscape*, London 1962.

HUBERT HOFFMANN

Townscape. Concept evolved in the late forties by analysing examples of consciously or unconsciously successful town design in terms of the progressive revelation of space and function to the moving spectator; influenced in part by the theories of English 18th-century landscape architects, which are transferred to an urban setting.

Invaluable discipline for the appreciation of historic towns, and the application of the lessons so learnt to the design of new ones.

Bibliography: Gordon Cullen, *Townscape.* London 1961.

HAROLD MEEK

Urbanism. *Town Planning.

USA. American architecture was for a long period an outpost of the European mainstream. During the colonial era (17th and 18th centuries) the styles were scarcely more than echoes of British practice at the same moment. With the coming of the Revolution, the influence of France became momentarily predominant. Then, for the first three-quarters of the 19th century, building developments in the United States followed the pace established both by British and French designers. The classical and Gothic revivals were succeeded by those mid-century Victorian fashions that were championed by Ruskin, Eastlake, *Morris and other writers, while Parisian influences in the guise of the Second Empire style were equally pervasive.

While it would be an exaggeration to maintain that American architecture had attained independence as well as maturity by the time of the Philadelphia Centennial Exposition of 1876, the date can be taken as symbolic of a new turn. At this juncture, American artists became aware of the unique character of their own colonial past, and, while in the process of making this discovery, they came under the influence of the new English taste for vernacular post-medieval styles, a revival movement that is generally if not especially accurately referred to as the Queen Anne. These two phenomena, in effect complementary manifestations of the same late 19th-century eclectic development, were present in varying degrees in the work of the three major American architects of the period, Henry Hobson *Richardson, Louis *Sullivan, and Frank Lloyd *Wright. Wright not only played a major creative rôle in the domestic architecture of the 1890s, but continued in both a creative and patriarchal capacity to mould and influence architecture in America and in Europe well past the middle of the 20th century.

It is conceivable that Richardson was the first architect of the post-Renaissance period to whom the word 'genius' is not inappropriate. In his ponderous, taciturn style were united the moralistic, revivalistic and rational principles of diverse earlier tendencies. However, above and beyond its manifold sources, the personal style of Richardson is remarkably fused, and the inner conflicts latent in its origins are so reconciled and submerged that it is eclectic and revivalistic only in methodology. In actuality these robust masonry or wood shingle forms are among the most disciplined and unified creations of the last century. It was the example of Richardson that helped to clarify the somewhat less certain taste of Louis Sullivan, who had been at first inspired by a Victorian architect of almost grotesque power, Frank *Furness, and only subsequently by the new technology of the steel-framed tall office building, which was invented and popularized in Chicago in the 1880s, a rational type of design that is identified by the sobriquet *'Chicago School'. Sullivan's most striking accomplishments of the 1890s in commercial architecture were echoed in the perceptive if less elegant skyscraper designs of Daniel H. *Burnham and John W. *Root, whether in the dense masonry structure of the Monadnock Building (1891) or in the expressive steel-framed Reliance Building (1890–4), a glazed thirteen-storey shaft. In contrast to these striking manifestations of commercial efficiency in a materialistic era, the early tall office buildings in New York were less boldly simplified in aspect, though their greater attention to variety of detail, as in Richard Morris Hunt's Tribune Building, New York (1873–5), was more original than is generally realized.

Frank Lloyd Wright is the third and most spectacular of this triumvirate in American architecture. An assistant of Louis Sullivan until he established his own practice in 1893, Wright subsequently devoted most of his efforts to domestic architecture, and if his position long went largely unrecognized in the USA—although his work always earned a degree of respect and admiration, if usually qualified in tone— the brilliant spatial inventions of his suburban Chicago houses of the period 1893–1909, culminating in the Robie House of 1909, were of immeasurable influence in Europe. These works were published and exhibited in Germany in 1910–11, and to judge from the works of the masters of the *International Style, together with their subsequent testimony, they had a tremendous impact. Wright's domestic architecture of 1900 was complemented by the work of others in his immediate circle, and his principles were echoed on the west coast in the domestic work of Charles and Henry *Greene, notably the Gamble House, Pasadena (1908–9), in which seemingly exotic oriental elements are successfully blended with an indigenous offshoot of the Queen Anne known as the 'Shingle Style', a mode originally popularized by Richardson. A similar independence was manifested by Bernard R. *Maybeck in his Christian Science Church, Berkeley (1910), in which a concrete structure is enriched by provocative medievalizing timber details. Equally picturesque effects, but in an academic, indeed, Imperial Roman garb, were produced by Maybeck in his Fine Arts Building for the 1915 San Francisco Exhibition, a temporary structure in pink stucco that still stands, albeit in a ruinous state.

Frank Furness. Pennsylvania Academy of Fine Arts. Philadelphia, 1872–6

Louis H. Sullivan. Auditorium Building. Chicago, 1886–9

Louis H. Sullivan. Getty Tomb. Chicago, 1890

The taste which stands behind the general style if not the personal feeling expressed in Maybeck's Fine Arts Building had earlier been crystallized at the World's Columbian Exposition, Chicago (1893), where a group of architects led by the fashionable academic firm of McKim, Mead and White (who had begun as disciples of Richardson) produced the famous 'White City' of Imperial Classicism in plaster and lath. Largely if not completely divorced from this *beaux-arts* design discipline was Sullivan's Transportation Building, with its intricately detailed round-arched portal which was admired by European if not by American visitors.

With this unmistakable 'revolution' in favour of the classical modes, which in a decade spread across the country, Sullivan and other independent-minded architects gradually lost contact with what seemed at the time to be the main stream of modern architectural design, a main stream which produced buildings such as the Pennsylvania Station, New York (1906–10), by McKim, Mead and White, which was not only stylistically neoclassical but went so far as to seek identity with a distant past through the imitation of certain portions of a typical Roman bath. Such accomplishments almost totally eclipsed for the moment the works of Sullivan's old age, such as the National Farmers Bank, Owatona, Minnesota (1907–8). Here the block-like design cut with a massive round arch bears analogies. not so much to the current academic fashion, as to the earlier idiom of Richardson. Sullivan's work of this period is in effect a vital, organic outgrowth of the late-19th-century traditions, whereas that of McKim, Mead and White is a largely sterile, even if scholarly, product of the same tradition.

If Wright, the Greene brothers, Maybeck and a few others clearly belong to an independent movement in architecture around 1900, along with Sullivan, the same

Charles and Henry Greene. Gamble House, Pasadena, 1908–9

cannot be said for a host of other interesting architects active during the first two or three decades of the 20th century in the USA. Among the domestic specialists of the period, few seem in retrospect to have been so able and craftsmanlike as the Philadelphia firm of Mellor, Meigs and Howe. Their abilities to produce a bland if arcane eclecticism are amply illustrated in the house of 1914 at Chesnut Hill, Pennsylvania, built for George *Howe, the junior member of the firm, who was later to reject this tentative style for a more forthright modernism.

Monumental architecture at this epoch is represented by Cass Gilbert's (1859–1934) Gothic skyscraper, the Woolworth Building, New York (1913); Bertram Grosvenor Goodhue's (1869–1924) tentatively 'modernistic' Nebraska State Capitol and Los Angeles Public Library of the 1920s, in which the departing spirit of 19th-century eclecticism makes one last effort to survive in a provocative compromise form; or in James Gamble Rodgers's (1867–1947)

numerous designs for Yale University, beginning in 1917, which depend for their sense of medieval authenticity upon a particularly luxuriant texture and carefully studied detailing. The classical tradition was maintained by Henry Bacon's (1866–1924) Lincoln Memorial, Washington (1914–22), and by John Russell Pope's (1874–1937) National Gallery of Art, Washington (1937), both extraordinarily pure revisions of the academic formula. Most of these able designers were nearly exact contemporaries of Wright, and it is therefore all the more interesting to compare the latter's idiosyncratically monumental Hollyhock House, Los Angeles (1920), with the more customary monumentalism of the others. Another contemporary of Wright, Albert *Kahn, had a rather different contribution to make to the growth of recent American architecture. From the first decade of the century his vast organization specialized in large-scale industrial work, and continued the process of developing the large office which had been inaugurated by the academically inclined firms of the 1880s and 1890s.

However, the work of the 1920s in the USA, curious and interesting as it is, completely lacks the forthright intensity of the new architecture that was then emerging in Europe. Indeed, the work of Wright at this time, even when viewed in the context of the more traditionally oriented buildings of the day, was less acutely creative than at an early or at a later period. But already there were signs that this era of somnolence was not destined to last. In 1923 the Finnish architect, Eliel *Saarinen, settled in America, representing the vanguard of a coming wave of distinguished European *émigrés*. While his work never quite fulfilled the promise of his earliest endeavours in Finland, and instead appears tentative in style if forthright in its programmatic solutions, a rather different and more unmistakable contemporaneity was to be found in the designs of Rudolph *Schindler and Richard *Neutra, two architects of Viennese origin whose particular dispositions were influenced by such disparate stimuli as Otto *Wagner, Adolf *Loos, and Frank Lloyd Wright. The houses built first by Schindler and, subsequently, by Neutra in and around Los Angeles, were the very earliest manifestations in the USA of the technique and taste that were later identified as the *International Style. The clear, unmistakably pure character of their works demonstrated that the tentative modernism of a Goodhue or an Eliel Saarinen would become outmoded along with the more literal sort of historicism as soon as the new architecture had spread.

The speed with which the new ideas and motifs took hold can be illustrated in the transformation of Raymond *Hood's widely admired skyscraper designs, which changed from a neo-Gothic mode in the Chicago Tribune (1923, with John Mead Howells, b. 1868), to a simplified abstract mode which is, albeit superficially, both functional and futurist, in the New York Daily News Buildings (1930). A much more profound essay in 'Skyscraper International' was the tower of the Philadelphia Savings Fund Society by George Howe and William *Lescaze of 1932, whose expression of vertical structural members on one side is set in contrast to the horizontal expression of cantilevers on

Henry Bacon. Lincoln Memorial. Washington, 1914–22

Raymond M. Hood. Daily News Building. New York, 1930

William Lescaze and George Howe. Philadelphia
Savings Fund Society Building. Philadelphia, 1932

another. Such integral relationships between the frame of the building and its
surface is analogous to the practice of the
earlier Chicago School, although the formal vocabulary conforms with the new
European fashion. This unusually frank
design is in distinct contrast with the tallest
of all tall office buildings, the Empire State
Building, New York, by Shreve, Lamb
and Harmon (1930–2), which manages to
be 'traditional' without being recognizably
revivalistic in style.

The 1930s were marked by two events
which had the dual effect of releasing
contemporary American architecture from
the predominantly tentative statements of
modernism, and of forming the basis from
which the post-Second World War leadership of the USA in the development of
world architecture would suddenly grow.
The first of these was the renaissance of

Frank Lloyd Wright (no other word will
suffice), which reached an initial climax
in the Kaufmann House, Falling Water
(1936), a building in which the organic,
naturalistic features inherent in Wright's
design philosophy were reconciled with the
machine-like clarity characteristic of the
European modern movement. Seconding
this noteworthy achievement in the reintegration and development of 20th-
century American architecture was the
arrival in the USA of several of the chief
mentors of the International Style itself:
Walter *Gropius and *Mies van der Rohe
were joined by others of more Expressionist
leanings like Erich *Mendelsohn or by
their younger disciples such as Marcel
*Breuer. Gropius continued his rôle as an
educator which he had begun in the
*Bauhaus by taking charge of the Archi-
tectural School at Harvard, while Mies
assumed a similar rôle at the Illinois
Institute of Technology, Chicago. Both
contributed to the development of American modernism at this juncture with distinctive and influential buildings. Mies's
master plan for the new campus of IIT,
perfected in 1940, did not exert a great
influence for perhaps a decade, and then,
suddenly, its cool, pristine, stately geometry became the paragon of new architecture in the 1950s. More immediately
influential were a series of houses designed
by Gropius in collaboration with Breuer
in the neighbourhood of Boston, Mass. in
the late 1930s and early 1940s, houses in
which the severe geometry of the International Style was tempered and transformed by the native wood-frame traditions
of New England domestic architecture.
This transplanted style quickly evolved in
the direction of something more organic
and romantic in the post-1945 houses of
Breuer, and was in fact anticipated in the
domestic architecture of the Western
States, generally known as the Bay Region
Style. The restrained manner of William
W. *Wurster and the more personal styles
of Hartwell Hamilton Harris and John
Yeon represented, throughout the 1940s,
one of the most vigorous schools of
domestic architecture; it remains far more
memorable than the much publicized
Scandinavian 'New Empiricism' of the
same epoch. However, few works of this
group were quite so remarkable as developments of the fluent, interlocking spatial

Frank Lloyd Wright. Kaufmann House, 'Falling Water'. Bear Run, Pa., 1936

schemes of the International Style as were the southern California villas of Richard Neutra that date from the late 1940s. At the same period there are other more novel developments in domestic architecture that are due to Frank Lloyd Wright, whose second house for Herbert Jacobs, Middleton, Wis. (1948), is, in its fortress-like, primitive character, an extraordinary reaction against the openness and sophisticated modernism of Neutra's contemporary dwellings. Indeed, in many of his more monumental designs of the 1940s and 1950s Wright seems to be continuing and reinterpreting the massive and closed 19th-century forms of Richardson and Sullivan, giving them a new contemporary relevance rather than merely 'reviving' them.

Other characteristics of this varied and formative period can be seen in two academic buildings in Cambridge, Mass.:

Alvar *Aalto's Dormitory for the Massachusetts Institute of Technology (1948) and Walter Gropius's Harvard Graduate Center of 1950. The former, a tawny brick serpentine slab, represents the continued growth of the romantic, empirical strain (as opposed to the more provocative personal mode of Wright) in American architecture. On the other hand, the layout and elevations of the Harvard Graduate Center are dependent upon the tradition of purged and simplified geometry that was earlier realized in the Bauhaus itself, but with one important difference: the contrasts between the shapes and locations of the various elements are less harsh and bold. Each of these buildings illustrates in its own way an aspect of 20th-century modernism that was on the wane in the late 1940s.

The immediate future was destined to be predicated upon two much more simple and intellectual domestic designs of the period: Mies van der Rohe's Farnsworth House (1946–51) and Philip *Johnson's Glass House, New Canaan, Connecticut (1947–9). In many respects the spatial and planning techniques of these two highly specialized dwellings are dependent upon a half-century of the machine aesthetic, and as such are outgrowths, if not ultimate manifestations, of the International Style. However, the reduction and simplicity of the cubic form, and the crystalline uniformity of the enclosing glass introduces a degree of regularity in both houses that is in contrast to the more diverse and irregular shaping and surfacing of the 'functional' architecture of the 1920s. The new architecture of the 1950s was to learn much from this carefully stated neoclassicization of the machine aesthetic. Equally, the precision with which these and other works by Mies and Johnson were rendered was an external and easy-to-imitate element that was swiftly turned into a popular fashion in the commercial architecture of the period. The firm of *Skidmore, Owings and Merrill—in effect a latter day successor to both the academicism of McKim, Mead and White and the utilitarianism of Albert Kahn—dominated this side of American

architecture, especially through the quality of its commercial designs, and it continued to be acutely sensitive to shifts of taste when, in the late 1950s, its manner edged away from the glass box to more solid-seeming forms.

The early 1950s also witnessed the emergence of Eero *Saarinen, son of the pioneer Finnish architect. His General Motors Technical Center, Warren, Michigan, has a superficial Miesian character, but the varied proportions indicate a certain freedom of stylistic disposition which would lead to a pronounced design eclecticism in the late 1950s. This direction is amply documented in his new residential colleges for Yale University (1962) in which an abstract and empirical design is made to blend subtly with the elegant historicism of James Gamble Rodgers's collegiate Gothic of a generation before. A similar testing of various modernist idioms, together with a tentative eclecticism, is revealed in the designs of Paul *Rudolph, who had achieved considerable success as a designer of houses about 1950, and who, in the subsequent decade, has made interesting contributions to the expansion of the contemporary idiom in larger buildings. In particular, Rudolph has

Alvar Aalto. Students' Hostel, Massachusetts Institute of Technology. Cambridge, Mass., 1948

Ludwig Mies van der Rohe. Lake Shore Drive Apartments. Chicago, 1950–1

recently made an effort to transpose the vigorous late style of Le Corbusier in designs for religious, educational and commercial buildings.

The most fashionable of recent architects have tended towards a certain decorative elaboration in the composition of façades. Perhaps the most successful of these designers a few years ago was Edward D. *Stone, whose American Embassy in New Delhi, India (1958), was the first of a series of endeavours to create an officially endorsed modernism. A more recent example is Saarinen's Embassy in London (1960). However, the opulent yet brittle mannerisms of Minoru *Yamasaki, with façades protected by metal grilles and thinly disguised historical motifs, is perhaps an even more potent fashion in the early 1960s. In spite of these somewhat frigid, superficial efforts to create a revisionist movement in contemporary archi-

tecture, the older practitioners have tended to hold fast to the creative basis if not to the external appearances of their previous work. In his ultimate works, Wright created a dazzling array of forms, but they were invariably imagined upon the basis of previous designs. Mies's latest projects have been for buildings abroad, notably in Mexico and Germany, and thus his tenacity in holding to the style he perfected twenty years ago, especially in the face of change reflected both in the ephemeral work of the 1960s, and of normal development in the work of direct followers such as Johnson, and Skidmore, Owings and Merrill, is particularly noteworthy.

As if to compensate for Mies's relative inactivity recently in the USA, *Le Corbusier, the most distinguished of the veteran modernists remaining in Europe, was invited to design a new Art Center at Harvard in 1960. The characterful forms of this new building will thus form a challenging comparison with the other significant contemporary works of the last decade in Cambridge, Mass., those of Gropius, Aalto and Eero Saarinen. However, to the dynamic inflections of a sculptural sort that are now being introduced into American architecture by way of Le Corbusier, there is another, equally rugged, manner that is to be seen almost exclusively in the new work of Louis I. *Kahn. Hardly known a decade ago, except to a loyal band of young students, by the

Paul Rudolph. Cultural Centre, Wellesley College, Mass., 1955–9

Edward Durell Stone. US Pavilion at the International Exhibition. Brussels, 1958

late 1950s his fame was already assured. Kahn's forthright concrete frame structures possess the semblance of a design philosophy relevant for their period and a final outward appearance which appeals both to a taste for contrasts of form and for certain kinds of justifiably accidental effects. Consequently, Kahn's few executed buildings may well turn out to be the most historically important if least typical designs of the early 1960s. Indeed, the nature of his style is such that it suggests the fulfilment of a century of American architecture, subsuming some of the profoundest lessons of Wright, Sullivan, and Richardson, and reaching so far back as to make relevant once again the century-old Victorian 'realism' of Sullivan's early mentor, Frank Furness.

The other side of the current picture is also traditionalist, but, it would seem, takes its cue from the alternate, academic current of the American development. The handsome, tasteful designs for Lincoln Center, New York, the work of several architects, including Wallace *Harrison, Max *Abramovitz, Philip Johnson, Skidmore, Owings and Merrill, and the late Eero Saarinen, seem to represent a blend of the challenging modernist discipline of a quarter-century ago with the half-century-old security of academicism as earlier represented by McKim, Mead and White. Of all the buildings at Lincoln Center, only Johnson's Theater of the Dance seems to

be the outcome of anything more than the most superficial decorative approach.

Under these confusing and rather inconsistent circumstances it is not easy succinctly to characterize the American scene in the 1960s. However, it is clear that an epoch of assimilation is past and the modern movement, brought to a climax in Europe in the 1920s and 1930s, has been incorporated into the evolving tradition of American architecture. The latter has, thereby, achieved new responsibilities through a generally recognized world-wide leadership which places new demands as well as a new dignity upon its subsequent development.

Bibliography: E. B. Mock, *Built in USA 1932–1944*, New York 1944; Henry-Russell Hitchcock and Arthur Drexler, *Built in USA: Post-war Architecture*, New York 1952; Lewis Mumford, *Roots of Contemporary American Architecture*, New York and London 1952; Ian McCallum, *Architecture USA*, London 1959; Wayne Andrews, *Architecture in America*, New York 1960; Esther McCoy, *Five California Architects*, New York 1960; 'America', *Zodiac 8* (special number), Milan 1961; John Burchard and Albert Bush-Brown, *The Architecture of America*, Boston and Toronto 1961; C. W. Condit, *American Building Art*, Vol. I, The 19th century; Vol. II, The 20th century, New York and London, 1960 and 1961.

                                        JOHN M. JACOBUS, JR

Utzon, Jørn, b. Copenhagen 1918. Utzon is the most original talent in modern Danish architecture. From the earliest years of his career he was possessed by an organic sense of architecture which was inspired by Frank Lloyd *Wright and Alvar *Aalto and strengthened by a period of study in the USA and six months' work in Aalto's Helsinki drawing office (1946).

For the young Utzon the functionalism of the thirties had ended in formalism, and the traditionalism of the forties, a consequence of the isolation and restrictions caused by the war, was totally lacking in relevance to the technical and scientific developments of the times. He considered that a progressive architecture could be learned from the laws of nature, and that new materials should be used in accordance with their own properties. He was himself able to live up to these very ambitious demands thanks to his originality, imagination and professional skill.

Utzon completed his secondary education in 1937 and entered the architectural school of the Academy of Arts, where he was taught by Kay *Fisker and Steen Ejler Rasmussen. He qualified in 1942 and then worked for three years in Stockholm, where his encounter with Gunnar *Asplund's architecture in particular influenced his development. In the following year he received prizes in a series of competitions for projects worked out in collaboration with Tobias Faber and submitted a design for the Crystal Palace in London together with Faber and Mogens

Jorn Utzon. House. Holte, 1952–3

Irming. Also important at this time was his friendship and collaboration with the Norwegian architect, Arne Korsmo.

In 1952 he built his own house in Hellebæk on a southward facing slope at the edge of a wood; the spaciousness and open ground-plan were quite new to Denmark at that time. A little later, 1952–3, he built a house in Holte, whose inspiration was more Japanese. Its concrete frame holds the otherwise timber-clad house a storey above the ground. During the first half of the fifties he received prizes in several Swedish competitions, including a plan for the Elineberg housing estate, which was subsequently realized (in collaboration with E. and H. Andersson).

Jorn Utzon. Opera House. Sydney, 1956. Model

In 1956 Utzon received first prize for a
highly original plan in the international
competition for a new Sydney Opera
House, to be placed on a mole in the middle
of the city's harbour. The opera house,
concert hall and foyers are to lie under
shells 200 feet in height on an extensive
stepped platform. This platform will serve
as the cover for a lower level with experimental theatre, access for vehicles, extra
space, etc. The shells are planned according to a bold and original scheme developed
in collaboration with Ove Arup in London.
The project was hailed by Harry *Seidler
as 'pure poetry', but the detailed planning
shows the presence of a logical and realistic
architect, able to turn his visions into
reality. In a number of projects from 1958 to
1960 Utzon varied the idea of raised plat-
forms or bastions, with vehicular access
below and the building proper above
(Højstrup Workers' High School, 1958; a
row of buildings in Frederiksberg, near the
centre of Copenhagen, 1959; International
Exhibition in Copenhagen, 1960). Smaller,
but no less characteristic, is the plan for the
Melli Bank in Teheran (1958).
While Utzon was working on these
dynamic and imaginative projects, two
housing estates in northern Zealand were
erected—Kingohusene near Helsingør
(1957–60) and the Danish Co-operative
Building in Fredensborg. Both are chains
of houses with courtyards or gardens,
staggered to fit the topography. Each
house and garden is enclosed by yellow
brick walls of various heights. The houses
are small and inexpensive and remind one
of a North African village.

TOBIAS FABER

Vago, Pierre, b. Budapest 1910. Came to
Paris at eighteen years of age to study
under Auguste *Perret at the École
Spéciale d'Architecture. While still a
student, in 1932, he became editor-in-chief
of the journal *L'architecture d'aujourd'hui*.
In 1934 designed a prefabricated all-metal
house. Town planning, schools, housing
(in Berlin 1957, with flat-units one and a
half storeys high), churches (Basilica of
Pius X at Lourdes, commenced 1954, with
*Freyssinet as engineer).

Van de Velde, Henry, b. Antwerp 1863,
d. Zurich 1957. Henry van de Velde was
the apostle in theory and practice of func-

tional aesthetics and 'pure form'; between
1900 and 1925 he exerted a decisive
influence on architecture and the applied
arts, particularly in Germany. Born of a
middle-class Flemish family, van de Velde
was attracted to music, literature and
painting before turning to architecture.
He was a student at the Académie des
Beaux-Arts at Antwerp in 1881, where he
attended the painting classes; he continued
with Carolus Duran in Paris from 1884 to
1885. He made contact with the Impres-
sionist painters and Symbolist poets, and
was particularly impressed by Seurat,
whose pointilliste technique seemed to
embody a spatial concept capable of opening up new prospects in architecture.
Returning to Antwerp, van de Velde took
part (1886) in founding the cultural circle
named *Als ik Kan* (after Van Eyck's motto),
and a year later, *L'art indépendant*, an
association of young neo-Impressionist
painters. From 1889 onwards he took part
in the international activities of the famous
avant-gardist Brussels group known as *Les
XX*, where he discovered the synthetical
art and flowing hand of Gauguin, the
English *Arts and Crafts Movement, and
the socially orientated work of William
*Morris. Towards 1890 he became asso-
ciated with the journal *Van Nu en Straks*,
for which he devised a revolutionary layout, new typography and woodcut ornaments in a style derived from Gauguin.
This undertaking, which played an important rôle in the renaissance of Belgian
book production, started van de Velde on
the road to the craft side of art. Henceforth,
following the example of William Morris,
he gave up painting (1893) and concentrated
on illustration. He designed a mural
tapestry, 'The Angels' Vigil' (1891, Zurich,
Kunstgewerbemuseum), and went on to
three-dimensional work with the creation
of his first pieces of furniture (1894), the
last stage before entering, shortly after his
marriage, on the royal road of architecture
proper.
In 1895 (two years after *Horta's Hôtel
Tassel) van de Velde built his own home,
'Bloemenwerf' at Uccle near Brussels. It
is designed as an organic whole and completely fitted out (joinery, hardware,
furniture, carpets, curtains, dinner service,
glasses, silver) in a uniform style of English
inspiration, thus conforming with the
theories which he set out in his own

Henry van de Velde. Folkwang Museum.
Hagen, 1900–2

structures imbued with the rhythm of a linear ornament. This failing that characterizes my first works has nothing to do with the rise of Art Nouveau, which certain writers have fathered on me, and which enshrined an amalgam of the type of ornamentation I was using around 1894 and the kind of floral ornament associated with the drawings of long-haired women that Otto Eckmann was turning out in Berlin at the same period, and which he had borrowed from the English Pre-Raphaelites.'

The fact remains that van de Velde's cult of linear ornament, of the undulating line, was strengthened by his enthusiastic adherence to the neo-romantic theory of empathy, formulated by Lipps in 1903. The originality of his designs soon caught the attention of the art historian Julius Meier-Graefe and the art dealer S. Bing, who helped to ensure their international popularity. In 1896 Bing invited van de Velde to fit out four rooms of a shop he was opening in Paris under the name of *L'Art Nouveau*. His robust and curvilinear furniture, in a style very like that introduced by the young Liége-born designer Georges Serrurier-Bovy in 1894, aroused much

publications (*Déblaiement d'art, L'art futur, Aperçu en vue d'une Synthèse d'art*). Noteworthy features include a return to a rational style that 'frankly and proudly' displays the processes of manufacture in all fields, an uncompromising logic in the use of materials, and a rejection of all ornament inspired by nature and all historic detailing. But van de Velde's renewed awareness of structural function, his desire to cast off dead tradition and his basic rationalism still retained sentimental overtones. His thought was instilled with German romanticism. 'Whether it was a matter of the works of German, Austrian or Dutch artists', he wrote later, 'we were all more attached than we thought to a kind of romanticism which would not allow us to consider form "without ornament", we were too much painters, too much wedded to literature, to glimpse the necessity of abandoning ornament and decoration . . . the temptations and subconscious insinuations of romanticism prompted us to bend and twist our structural schemes and present them as ornaments acting as structural elements, or as

Henry van de Velde. Art School. Weimar, 1906

Henry van de Velde. Werkbund Theatre.
Cologne, 1914

enthusiasm at the Dresden Exhibition of
Applied Arts in 1897.
Henceforth, van de Velde's path was clear:
he would make his career in Germany.
Before he left Belgium (1899), Meier-
Graefe commissioned him to do the
interior decoration of the *Maison Moderne*
he had founded in Paris, and introduced
him to the *Pan* group in Berlin, where he
also won many commissions (Hohen-
zollern Craftwork Shop, 1899; Haby's
barber shop, 1901; premises for the
Habana Tobacco Co., 1900; Esche House,
Chemnitz, 1902). During the winter of
1900–1, he undertook a lecture tour in
Germany, during which he explained his
artistic principles (published in 1902 under
the title of *Kunstgewerbliche Laienpredigten*).
At the instance of K. E. Osthaus, he undertook the internal layout and decoration of
the Folkwang Museum at Hagen (1900–2;
exhibition rooms, glass cases, stairs, handrails, decorative glazing, mouldings, furniture, etc). The strong modelling and curved
ornamentation of this building are typically Art Nouveau, and mark the culminating point of the first phase of van de
Velde's career, which closes with the rest
room he designed for the Dresden Exhibition of Applied Arts in 1906.
The second phase, from 1906 to 1914, is
opened by the foundation and building of
the Weimar School of Applied Arts,
thanks to van de Velde's influence with the
Grand Duke of Saxe-Weimar, to whose
court he had been attached since 1901 as

artistic counsellor, charged with raising the
level of design in local industry. Here he
found an ideal field for exercising his
vocation as a teacher. He introduced a new
system of instruction based on the development of spontaneous feeling and a constant
recourse to the student's powers of invention, avoiding the use of models from
the past and the study of historic styles.
These methods gave rise to new forms,
which German industry was not slow to
adopt. 'We shall be obliged to recognize
one day,' van de Velde subsequently
observed, 'that these objects with their
rational shapes prepared the way for the
advance of a rational type of architecture,
and largely contributed to its general
diffusion. Their principles are the same as
those that modern architecture was based
on afterwards.'
The design of the Weimar school buildings
clearly expresses in itself the development
of van de Velde's architectural thought.
Although traditional building methods are
employed, a surer sense of space and
volume is evinced. The straight line returns,
ornament is purified and stress laid on
plastic expression, as in the Werkbund
Theatre. This celebrated building, now
destroyed, was built for the Werkbund
Exhibition of 1914, in Cologne. Laid out
on a symmetrical plan, with a heavy traditional shell, albeit of original appearance,
it embodied numerous innovations that
provided a brilliant answer to the requirements of the dramatic art of its day:
auditorium in the shape of an amphi-
theatre, independent proscenium, circular
horizon, and, in particular, tripartite stage.
Van de Velde, who was friendly with
Gordon Craig and Max Reinhardt, had
already in 1911 drawn up the first plans
for the Théâtre des Champs-Élysées,
Paris.
The outbreak of the First World War marks
the commencement of the third and final
phase of van de Velde's career (1914–57).
He moved to Switzerland in 1917, where
he became intimate with Romain Rolland
and E. L. Kirchner. In 1921 he transferred
to Holland, where he was commissioned by
the Kröller-Müller family to design a
museum, which he ultimately built, to a
modified plan, at Otterlo (1937–54). This
building is a work of great simplicity and
harmony, free of all rhetorical efforts; it is
perfectly adapted to its site and function

(one level throughout, main and secondary circulation, top lighting, etc.).

Van de Velde returned to Belgium in 1925. With the support of the Minister C. Huysmans, he was given the opportunity once more of carrying out the experiments he had conducted at Weimar: in 1926 he founded the Institut des Arts Décoratifs de la Cambre, which later became the École Nationale Supérieure d'Architecture et des Arts Décoratifs. He was the principal of this school until 1935; in addition, he occupied the chair of architecture at the University of Ghent from 1926 to 1936. He settled at Oberägeri in Switzerland in 1947, where he began writing his memoirs.

Van de Velde's work is dominated by his controversial and acute writings. His thought is condensed in the *Formules de la Beauté architectonique moderne* (Weimar 1917), revised and re-issued as *Formules d'une Esthétique moderne* (Brussels 1923), which stands to early-20th-century architecture as do Maurice Denis's *Théories* (1890) to the painting of his time. Among van de Velde's most important collaborators and pupils may be mentioned Victor *Bourgeois, J. J. Eggerick, R. Verwilghen, and L. Stynen.

Bibliography: Henry van de Velde, *Déblaiement d'art*, Brussels 1894; Henry van de Velde, *L'art futur*, Brussels 1895; Henry van de Velde, *Aperçu en vue d'une Synthèse d'art*, Brussels 1895; Henry van de Velde, *Geschichte meines Lebens*, Munich 1962; Karl Ernst Osthaus, *Henry van de Velde. Leben und Schaffen des Künstlers*, Hagen 1920; J. Mesnil, *Henry van de Velde et le Théâtre des Champs-Elysées*, Brussels; O. J. Maurice Casteels, *Henry van de Velde*, Brussels 1932; 'Henry van de Velde', Special Issue of *La Cité*, Brussels 1933, No. 5–6; Herman Teirlinck, *Henry van de Velde*, Brussels 1959.

ROBERT L. DELEVOY

Viganò, Vittoriano, b. Milan 1919; garduated there 1944. Residential and sports buildings. His Istituto Marchiondi (Milan 1957) with its dramatically accentuated structure, heavy massing and untreated, exposed concrete is regarded as the Italian variation of *Brutalism.

Villagran Garcia, José, b. Mexico City 1901. Studied architecture at Mexico University. Teacher of most modern Mexican architects and pioneer of modern architecture in *Mexico. Numerous schools, public and welfare buildings.

Villanueva, Carlos Raúl, b. Croydon, England 1900. More than any other individual architect Villanueva has been responsible for the impressive development of modern architecture in Venezuela. He studied at the *École des Beaux-Arts in Paris. In a way typical of his generation throughout Latin America, his early work was an attempt to renew, with discriminating connoisseurship, the traditions of local colonial architecture. Quite soon, however, he came to a deep understanding of the new ways of thought in architecture and devoted himself with a missionary ardour to the spread of modern architecture in his own land.

To the inspiration received from the great masters of his time Villanueva adds characteristic personal elements: a dynamic and spontaneous quality in structural design, forcefully expressed in exposed concrete; a catholicity of taste reflected in extensive collaboration with many painters and sculptors as well as in a daring use of polychromy; and a feeling for large-scale composition which enables him to cope with the enormous building programme resulting from the rapid development of the country. Villanueva's impact is also felt in the fine architectural tradition established by the housing authority, the *Banco Obrero*, whose gigantic operations on a consistently high level have enabled many younger architects to start promising careers. Among Villanueva's most important work the buildings for the University City in Caracas obviously come first. The Olympic Stadium (1950–1), with its daringly cantilevered marquees, built in shell concrete, with exposed ribs, and the Auditorium and the Covered Plaza (Aula Magna and Plaza Cubierta, 1952–3) are the best known. The Aula Magna, one of the most beautiful assembly rooms in the world, has a clean white curved ceiling against which float a large number of variously coloured and shaped panels, designed by Alexander Calder (with R. Newman as acoustics specialist). The austerity of the exterior, emphatically expressing the structural framework, is compensated by the gaiety and airiness of the Plaza Cubierta, the large semi-enclosed

Carlos Raúl Villanueva. Olympic Stadium. Caracas, 1950–1

foyer, displaying works of art by Arp, Léger, Vasarely, and others. In all the other buildings, such as the library, the hospital, the various schools, an individual theme is carried through, the result of special research into each particular programme, boldly expressed in a framework of exposed concrete, often filled in with variously coloured panels covered with mosaic.

Of Villanueva's huge housing projects, called for by the rapid growth of Caracas (163,000 inhabitants in 1936, 359,000 in 1941, 718,000 in 1951, and 1,300,000 today) at least two, located in this city, must be mentioned as examples: the 'Dos de Diciembre' Housing Estate, with 2,366

dwellings for 12,744 people—400 persons per hectare—designed in collaboration with José Manuel Mijares, José Hoffman and Carlos Branco; and the 'El Paraiso', a smaller estate, with duplex units in a four-storey and a sixteen-storey building, (the density only 200 people per hectare), designed in collaboration with Carlos Celis and José Manuel Mijares. In both, the provision of ancillary facilities, social and commercial, is typical of the architect's humanistic approach. The extremely frank expression of the structure distinguishes these buildings, like most of Villanueva's, from the work of other Venezuelan architects such as Bernardez, Vegas and Galia, or Guinand and Benacerraf, which seems closer to an international idiom. But it is precisely this distinction that lends to Villanueva's work its characteristic pioneering and dynamic spirit.

Bibliography: Henry-Russell Hitchcock, *Latin-American Architecture since 1945*, New York 1955.

HENRIQUE E. MINDLIN

Viollet-le-Duc, Eugène Emmanuèle, b. Paris 1814, d. Lausanne 1879. In 1840 began a series of important restorations of medieval buildings, of doubtful quality, however, by current standards of conservation; these include Vézelay, Carcassonne, Amiens, Pierrefonds, Notre-Dame de Paris. He had controversies with the *École des Beaux-Arts, to which he was appointed in 1863. His influential writings (*Dictionnaire de l'Architecture*, 1854f., *Entretiens sur l'Architecture*, 1863–72), although supporting the tendencies to stylistic copyism of the times, went far beyond Viollet-le-Duc's own work in their demand for rationality of structure.

Vlugt, L. C. van der, b. Rotterdam 1894, d. Rotterdam 1936. Housing and schools. From 1925 onwards in partnership with Johannes Andreas *Brinkman.

Voysey, Charles Annesley, b. Hessle, Yorkshire, 1857, d. Winchester 1941. Architect and designer of great influence on English and Continental *Art Nouveau. His private houses, mostly small, go back to the tradition of the English country house and are examples of building 'from the inside out' in their functional design.

Carlos Raúl Villanueva, Carlos Celis and José Manuel Mijares. El Paraiso Flats. Caracas

Carlos Raúl Villanueva. Building for the Faculty of Architecture and Town Planning of the University. Caracas, 1957. Large Hall.

Wachsmann, Konrad, b. Frankfort on the Oder 1901. Wachsmann has been a pioneer of industrialized building in theory, practice and teaching. He has always advocated that the scientific and technical resources of mass production should be applied to the processes of building, and he holds a corresponding structural and aesthetic conception of architecture. He came straight from building in timber to the problems of prefabrication. Trained as joiner and carpenter, Wachsmann was a student at the Arts and Crafts Schools of Berlin and Dresden (under Heinrich Tessenow) and at Berlin Academy of Art, where he was a star pupil of Hans *Poelzig's. From 1926 to 1929 he worked as chief architect for the firm of Christoph and Unmack who were the largest manufacturers of timber buildings in Europe at the time. In 1932 he was awarded the Rome Prize by the German Academy in Rome. In the years following, which he spent in Rome, he was occupied with building blocks of flats in reinforced concrete. Emigrating to the United States, he founded a partnership with Walter

Konrad Wachsmann. Structural system for halls.
1950-3. Model

*Gropius from 1941 to 1948, from which
emerged the General Panel Corporation,
the first fully automated factory for the
production of prefabricated building components. In 1950 Wachsmann, who has
been an American citizen since 1946 and
who lives partly in America and partly in
Europe, was appointed professor at the
Illinois Institute of Technology at Chicago
and director of the Department of Advanced Building Research. Since then,
with the support of the American Government, he has directed architectural semi-

Konrad Wachsmann. Perspective of a structural
unit. 1953

nars at universities and colleges in Japan,
Israel, Austria and Germany. In recent
years he has conducted research on town
and country planning in the United States,
and on multi-storey building in Europe.
Wachsmann's research has concentrated on
the basic character of universal elements in
building construction which can be mass
produced. His starting point is 'modular
coordination', which governs the relationship of the various building components to
each other. These components should be
as simple as possible and capable of as
many different combinations as possible.
A 'universal module', identical with the
'planning module', comprises all the
modular categories (material, performance,
construction, installation, etc.). The resulting abstract data are carried over into the
concrete conception of a standard form.
Wachsmann's research has found a practical
application above all in the General Panel
System, which is made up of prefabricated
timber units. In the forties, he was commissioned by the US Air Force to develop
the 'Mobilar Structure', a system for the
construction of aircraft hangars to any
required size by the addition of steel
struts, whose tubular diameter possesses
extremely favourable static properties. He
made a special study of the nature of the
connections and joints of cellular structures
such as Buckminster *Fuller's geodesic
domes or Le Ricolais's space structures,
built up from similar elements. In 1951,
he worked out a classification system for
modular coordination for the Federal
Housing Agency in Washington as an
example of the rational planning of vast
building programmes.
Wachsmann carried out part of his research
in the form of team-work with his students
in the course of his teaching activities. On
the rôle of the architect within the industrialized building process he says: 'It will
be the task of the universal planner to
combine the requisite technological components by a creative act into a complete
whole. The universal planner becomes part
of the creative team, combining prefabricated parts and planning with them in the
widest sense.' He has anticipated the future
time and again with his apparently utopian
projects, and has stimulated discussion,
beyond the limits of architecture, on the
problem of the spirit in a technical
civilization.

Bibliography: Konrad Wachsmann, *The Turning Point of Building*, New York 1961; Konrad Wachsmann, *Aspekte*, Wiesbaden 1961.

MARGIT STABER

Wagner, Martin, b. Königsberg 1885, d. Cambridge, Mass. 1957; 1926–33 City Architect of Berlin, where he was closely associated with *Gropius, *Häring, *Mies van der Rohe, *Poelzig, *Scharoun. Emigrated to the United States. Lecturer at Harvard University (1936–50).

Wagner, Otto, b. Penzing, near Vienna 1841, d. Vienna 1918. A precursor of 20th-century architecture and town planning, Wagner was the founder of the Vienna School, which rose to fame through its most brilliant disciples: Adolf *Loos, Josef *Hoffmann and Joseph Maria *Olbrich. He was the spiritual heir of *Viollet-le-Duc, and played a part in Austria equivalent to that of *Sullivan in the United States, van de *Velde in Belgium and *Berlage in the Netherlands. His work is based fundamentally on a renewed awareness of the plan, adapted to the requirements of social progress and current advances in technology; it expresses an unerring renewal of architectural thought and symbolizes the great changes in taste that were taking place at the turn of the 19th and 20th centuries.

Wagner began his studies in 1857 at the Vienna Technical College. He spent some time in 1860 at the Berlin Academy of Building, and completed his training at the school of architecture of the Vienna Academy from 1861 to 1863. The first phase of his career is marked by a historical outlook. He adopted a form of classicism derived from the Tuscan and Florentine High Renaissance: closed plans that were lucid, logical and very severely geometrical. His work earned him such a reputation that he was commissioned in 1890 to draw up a scheme for completely remodelling the city of Vienna. Of this, the only item to be carried out was the construction (1894–7) of the Stadtbahn, or metropolitan railway network, intended to provide rapid communication with the suburbs and to thin out city traffic.

In 1894 he was appointed head of a special class in architecture at the Vienna Academy. This year also marked the opening of a

Otto Wagner. Majolika-Haus. Vienna, *c.* 1898

second phase in the development of his work (1894–1901), characterized firstly by his assumption of a definite theoretical standpoint and next by his adherence to the system of aesthetics proclaimed at Brussels, Paris and Munich by the adepts of *Art Nouveau. While van de Velde was

Otto Wagner. Post Office Savings Bank. Vienna, 1904–6

opening his famous campaign in Brussels to purify the language of architecture (*Déblaiement d'art*, 1894), Wagner put forward in his inaugural lecture at Vienna Academy (1894) a doctrine that has become famous under the title of *Moderne Architektur*. In his view, the new architecture must take the requirements of modern life as its point of departure, and find adequate forms to express them. Two years after Sullivan's plea (*Ornament in Architecture*, 1892), and three years before the first statements of Loos, Wagner was extolling horizontal lines, flat roofs, and a stripped-down style that would draw its powers of expression from a striking affirmation of structural principles and the loyal use of materials, with steel in particular affording solutions that were new and bold.

The Stadtbahn station in the Karlsplatz (1899–1901) may serve to illustrate this transitional period. The use of a steel frame, in accordance with current French practice at the time, requires all archaeological reminiscences to be dispensed with; but by combining the straight line and the curve in floral ornamentation, a compromise is struck between doctrinal rigour and the inflections made fashionable by Art Nouveau.

Wagner went on to adopt a more radical attitude in full conformity with the principles he defended. The Post Office Savings Bank in Vienna (1904–6) dominates the third and last phase of his career; the economy of its trapezoidal plan, developing harmoniously around a central hall, the feeling for monumentality, the flexible handling of space, the complete eschewal of ornament and the perfect integration of steel and glass all go to make this building an unmistakable landmark in the history of contemporary architecture.

Bibliography: Otto Wagner, *Moderne Architektur*, Vienna 1896; 4th Edition: *Die Baukunst unserer Zeit*, Vienna 1914; Joseph August Lux, *Otto Wagner*, Munich 1914; Hans Tietze, *Otto Wagner*, Vienna 1922.

ROBERT L. DELEVOY

Warchavchik, Gregori, b. Odessa 1896. Trained in Rome. Warchavchik, who published a 'Manifesto of Functional Architecture' in 1925, built private houses in Brazil in the *International Style in the late twenties.

Webb, Philip, b. Oxford 1831, d. Worth, Sussex 1915. Assistant of G. E. Street, in whose office he met William *Morris. Associate in the Morris Company. Webb built town and country houses, in which he employs late-medieval building methods to create unconventional designs without resorting to historical copyism. The Red House near Bexley Heath, Kent (1859).

Weese, Harry, b. Chicago 1915. Trained at Massachusetts Institute of Technology and at Harvard University, Cambridge, Mass. Collaborated with Gordon *Bunshaft (*Skidmore, Owings and Merrill). Houses, schools, project for US Embassy at Accra (Ghana).

Wendingen. Dutch architectural journal (until 1936) which served as the focus for a group of architects in Amsterdam.

Werkbund. *Deutscher Werkbund.

Williams, Sir E. Owen, b. Tottenham, London 1890. Reinforced concrete structures important in the development of modern English architecture. Boots' factory at Beeston near Nottingham (1932), Empire Swimming Pool, Wembley (1934), Peckham Health Centre (1936), aircraft hangars in London (1955).

Wright, Frank Lloyd, b. Richland Center, Wis. 1867 or 1869, d. Taliesin West, Ariz. 1959.

After Frank Lloyd Wright's death at the end of an architectural career that had continued for more than seventy years, he was very generally considered the greatest American architect and one of the three or four greatest architects of the 20th century. Yet recurrently, and to the end, his work had been the subject of controversies and it is unlikely that in the future all those controversies will be resolved in his favour —nor perhaps would he have wished it to be so. Even the date of his birth is disputed —he believed he was born in 1869, but evidence in the family records indicates 1867. Of English origin on his father's side and Welsh on his mother's, it was the Celtic strain in his temperament that dominated; at the same time he considered himself the most American of Americans, or as he was inclined to put it, Usonians. His remarkably long career not unnaturally

Frank Lloyd Wright

divides into a succession of phases, from his education in the 1870s and 1880s in which his exposure to the Froebel kindergarten system and his reading of such architectural writers as *Ruskin and *Viollet-le-Duc seem to have played as great a part as the two years he spent studying engineering at the University of Wisconsin, to the final florescence of the 1950s. Nor, on the testimony of his remarkable autobiography can the ambience of his grandfather's farm near Spring Green, Wisconsin, be ignored in the early formation of his agrarian preferences and his special attitude towards nature and the nature of materials.

After a very brief initial period of work in the office of the minor 'Shingle Style' architect J. L. Silsbee in Chicago, he entered in 1888 the employ of Louis *Sullivan, the greatest American architect of the day, always to Wright the *Lieber Meister*. In that office he was early entrusted with the domestic commissions, notably the Charnley House in Chicago of 1892. But in his personal work, which began with the construction of his own house in Oak Park, Illinois, in 1889 and

which naturally increased in volume after his break with Sullivan in 1893, many influences other than Sullivan's are evident, notably from such architects of the eastern seaboard as *Richardson, Bruce Price, and McKim, Mead and White. Following on the apprentice work of the nineties, in which his own studio in Oak Park (1895), the windmill for his aunts at Spring Green (1896), and the River Forest Golf Club (1898) may be cited as especially significant, he came to maturity almost precisely in 1900.

In that year the Bradley and Hickox Houses in Kankakee, Ill. and the design for 'A Home in a Prairie Town' (published in the *Ladies Home Journal* in February 1901) initiated the series of his Prairie Houses, his earliest major contribution to modern architecture. In the Prairie Houses, of which the most notable were perhaps the Willitts House in Highland Park, Ill. and the Heurtley House in Oak Park (1902), the Martin House in Buffalo, New York (1904), the Glasner House in Glencoe, Ill. (1905), the Coonley House in Riverside, Ill. and the Isobel Roberts House in River Forest, Ill. (1908), and above all the Robie House in Chicago and Mrs Thomas Gale's House in Oak Park (1909), the American house was revolutionized with results that later affected house-design internationally. Characteristically the plans of these houses were articulated in X, L, and T shapes, with free spatial flow between the principal living areas. Externally they were low and horizontal, with windows arranged in continuous bands under the wide-spreading eaves of low hipped or gabled roofs which also subsumed porches within the carefully ordered compositions. Except for leaded-glass windows with delicate geometrical patterns, there was usually no ornament whatsoever and, except for occasional bold cantilevering of the roofs, no real modification of standard American building methods.

Already in 1901, however, he had published in *The Brickbuilder* a project for a cast-concrete bank and in non-domestic work was soon exploiting *reinforced concrete structure. When his work was brought to the attention of European architects by the Wasmuth publications of 1910 and 1911, the Larkin office building in Buffalo, New York (1904), the Unity Church in Oak Park (1906) and even the small hotel in Mason City, Iowa (1909) were perhaps more influential than the domestic work. Their complex cubic forms, spatial development in three dimensions, and expressive exploitation of new building materials and methods appealed strongly to younger architects abroad, and this influence played some part in the adumbration of the *International Style in Europe in the following fifteen years.

For various reasons personal and general the next decade was less productive for Wright. But to these years, often considered his 'Baroque' period, belong the destroyed Midway Gardens in Chicago (1913), in which the sculptured and painted decoration paralleled and even prefigured aspects of post-Cubist art in Europe, and the big Imperial Hotel (1916–22) in Tokyo.

With his return to America in the early 1920s came a group of concrete-block houses in California, the most notable the Millard House in Pasadena (1923). Here a new setting and a new material induced a total revolution in his house design, with crisper forms, all-over patterned surfaces and invisible flat roofs. His own house, Taliesin, near Spring Green, Wisconsin, first built in 1911 and rebuilt after fires in 1914 and 1925, was more in the line of the earlier Prairie Houses, but characteristically adapted to a hillside and making expressive use of the local limestone.

In the mid and late 1920s Wright's career seemed for some years to have come to an end and he was already considered an 'old master', left behind by the new developments in architecture of that decade. Projects, however, notably that for the Noble apartment house in Los Angeles of 1929, indicated his will to rival, if not to imitate, the new architecture that he scorned as mere 'boxes on stilts'; and when the curve of his production turned up once more in the mid 1930s two extraordinary works, Falling Water, the Kaufmann House in the Pennsylvania woods (1936) and the S. C. Johnson & Son administration building in Racine, Wis. (1936–9) indicated in

Frank Lloyd Wright. Robie House. Chicago, 1909

Frank Lloyd Wright. Unity Church. Oak Park, 1906

Frank Lloyd Wright. Millard House. Pasadena, 1923

their totally different ways—extravagant exploitation of cantilevering; utilization of free-standing mushroom columns—the assurance with which he was now ready to handle reinforced concrete. In their almost total avoidance of ornament, in the subtle handling of a wide gamut of materials—from the Taliesin-like stonework of the core of Falling Waters to the metallic slickness of the glass-tube fenestration of the Johnson Building—these works displayed the ever-increasing range of his sensitivity to materials both old and new. Also to the late 1930s belong his 'Usonian' houses with walls of wooden-sandwiches and flat roofs of crossed wooden scantlings, modest dwellings built at surprisingly low cost in which his planning reached its extreme of openness with the substitution of clerestory-lighted 'work-spaces' attached to the main living areas for conventional kitchens. The range and size of his commissions was already widening. But more significant perhaps for the final florescence of his last twenty years than the large project of 1938 for a new campus for Florida Southern College in Lakeland, Fla., where construction started in 1940 and continued into the 1950s, was the variety of response evoked by the opportunity to work in sharply contrasted natural settings: the desert of Arizona, where he began his own winter establishment 'Taliesin West' at Scottsville in 1938 and the exemplary Pauson House of 1940 at Phoenix, making use of 'desert concrete' in which large rough blocks of local stone were laid up loosely in forms with a minimum of cement binding; the hills of Los Angeles, where the Sturgis House (1939), a 'box without stilts', although visibly of brick and redwood, was cantilevered by hidden stall beams even more boldly than the terraces of 'Falling Water'; not to speak of Florida, where the warm climate and the lush foliage encouraged a return to the patterned block-work of the earlier California years.
Parallel to this was an extraordinary increase in the range of geometrical and structural themes which he was to continue to develop to the end of his life. In addition to the rectangular forms characteristic of his work in the first quarter of the century, he now became fascinated with plan-patterns based on 60°–30° angles, on circles, and even on spirals. Early instances

Frank Lloyd Wright. Kaufmann House, 'Falling Water'. Bear Run, Pa., 1936

of these new approaches can be found in the projects of his fallow 1920s, but their full exploitation came only with the years after the Second World War. The 60°–30° angles appeared first in the San Marcos project for a resort in Chandler, Ariz. in 1927 and were first carried to execution in the Hanna House in Palo Alto, Calif., in 1937. The circle and the helix were the theme of the Strong Automobile project for Maryland (1925), but came to ultimate realization in the Guggenheim Museum, designed 1943–6 and built 1956–9.

Frank Lloyd Wright. Taliesin West. Scottsville near Phoenix, Ariz., 1938

The remarkably prolific and varied production of Wright's last decade of activity, including several major works such as the County Buildings for Marin County, California, which are still in construction, has not yet been sorted out and published in dated sequence.

In the vast variety of his plans, which included fantastic urban projects for Bagdad as well as for Pittsburgh and Madison, Wis., not to speak of a Mile High Skyscraper, it is difficult to see what were the main lines along which he was moving. Responsive, perhaps, to the new international architectural climate of the 1950s, as he had once before been to the climate of the late 1920s and early 1930s, he seemed ready to initiate a new style with each major project. Yet more careful study of the drawings of his earlier periods of activity often reveal that what seemed to be wholly new developments of his later decades were in fact the realizations of ideas long nurtured; thus the design of the Price Tower at Bartlesville, Okla. (1955) can be traced back through several intervening versions to the St Mark's Tower project for New York (1929).

In conclusion it should be noted that Wright was not a silent creator. Difficult as it may be sometimes to see precisely how, in detail, his ambitions for a universal

Frank Lloyd Wright. Price Tower. Bartlesville Okla., 1955

Frank Lloyd Wright. Beth Sholom Synagogue. Elkins Park, Pa., 1959

'organic architecture' of the 20th century reached the particular expression that they did in his own works, his career owed much to what he said and wrote. Posterity will have more material concerning Wright than can be readily digested for a long time in a ·tremendous *œuvre*, a vast volume of intrinsically fascinating drawings, and a written gospel, on which to base a later judgement on this great architect, who was also perhaps the greatest American of his generation.

Bibliography: Frank Lloyd Wright on Architecture, ed. Frederick Gutheim, New York 1941; Henry-Russell Hitchcock, *In the Nature of Materials, 1887–1941, The Buildings of Frank Lloyd Wright*, New York 1942; Frank Lloyd Wright, *Auto-*

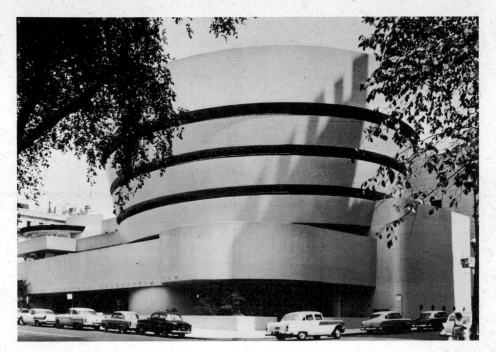

Frank Lloyd Wright. Guggenheim Museum. New York. Designed 1943–6, built 1956–9

biography, New York 1943; Frank Lloyd Wright, *Testament*, New York 1957; *Drawings, Frank Lloyd Wright*, New York 1959; *The Drawings of Frank Lloyd Wright*, ed. Arthur Drexler, New York 1962; Vincent J. Scully, Jr, *Frank Lloyd Wright*, New York 1960, Ravensburg 1961.

HENRY-RUSSELL HITCHCOCK

Wurster, William Wilson, b. Stockton, Calif. 1895. Studied at the University of California. Independent practice from 1926; since 1945 in partnership with Bernardi and Emmons. Wurster, who was influenced by *Maybeck, is an exponent of the 'Bay Region Style', the Californian variant of modern American architecture. He became known through his town and country houses which are distinguished by their modesty, adaptation to environment and consideration of locally prevailing social, economic and climatic conditions. Wurster, who thinks of *Aalto as a like-minded person, talks of an 'every-day-architecture' which is more concerned with function than form.

Yamasaki, Minoru, b. Seattle 1912. Studied at the Universities of Washington and New York. Worked in the offices of the Empire State Building architects Shreve, Lamb and Harmon; with *Harrison, Fouilhoux and *Abramovitz; and with Raymond Loewy Associates. He achieved international notice together with Hellmuth and Leinweber, his partners at the time, for the airport at St Louis (1953–5) whose reception halls consist of a series of intersecting barrel vaults.

Yamasaki is an admirer of *Mies van der Rohe, although he aims increasingly at a 'richness' which 'would make Mies frown' (Yamasaki). A characteristic feature of his style is the dissolution of the wall into an apparently textile-like fabric, which veils the structural members: umbrella walls made of profilated blocks at the Society of Arts and Crafts and at the American Concrete Institute (1958) at Detroit; metal grilles in the Reynolds Metals Office in Detroit (1959). Axial plans, silhouettes enlivened by turrets or top lighting visible from the exterior, and exuberant layouts

Minoru Yamasaki. Century 21 Exposition.
Seattle, 1962. Model

Yorke, Rosenberg and Mardall. London
(Gatwick) Airport, Stage 1. 1958. Terminal
Building and Central Pier

with gardens and pools contribute to the impression of contrived elegance which is typical of Yamasaki's later designs. Canopied structures for the American pavilion at the New Delhi Fair (1960) and the Century 21 Exposition at Seattle (1962).

Yorke, Francis Reginald Stevens, b. 1906, d. 1962. Studied at Birmingham University School of Architecture. Founder member of MARS (British section of *CIAM) and pioneer of modern architecture in *Great Britain, with his reinforced concrete houses at Gidea Park, Essex (1933, with W. *Holford, G. Stephenson and A. Adam) and house at Nast Hyde, Hatfield (1935). In partnership with Marcel *Breuer, 1935–37, and from 1944 with Eugene Rosenberg and Cyril Mardall, in the firm of Yorke, Rosenberg and Mardall, which has been responsible for many important projects, including schools at Stevenage (1947–9), Oldbury, and Pool Hill, Salop. (1955–7, with extensive use of timber cladding), academic buildings in London, Merthyr Tydfil and Leeds; housing at Stevenage, Harlow and the Hansa district of Berlin; hospitals at Londonderry, Crawley and Hull; a department store at Sheffield, and Gatwick Airport, Sussex. The firm's own office in London, a restrained but finely proportioned and detailed building, was awarded the RIBA Bronze Medal for 1962. Yorke was the editor of the annual volume *Specification* from 1935 to the time of his death, and was the author of standard works on modern houses and (with Frederick *Gibberd) modern flats.

HAROLD MEEK

Zanuso, Marco, b. Milan 1916; graduated there 1939. Olivetti factory at São Paulo (1956–8), a scheme consisting of honeycomb cells, roofed with thin shell vaults. Also worked as a journalist.

Zehrfuss, Bernard, b. Angers 1911. Studied at the École des Beaux-Arts, Paris. Awarded the Rome prize of the French Academy in 1939. Unesco building, Paris (1953–7, in collaboration with *Breuer and *Nervi). Exhibition building of the Centre National des Industries et Techniques, Paris (1958, in collaboration with Camelot and De Mailly). Industrial buildings (Renault Works at Flins, 1953; Mame Printing Works at Tours).

Selected bibliography on the history of modern architecture

See also the bibliographies at the end of individual articles

Banham, Reyner, *Theory and Design in the First Machine Age*, London 1959.

Banham, Reyner, *Guide to Modern Architecture*, London 1962.

Behrendt, Walter Curt, *Modern Building. Its nature, problems and forms*, New York 1937.

Benevolo, Leonardo, *Storia dell'architettura moderna*, 2 volumes, Bari 1960.

Blake, Peter, *The Master Builders*, New York 1961.

Conrads, Ulrich and Hans G. Sperlich, *Phantastische Architektur*, Stuttgart 1960.

Darmstaedter, Robert, *Künstlerlexikon. Maler-Bildhauer-Architekten*, Berne and Munich 1961.

Dorgelo, A., *Modern European Architecture*, Amsterdam 1959.

Enciclopedia Universale dell'Arte. Encyclopaedia of World Art. Venice, Rome, New York, Toronto, London 1959 ff.

Francastel, Pierre (editor), *Les Architectes Célèbres*, 2 volumes, Paris 1959.

Giedion, S., *A Decade of New Architecture—Dix Ans d'Architecture Contemporaine*, Zurich 1954, 1st edition 1951.

Giedion, S., *Space, Time and Architecture*, Cambridge, Mass. 1956, 1st edition 1941.

Gropius, Walter, *Internationale Architektur*, Munich 1925.

Handbuch moderner Architektur, Berlin 1957.

Hilberseimer, Ludwig, *Internationale Neue Baukunst*, Stuttgart 1926.

Hilberseimer, Ludwig, *Grossstadt-Architektur*, Stuttgart 1927.

Hitchcock, Henry-Russell, *Modern Architecture, Romanticism and Reintegration*, New York 1929.

Hitchcock, Henry-Russell, *Architecture: Nineteenth and Twentieth Centuries*, Harmondsworth 1958.

Hitchcock, Henry-Russell and Philip Johnson, *The International Style. Architecture Since 1922*, New York 1932.

Joedicke, Jürgen, *A History of Modern Architecture*, London 1959.

Jones, Cranston, *Architecture Today and Tomorrow*, New York 1961.

Kultermann, Udo, *Baukunst der Gegenwart*, Tübingen 1958.

Pevsner, Nikolaus, *Pioneers of Modern Design. From William Morris to Walter Gropius*, London 1936.

Platz, Gustaf Adolf, *Die Baukunst der neuesten Zeit*, Berlin 1927.

Richards, J. M., *An Introduction to Modern Architecture*, London, Baltimore 1953.

Roth, Alfred, *La Nouvelle Architecture—Die neue Architektur—The New Architecture*, 4th edition, Zurich 1948.

Sartoris, Alberto, *Gli elementi dell'architettura funzionale*, 3rd edition, Milan 1941.

Sartoris, Alberto, *Encyclopédie de l'architecture nouvelle*, 3 volumes, Milan 1954–57.

Sartoris, Alberto, *Introduzione alla architettura moderne*, 3rd edition, Milan 1948.

Scully, Vincent, *Modern Architecture*, New York 1961.

Siegel, Curt, *Strukturformen der modernen Architektur*, Munich 1960.

Smith, G. E. Kidder, *The New Architecture of Europe*, London 1961.

Taut, Bruno, *Die neue Baukunst in Europa und Amerika*, Stuttgart 1929.

Thieme, Ulrich and Felix Becker (editors), *Allgemeines Lexikon der Bildenden Künstler von der Antike bis zur Gegenwart*, 37 volumes, Leipzig 1907–50.

Wasmuths Lexikon der Baukunst, 5 volumes, Berlin 1929–37.

Whittick, Arnold, *European Architecture in the Twentieth Century*, First Vol.: *1800–1924*. Second Vol.: *1924–1933*, London 1950–53.

Zevi, Bruno, *Architecture as Space*, New York 1957.

Zevi, Bruno, *Storia dell'architettura moderna*, 3rd edition, Turin 1955.

328

Photograph sources

The publishers are indebted to all individuals and institutions listed below who have kindly supplied photographs for publication in this book and especially to the Rijksvoorlichtingsdienst, The Hague; the Suomen Rakennustaiteen Museo, Helsinki; and to Mr Edgar Kaufmann jr., New York.

A.C.L., Brussels; Agtmaal, van, Hilversum; Aistrup, Wedboek; Annan, Glasgow; Apollo, Helsinki; Architectural Photographing Company, Chicago; Architectural Review, London; Beider, Basel; Bentham-Moxon Trustees, London; Beratungsstelle für Stahlverwendung, Düsseldorf; Bildarchiv Foto, Marburg; Bladh, Bromma; Borremans, Cachan; British Features, Bonn; Bulloz, Paris; Casali, Milan; Cellard, Bron; Cetto, Mexico City; Checkman, Jersey City; Chevojon, Paris; Deutsche Presse-Agentur, Frankfurt; Diederichs, Berlin-Lankwitz; Dino, Milan; Doeser, Laren; Dotreville, Brussels; Dumont, Royan; Dupain, Sydney; Dyckerhoff und Widmann, Munich; Faigle, Stuttgart; Farbwerke, Hoechst; Finsler, Zurich; Fortunati, Milan; Fotogramma, Milan; Friedrich, Berlin-Lichterfelde; Futagawa, Tokyo; García Moya, Madrid; Gasparini, Caracas; Gautherot, Rio de Janeiro; Georges, New York; Gerlach, Vienna; Giraudon, Paris; Gmelin, Dornach; Grünert, Zurich; Guerrero, New York; Hanley; Havas, Helsinki; Hedrich-Blessing, Chicago; Heidersberger, Braunschweig; Held, Weimar; Helmer-Petersen, Copenhagen; Hervé, Paris; Høm, Copenhagen; Hubmann, Vienna; Ingervo, Helsinki; Jacobs, Berlin-Lichterfelde; Joedicke, Stuttgart; Jonals, Copenhagen; Josuweck, Cologne; Kersting, London; Kidder Smith, New York; KLM Aerocarto, Amsterdam; Köster, Berlin-Lichterfelde; Korab, Birmingham, Alabama; Kunstgewerbemuseum, Zurich; Laboratorio Fotografico, Rome; Landesbildstelle, Hamburg; Larson, Stockholm; Lazi, Stuttgart; Lens Craft, New York; Library of Congress, Washington; Luckhaus, New York; Madenskey, Vienna; Mäkinen, Helsinki; Maltby, London; Manchete, Rio de Janeiro; Mango, Neapel; Maré, London; Mari, Rome; Martin, Paris; MAS, Barcelona; Michel, Rio de Janeiro; Møller, Århus; Moisio, Turin; Molitor, Ossining; Moosbrugger, Basel; Moncalvo, Turin; Moscardi, São Paulo; M.R.L., Strassburg; Müller, Alfred, Rio de Janeiro; Murasawa, Tokyo; Museum of Modern Art, New York; National Buildings Record, London; New York Daily News; Nilsson, Stockholm; Ojen, van, The Hague; Österr. Nationalbibliothek, Vienna; Pfau, Mannheim; Pietinen, Helsinki; Pfriem, Paris; Publicam, Hilversum; Reens, New York; Renes, Amsterdam; Roos, Helsinki; Roubier, Paris; Ryan, Minneapolis; Schiller, Mill Valley; Schwab, Stuttgart; Science Museum, London; Shokokusha, Tokyo; Shulman, Los Angeles; Sibbelee, Amsterdam; Smith, Wilton; Sörvik, Göteborg; Souza, Rio de Janeiro; Spaziani, Rome; Spreng, Basel; Steiger, Stuttgart; Steuer, Chicago; Stillman, Litchfield, Connecticut; Stoedtner, Düsseldorf; Stoller, Rye; Strüwing, Copenhagen; Sturtevant, San Francisco; Sundahl, Stockholm; Syndicat d'Initiative, Évian; Szarkowski, Ashland, Wisc.; Urbschat-Fischer, Berlin-Charlottenburg; USIS, Bad Godesberg; Vasari, Rome; Velin, Helsinki; Versnel, Amsterdam; Victoria and Albert Museum, London; Villani, Bologne; Viollet, Paris; Volkart, Stuttgart; Vriend, Amsterdam; Vrijhof, Rotterdam; Wåhlén, Stockholm; Wahlström, Helsinki; Wasastjerna, Helsinki; Whittick, Crawley; Wickberg, Helsinki; Winkler, Stuttgart; Wölfl, Vienna; Wrubel, Düsseldorf; Zerkowitz, Barcelona; Zumstein, Berne.

Index of names

Architects whose names appear in italic have individual entries. Figures in roman type indicate text references; those in bold type refer to the illustrations.

Aalto, Aino 64
Aalto, Alvar 19–20, 28–32, 64, 100–1, 103, 147, 240, 307, 309, 311, 325, **18, 28–31, 103, 154, 220, 308**
Abel 126
Aberdeen 32
Abildgård 160
Abramovitz 32, 81, 147, 310, 325, **81**
Adam, A. 326
Adam, H. G. 108
Adler 32, 69, 128, 275–6
Åhrén 283
Aillaud 107
Albers 46
Albert, Edouard 107
Albini 32–3, 155, 158, **33**
Albuquerque 54
Alexander 215
Allison, J. T. 88
Almqvist 33, 282–3
Alvarez 188
Amis 151
Andersson, E. 311
Andersson, H. 311
Angeli 208
Antonelli 33
Apel 127
Arbeitsgruppe 4, 42, **42**
Arcon 98
Arnodin 105
Aronco, d' 34, 155, 262, **156**
Arp 87, 316
Arsène-Henry 108
Artaria 286, **286**
Artigas 55, 188
Arup 312
Ashbee 12, 36–7, **37**
Ashihara 164
Aslin 38, 73, 136, **136**
Asplund 17, 21, 33, 38–40, 133, 160, 282–5, 311, **38, 39, 281**
Astengo 158
Atelier 5, 287
Attolini Lack 188

Aubert **20**
Auböck 42, 232

Backström 285, **283–4**
Bacon 304, **305**
Badovici 105–6
Baines 98
Bakema 42–3, 60, 73, 212–13, **42, 61, 212, 297**
Balat 149
Baldessari 43, 156, 158
Balla 114
Baltard 130
Banfi 47, 158
Bardi 156
Barillet 133
Barnes 58
Baroni 257
Barragán 188
Bartning 43, 97, 126, 133, 244 **271**
Bartoli 208
Baruel 31
Basile 34, 43, 155, 262
Bassi 158
Baudot, de 43, 208, 234, **235**
Bauersfeld 257, **256**
Baumgart 216
Baumgarten 126
Baur, Hermann 287, **286**
Baur, H. P. 287
Bauschinger 234
Bayer 46, 87
BBPR 47, 158, 240, 244, **25, 159**
Beaudouin 47, 106–7, 177, 231, 240, **106, 108**
Bega 132, 240
Behrens 14, 20, 34, 36, 47–8, 50, 79, 85–6, 93, 97, 123–4, 132–3, 139, 145, 152, 170, 189–91, 202, 238, 244, 271, **48–50**
Bélanger 267
Belgioioso 47, 158
Belluschi 50, 80, **81**
Belmont **232**

Benacerraf 316
Bentsen 82
Berg 50, 93, 123, 236, **124, 237**
Berghoef 212
Bergsten 33, 280, 282, **280**
Berlage 14, 33, 50–1, 104, 130, 169, 191, 209–10, 222, 242, 271, 280, 319, **51, 209**
Bernardes 55
Bernardez 316
Bernardi 325
Bernasconi 80, 158, 219, **80, 157**
Bernoulli 285
Beuté 107, 177
Beyaert 145
Bieber 40
Bijvoet 88, 210
Bill 51, 286–7, **287**
Bindesbøll 82–3, **82**
Bing 313
Black **99**
Blomstedt, Aulis 103, **104**
Blomstedt, P. E. 100
Bo 84, **84**
Boberg 279–80
Boccioni 114
Bodiansky 67, 107, **108**
Bogardus 51, 132, 268, **267**
Böhm 51–2, 126
Boileau 130, 268, **268**
Bolonha 55
Bon 68, 137
Bonatz 52, 93, 248, **96**
Bordenave 235
Borromini 166
Bottoni 158
Boullée 9
Boulton 266, **266**
Bourdon 267
Bourgeois 52, 71, 315
Bradshaw 258
Bragaglia 115
Bramante 204
Branco 316
Bratke 55

Bräuning 287
Brechbühler 287
Brenner 40
Brett 299
Breuer 46, 57–60, 76, 87–8,
    125, 133, 135, 142, 164–5,
    205, 208, 212, 219, 240,
    255, 258, 306, 326, **57–9,
    77**
Brinkman 60, 133, 317, **211**
Broek, van den 43, 60, 212–13,
    42, 61, 212, 297
Brown 98
Brugger 286
Brunel 130, 267
Brunet 267
Bryggman 28, 64–6, 100–1,
    65
Bunshaft 66, 168, 261, 320
Burckhardt 286
Burle Marx 56
Burnham 6, 66, 69–70, 79,
    132, 177, 245, 270, 278,
    301, **68–9**
Burton 129, **129**
Bürck 48

Caccia Dominioni 158
Calder 315
Calini 157, **157**
Camelot 109, 231, 326
Camenzind 286
Camus 32
Cancellotti 157
Candela, Antonio 66
Candela, Félix 66–7, 188, 240,
    258, **66–7**
Candilis 67, 73, 107, **108**
Capon 34
Cardoso 215
Caretta 288, **288**
Carloni 286
Carminati 292
Casson 67, 98, 134
Castañedo 188
Castellazzi **157**
Castiglioni 67, 158
Castrén 241
Castro Mello 55
Celis 316, **317**
Celsing 285
Cessart, de 267
Cetto 188
Cézanne 30, 35, 74
Chamberlin 68, 137
Chance 223

Chareau 106
Chemineau 107
Chermayeff 185
Chiattone 68, 114, 116, 250,
    114
Chitty 291
Choisy 105, 165
Christiansen 48
Cocchia 158
Cocke 34
Coignet 234, 235
Colbert 89
Conder 67, 134
Connell 135
Contamin 7, 35, 79, 130,
    234–5, **235, 269**
Cook 258
Cooke-Yarborough 34
Correia Lima 54, **52**
Costa 20, 54–6, 77–8, 172,
    215–16, 219, 232, 238, **53,
    78**
Coulon 108
Coyne 107
Crabtree 136, 138, **136**
Cragg 266
Craig 314
Crane 37
Cret 167
Cuijpers 78, 208, **208**

Damaschke 295
Daniel 138
Dark 98, 138, 204
Dastugue **20**
David 254
Davies 204
Davis 138
Debat-Ponsan 118
Deilmann 82
Deitrick 82, 219, 240, 278,
    279
Delaunay 91
Denis 315
Depero 114–15
Dichinger 66, 257–8
Dickens 36
Dillon 267
Diulgheroff 114
Dixon 138
Döcker 86, 125, 244
Dodd 266
Doesburg, van 75, 87–9, 177,
    210, 222, 242, 272–3, **88,
    272**
Dondel **20**

Dony 67
Drake 111, 291
Drew 88, 98, 111
Drexler 198
Dubuffet 62
Dubuisson 107
Dudok 79, 88, 211, **210**
Dugdale 291
Duiker 88, 133, 210, 238
Duran 312
Durand 9, 202
Duret 286
Dürig 287
Dutert 7, 35, 79, 130, **269**
Duthilleul 108
Düttmann 127

Eames, Charles 89
Eames, Ray 89
Eastlake 301
Easton 134
Eastwick-Field 274
Eberstadt 295
Ebert **144**
Eckmann 92, 313
Ecochard 107
Eesteren, van 43, 71, 73, 75,
    87, 89, 210, 242, **272**
Egender 286, 287
Egger 107
Eggerick 315
Ehmcke 85
Eiermann 89–90, 127, **89–90**
Eiffel 6, 35, 90–2, 105, 130,
    268, **90–1, 268**
Eijck, van 73, 92, 213, **212**
Einstein 201, 221
Ekelund 101
Ellis 179
Ellwood 92
Emberton 135
Emmons 325
Endell 34, 92, 123, **35, 123**
Enfantin 5
Eriksson 284
Ervi 92, 101
Esquillan 258
Estellita 218
Estrella 54
Eyck, van 312

Faber 311
Fadigati **157**
Fahrenkamp 96
Fairbairn 234, 266
Farmer 98, 138, 204

Feininger 15, 45, **15**
Fellerer 42
Ferreira 54
Fietz 287
Figini 99, 104, 145, 157–8, 226, 291, **159**
Fillía 114–15
Finsterwalder 66
Fiocchi 80, 104, 158, 219, **80, 157**
Fischer, Florian 286
Fischer, Theodor 51–2, 85, 93, 104, 146, 183, 221, 290
Fischli 286
Fisker 82, 104, 282, 312, **83**
Fletcher 288
Fontaine 129
Fontseré 119
Förster 10, **10**
Fouilhoux 147, 325
Fox and Henderson 223
Frank 40, 86, 253
Frette 145, 291
Freyler 42
Freyre 52
Freyssinet 107, 109–11, 206, 225, 236, 257, 294, 312, **110**
Friedhoff 211
Fritsch 295
Frosterus 28, 100
Fry 88, 98, 111, 135, 142
Fuller 64, 111–12, 229, 264, 272, 318, **111–12, 229, 264**
Furness 113–14, 275, 301, 310, **302**

Gabo 74, 76
Gabriel 225
Galia 154, 316
Gallé 34
Gallén-Kallela 99
Garcia Roza 55
Gardella 20, 116–17, 133, 158, **116**
Garden 70, 237
Garnier 7, 105, 117–19, 170–1, 202, 235, **9, 117–18, 236, 299**
Gärtner 8
Gaudi 14–15, 35, 67, 119–23, 151, 262, **13, 36, 119–21**
Gauguin 35, 312
Gellner 158
George 295
Gerson, Hans 96–7
Gerson, Oskar 96–7
Gesellius 99, 248

Gibberd 128, 138, 299, 326, **128**
Gibson 73 128, **99, 128**
Giedion 61, 70–3, 203
Gieselmann 127
Gilbert 304
Gill 128
Gillet 107, 231, **108**
Gilly 9, 122, 254, **9**
Ginsberg 107
Godwin 12
Goeritz 188
Goff 134
Gollins 134, 138
Gomis 107
Goodden 98
Goodhue 304–5
Goodwin 274
Gores 58
Gottwald 40, 42
Gowan 274
Granpré Molière 211
Gravereaux 80, 107
Greene, Charles Sumner 139, 302–3, **304**
Greene, Henry Mather 139, 302–3, **304**
Greenham 188
Grice 34
Groenewegan 210
Gropius, Martin 139
Gropius, Walter 14, 16–17, 20–2, 24, 35, 43–6, 50, 57–8, 73, 79–80, 86–7, 95–6, 111, 116, 124–6, 132, 134–5, 139–46, 148, 152, 155, 162, 164, 189–90, 194–5, 205, 212, 219, 229, 237–8, 244–5, 258, 274, 282, 288, 306–7, 309, 317–19, **15, 45–6, 80, 139–41, 144, 152, 229**
Gruen 145
Guadet 202, 225
Guevrekian 106
Guimard 12, 34, 105, 123, 145, **35, 105**
Guinand 316
Gunnløgsson 84
Gutbrod 126
Gutmann 73

Hack 82
Haefeli 286–8, **286, 288**
Haertl 40
Haesler 125, 244
Hahr 282
Haller von Hallerstein 9

Hankar 34, 145–6, **145**
Hansen 83
Harding 291
Häring 97, 124, 146–7, 244, 319, **146**
Harkness 288
Hartley 266
Harmon 306, 325
Harris 306
Harrison 32, 80–1, 132, 147, 310, 325, **81**
Hausen, von 82
Haussmann 10, 147, **295**
Havlicek 147
Hawksmoor 61
Helg 32
Hellmuth 258, 325, **259**
Henderson, W. A., 136
Hennebique 234–6, **235**
Henrion 98
Hentrich 80, 126, **126**
Hepworth 122
Herbé 107, 231
Herholdt 82
Hermant 108
Hilberseimer 86, 125, 147, 244, 253
Hitchcock 17, 165
Hittorff 8
Hoch 42
Hoff 83, **83**
Hoff, van't 210, 242, 272, **273**
Hoffmann, Josef 34, 40, 85–6, 147–9, 155, 170, 178, 248, 319, **148**
Hoffmann, Ludwig 93, 146
Hofmann 286
Höger 96–7, **95**
Holabird 69–70, 149, 214, 270
Holford 149, 326
Holzbauer 42
Holzmeister 41, 149
Honegger 107, 177, 288
Honeyman 179
Hood 147, 149, 305, **305**
Horeau 5
Horiguchi 162–3
Horta 12, 34, 79, 104, 123, 132, 145, 149–51, 270, 312, **36, 129, 149–51, 270**
Hottinger 287
Howard 100, 151, 295
Howe 151, 167, 177, 271, 304–5, **306**
Howell 73, 151
Howells 305
Hruban 258

Hubacher 286, **286**
Huber 48
Hubsch 122
Hunt 69, 301
Huszar 272
Hutchinson 179
Huttunen 100
Huysmans 315
Hyatt 234

Imai 162
Irming 311
Ishimoto 162
Israel 179
Israels 47
Ito 162
Itten 44–6

Jacobsen 83–4, 154, 159–61,
    160–1
Jäntti **102**
Järvi **101**
Jeanneret, C.E. *Le Corbusier
Jeanneret, P. 106, 170, 256
Jefferson 167
Jenney 6, 69, 79, 132, 149,
    164, 177, 270, **6**
Johansen 58, 164, 204
Johnson 17, 58, 165–8, 195,
    205, 245, 308–10, **165–7**,
    204
Johnson-Marshall 183
Josephson 280
Josic 67
Jourdain 79, 105
Jung **99**

Kahn, *Albert* 167, 304, 308
Kahn, *Louis* 62, 147, 167–9,
    205, 309–10, **168–9, 205**
Kampmann 82
Kandinsky 45, 97
Karsten 210
Kaspé 188
Kaufmann 9
Kazis 108
Keppie 179
Ketterer 42
Khnopff 34
Kikutake 164, **164**
Killick 151
Kirchner 95, 97, 314
Kishida 163
Klaarhamer 242
Klaudy 42
Klee 45

Klenze 8
Klerke, de 33, 169, 209–10, **14,**
    96, 210
Klimt 34, 147, 178, 180
Klint, Jensen 82, 169, **83**
Klint, Kåre 82
Kneese de Mello 218, **55, 216**
Koch 180
Koechlin 91
Koike 163
Kok 272
Kokko 240
Kokoschka 95
Kolbe 194
Korsmo 311
Kosaka 162, **162**
Kraemer 126, 169, **127**
Krahn 126
Kramer 33, 209
Kreis 96
Kröller 191
Kromhout 34
Küpper *Doesburg, van
Kurrent 42

Labrouste 6, 43, 105, 133, 169,
    242, 268, **105**
Lafaille 107, 257
Lagneau 107
Lamb 306, 325
Lambot 234
Larco 145, 291
Larsson 279
Lasdun 111, 137, 291, **138**
Lassen, Flemming 160
Lassen, Mogens 83
Latis 158
Laugier 205
Laurence 133
Lauritzen 83, **83**
Leão 54
Leck, van der 272
Le Corbusier 9, 11, 15–20, 22,
    24, 26, 47, 50, 54, 58, 61,
    67, 70–1, 73, 75–80, 83,
    86–8, 104–7, 111–13, 119,
    126, 130, 132–3, 137, 139,
    146–8, 150, 152, 155, 160,
    162–3, 168–76, 181, 183,
    187, 190, 200–3, 206–7, 215,
    217, 225, 236–8, 240, 246,
    256, 258, 271, 282–4, 286,
    288, 309, **16, 19, 27, 53, 62,**
    106, 132, 152, 169–76, 201,
    203, 238, 300
Le Couteur 107
Ledoux 9, 166–7

Leemann 288
Léger 133, 316
Legorreta 187
Lehmbrock 126
Leibl 47
Leinweber 258, 325, **259**
Lemmen 34
Lemos 218
Leonhardt 127
Leonidow 17
Lepère 8
Le Play 7
Lequeu 9
Le Ricolais 92, 264, 279, 318
Lescaze 151, 167, 177, 271,
    305, **306**
Lethaby 37
Leuzinger 182
Levi 54, **52**
Lewerentz 33, 38, 177, 282,
    284–5, **284**
Libera 145, 291
Lichtblau 40
Lindegren 30, 100, 103, **102**
Lindgren 99, 248
Lindqvist 99
Lindström 285
Lingeri 156, 158, 292
Lipps 313
Lipschitz 165
Lissitzky 17, 74–6, 177, **76**
Llorens y Barba 119
Lodoli 63
Lods 47, 106–7, 177, 231, 240,
    106
Loewy 325
Loghem, van 210
Loos 14, 40, 42, 105, 118, 128,
    147–8, 150, 152, 155, 177–8,
    180, 202, 213, 250, 305,
    319–20, **14, 40, 177–8**
Lopez 80, 107, 231
Lorenz 42
Lotufo 218, **55, 216**
Louis 267
Lozeron 288
Lubetkin 291
Luccichenti 157
Luckhardt, Hans 96, 124, 178,
    244
Luckhardt, Wassili 96, 124,
    178, 244
Lund 83
Lundsten 241
Lundy 179
Lurçat 106, 148, 179, **107**
Lutyens 37, 264

Lynn 62, **62**
Lyons, Edward D. L. 179
Lyons, Eric Alfred 179

Maaskant 43
Macdonald, Frances 180
Macdonald, Margaret 180
Machado Moreira 54, 55, **53, 54**
Mächler 124, 252
Mackintosh 12, 14, 35–7, 48, 123, 179–81, 248, **180–1**
Mackmurdo 34
Maekawa 163–4, 181, 288, **163**
Magistretti 158
Magnant 107
Maillart 181–3, 206, 225, 236, 240, 258, 285, **182**
Mailly, de 109, 231, 258, 326
Makkinheimo 31
Makowski 264
Malevich 17, 74, 183, 278, **76**
Mallet-Stevens 106, 183
Mandrot, de 70
Mangiarotti 158
Marc 97
Marchi 114–15
Marcks 45–6
Marcos 188
Mardall 326, **326**
Marinetti 114, 116, 202, 251
Marinho 54–5
Markelius 183, **282, 298**
Marot 108
Marsio *Aalto, Aino 28
Martin 70, 237
Martinez de Velasco **188**
Matisse 133
Matthew 137, 183, **137**
Maus 34
May 71, 125, 183, 244
Maybeck 183, 226, 302–3, 325
Mayer 219
McKim 303, 308, 310, 321
McMillan 288
McMillen 288
McNair 179
Mead 303, 308, 310, 321
Meier-Graefe 313–14
Meigs 151, 304
Mellor 151, 304
Melvin 134, 138
Mendelsohn 15, 17–19, 48, 95, 97, 124–5, 133, 135, 140, 183–6, 214, 220–1, 237, 244, 271, 306, **97, 184–6, 220**

Merkelback 210
Merrill (SOM) 23, **23**
Mesquita dos Santos 54
Messel 93, 186
Meuli 288
Mey, van der 33, 209
Meyer, Adolf 80, 86, 139–41, 152, 189, **15, 140, 152**
Meyer, Hannes 46, 71, 125, 189, 286, **189**
Michelangelo 220
Michelucci 158, 189
Mies van der Rohe 15–17, 20–4, 46, 50, 61–2, 78, 80, 84, 86–7, 89, 92, 95, 107, 122, 124–6, 132–3, 139, 146, 152, 155, 160, 162, 165–8, 177, 189–99, 202, 204–5, 212, 214, 224–5, 231, 237, 240, 244–6, 250, 252, 255, 261, 271, 282, 306, 308–9, 319, 325, **21–2, 95, 125, 130, 133, 153, 190–9, 203–4, 272, 309**
Mijares, José, 316, **317**
Mijares, Rafael **187**
Milà y Fontanals 119
Miljutin 252
Mills, Edward David 98, 200
Mills, Mark 262, **263**
Mindlin 55, **55**
Mirabaud 107, 231
Mizutani 163
Moberley 136, **136**
Moholy-Nagy 45–7, 87
Moll 252
Møller, C. F. 82, 84, 104, **83**
Møller, Erik 84, 160
Mollino 158
Moltke, von 58
Monaco 157
Mondrian 75, 206, 243, 272–3
Monier 234
Montuori 157, **157**
Moore 122
Mora, de la 187, **67**
Moral, del 187–8, **187**
Morancé 105
Morandi 158
Moretti 157
Morgenthaler 287
Morisseau 258
Morris 11, 34–7, 84–5, 202, 280, 301, 312, 320
Moser, Karl 177, 202, 238, 285, **285**
Moser, Koloman 147

Moser, Werner 286–8, **286, 288**
Moya 137, 228
Muche 45, **44**
Munch 35
Murata 164
Muthesius 37, 48, 84–7, 123, 202, 211
Muzio 157

Nairn 274
Nash 8, 202, 267, **8**
Nelson 202
Nervi 20, 58, 77, 111, 155, 158–9, 181, 206–9, 225, 227, 240, 258, 272, 326, **158, 206–8, 229, 239, 258**
Neutra 17, 40, 133, 148, 213–15, 271, 305, 307, **213–14**
Newman 73, 315
Nicholson 67
Nielsen 84
Niemeyer 20, 54–6, 77–8, 128, 172, 215–19, 238, 255, **53, 55–6, 216–18**
Nilsson 280
Nizzoli 80, 104, 158, 219, **80, 157**
Nolde 97
Nouguier 91
Novarina 133, **231**
Nowicki 82, 219, 240, 278, **279**
Noyes 219
Nunes 54
Nyrop 82
Nyström 99

Obrist 11, 92
Oddie 61
Oesterlen 126
O'Gorman 63, 187–9, 219, **188**
Olbrich 34–5, 40, 48, 92, 147, 178, 219–20, 319, **12, 219**
Oliveri 104, 219
Olivio D' 158
O'Rorke 98
Östberg 282
Osthaus 314
Otaka 164
Otto 127, 221, 279
Oud 18–19, 86–7, 133, 152, 155, 210–12, 221–2, 272–3, **14, 221–2, 273**
Overbeck 119
Owings (SOM) 23, **23**
Ozenfant 105, 170

Pagani 158
Pagano 156–7, 227, 292
Paillard 288
Paine 267
Palanti 55
Palladio 61
Pani 188
Pankok 92
Pannaggi 114
Partridge 151
Pasmore 138
Paul 190
Pacton 5–6, 79, 111, 129, 207,
    223–4, 267, **5, 223, 228**
Pei 224
Peressutti 47, 158
Perkins 70
Perrault 234
Perret 79, 83, 104–6, 118, 133,
    152, 170, 202, 224–5, 235,
    238, 240, 312, **224–5, 237**
Perriand 108
Perrin-Fayolle 231
Persico 156–7, 227
Petäjä 241, **241**
Petersen 82
Petschnigg 40, 80, 126, **126**
Pevsner, Antoine 74, 91
Pevsner, Nikolaus 203
Pfeffer 42
Phidias 202
Piacentini 156–7, 203, 258
Piccinato 157
Pickett 6
Pingusson 106
Pintonello **157**
Piot 67, **108**
Piscator 141
Pison 106
Poelzig 48, 85–7, 93, 97, 124,
    226, 244, 255, 271, 317, 319,
    93, 226, 270
Polk 79, 132, 226
Pollini 99, 104, 145, 157–8,
    226, 291, **159**
Pollock 62
Ponti 156, 158, 208, 226–7,
    240, **226–7**
Pope 304
Popp 133
Portinari 56
Powell, Geoffrey 68, 137
Powell, Philip P. 137, 228
Powers, M. A. R. 34
Prampolini 114–15
Price 321
Prieto 188

Prouvé, Henri **231**
Prouvé, Jean 106–7, 230–2,
    231–2
Prouvé, Victor 231

Quaroni 157

Rabut 109
Rading 86, 252
Rafn 82
Rainer 41–2, 232, **41**
Ramirez Vázquez 189, **187**
Rasmussen 311
Rava 145, 291
Rave 82
Redig de Campos 55
Redslob 45
Reichow 126
Reidy 54–5, 232–4, 238, **53,
    55, 233**
Reifenberg 98
Reilly 136, **136**
Reinhardt 226, 314
Reinius 285, **283–4**
Repton 267
Revell 101, 240–2, **104, 241–2**
Ribeiro 55
Ricci 63
Richardson 6, 50, 69, 104, 242,
    248, 276, 279, 301–3, 307,
    310, 321, **68**
Rickman 267
Ridolfi 157
Riemerschmid 85, 92, 123, 242
Rietveld 75, 148, 152, 155,
    210, 213, 242–4, 272–4,
    243–4
Riihimäki 240
Rivera 188
Roberto, Marcelo 54
Roberto, Milton 54
Roberts 258
Robertson 134
Robson 258
Roche 69, 70, 149, 214, 270
Rocher 133
Rodgers 304, 308
Rogers 47, 72, 158, 244
Rolland 314
Root 6, 66, 69–70, 79, 132,
    177, 245, 270, 301, **68–9**
Rosen 83, 188
Rosenberg, Eugene 326, **326**
Rosenberg, Léonce 105
Roth, Alfred 286, **57**
Roth, Emil 286–7, **57, 286**
Rouhault 129

Roux-Spitz 106
Rowe 204
Rudolph 26, 58, 245, 308, **309**
Ruf 90
Ruhnau 82
Ruskin 5, 35–7, 301, 321
Russell 98

Saarinen, Eero 26, 155, 167–8,
    225, 245–8, 258, 272, 308–
    10, **24, 154, 245–7, 250**
Saarinen, Eliel 99–100, 245,
    248–50, 305, **249–50**
Saarnio 30
Saavedra **188**
Sakakura 164
Saldanha 55
Salvisberg 286
Samonà 158
Sánchez 188
Sant'Elia 15–16, 68, 114, 116,
    152, 155, 171, 202, 250–2,
    115, 251
Sarger 258
Sartoris 114–15, 158
Saskelin 64
Sato 163
Saturnino de Brito 54
Saugey 286, 288
Saulnier 79, 268, **79**
Sauvage 106
Scalpelli 157
Scarpa 133, 158, 252
Schader 287
Schaefer 258
Scharoun 86, 89, 96, 124,
    126–7, 147, 244, 252–4,
    319, **94, 125, 253–4**
Schein 107
Scheper 46
Schimka 42
Schindler 17, 40, 214, 254,
    305
Schinkel 7–9, 21, 122, 165,
    191, 193, 202, 225, 254–6,
    123
Schleget 83
Schlemmer 45, **43**
Schmidt, Friedrich 8
Schmidt, Hans 286, **286**
Schmidt, Joost 46
Schmidt, Karl 85
Schmidt, Richard E. 70, 237
Schneck 86
Schneider 96
Schneider-Esleben 132
Scholer 52, 93

Schröder-Schräder 242
Schumacher 93, 97, 125, 295
Schuster 40–1
Schütz 287
Schwanzer 42, **41**
Schwarz 126–7, 255, **127**
Schwippert 255
Séguin 267
Seidler 40, 255, 312, **255**
Sekino 162
Sekler 42
Semper 256, **9**
Senn, Otto 286
Senn, Rainer 108
Serrurier-Bovy 34, 313
Sert 72–3, 205, 256
Seurat 312
Severud 82, 219, 240, **279**
Shaw 12, 84, 134–5, 248, 256,
    256
Sheppard 258, 260
Shreve 306, 325
Silsbee 321
Silvy **232**
Simberg 30
Simon 258
Sipari 241
Siren, Heikki 101, 260, **103,**
    230
Siren, J. S. 100
Siren, Kaija 101, 260, **103,**
    230
Sirvin 107
Sitte 118
Sive 107, **231**
Sjöstrom 65
Skidmore, Owings and Merrill
    (SOM) 23, 66, 80, 126, 132,
    164, 245, 260–2, 308–10,
    320, **23, 81, 260–2, 271**
Slater 136, **136**
Sluyterman 34
Smith 62, **62**
Smithson, Alison 61, 64, 73,
    137, 204, 262, **63, 205**
Smithson, Peter 61, 63–4, 73,
    137, 204, 262, **63, 205**
Soane 8, 9, 12, 166, 205, 262
Sobre 9
Soeiro 54
Soleri 63, 262, **263**
Sommaruga 34, 155, 262
Sonck 99, **99**
Sonrel 108
Soraja y Matyas 252
Sordo Madaleno 188
Soufflot 234

Spalt 42
Spence '98, 133, 138, 264, 266,
    265
Stam 60, 75–6, 86, 177, 210,
    286, **76**
Stegmann 82, 104, **83**
Steiger, Peter 288, **287**
Steiger, Rudolf 286–8, **286–8**
Steinbüschel 40
Steiner 14, 96, 237, **97**
Stenhammar 280
Stephenson G. 326
Stephenson, Robert 267
Stillman 274
Stirling 274
Stone 24, 26, 90, 274, 309, **23,**
    310
Stonorov 167
Street 202, 320
Strengell 100
Strnad 40
Stubbins 26, 274, **274**
Stucky 288
Studer 288, **288**
Stuijt 221
Stynen 315
Sullivan 6, 32, 69–70, 113–14,
    128, 132, 151, 177–8, 220,
    248, 270, 275–9, 301, 303,
    307, 310, 319–21, **275–8,**
    302–3
Summerson 63
Sundahl 283
Syllas, de 34

TAC 23, 144, 288, **143–4**
Takizawa 162
Tange 164, 181, 288–90, **163,**
    289–90
Taniguchi 163–4
Tarjanne 99
Tassel 34
Tatlin 74, 76, 177, 290, **75**
Taucher 100, **101**
Taut, Bruno 15–16, 19, 22, 86,
    124, 163, 244, 252, 290,
    130
Taut, Max 86, 124, 244, 290
Tavio 30
Tecton 135, 137, 291, **135–6**
Tedesco, de 235
Telford 266–7, 291, **6**
Tengbom 282
Terragni 64, 145, 155–6, 158,
    203, 291–2, **291–2**
Tessenow 85, 211, 317
Thiersch 183

Thompson 288
Thomson **8**
Tijen, van 43, 60
Torroja 20, 66, 240, 258,
    292–4, **257, 293–4**
Trucco 156, 236, **156**
Tschernykhov 76
Tsuchiura 164
Tubbs 98
Turner 129, **129**
Turnock 133
Tyrwhitt 72

Uchôa 218, **55, 216**
Ungers 127
Unwin 295
Ursault 107
Utzon 84, 311–12, **311**

Vago 107, 312
Välikangas 100–1
Valjus 241
Vanbrugh 61
Van Gogh 35
Vantongerloo 75, 272
Vasarely 316
Vasari 220
Vasconcellos 54, 238, **53**
Vegas 154, 316
Vegter 212
Velde, van de 11, 34–5, 37, 43,
    47–8, 85–6, 92–3, 100,
    123–4, 145, 220–1, 312–15,
    319, **313–14**
Verwilghen 315
Vesnin, Alexander 76, **75**
Vesnin, Vladimir 76, **75**
Viard **20**
Viénot 108
Viganò 63, 158, 315, **24, 63**
Villagrán Garcia 187–8, 219,
    315
Villanueva 315–17, **26, 316,**
    317
Villar 119–20
Viollet-le-Duc 43, 78, 104,
    112, 119, 149, 183, 209, 225,
    317, 319, 321, **266**
Vital Brasil 54
Vitellozzi 258, **157–8, 258**
Vitruvius 220
Vlugt, J. A. van der 210
Vlugt, L. C. van der 60, 133,
    210, 317, **211**
Voelcker 73, 204
Voysey 12, 35, 37, 84, 134–5,
    151, 202, 248, 317, **11**

Wachsmann 92, 144, 229, 264, 272, 317–19, **263, 318**
Wagner, Martin 125, 252, 319
Wagner, Otto 34, 40, 130, 147, 155, 178, 213, 219, 250, 254, 271, 305, 319–20, **40, 319**
Wahlman 282
Wallot 104, 202
Walton 37
Warchavchik 54, 77, 232, 320
Ward, Basil 135
Ward, Edmund Fisher 134, 138
Ward, Ronald 138–9
Wasmuth 321
Watt 266, **266**
Wayss 234
Webb 84, 134–5, 202, 248, 320, **37**
Weber 127
Weese 320
Weideli 287
Weinbrenner 9

Westman 280
White 303, 308, 310, 321
Wickman 279, 282
Wiebinga 210
Wiener 54
Wilde 35
Williams 134–5, 238, 320, **134**
Wils 87, 210
Wimberley 258
Windbrechtinger 42
Windinge 83, **83**
Wittkower 204
Wittwer 189, **189**
Wogenscky 107
Wohlert 84, **84**
Wolf 34
Wolske 127, **127**
Woods 67, **108**
Wörle 42
Wren 34
Wright 12, 14, 18, 20, 22, 68, ·70, 84, 104, 112, 133–4, 146, 152, 163, 168, 176, 214,

220–1, 238, 248–9, 252, 254, 262, 274, 280, 288, 293, 301–7, 309–11, 320–5, **12, 19–20, 131, 220, 307, 321–5**
Wurster 306, 325
Wyatt 130

Yamada 162, 164
Yamasaki 25–6, 258, 309, 325–6, **25, 259, 326**
Yamawaki 163
Yáñez 187
Yeon 306
Yorke 58, 326, **326**
Yoshida 162, 164, **162**
Yoshimura 164

Zanuso 158, 326
Zavanella 158
Zehrfuss 58, 109, 208, 231, 240, 258, 326
Zevi 157, 159, 203
Zweifel 286